PRAISE FOR *DIGIT*
MARKETING IN PR

CW00796868

"Technology is driving marketing impact like never before. This book adds the missing link for future marketeers on how to use digital technologies responsibly and achieve long-term market development success."
Mark A A M Leenders, Professor of Marketing and Innovation, Graduate School of Business and Law, RMIT University, Melbourne, Australia

"The book takes readers on a compelling journey through the digital marketing landscape with a strong focus on the important role of market research."
Lena Hochstrat, Senior Manager, Global Account Development, NielsenIQ Services Germany GmbH

"A valuable resource which gives the reader an all-encompassing review of what aspiring digital marketers need to know. This is not a text that majors solely on the current 'on trend' digital channels; it instead gives them an overview of critical ideas such as customer journey mapping and digital marketing metrics, all written in a manner that helps the reader understand the topics and apply them to practical scenarios."
David Hart, Associate Professor of Marketing and Deputy Head of Department (Marketing, Operations and Systems), Northumbria University, UK

"This text provides its readers with key insights into the strategic and operational dimensions of digital marketing. The book is a valuable resource for those engaged in and studying and practising digital marketing at all levels. Its focus on responsible and sustainable marketing in the digital world presents a fresh take on the main issues that need to be considered by digital marketers in contemporary business environments."
Phil Megicks, Associate Professor of Marketing, Southampton Business School, University of Southampton, UK and Chief Examiner, *Chartered Institute of Marketing* Awards

"This book is a delightful guide full of important information for those who want to understand digital marketing, whether they are students with no prior experience, researchers who want to understand current digital marketing practices, or practitioners looking for best-practice examples and inspiration for their own business."
Wassili Lasarov, Department of Marketing, Audencia Business School, Nantes, France

"Knight and Vorster provide an interesting and easy-to-read introduction into the field of digital marketing. The comprehensive book covers a wide range of topics, including the highly timely and relevant, but often neglected chapters on responsible digital marketing or the use of technology to achieve sustainable business development."
Stefan Hoffmann, Department of Marketing, Kiel University, Germany

"Finally, the digital marketing book we all needed! Knight and Vorster have created a must-read for marketing students and anyone who wants to get involved in (digital) marketing. The text is comprehensive without being overwhelming: from digital marketing history to the mysterious crypto, and how to conduct a digital marketing audit, without ignoring ethical, legal, and responsible digital marketer behaviour. This masterpiece is reader-friendly, intuitively structured, easy to follow, and contains relevant examples and comments from practitioners, engaging hands-on activities, and up-to-date case studies. A book worth reading, keeping, and teaching."
Verónica Martín Ruiz, Assistant Professor of Marketing, UMass Amherst, USA

"This is a comprehensive text that delivers all you need to know about digital marketing in practice. The book strikes a good balance between theory and application that is reinforced by the excellent case studies in every chapter. I would highly recommend this book to both undergraduate and postgraduate students."
Michael Kong, Programme Director, HKU SPACE College of Business and Finance, Hong Kong

Digital Marketing in Practice

Design, implement and measure effective campaigns

Hanne Knight and Lizette Vorster

Publisher's note

Every possible effort has been made to ensure that the information contained in this book is accurate at the time of going to press, and the publishers and authors cannot accept responsibility for any errors or omissions, however caused. No responsibility for loss or damage occasioned to any person acting, or refraining from action, as a result of the material in this publication can be accepted by the editor, the publisher or the author.

First published in Great Britain and the United States in 2023 by Kogan Page Limited

Apart from any fair dealing for the purposes of research or private study, or criticism or review, as permitted under the Copyright, Designs and Patents Act 1988, this publication may only be reproduced, stored or transmitted, in any form or by any means, with the prior permission in writing of the publishers, or in the case of reprographic reproduction in accordance with the terms and licences issued by the CLA. Enquiries concerning reproduction outside these terms should be sent to the publishers at the undermentioned addresses:

2nd Floor, 45 Gee Street	8 W 38th Street, Suite 902	4737/23 Ansari Road
London	New York, NY 10018	Daryaganj
EC1V 3RS	USA	New Delhi 110002
United Kingdom		India

www.koganpage.com

Kogan Page books are printed on paper from sustainable forests.

© Hanne Knight and Lizette Vorster 2023

The right of Hanne Knight and Lizette Vorster to be identified as the authors of this work has been asserted by them in accordance with the Copyright, Designs and Patents Act 1988.

ISBNs

Hardback	978 1 3986 0889 4
Paperback	978 1 3986 0887 0
Ebook	978 1 3986 0888 7

British Library Cataloging-in-Publication Data

A CIP record for this book is available from the British Library.

Library of Congress Control Number
2023931348

Typeset by Integra Software Services, Pondicherry
Print production managed by Jellyfish
Printed and bound by CPI Group (UK) Ltd, Croydon, CR0 4YY

CONTENTS

PART FOUR Implementation of a digital strategy 205

LIST OF FIGURES AND TABLES

Figures

Tables

ABOUT THE AUTHORS

Hanne Knight is a lecturer in Marketing at the University of Plymouth and a practitioner providing strategic solutions to digital marketing questions. Hanne gained her Bachelor and Masters degrees in the Netherlands, while her Masters in Business Studies from the University of Amsterdam and her PhD in Marketing from the University of Plymouth focus on the successful adoption of sustainability messaging in business communications. She has been awarded a Professional Diploma with Distinction from the Digital Marketing Institute. Hanne is an active member of the Chartered Institute of Marketing where she examines Sustainable Business Modules, and is acting as Programme Leader for the MSc in Digital Marketing at the University of Plymouth and at the HKU School of Professional and Continuing Education, which is part of the University of Hong Kong.

Hanne has been acting as board member for several institutions and charities, including the Chartered Management Institute, and is a Fellow of Advanced HE. She is a keen academic journal reviewer and has worked for the *Journal of Business Ethics* and *Journal of Cleaner Production* among others. Hanne's research interests include the effectiveness of corporate sustainability messages on social media and cultural differences in the use of social media for sustainability message sharing. She is currently developing models that help to combat the spread of sustainability misinformation on social media channels.

Lizette Vorster is an assistant professor in Strategic Business Communication at Aarhus University in Denmark. She teaches across various subjects spanning marketing, communication theory and practice as well as digital communication. Her previous positions include academic and professional marketing practice. Lizette gained her Bachelor degree in Information Design from the University of Pretoria in South Africa, with subject areas spanning design, marketing and visual communication. She worked in various advertising and marketing roles in South Africa and the UK, from graphic designer to creative director. She obtained her PhD in Marketing and Consumer Psychology from Coventry University in the UK, specializing in responsible marketing strategy in culturally diverse marketplaces. Before moving to Denmark, she was a lecturer in Digital Marketing at Northumbria University and Programme Lead for the Digital Marketing Degree Apprenticeship programme.

Lizette is a Fellow of the Higher Education Academy, and a member of the Academy of Marketing Science and the Institute of Data and Marketing. Lizette's research interests include the social role of marketers and the impact of their marketing communications on intercultural interactions and marketplace well-being in traditional and digital spaces. She is also an active member of the Multicultural Marketplaces Network, a research-based group where marketers aim to improve marketplaces via transformative consumer insights, policy development and educational tools.

PREFACE

How do you create and measure digital marketing campaigns? How can you analyse competitor and consumer behaviour? How can digital marketing be conducted in a responsible and accountable way? These are some of the questions that this textbook aims to answer. The content is understandable and applicable for those without any prior knowledge of digital marketing and is therefore useful to digital marketing students as well as practitioners who would like to learn more about best practice, tools, channels and platforms.

The textbook combines academic sources and industry voices to provide you with a well-rounded view on how to execute successful digital marketing campaigns. One of the main features of *Digital Marketing in Practice* is its focus on the responsible and ethical execution of digital marketing. Each chapter looks at the content through a responsibility lens, ensuring that the reader understands the ethical implications and boundaries that should guide successful digital marketing campaigns in contemporary marketplaces.

This textbook is divided into six parts. Part One deals with basic concepts and understanding of digital marketing. Part Two establishes how to research the digital environment, and in Part Three we discuss online consumer behaviour. Once you understand the digital marketing environment and its players, Parts Four and Five show you how to create plans and set objectives, design digital marketing campaigns and evaluate their success for improvement. The final part focuses on reviewing legal and ethical constraints and how and why sustainability matters in the digital age. Depending on your level of knowledge, you might want to start with Part One or decide to jump straight into Part Six.

Featuring interviews with industry practitioners, case studies and examples from a range of brands including Nielsen and the UK Met Office, the book also contains how-to guides, checklists, key term definitions and critical thought pieces. The book is also supported by online resources consisting of lecture slides, self-test questions, group activities, worksheets, additional interactive case studies and further resource links. These bonus materials will equip you with the tools to develop and implement successful and responsible digital marketing campaigns.

Enjoy the journey to becoming a successful digital marketer!

PART ONE
Basic concepts and understanding of digital marketing

Introduction to digital marketing   01

By the end of this chapter, you should be able to:

- briefly explain the history of the web
- explain how the 4Ps of marketing have to be adjusted to fit the digital context
- distinguish between earned, owned and paid media
- justify the benefits of digital marketing in comparison to conventional marketing

Introduction

Marketing can be defined in numerous ways. The main goal of *marketing* is to satisfy consumers. Most definitions say that to satisfy consumers, we need to know what they want and need. This identification of wants and needs can be based, for example, on past data (e.g. sales data). Ideally, marketing managers should be able to anticipate consumers' needs to satisfy those needs.

KEY TERM
Marketing

Marketing is the management process responsible for identifying, anticipating and satisfying customer requirements profitably.

SOURCE Chartered Institute of Marketing, 2015

Digital technologies greatly influence how the goals of marketing (identification, anticipation and satisfaction of consumers' needs) can be achieved. Several different technologies contribute to the identification of consumers' needs. Review sites are just one example that enable businesses to identify such needs easily. Businesses can gain more customer knowledge by reviewing what is talked about on social media sites. These new channels of identifying needs and wants allow for better prediction of future consumers' needs. The overall satisfaction of consumers is simplified through a plethora of online channels that allow for personalized product and service delivery.

The history of the web

To understand how digital marketing works in practice today, we need to understand how far we have come. In the 1980s and 1990s, the first access to the internet was termed Web 1.0. This was all about information sharing. Businesses shared on the web what they would normally have shared on their printed marketing collateral. There was no real interaction between the business and the consumer. Consumer information (e.g. order forms) was collected but that was the extent of it.

Web 2.0 introduced the interactive relationship between consumers and businesses. Web 2.0 was all about the introduction of social media channels, and interaction was the main aim. Consumers felt empowered to have their voices heard. Business communications were not just presented online but interaction with the consumer was encouraged. Web 2.0 was all about two-way communication.

Web 3.0 involves a third party of interaction, namely the involvement of machine learning. Things like product recommendations on websites based on the consumers' browsing history or past purchase behaviour are examples of such machine learning. Hence, Web 3.0 has three players: the web, the user and the machine.

Web 4.0 takes the web to another level by introducing the *Internet of Things (IoT)*. Now we have machine learning on another level. We do not just access the internet on our computers, but instead, our smartphones as well as devices such as smart speakers, smartwatches and more form a whole net that collects and distributes information.

KEY TERM
Internet of Things (IoT)

The Internet of Things (IoT) is a name for the aggregate collection of network-enabled devices, excluding traditional computers like laptops and servers. Types of network connections can include Wi-Fi connections, Bluetooth connections, and near-field communication (NFC). The IoT includes devices such as 'smart' appliances, like refrigerators and thermostats; home security systems; computer peripherals, like webcams and printers; wearable technology, and smart speaker devices.

SOURCE Kenton, 2021

Activity 1.1

The Internet Archive's main goal is to save images of important websites to ensure the internet is being captured historically. It developed a tool called The Wayback Machine in which screenshots of websites have been taken since 1996 and are freely accessible to the public.

i   Visit the Internet Archive (2022) website (listed in the References).

ii Type a web address of your choice.

iii Click browse history.

iv Look at the Calendar view.

v   Discover older versions of your chosen website.

The 4Ps of marketing in a digital world

The 4Ps of marketing (also referred to as the marketing mix) are one of the most commonly applied marketing principles. They describe product, place, promotion and price and help to set marketing strategies. The 4Ps have been around since the 1950s and were established by Neil Bordon (Twin, 2021). Despite the marketing mix being around for a long time, it has not lost its relevancy. However, given the shift of marketing into the online world, certain adjustments need to be made. Here is how to understand the 4Ps of the marketing mix and how it needs to be adjusted to remain relevant in the digital world.

Product

Product describes the product a company is selling. A product can be a tangible good or an intangible service. Companies need to establish what it is they are trying to sell. Companies that do well often develop new products according to consumer demand. Amazon is an example of a company that develops its products based on what its users want. It started as a book store in the early 1990s and is now the world's largest online platform, selling thousands of different products. The first P of the marketing mix establishes the main benefits of a product or service to the consumer.

The digitalization of marketing has impacted products in numerous ways. Completely new products (goods and services) are available now that were previously unthinkable. For example, streaming platforms such as Netflix and Amazon Prime are completely new products. Other impacts of technology on a product are in the form of new product development. Digital technologies have now made it much easier to track changing consumer demand.

Place

Place refers to the place where consumers can buy a product. This includes deciding in which stores the products are sold. This also requires businesses to consider where exactly in the stores the products should be placed (in-store location). For example, a lot of businesses that sell FMCGs (fast-moving consumer goods) are fighting for shelf space in supermarkets that are at eye level to ensure the best exposure.

The internet has opened up a completely new form of place to sell products and services. E-commerce has boomed in recent years and allows anybody to sell something online. With such immense opportunities comes a lot of competition too. The online marketplace is very competitive and businesses need to work hard to be noticed by their consumers.

Promotion

Promotion describes the promotional techniques available to businesses to communicate their product features to an audience. Promotion can include several different promotional channels and varying activities. Advertising, sales promotion, public relations and product placement are some of the different activities available to businesses.

Promotional activities have numerous new digital channels to work with. For example, advertising used to be seen through mass media such as television or print magazines. The digital landscape has made it possible for highly targeted advertising on different platforms. For example, display advertisements on websites can be highly targeted based on someone's interests or previous shopping behaviour. Some companies only exist to offer sales promotion. For example, Groupon or Wowcher offer sales promotions for numerous products and services from third parties.

Price

Price refers to the amount of money businesses can charge for a product. Successful businesses have a clear understanding of how much their consumers are willing to pay for their products. The more market demand there is for a product, the higher the price businesses can charge and consumers are willing to pay. Such higher willingness-to-pay can be due to the limited availability of innovative product features. It is the role of promotional activities to ensure that consumers are willing to pay the price for a product charged by a business.

The pricing of products has also been massively influenced by technology. Price transparency through price comparison sites and the ability of consumers to find competitors' prices only one click away has led to a lot of businesses offering price matching. This means that if consumers find a product cheaper elsewhere, the price would be matched.

Media division: owned, earned and paid media

A common model that helps to understand the digital landscape that today's marketers are facing is the owned–earned–paid media model. Often loosely applied, Corcoran (2009) clarified what each of these segments mean and why it is so important for businesses to view their media landscape in these three key areas:

- **Owned media** refers to the media that a business controls. One needs to differentiate between media that is completely owned by a business (for example, a website) as opposed to media that is only partially owned (for example, social media pages).

- **Earned media** is a term that originates from public relations activities and is used to describe getting a brand into a media outlet without having to pay for advertising. Nowadays, this is extended by the process of people (professionals or consumers) talking positively about a brand or product without being paid to do so referring to word of mouth (WOM). With social media channels giving everyone a voice, businesses need to learn how to respond to positive and negative mentioning online.

- **Paid media** is all the media that a business pays for to be seen. This can be in the form of paid advertising or influencer marketing (where businesses pay someone for positive WOM). The digital landscape allows for a plethora of different forms of paid media and enables highly targeted and personalized advertising campaigns.

A business needs to classify its media and link these classifications to its objectives. For example, earned media is very useful to foster trust and engagement with existing consumers. Paid media on the other hand is very useful when it comes to reaching new clients.

Activity 1.2

Earned media is a term that has been used by public relations departments to get brands and businesses mentioned on media outlets without having to pay for it.

i   Discuss how digital technologies have changed how earned media can be achieved.

ii Write down two advantages and two disadvantages of digital technologies for earned media.

Key benefits of digital marketing

Digital technologies have impacted the way businesses do marketing. As you remember, marketing is all about identifying, anticipating and satisfying customers' needs profitably. The following provides an overview of the main advantages of digital marketing:

- consumer data
- consumer access
- consumer involvement
- speed
- sustainability
- savings

Digital technologies allow for easier collection of consumer data and therefore enable businesses to make better informed decisions. The data collected can range from general consumer interests collected on social media to product-specific reviews. Better consumer access is gained through the use of additional channels. For example, a traditional brick-and-mortar store can extend its product offer by establishing an e-commerce store. Digital channels allow businesses to get closer to their consumers by involving them in a two-way conversation. This means that consumers' voices can be heard and businesses can establish a voice of their own.

Digital campaigns can be implemented and adapted much more quickly than conventional print-based campaigns. Think of an email campaign for example. It is much quicker to send out an email than it would be to send out a mail campaign. Also, it is possible with email marketing to send out two versions of the same message and test which of those receives better results. Digital marketing is more sustainable as it prevents a lot of paper-based communication and thus allows for more resource-efficient marketing.. Overall, one can argue that digital marketing is more cost-effective than conventional marketing as fewer resources are wasted due to its digital nature, and marketing efforts can be more targeted and therefore have less wastage. Digital technologies allow for improved self-service which could mean reduced staffing costs.

Summary

Digital marketing can be defined as *achieving marketing objectives through the application of digital technologies*. In this chapter, we have learnt how the internet has developed from its humble beginnings of just sharing information to being a complete network of interrelated devices that people use in their daily lives. We have learnt how the marketing mix has been influenced by technologies. While all 4Ps have been influenced, one of the major shifts has taken place in the numerous promotional techniques that have been newly developed in the online space. A useful tool to review a business's media landscape is to divide it into owned, earned and paid media. This division aids businesses to review which of their media outlets requires attention. Finally, we have reviewed the benefits of applying digital technologies to marketing.

Chapter review

Reflective questions

Q1 How has the role of the consumer changed throughout the development of Web 1.0 to Web 4.0?

Q2 How have the 4Ps of the marketing mix been impacted by digital technology?

Q3 How could the media landscape of a business be divided and what are the benefits of doing so?

Q4 How would you describe the main benefits of digital marketing compared to conventional marketing?

Key learning points

- The history of the web ranging from Web 1.0 to Web 4.0.
- The 4Ps of marketing (also referred to as the marketing mix) in a digital world.
- The media division: owned, earned and paid media.
- The key benefits of digital marketing.

References

Chartered Institute of Marketing (CIM) (2015) A brief summary of marketing and how it works, www.cim.co.uk/media/4772/7ps.pdf (archived at https://perma.cc/2L7Q-JYV9)

Corcoran, S (2009) Defining earned, owned and paid media, 16 December, Forrester, www.forrester.com/blogs/09-12-16-defining_earned_owned_and_paid_media/ (archived at https://perma.cc/G52P-5LVG)

Internet Archive (2022) About the Internet Archive, archive.org/about/ (archived at https://perma.cc/DS7N-9LQM)

Kenton, W (2021) The Internet of Things (IoT), Investopedia, 28 May, www.investopedia.
    com/terms/i/internet-things.asp (archived at https://perma.cc/HD9A-5FMZ)
Twin, A (2021) The 4Ps, Investopedia, 21 July, www.investopedia.com/terms/f/four-ps.
    asp#:~:text=Jerome%20McCarthy%2C%20a%20marketing%20professor,idea%20
    of%20the%204%20Ps (archived at https://perma.cc/BT2U-7CBG)

Planning a digital marketing strategy 02

By the end of this chapter, you should be able to:

- explain in detail why a strategic approach to digital marketing is essential to succeed
- differentiate between digital business models
- distinguish between the different layers of business objectives
- understand challenges when planning a digital marketing strategy
- describe the individual steps of a digital marketing plan

Introduction

Any business should have a plan of where they are heading. This helps to set the direction and focus of the business for the future. A good strategy should clearly outline measurable goals to evaluate progress against. This means that setting a strategy allows a business to see whether they are successful and can change their course if they realize that they are not successful. Planning a strategy requires work and time. Some managers and business owners decide to make ad hoc decisions rather than designing a business strategy. This can be problematic as research has shown that businesses that plan strategically perform better than those that do not (Rudd et al, 2008). In this chapter, you will learn why digital marketing requires strategic planning and how general strategy can be applied in the digital context. We will then review the different layers of setting businesses objectives. After that, we will look at challenges when planning digital marketing strategies. The chapter will conclude with the individual steps needed to draft a digital marketing plan.

Strategic planning

One of the main reasons *strategic planning* contributes to a business's success is that a plan can anticipate external and internal forces and address them accordingly before they turn into a problem (Rogers et al, 1999).

KEY TERM
Strategic planning

Strategic planning is a deliberative, disciplined effort to produce fundamental decisions and actions that shape and guide what an organization (or other entity) is, what it does and why.

SOURCE Bryson, 2011

As the key term definition shows, one of the most critical aspects of strategic planning is knowing your business's reason for being and where you are planning to take your business. These decisions can be described as setting your vision and mission.

A *business mission* sets out what the purpose of a business is. This is usually written in the form of a mission statement. A mission statement can be defined as 'an action-based statement that declares the purpose of an organization and how they serve their customers' (Tsang, 2020). Businesses doing well usually know precisely their purpose and use their mission statement to guide decision-making and planning. The following are two examples of powerful mission statements:

- 'To accelerate the world's transition to sustainable energy' (Tesla, 2022)
- 'Spread ideas' (Ted Talks, 2022)

Both mission statements set out precisely the companies' purpose. Both statements are clear and concise, and both guide the businesses and inform consumers what they are all about.

Activity 2.1

A mission statement is meant to set out the purpose of a business. Patagonia is an outdoor clothing company that was founded in 1973. The following mission statement has guided Patagonia for 45 years:

Build the best product, cause no unnecessary harm, use business to inspire and implement solutions to the environmental crisis.

It has recently changed its mission statement to:

   We're in business to save our home planet.

i   Visit Patagonia's website (Patagonia, 2022) and try to find out why they seemed to have changed their mission statement after such a long time.

ii   Why did the initial mission statement seem outdated?

The *vision of a business* sets out what a business wants to achieve. Often the vision goes hand-in-hand with the mission statement but extends it into the future. The vision of a business should be motivational and aspirational. It should give the business a clear direction of where it wants to get to in the future. Imagine a business with a strong mission (purpose) but which does not extend its planning further than a few months at a time. It would be like a journey without a destination. A mission is all about how a business can serve its customers best, and the vision is all about why a business is serving its customers.

To demonstrate the difference, look at Tesla's mission and vision:

- Mission: 'To accelerate the world's transition to sustainable energy.'

- Vision: 'To create the most compelling car company of the 21st century by driving the world's transition to electric vehicles.'

As discussed earlier, you see how the mission perfectly describes Tesla's purpose. On the other hand, the vision emphasizes the aspiration of what Tesla wants to become.

Strategy framework

Businesses have to decide which strategy to pursue once they have chosen their overall mission and vision. Numerous frameworks can help businesses to determine which strategy to follow to fulfil their mission. One framework often applied is the Ansoff Matrix (Figure 2.1).

This matrix was developed by Igor Ansoff in 1957 and is still very relevant today. Often praised for its simplicity, the Ansoff Matrix presents four strategies that a business can pursue to grow. The framework is also used to analyse risk. The idea is that when a business changes its strategy by moving into another quadrant (horizontally or vertically), risk increases. The four strategies are:

- **Market penetration:** This strategy has the lowest risk associated with it as businesses choose to expand sales of existing products to markets they already know. With this strategy, businesses need to find a way for consumers to purchase products more frequently.

Figure 2.1   The Ansoff Matrix

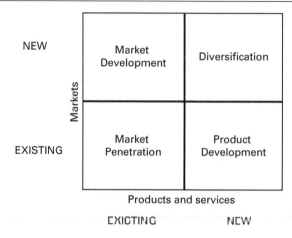

SOURCE Ansoff, 1957

- **Market development:** This strategy is somewhat riskier as businesses are planning to sell an existing product to a new consumer group. This can be done by, for example, targeting a new geographical area or repositioning the product to appeal to a new consumer group.

- **Product development:** Here, businesses would introduce a new product into an existing market. The benefit is that they know their market, but new product development is risky and requires a lot of research and planning.

- **Diversification:** This is the riskiest of the strategies as it means that businesses would develop a new product and introduce it to a new market. The main advantage of diversification is that businesses become less vulnerable – if one product fails or a market becomes saturated, the diversified product portfolio means that such circumstances can be mitigated.

The Ansoff Matrix can also be functional in the digital context as digital technologies can be utilized to achieve the chosen strategy. Market penetration can be enhanced through automatic orders and repeat purchases on websites. Amazon, for example, offers simple repeat purchasing options. Digital technologies can support market development such that new markets are more easily accessible. For example, geographical borders are more fluid online and allow a swifter transition into a different target market. New product development can be achieved through digital technologies by offering additional services.

Digital marketing strategy

Now that we have covered strategic planning on the overall business level, we need to understand why a digital marketing strategy is essential and how we can draft a digital marketing strategy. Let me remind you that one of the critical advantages of strategic planning is to set out a clear direction for a business. This fundamental advantage is just as essential for digital marketing activities.

The rapid growth of the internet has led to many businesses making ad hoc decisions on which digital marketing channels to use. Businesses thought it essential to be represented on popular social media channels without knowing HOW and WHY it would help them and their consumers. Such rushed actions often fail to be aligned with the overarching business strategy. The following list summarizes some of the advantages of strategic planning, as it:

- establishes goals to plan against
- communicates a clear purpose for employees, consumers and shareholders
- sets an aspirational direction for the future
- allows businesses to anticipate and address external and internal issues
- enables correct resource allocation

The advantages of strategic planning can all be put in a digital marketing context and are just as relevant. Any digital marketing strategy has to have clear overarching goals. These *goals* should be at the business level rather than tactical, operational goals. For example, reaching a larger audience or engaging current consumers would be overarching goals. On the other hand, *tactics* would be a specific channel goal such as 'increase followers on Instagram'.

A digital marketing strategy should be aligned to the *overall mission and vision*. This ensures continuity of communicating the purpose and aspiration of the business. For a digital marketing strategy to be successful, every bit of content created should consider the mission and vision of the business. Imagine if a business such as Tesla, whose mission is to transition the world to sustainable energy, chose to run a display advertising campaign on an oil company's website. This would not go down well with consumers, shareholders or employees of Tesla.

Setting aspirational goals requires planning for digital marketing strategies. Rather than thinking of short-term gains such as gaining more followers on Facebook, a successful digital marketing campaign has to have an overarching direction guiding every lower-level decision made. If we revisit Tesla's example, its vision is to create the most compelling car company by driving the world's transition to electric vehicles. Every bit of content produced by Tesla should have that vision in mind. To be true to that vision, one aspect of their digital marketing strategy could be to change the perception of electric vehicles in the minds of consumers. Such content would align with Tesla's vision, even though it might not 100 per cent benefit them as a business as consumers might choose competitors.

Activity 2.2

Tesla is one of the first companies whose aim is to make electric cars accessible to the mass market. Their overarching goal is to drive the world's transition to electric vehicles.

i   Visit Tesla's social media channels and review their posts.

ii Can you find any posts about general electrical vehicle facts (e.g. advantages of electric vehicles) rather than specifically about Tesla?

iii Do you think Tesla's representation on social media channels aligns with its overall mission and vision?

A good digital marketing strategy has the collection of data at its core. In other words, digital marketing decisions should be *rooted in data* rather than based on ideas only. Therefore, the advantage of strategic planning to anticipate and address changes is very applicable to a digital marketing strategy. It has never been easier for businesses to access information. Such data could be collected by reviewing trending topics on social media channels or collecting product reviews. For example, in 2013, electric vehicles were often mentioned in social media posts for supposedly having a higher fire risk than petrol cars. This fact has been noticed by Tesla, who published a blog entry that highlighted the general fire safety of electric vehicles versus petrol vehicles (Musk, 2013).

One advantage of digital marketing is that it can save costs. This can be, for example, due to limited print and postal costs. Also, many social media channels are free for businesses and consumers to sign up to. For these reasons, businesses are still often under the impression that a successful digital marketing campaign should not cost much. Yet, planning for sensible outgoings that are crucial to achieving the set goals is essential. So the advantage of strategic planning to allow for *correct resource allocation* is just as fitting for a digital marketing strategy.

Business models

We have reviewed strategic planning and its application to the digital context. We now need to recognize that varying **business models** contain different strategies on how a business plans to make a profit.

KEY TERM
Business model

The business model refers to a company's plan for making a profit. It identifies the products or services the business plans to sell, its identified target market and any anticipated expenses.

SOURCE Kopp, 2020

Now that we know how a business model is defined, we can set the term business model in the digital context. A *digital business model* includes the application of digital technologies to create value and enhance businesses' profitability. One way of categorizing business models is to divide them into the groups the business directs its sales efforts towards. This works for conventional businesses as well as digitally focused businesses.

B2C: business-to-consumer

This is the most common business model and describes transactions between a business and the end-consumer/-user. B2C transactions occur most frequently, and each individual transaction is generally of lower value. Therefore, businesses require a high quantity of B2C transactions to be profitable. Digital technologies have extended the B2C market tremendously as there are many new routes for businesses to connect to the end-user. For example, businesses no longer need a brick-and-mortar outlet to sell their products but rely entirely on e-commerce solutions.

B2B: business-to-business

In this business model, a business sells its products (goods or services) to another business. The buyer (in this case, another business) might be the product's end-user or sell the product to another consumer. B2B transactions are usually less frequent but of higher sales value to a business. Digital technologies have opened up a whole new market for B2B transactions as it is much quicker, easier and cheaper to set up a business online. Therefore, the B2B market has grown tremendously, especially among young entrepreneurs taking part in B2B transactions.

C2B: consumer-to-business

This business model describes transactions when consumers are providing value in the form of services or products to businesses. In the digital world, this is often done through paid testimonials, data sharing or referral programmes (Ward, 2022). For example, a consumer might have a lot of followers, which makes it valuable for a business to be mentioned on that consumer's online presence.

C2C: consumer-to-consumer

In this business model, businesses facilitate the exchange of products and services between consumers. Value is created by consumers doing transactions with each other. For example, websites like eBay were some of the very early providers of C2C. This is one of the preferred digital business models and made companies such as Uber and Airbnb big players in the online world.

Charities and not-for-profit

Charities and not-for-profit organizations cover another model of doing business. For these organizations, value is created not in monetary gain but rather by contributing to categories that the government has deemed charitable. This includes education, human rights, animal welfare and protection of the environment. Digital technologies had massive impacts on charities by creating a broader and faster spread of information and more accessible donating methods.

Activity 2.3

Digital technologies have revolutionized the marketplace for C2C transactions. Many of the big players in the online world benefit from some C2C interaction. One website that has made use of facilitating C2C transactions is Etsy.

i   Visit Etsy.com's website.

ii   Try to think of three reasons why the C2C business model works so well in the arts and craft context.

Types of digital business models

By now, you should be able to differentiate between the different business models. These are very broad groupings, and many businesses fall into more than one category. For other businesses, it might be difficult to be put into any of those boxes. Nevertheless, these divisions of categories into who a business is trading with provide a valuable tool for making strategic decisions and planning for the future. The categorization works for conventional as well as online businesses. It is essential to understand how digital technologies, in particular, can help to provide value for businesses. The following list shows specific types of digital business models, according to Cuofano (2022):

- **Free** (also hidden-revenue or ad-supported model): companies such as Facebook and Google offer their product for free and generate money differently (e.g. by selling advertising).
- **Freemium:** commonly used online, essential services are offered for free, but a paid version is available for additional benefits (e.g. no adverts, more extensive storage, etc).
- **Subscription:** a widespread business model whereby consumers pay a monthly fee to subscribe to a service. A significant advantage of this business model is a guaranteed stream of income.
- **E-commerce:** the most common type of digital business model is where companies sell physical products to consumers through online marketplaces.

Value proposition

We have learnt so far that a digital marketing strategy has to be aligned with the overall vision and mission to be successful. Businesses also have to set out a plan for being profitable by determining a business model that enables them to do so. Another step towards planning a successful digital marketing strategy is to define a compelling *value proposition*.

KEY TERM
Value proposition

A value proposition refers to the value a company promises to deliver to customers should they choose to buy their product. The value proposition provides a declaration of intent or a statement that introduces a company's brand to consumers by telling them what the company stands for, how it operates and why it deserves their business.

SOURCE Twin, 2022

A digital marketing strategy must demonstrate that the business is aware of and has planned a compelling value proposition. Let us revisit Tesla to show you an example of a value proposition. Li et al (2021) describe how Tesla's value proposition is divided into three aspects:

1 innovation towards vehicle: high-performance and intelligent services
2 innovation towards battery: high capacity and low-cost battery
3 innovation towards infrastructure system: high-performance recharging station

This value proposition clearly shows what the customer can expect if they buy a Tesla car. Part of the digital marketing strategy is establishing an online value proposition (OVP). This should reinforce the overall value proposition of the company. An OVP should communicate a business's value to its customers through digital technologies. It should answer questions such as: Why do business with us online? How are we better at providing an online service to our consumers than our competition?

Uber is one business that excels in its simple OVP. It states its service as three simple steps and indirectly highlights its value over using a traditional taxi service (Shewan, 2022):

- One tap and a car comes directly to you.
- Your driver knows exactly where to go.
- Payment is completely cashless.

Business planning (annual – digital marketing plan – campaigns)

By now, you should have learnt that a strategy is the business's plan to realize its mission and vision. Part of that plan is to set measurable goals. Goals are usually specified as objectives and need to happen at different layers and for different time frames within a business. Usually, we would differentiate between long-term strategic goals and shorter-term tactical (operational) objectives.

Strategic goals are usually decided in the top layer of an organization and often contain growth ambitions. For example, a car company might set the goal to gain 20 per cent market share in the next five years. The tactical objective would then be decided within the individual departments. For example, the research and development (R&D) department might set goals that feed into the overall strategic objective, such as developing three new cars within the next two years. Another department, such as the marketing department, would then write its operational objectives to reach 100,000 new customers within the next six months.

The previous examples can also be applied to the digital marketing department. The hierarchy and timings would be similar to those shown in the figure below. Time frames can vary significantly, so Figure 2.2 is just an indication. It illustrates that the strategic objective is much longer term. The digital marketing objectives and digital marketing campaign objectives can also be seen as the tactical and operational objectives and are usually set for the shortest time frame. These require constant checking and adjustment. Setting specific, measurable, achievable, realistic and timely (SMART) objectives is crucial for any successful strategy. Chapter 14 will describe in further detail how objectives should be set.

Figure 2.2   The hierarchy of business objectives in digital marketing strategy

```
┌─────────────────────────────────────────┐
│        Strategic Business Objectives      │
│                                           │
│           Timeframe: 3–5 years            │
└─────────────────────────────────────────┘

      ┌─────────────────────────────────────┐
      │         Marketing Objectives         │
      │                                      │
      │         Timeframe: Annually          │
      └─────────────────────────────────────┘

        ┌─────────────────────────────────┐
        │    Digital Marketing Objectives  │
        │                                  │
        │        6 months –1 year          │
        └─────────────────────────────────┘

          ┌─────────────────────────────┐
          │   Digital Marketing Campaign │
          │          Objectives          │
          │                              │
          │      Timeframe: Monthly      │
          └─────────────────────────────┘
```

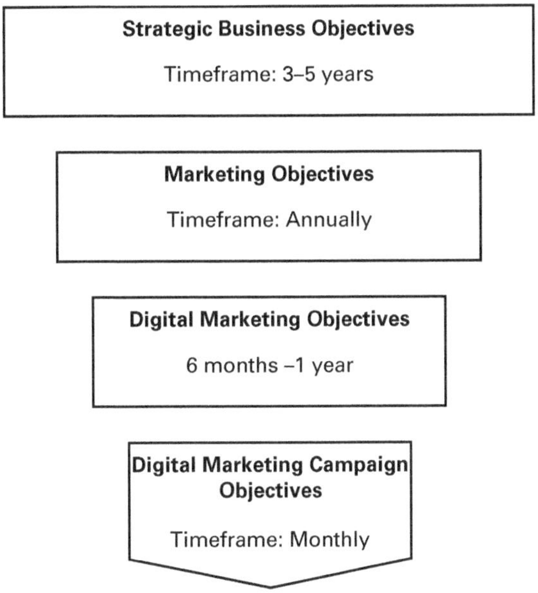

Activity 2.4

You are the marketing manager of a global fashion retailer. You have brick-and-mortar shops as well as a very successful e-commerce platform. As a five-year plan, the business aims to increase its market position to become the best-selling fashion retailer in the UK market. You are now tasked to write the following objectives:

i   marketing objectives

ii digital marketing objectives

iii digital marketing campaign objectives

Bear in mind that these objectives should contribute to the overall goal of growing the business.

Challenges when planning a digital marketing strategy

We have discussed plenty of advantages of planning a digital marketing strategy and have learnt how to differentiate between the layers of objective setting. Not every business performs successful strategic planning. Quite on the contrary, most businesses do not manage their strategic planning as detailed as necessary. There are several challenges associated with planning a digital marketing strategy. Businesses might experience some of the following when preparing their digital marketing strategy:

- lack of support from senior management
- misalignment between digital marketing planning and overarching business strategy
- limited knowledge of the market
- restricted access to data to inform decision-making

Digital marketing plan

We will now move on to the operational function of drafting digital marketing plans. A digital marketing plan helps businesses to structure the execution of a strategic plan by setting out individual steps. One can find several different digital marketing templates in textbooks and online sources. The structure of such plans does not differ significantly from traditional marketing plans. The following overview shows the main steps of a digital marketing plan based on a standard marketing plan model highlighted by Cohen (2001):

1 executive summary
2 table of contents
3 introduction
4 situation analysis
5 target market
6 digital marketing goals and objectives
7 digital marketing strategy
8 digital marketing tactics
9 implementation and control

Executive summary

The executive summary should first introduce your plan's purpose and main findings. You should then go on to discuss the key points. It is sufficient to write a concise paragraph for each key point. You should also highlight any recommendations that you would make based on your findings. It is good practice to explain the benefits of your recommendations. The executive summary must contain enough information that anybody can understand your plan without thoroughly reading it.

Table of contents

The table of contents should be detailed enough so that the reader of your plan can easily access the information they are looking for. Often digital marketing plans are written to secure funding for the planned activities (either externally or internally). People reviewing the plan are usually very busy and rely on the executive summary and reading critical points in your plan. These key points need to be readily available and easy to find. Thus, the table of contents is more important than you might think. You will save yourself a lot of work if you diligently work with clear headings and subheadings while writing your plan, as these will help navigate the reader through the content.

Introduction

The introduction explains the details of your plan rather than a summary of your findings. You might want to use the introduction to outline how your digital marketing plan fits into your overall business strategy. You might also want to highlight your key business objectives. Referring back to the overarching strategy of the business helps to ensure alignment between the business and the digital marketing strategy. The introduction should contain the background of your plan and set out what you are trying to achieve with your plan.

Situation analysis

The situation analysis of a digital marketing plan analyses the current situation that a business faces. It usually contains an analysis of a business's internal and external environment. The overarching aim of a situation analysis is to understand internal capabilities, customers and the business's environments.

The situation analysis often starts by examining a business's external macro-environment. The macro-environment includes forces that potentially have an impact on the business. A lot of scholars apply frameworks such as the *PESTEL analysis*. There are different names for similar analyses, such as PEST, STEP or STEEPLE analysis. They are all doing very similar things. They review external forces according to the letters in the acronyms. PESTEL stands for political, economic, social, technological, environmental and legal forces. Technological forces are usually critical for a digital marketing plan as it is essential to review how technological advances in its environment might impact a business.

The next step of the situation analysis would be reviewing the *internal capabilities*. This is often done by considering a business's strengths and weaknesses (S+W).

Following the internal analysis, businesses need to conduct a *consumer analysis*. They should review their current target audience. Who are they? What do they currently buy? Where do they buy our product? These are just some considerations to make when reviewing the current customer base.

Another crucial part of the situation analysis is the *competitor analysis*. This part of the digital marketing plan is vital for understanding where the competition operates. A lot of data for this analysis is readily available online. How effective the competition is in the digital space is a common consideration during this part of the plan.

The situation analysis should ideally be concluded with a *SWOT analysis*. A SWOT analysis summarizes the factors of the internal analysis (strengths and weaknesses of the business). It can also contain elements from the consumer and competitor analysis. The opportunities and threats (O+T) should be founded in the external analyses. Overarching forces identified in the PESTEL analysis should be summarized as either presenting opportunities or threats for the business.

Chapters 5, 6, 7 and 8 provide a detailed description of how the above mentioned analyses can be executed.

Target market

You have already identified your current target audience in the previous section. This section of your digital marketing plan should specify how you plan to adapt your target audience to achieve your new goals. Are you planning on extending your reach, or are you maybe planning to narrow down your target audience? As you have learnt at the beginning of this chapter, strategic planning is all about allocating your resources to have the most significant impact on your business. This is essential to consider when establishing your target market, as it would be costly to waste your digital marketing efforts on everybody. Cohen (2001) suggests segmenting your market according to the following terms:

- demographics
- geography
- psychographics
- lifestyle

The above terms are a valuable way of dividing your market into smaller segments on which to focus your efforts. However, given that this is a digital marketing plan, you will have to extend your analysis to understand the digital consumer. One of the earliest models that helps to analyse the digital consumer is the technology acceptance model (TAM), initially developed by Davis (1989). Attitudinal variables such as *perceived usefulness, perceived ease of use* and *acceptance of information technology* can be used to describe your target audience. Are your customers technology savvy?

Do they perceive online channels to be useful? These are some of the questions you should ask yourself when drafting your target audience. Common practice among digital marketing practitioners is to draft your target audience as *personas*.

KEY TERM
Persona

A persona is a representation of a target customer, typically based on real consumer insights and built using research into user demographics, goals, needs and interests. These fictional characters are then used as a model to target marketing strategies.

SOURCE Data and Marketing Association, 2016

Chapter 10 will discuss the digital consumer, including how to draft personas.

Digital marketing goals and objectives

This section of the digital marketing report is critical as it combines all of the information collated in the earlier part of the report and sets objectives for the future. If you refer to earlier in this chapter, we have distinguished between strategic business objectives, marketing objectives, digital marketing objectives and digital marketing campaign objectives.

This report should contain the digital marketing objectives. These should support the overall strategic and marketing objectives but should be more specific to the digital marketing context. Digital marketing objectives often relate to growing your online following, converting followers into more frequent purchasers, or engaging your consumers. Chapter 14 will elaborate further on how to set SMART objectives.

Digital marketing strategy

This section of your digital marketing plan should outline what you plan to do to reach your goals. Here you should highlight your business model (e.g. B2B or C2C?) and digital business model (e.g. e-commerce or subscription-based model?). Furthermore, it is worth making strategic decisions regarding your product/service and your market by applying the Ansoff Matrix. Are you planning to work with your existing products and markets, or are you planning on developing either market or product? You might also want to consider how your competitors might react to your new strategy.

Digital marketing tactics

While your strategy demonstrates what you are planning to do, the tactics should establish how you will carry out your strategy. You should write down exactly which actions you plan to execute to reach your goals. Tactics should also always include an idea about timing. One common way of dividing your tactics section is to apply the digital marketing mix. What decisions will you make in terms of product, promotion, place and price? The digital marketing mix will be discussed in great detail in Chapter 15.

Implementation and control

This is the final section of your digital marketing plan. Here you should outline how and when you will implement your tactics. Planning should specify information such as who is doing what and how you plan to allocate resources. Implementation should also contain a budgeting plan. The breakeven point should be calculated to ensure the feasibility of the project. Measurement and evaluation tools should be applied, and a corrective course taken if needed. Chapters 19 to 22 outline how success can be measured and evaluated.

Summary

This chapter has taught you how a digital marketing strategy fits the overarching business strategy. We have stressed the importance of planning for success and reviewed various business models to help decide how best to create value for customers and the business alike. Setting objectives is another way of setting goals for a business. We have reviewed how the objectives need to be set on different business levels. We have learnt that many businesses do not take part in strategic planning. This can be for numerous reasons. We have learnt about the various challenges that might prevent a business from planning its future strategically. The final part of this chapter contains a step-by-step guide to writing a digital marketing strategy plan.

Chapter review

Reflective questions

Q1 Why is it necessary to plan strategically?

Q2 What are business models, and what do they set out to do?

Q3 What differentiates strategic business objectives and marketing campaign objectives?

Q4 What are the challenges when planning a digital marketing strategy?

Key learning points

- Strategic planning is essential to provide businesses with a clear direction for the future.

- An essential part of strategic planning is to design a mission and vision for the business.

- There are a number of digital business models that can be applied in a digital context.

- Different layers of business objectives need to be set to have a clear direction.

- Individual steps of a digital marketing plan help to strategically plan digital marketing activities.

References

Ansoff, H I (1957) Strategies for diversification, *Harvard Business Review*, 113–24

Bryson, J M (2011) *Strategic Planning for Public and Nonprofit Organizations*, Jossey-Bass, San Francisco, CA

Cohen, A C (2001) *The Marketing Plan*, John Wiley & Sons Inc, New York

Cuofano, G (2022) Digital Business Models Map, FourweekMBA, fourweekmba.com/digital-business-models/ (archived at https://perma.cc/S77B-BMZF)

Data & Marketing Association (2016) The persona building game: why traditional marketers are losing, DMA, 9 September, dma.org.uk/article/the-persona-building-game-why-traditional-marketers-are-losing (archived at https://perma.cc/KBS2-4UVG)

Davis, F (1989) Perceived usefulness, perceived ease of use, and user acceptance of information technology, *MIS Quarterly*, 13(3), 319–40

Kopp, C (2020) What is a business model? Investopedia, 3 July, www.investopedia.com/terms/b/businessmodel.asp (archived at https://perma.cc/3JSG-7LLV)

Li, Y, Lin, J and Xu, S (2021) Analysis of Tesla's business model: A comparison with Toyota, *Advances in Economics, Business and Management Research*, 190, 30–39

Musk, E (2013) The mission of Tesla, www.tesla.com/en_GB/blog/mission-tesla (archived at https://perma.cc/DTB9-DKUR)

Patagonia (2022) Home page, eu.patagonia.com,gb/en/home/ (archived at https://perma.cc/S7JM-WZ55)

Rogers, P R, Miller, A and Judge, W Q (1999) Using information-processing to understand planning/performance relationships in the context of strategy, *Strategic Management Journal*, 20, 567–77, doi.org/10.1002/(SICI)1097-0266(199906)20:6<567::AID-SMJ36>3.0.CO;2-K (archived at https://perma.cc/2BTH-PWTU)

Rudd, J, Greenley, G, Beatson, A and Lings, I (2008) Strategic planning and performance: Extending the debate, *Journal of Business Research*, 61(2), 99–108, doi.org/10.1016/j.jbusres.2007.06.014 (archived at https://perma.cc/CMB4-XRWG)

Shewan, D (2022) 7 of the best value propositions examples we've ever seen, Wordstream 2022, www.wordstream.com/blog/ws/2016/04/27/value-proposition-examples (archived at https://perma.cc/FD42-H6A7)

Ted Talks (2022) About Ted, www.ted.com/about/our-organization#:~:text=Our%20Mission%3A%20Spread%20ideas&text=On%20TED.com%2C%20we',the%20world%2C%20all%20year%20long (archived at https://perma.cc/W697-369M)

Tesla (2022) About Tesla, www.tesla.com/about#:~:text=Tesla's%20mission%20is%20to%20accelerate%20the%20world's%20transition%20to%20sustainable%20energy (archived at https://perma.cc/32SN-248T)

Tsang, S (2020) Best mission statements: 12 examples you need to see, Fond, www.fond.co/blog/best-mission-statements/ (archived at https://perma.cc/2N82-HW78)

Twin, A (2022) Value proposition, Investopedia, 9 March, www.investopedia.com/terms/v/valueproposition.asp (archived at https://perma.cc/7BZU-6PAF)

Ward, P (2022) C2B Business definitions and examples, NanoGlobals, 3 March, nanoglobals.com/glossary/c2b-consumer-to-business/ (archived at https://perma.cc/C2YX-MAC4)

Digital marketing campaigns 03

By the end of this chapter, you should be able to:

- explain the difference between a digital marketing strategy and a digital marketing campaign
- identify descriptors of digital marketing campaigns
- describe how the unique features of digital technologies aid campaign success
- examine how project management is part of digital marketing campaign execution
- determine challenges when planning and executing a digital marketing campaign
- describe the individual steps to execute a digital marketing campaign

Introduction

Successful businesses tend to invest a lot of time and effort into planning their marketing strategy. We have learnt that careful planning can help reach profitable consumers and ensure resource allocation for maximum profit. However, planning an appropriate marketing strategy is just one piece of the puzzle. Once the general direction of the business is set, marketing campaigns are crucial to executing decision-making on the operational, more tactical level. Digital technologies have long helped manage those decisions by reaching new customers on numerous new channels. New digital technologies enable vastly different campaign execution, but the need for careful management arises with so many different opportunities. Project management is one area that is very helpful when it comes to successful campaign execution. This chapter will highlight and explain five essential steps that can be followed to plan and execute a successful digital marketing campaign.

Digital marketing strategy vs digital marketing campaign

There seems to be some confusion among marketing professionals about what constitutes a digital marketing strategy/ plan instead of a digital marketing campaign. It is essential to differentiate between the two, though, as there are different reasons for executing both. A digital marketing plan is part of the overarching marketing strategy and is conducted over a more extended period, sometimes even continuously. On the other hand, *digital marketing campaigns* are more operational and tactical in their execution and usually run over a much shorter time frame.

KEY TERM
Digital marketing campaigns

A digital marketing campaign is a focused, tactical initiative to achieve specific digital marketing goals.

SOURCE Rego, 2017

This key term definition highlights one of the essential differences: the time factor. Whereas a digital marketing strategy should be set for several years, a digital marketing campaign can be executed in a few weeks. Some campaigns are instantaneous and last only a few hours to a couple of days. This can be the case when businesses aim for content to go viral within a brief period. Overall, one can describe digital marketing campaigns as the individual building blocks that together form the execution of the overarching marketing strategy.

Unique features of digital technology in marketing campaigns

Digital technology enables many different channels and forms of execution to be used when it comes to digital marketing campaigns. The opportunities that digital technologies offer in executing digital marketing campaigns are endless. In the following section, we will discuss the unique features of digital media and how they aid in running a successful digital marketing campaign.

Activity 3.1

Digital media provide numerous advantages over traditional media when executing marketing campaigns.

i.   Try to think of the last campaign of your favourite brand that you have noticed on your social media channels.

ii. What features made the campaign successful?

iii. Would it have been possible to execute the same campaign with traditional media such as TV and print publications?

iv. If not, why not?

Data availability

The collection of data is one of the key advantages of digital media, and can be done in several forms. Data is necessary for digital marketing campaigns in two ways.

First, consumer data is collected when identifying which consumer segment to target. Marketers can use data provided by the consumer and data that can be gathered by social media providers. For example, consumers are willing to give a lot of their private data away to access social media platforms. Consumers are also willing to share their thoughts and views about products on numerous channels. Businesses can collect this data to build a detailed picture of the current or prospective consumers.

Second, data is crucial for measuring the success of a digital marketing campaign. Businesses need to think of how meaningful data can be collected once a campaign is over to determine its success.

Data accessibility in traditional channels is much trickier and usually takes longer. Often market research through interviews or surveys informs marketers of the success of conventional marketing campaigns. This form of data collection is much slower and more expensive.

Extended consumer reach

Digital media allows for numerous ways to reach and engage with consumers. Just think of the multiple touchpoints a consumer might have with a business. A consumer might be searching for a particular product. The search likely starts with a search engine. The consumer might then use social media channels to find out more about a specific product. Market research suggests that 64 per cent of internet users use their social media accounts to discover new brands and products (GWI, 2022).

The same report shows that almost 30 per cent find new brands by being exposed to ads on social media networks.

After coming across a new brand or product on social media, they may be exposed to the same message on display advertising on different websites and potentially be targeted through an email campaign. As you can see, there are numerous channels that businesses can use to reach new consumers. By comparison, the options available in traditional media channels are limited and pricey.

Customer involvement

Digital technology enables the involvement of consumers by creating two-way conversations with them. This means that businesses do not just publish their messages to be received by potential and existing customers. Instead, a dialogue between the business and its consumers can be initiated and sustained. The majority of marketing campaigns that do not use digital technologies are directed at the mass market. For example, think of a campaign that is rolled out in the form of billboards on bus shelters and other visible spots. These billboards are seen by anyone who drives or walks by. Yet the involvement of the consumer is minimal.

Now consider an advertising campaign on social media. Social media campaigns encourage customers to interact with the brand in the form of liking, sharing or commenting on content. Another advantage of digital marketing campaigns enabled through digital technology is conversations among consumers. Whereas consumers might have talked about a new brand or product with their immediate peer group, digital channels would allow consumers to speak to each other without knowing each other in the real world.

Speed

Another unique aspect of digital marketing campaigns is that they can be implemented and adjusted very swiftly. It takes a lot of planning to create a successful campaign, which might take a while, but the actual execution can be done quickly once the plan is written. Consumers' reactions and feedback are almost instantaneous. This swift execution has the advantage that things can be changed/adjusted if the consumer reaction differs from what was expected. Take, for example, an email campaign. Businesses get to access a report as soon as the emails have been sent out. This report shows analytical data such as how many emails have bounced, the opening rate, and how many people clicked on any links within the email. Businesses often use *A/B testing*, also referred to as 'split testing' in email marketing, whereby two versions of an email are sent before deciding which one will be chosen for the primary campaign. The analytics previously discussed will be analysed once both email versions have been sent out, and the more successful email will then be selected.

KEY TERM
A/B testing

A/B (or split) testing in email marketing describes having two different versions of the same content and testing whether consumers prefer option A or B. This allows marketers to choose the better-performing email to be sent in the main email campaign. Tests can vary in complexity: simple tests involving sending multiple subject lines to test which ones generate more opens; or more advanced tests which include completely different email templates to see which one generates more click-throughs. Variations can include headlines, email subject lines, images, colours, fonts, buttons or calls to action.

SOURCE Campaign Monitor, nd

Choice of media channels

Digital technologies have opened a whole plethora of new channels to reach customers. Think of traditional marketing campaigns limited to promotions only through mass media such as TV, print publications or billboards. With digital media come a whole other level of reaching the masses. Think of all the different social media channels, search engines, emails, etc. The campaign execution channels are endless.

Meaningful data

Digital marketing campaigns can generate masses of consumer data that can be analysed and used to inform future campaigns. One significant advantage of using digital technologies for your marketing campaign is quantifiable results. For example, you might run a campaign on one of your social media channels. You will be able to measure how many people have visited your website and purchased something due to your campaign. *Web analytics* can provide a lot of meaningful data to evaluate the success of a campaign.

KEY TERM
Web analytics

Web analytics describes the reporting of activities on websites. It gets its information from traditional business intelligence and data mining processes. It provides information on how many visitors your site gets, how much time they spend on your website, and what they do while they are on your website.

SOURCE Lippa, 2012

PRACTITIONER INPUT
Ross Middleham (1)

Ross Middleham is Creative Lead for the UK Meteorological Office (the Met Office), the home of weather and climate science.

Would you introduce the organization that you're working for?

The Met Office is funded by government to provide a national weather service for all citizens of the UK. A critical part of this remit is to equip them with information to take appropriate decisions/actions to stay safe, particularly during severe weather.

I oversee design, video and social media production, setting the direction for our social channels and ensuring we publish timely and engaging content. I deliver positive creative leadership and clear brand direction by visibly encouraging future thinking and championing a culture of creativity. I work to empower the creation of consistent, accessible, high-quality interactions across all Met Office products and services.

Could you give us an example of a successful digital marketing campaign from the Met Office?

In February 2022, three named storms (Dudley, Eunice, Franklin) affected the UK within a week – an unprecedented event with two rare red warnings issued. Our objective during this crisis was to fulfil our remit as detailed, using social media channels. Quantifiably, we wanted to increase followers by 80k across channels.

The strategy included:

- Identifying areas we could make the most impact and get the most reach/engagement, focusing resource in a short space of time by making sound channel, format and posting schedule decisions.

- Setting the news agenda using storm name hashtags making the Met Office the authoritative source and go-to place for updates, cutting through the noise, whatever channel people were on, countering fake news, rife in the weather sector.

- Leveraging increased eyeballs while high on the news agenda, converting these into new followers to achieve year-round engagement, not just during severe weather.

- Increasing brand awareness and trust.

- Identifying and leveraging strategic channel partners/brands to amplify content, accessing new audiences via their channels and maximizing authoritative, specialist safety messages.

Content was predominantly organic, but alongside this we also used carefully geographically targeted advertising to reach the right people in the most impacted areas. This also meant people weren't seeing warnings content not relevant to them, avoiding confusion.

How important is access to consumer data for you when designing a digital marketing campaign? What type of consumer data do you use to inform your campaigns?

Our challenge at the Met Office is quite unique. Unusually for many campaigns, our target is often to get safety information to as many people as possible. For example, when the February storms hit, our audience was every citizen of the UK, to ensure our forecasts/warnings helped as many people as possible. With storms this severe, it really was a case of life and death information. Emphasis was given to the harder-to-engage demographic (18–24) who are less likely to see weather warnings via traditional channels like TV.

We use in-app data to understand what the breakdown of our audience is across our channels. That way we are able to tailor the content per channel to suit.

Equally as important as data is being able to spot emerging opportunities and that can be achieved by simply being on social channels and absorbing what others are doing. It also helps to follow social media commentators or groups who often share new features. At the Met Office I have helped to build strong relationships with the channels themselves in order to help us spot what features they are placing emphasis on. For example, we worked with our Twitter contact to trial Twitter Spaces, helping to feed back on functionality. Knowing what features are coming up can help you be in a position to ride the wave of popularity and achieve the maximum reach for your content.

The speed by which digital marketing campaigns are executed is an advantage of digital media. Is this something you can relate to?

Responding quickly to the situation and devising a strategy to utilize our social media presence ultimately resulted in lives and property being protected.

Communicating weather is a unique challenge at the best of times but, in a storm situation, it's important to keep updating the public at the right time, messaging appropriately despite uncertainty in the forecast, media sensationalism and misinformation. Weather information also dates quickly so requires clear titles and date stamps while encouraging people to stay up to date with changing events via our other channels, including our app.

We had to carefully consider tone of voice, making sure we were neither alarmist nor playful. Timing of content is critical, and this was managed through our daily editorial process. Having an in-house creative team, alongside subject experts, makes it much easier to produce and publish content quickly.

Our presenters are also trained meteorologists, and they create and tell the stories in various formats. That might be a longer video for YouTube, where they can highlight any uncertainty in the forecast, or live on Facebook where they can answer questions from people.

Reacting to the weather or trending topics and being able to publish accurate, timely and relevant content makes our information more useful to people. It helps them be aware, understand and take the appropriate action if needed.

Is adjusting campaigns through A/B (split) testing something that is important to the success of your digital marketing campaigns?

As turnaround times were very tight around the named storms, we didn't use any split testing in this instance. However, split testing has been important for us on other campaigns, where we are pushing other messages. For example, to help highlight our accuracy, we ran a number of campaigns across our social channels using A/B testing. This helped us to identify what 'creatives' were most effective at driving action, and ensured budget was focused on getting the most value by pushing the best-performing posts.

Split testing can also be a great way to learn what works for your channels and audience. For example, by looking at comments you can quickly judge sentiment as well as the typical monitoring of reach, views and click-throughs.

Are there any other advantages of digital media for your marketing campaigns that you would say are important to your organization?

At the Met Office we also syndicate all of our social content to news and media outlets each day. This helps to extend our reach and get a consistent, authoritative message out to the public.

Omnichannel marketing

Some of the unique features of digital marketing campaigns result from and have implications for changing consumption patterns. Consumers used to be relatively predictable in how they would do their shopping. Consumers tend to have their favourite shops and complete their shopping there. With digital technologies came the option of choice. People have much greater price transparency as prices can be easily compared online. The term *price transparency* has its roots in behavioural economics and is often used in financial trading cycles (Forex Traders, 2022).

KEY TERM
Price transparency

Price transparency typically refers to a process that guarantees all market participants have the same access to prices. High price transparency would allow the public access to different prices. Low price transparency would limit public access.

SOURCE Forex Traders, 2022

Consumers tend to use multiple channels to complete their shopping. For example, they might search for information about their favourite product on social media channels; they might then visit review sites to read different reviews. Once they decide which brand to purchase, they might shop online to compare prices. They might then go into an actual store to touch and feel the product. They might then revisit a website to get the best deal. As you can see from the previous example, consumers have approached their shopping through an omnichannel lens during this one transaction.

This has two implications for marketers. First of all, marketers have to understand where to find their consumers. Second, they cannot afford only to target one or two channels, given that consumers use every channel that is most convenient to them. Therefore, digital marketing campaigns need to consider *omnichannel marketing*.

KEY TERM
Omnichannel marketing

Omnichannel marketing is defined as the synergistic management of all customer touchpoints and channels both internal and external to the firm to ensure that the customer experience across channels as well as firm-side marketing activity, including marketing mix and marketing communication (owned, paid and earned), is optimized for both firms and their customers.

SOURCE Cui et al, 2021

It is important to note that not every business should focus on omnichannel marketing. If a business realizes that almost all of its customers engage through a single channel, it might be worth considering putting all its resources into that one particular channel.

Activity 3.2

i. Review your favourite digital marketing campaign and write down all of the various channels you have been exposed to the marketing message of your favourite brand.

ii. Do you think your campaign would have been as successful if fewer channels had been selected?

Categorizing customers

Marketers need to group customers into different types to allocate resources accordingly. As businesses usually have a finite pool of resources, these need to be allocated successfully. There are numerous ways in which a business can divide its customer base.

One of those was introduced by Parasuraman (1997) who divides customers into four main types that can be considered when planning a digital marketing strategy:

- new customers
- short-term customers
- long-term customers
- win-back customers

Marketers need to make decisions about these different types of customers based on purchase propensity, resource intensity (Nguyen et al, 2018), and value contribution. *Purchase propensity* would involve questions such as how likely this consumer is to purchase something from us. *Resource intensity* includes considerations regarding how much time, effort and money we have to put into this consumer to get a purchase in return. *Value contribution* is a weighted consideration around whether the investment is worth the hassle. Table 3.1 demonstrates how the different types of customers fall into different categories and require different levels of attention from a business.

Table 3.1 Decision-making for different types of customers

	Purchase propensity	Resource intensity	Value contribution	Campaign execution example
New customers	low	high	unknown	Focus on reaching high quantity through paid ad and paid search campaigns
Short-term customers	high but might be one-off transaction	medium	relatively little	Focus on encouragement of repeat purchase through email marketing, paid ads campaigns
Long-term customers	high	medium-low	high	Focus on engagement through social media campaigns
Win-back customers	low	high	unknown	Focus on prevention of bad review through service recovery campaigns via different channels

Project management in digital marketing campaigns

As we have learnt initially, digital marketing campaigns are the individual building blocks that help fulfil an overarching marketing strategy. Each campaign can be viewed as a project and therefore can benefit from applying *project management* principles.

KEY TERM
Project management

Project management is the application of processes, methods, skills, knowledge and experience to achieve specific project objectives according to the project acceptance criteria within agreed parameters. Project management has final deliverables that are constrained to a finite timescale and budget.

SOURCE APM, 2022

As you can see from the project management definition, one of the critical factors is that a project has a finite time span. So, the difference between project management and general management is that management is an ongoing process. It is important to note that digital marketing management is also an ongoing process, but the execution of a digital marketing campaign should have a clearly defined timescale and budget.

The following outlines principles of successful project management as published by Bing (1994):

1 There must be a defined project and not just a task or an ongoing activity.

2 There must be a single leader (project manager), one who is experienced and willing to take responsibility for the work.

3 There must be an informed and supportive management that delegates appropriate authority to the project manager.

4 There must be a dedicated team of qualified people to do the work of the project.

5 The project goal must be clearly defined along with the priorities of the 'shareholders'.

6 There must be an integrated plan that outlines the action required in order to reach the goal.

7 There must be a schedule establishing the time goals of the project.

8 There must be a budget of costs and/or resources required for the project.

All of the above principles are highly relevant to digital marketing campaigns. While digital marketing management is an ongoing process, a digital marketing campaign should have a clearly defined timescale and not be an ongoing activity. This is important as it helps marketers clarify how to plan a campaign.

Any digital marketing campaign requires having one person responsible for the execution of the campaign. While primarily a whole team is involved in the planning and executing of a campaign, it is crucial to have one central person who can be held responsible should something go wrong.

Senior management should be aware of any planned campaign, and appropriate support should be given. This ensures that the campaign is aligned with other marketing activities within the business, and authority needs to be granted that allows swift decision-making in lower ranks. This is especially important given the opportunity to adjust campaigns in real time should they not achieve the desired outcome.

This brings us to the next point of having a dedicated team to execute the digital marketing campaign.

One of the main factors of successful digital marketing campaigns is having a clear goal. This means that every member working on the campaign should be aware of what the campaign aims to achieve.

Planning is another principle that applies well in project management and the digital marketing campaign sphere. Planning is crucial for the successful execution of campaigns. If a company sets clear goals but doesn't clarify the route to achieving those goals, problems will occur. Planning helps break the end goal into multiple minor actions to outline precisely what requires execution.

A clearly defined schedule and budgeting of costs and resource requirements are crucial to completing a successful digital marketing campaign.

Digital marketing campaigns can 'borrow' a lot of principles on how to be successful from the project management discipline. However, sometimes it is not only the proper planning that makes a campaign successful.

Activity 3.3

The Digital Marketing Institute (DMI, 2019) has reviewed six of the most successful campaigns. They show that there are many different reasons why some campaigns just work.

i. Visit the DMI's website and search for the article '6 of the best digital marketing campaigns you can learn from'.

ii. Make a list of reasons why these campaigns have been successful.

iii. Which one of the six campaigns resonates with you the most and why?

Challenges in digital marketing campaign planning and execution

We have established that digital marketing campaigns share common characteristics with project management in planning and execution. This is helpful as it highlights some of the principles that must be adhered to for a digital marketing campaign to be successful. However, internet usage is still increasing worldwide, and businesses have to quickly adapt to the digital environment. The speed of these developments is still causing numerous challenges for marketers.

Dey (2021) states the three most prominent digital marketing mistakes are:

- starting without a clear strategy
- not setting clearly defined goals
- targeting the wrong audience

These three challenges are essential to consider, and all three points would be avoidable if thoughtful planning were done before executing a campaign. One of the most prevailing challenges concerns the collection and analysis of data. Leeflang et al (2014) studied 777 marketing executives across the world, and their study confirmed that the main challenge facing digital marketers involves data.

They find that the majority of marketers see problems in:

- how to use consumer insights to compete effectively
- the analysis of new digital metrics, and
- the increasing talent gap in analytical capabilities within firms

Most respondents blamed constraints on funding and lack of infrastructure and IT tools as challenges to build a robust analytical function. Another interesting challenge for digital marketing campaigns is the lack of control to position a brand (Leeflang et al, 2014). This is explained by the fact that consumers are empowered through social media to have their voice and their thoughts on brands' positioning. In other words, what consumers say to other consumers about brands online is much more powerful than what a business tells the consumer the brand should be about. This requires companies to focus on building relationships with consumers.

Overcoming these challenges is crucial in any digital marketing campaign. Planning your digital marketing campaign carefully should prevent most of these challenges.

Individual steps of a digital marketing campaign

A digital marketing campaign plan is a more condensed form of an overall digital marketing plan. Some of the steps necessary are similar and can use practices as outlined within specific chapters of the book. The outline below describes five steps of a digital campaign plan and common questions to consider. Relevant chapters that should be considered when completing a digital marketing campaign plan will be highlighted.

1. Choose your target audience

Who is your customer? Who do you want to attract? Where do you reach them? What do they do online? Chapters 9 to 13 cover online customer behaviour in great detail and should be consulted when choosing your target audience. Chapter 7 will cover how to segment your overall market and target the right audience for your campaign.

2. Set your goals and how to evaluate success (KPIs)

What aims do you want to achieve? How will you measure performance? Chapter 14 will help with objective setting for digital marketing strategy planning and campaigns. Chapters 19 and 20 will cover the evaluation of success.

3. Design your offer/message and choose your channel

How will you attract attention? Which media channel will be most appropriate to promote your offer? Chapters 17 and 18 covers all the different channels necessary to execute a successful digital marketing campaign.

4. Measure results

How will you measure success? Which data will be available to you? Who can analyse the data? Chapters 21 and 22 will highlight in detail how success can be measured.

5. Integration into digital marketing strategy

Where does the campaign fit into the overall digital marketing strategy? Which overarching goals does the campaign help to achieve?

CASE STUDY   Heineken

In 2017, Heineken launched the World's Apart campaign, where people of opposing views met as part of a social experiment (Hunt, 2017). Two strangers were put in a warehouse and asked to complete a task together – building a bar from scratch. These people knew nothing about each other. Only at the end of their completed task were they asked to watch a short clip about each other. These clips would show their opposing views. For example, a member of the "new right" was paired with a feminist and a climate change denier with an environmental activist. After watching the clip, both participants were asked whether they wanted to stay and discuss their differences over a beer or whether they chose to leave (see the full clip on YouTube (Heineken, 2017)).

The following outlines how Heineken might have planned the five steps of a digital marketing campaign for this successful campaign.

1 Choose your target audience

At first glance, this campaign seems to have a broadly defined target audience. Given the digital focus of this campaign, the target audience should be reviewed from a digital perspective. Heineken seems to have chosen an audience that is widely connected online to ensure exponential growth of sharing opportunities. In terms of channel usage, Heineken targeted channel users that prefer video consumption. They probably tried to reach and engage an audience that is being kept up to date with current events as all of the covered subjects were very relevant topics in 2017. The diverse topics will appeal to a lot of different people. One of the critical aspects of this campaign is that it's not very obvious that it is a) an ad at all, and b) an ad for a beer.

2 Set your goals

While the campaign is all about connecting people with different viewpoints, the business's end goal would be to grow sales. However, the campaign-specific goals were likely around reach, and with that, social media metrics would be critical. Things like views, shares and comments would provide a solid understanding of how successful the campaign would be.

3 Design the offer and choose your channel

The output of the campaign is a four-minute video posted on numerous social media channels. Heineken chose a concept called storytelling in marketing. Storytelling is a powerful tool to get an emotional response from viewers and an effective way to create viral content (Tellis et al, 2019).

4 Measure results

According to the DMI (2019), the video has received more than 17.7 million views, more than 138,000 shares, and 324,000 engagements on Facebook. Also, people tweeted more than 22,000 about the ad, and of those tweets, 85 per cent were positive. In addition to these results, more than 624 articles were written about the campaign in different magazines.

Summary

This chapter establishes the difference between a digital marketing strategy and a digital marketing campaign. You have learnt how digital marketing campaigns are individual building blocks that help fulfil the aims of the overall digital marketing strategy. Digital marketing campaigns can apply project management concepts as every campaign can be seen as an individual project. One of the primary descriptors of campaigns is that they need to have a finite timescale and budget. We have reviewed the challenges of digital marketing campaigns, mainly about the lack of knowledge of analysing data and metrics. Finally, individual steps of a digital marketing campaign are outlined and applied in the case study.

Chapter review

Reflective questions

Q1 What are the differences between a digital marketing strategy and a digital marketing campaign?

Q2 How would you describe the key points of digital marketing campaigns?

Q3 How does knowledge of project management help when it comes to planning and executing digital marketing campaigns?

Q4 What are the challenges when planning a digital marketing campaign?

Key learning points

- The difference between a digital marketing strategy and a digital marketing campaign.
- Descriptors of digital marketing campaigns.
- Unique features of digital technologies aiding campaign success.
- Project management as part of digital marketing campaign execution.
- Challenges when planning and executing a digital marketing campaign.
- Individual steps of a digital marketing campaign.

References

APM (2022) What is project management, www.apm.org.uk/resources/what-is-project-management/ (archived at https://perma.cc/33FF-FGLQ)

Bing, J A (1994) Principles of project management, *PM Network*, 8(2), 38–41, www.pmi.org/learning/library/pm-project-management-principles-3400 (archived at https://perma.cc/7UHE-PZCC)

Campaign Monitor (nd) A/B test your email campaigns, www.campaignmonitor.com/resources/guides/ab-test-email-marketing-campaigns/ (archived at https://perma.cc/5ZLB-G58M)

Cui, T H, Ghose, A, Halaburda, H, Iyengar, H, Pauwels, K, Sriram, S, Tucker, C and Venkataraman, S (2021) Informational challenges in omnichannel marketing: Remedies and future research, *Journal of Marketing*, 85(1), 103–20

Dey, J (2021) The 3 biggest digital marketing mistakes and how to avoid them, LinkedIn, 28 April, www.linkedin.com/pulse/3-biggest-digital-marketing-mistakes-how-avoid-them-joydeep-dey/ (archived at https://perma.cc/877Z-E2CX)

Digital Marketing Institute (2019) 6 of the best digital marketing campaigns you can learn from, The Digital Marketing Institute, 19 February, digitalmarketinginstitute.com/blog/6-of-the-best-digital-marketing-campaigns-you-can-learn-from (archived at https://perma.cc/8CPM-PN6F)

Forex Traders (2022) What is price transparency? www.forextraders.com/forex-education/forex-glossary/what-is-price-transparency/ (archived at https://perma.cc/N5S7-8BWW)

GWI (2022) The biggest social media trends for 2022, GWI, www.gwi.com/reports/social (archived at https://perma.cc/6R4X-ND5Q)

Heineken (2017) Worlds Apart [video], YouTube, www.youtube.com/watch?v=dKggA9k8DKw (archived at https://perma.cc/2YYF-5T3Z)

Hunt, E (2017) That Heineken ad: brewer tackles how to talk to your political opposite, *The Guardian*, 28 April, www.theguardian.com/media/2017/apr/28/that-heineken-ad-does-it-land-with-the-audiences-other-beers-cannot-reach (archived at https://perma.cc/S3BG-3GPN)

Leeflang, P S H, Verhoef, P, Dahlström, P, Freundt, T (2014) Challenges and solutions for marketing in a digital era, *European Management Journal*, 32, 1–12

Lippa, G (2012) FAQ's web analytics, Data and Marketing Association, 14 June, dma.org.uk/article/faqs-web-analytics (archived at https://perma.cc/EY7J-YB3K)

Nguyen, T D, Paswan, A, Dubinsky, A J (2018) Allocation of salespeople's resources for generating new sales opportunities across four types of customers, *Industrial Marketing Management*, 68, 114–31

Parasuraman, A (1997) Reflections on gaining competitive advantage through customer value, *Journal of the Academy of Marketing Science*, 25(2), 154–61

Rego, B (2017) Marketing plans vs marketing campaigns, Imagine Media Consulting, 11 April, www.imaginemediaconsulting.com/blog-all-posts/staysocialcampaign (archived at https://perma.cc/4D7S-K55V)

Tellis, G, MacInnis, D, Tirunillai, S, and Zhang, Y (2019) What drives virality (sharing) of online digital content? The critical role of information, emotion, and brand prominence, *Journal of Marketing*, 83 (4), 1–20

Accountability in the digital age　04

By the end of this chapter, you should be able to:

- distinguish between marketing and digital marketing accountability
- explain the primary sources of concern for accountability in the digital world
- briefly outline the main groups of accountable online users
- elaborate on the importance of corporate digital responsibility

Introduction

Accountability usually means that individuals and businesses are held accountable for their actions. Accountability in marketing is applied in varying contexts. One application of marketing accountability is using metrics to establish the contribution of marketing activities to business outcomes such as growth or profit. This is pertinent in digital marketing as digital media's main advantage is data availability. Therefore, accountability has always been a promising feature of digital marketing activities. However, with the availability of data comes responsibilities of how to treat such data fairly. Accountability in the digital world describes both rights and responsibilities that people and businesses have online. Both businesses and people are held accountable for what they do in the real world, and the same should apply in the digital world.

Therefore, another major area of accountability in digital marketing refers to firms being held accountable for their actions on digital media. Due to the rapid development of new technologies, both legislation and standards have been slow to develop that would regulate behaviour in the digital world. With that, critical voices become apparent. For example, Facebook came under great scrutiny in 2021 when a former employee raised questions about the business's potential lack of keeping its users safe (Waterson and Milmo, 2021). This chapter will review the roots of accountability in the general marketing literature. We will then examine how accountability is essential in digital marketing. Different levels of accountability regarding specific digital marketing channels are assessed. Finally, we will evaluate the concept of corporate digital responsibility and how it is an essential strategic tool in the absence of legal guidelines.

Marketing accountability

Marketing accountability refers to a number of different activities undertaken in the marketing discipline.

KEY TERM
Marketing accountability

Marketing accountability refers to metrics to link a firm's marketing actions to financially relevant outcomes and growth over time. This accountability allows marketing to take responsibility for the profit and loss from investments in marketing activities and demonstrate the financial contributions of specific marketing programmes to the overall financial objectives of the firm, including brand asset value.

SOURCE MASB, 2016

As you can see from this definition, some scholars see marketing accountability as a purely financial concept. While this is a crucial aspect of marketing accountability, plenty of voices perceive marketing accountability to have a broader focus. The Data and Marketing Association (D&MA, 2019), for example, reviews the accountability concept of the *General Data Protection Regulation (GDPR)* and states three core accountability considerations for marketers:

1 accountability as a core principle
2 accountability at the heart of operations
3 accountability goes right to the top

These considerations show that accountability should not just be restricted to the financial return of marketing activities. Instead, it should be emphasized throughout the organization by placing the customer as the foundation for good marketing.

KEY TERM
General Data Protection Regulation (GDPR)

The General Data Protection Regulation (GDPR) is a legal framework that sets guidelines for the collection and processing of personal information from individuals who live in the European Union (EU).

SOURCE Frankenfield, 2020

Activity 4.1

The Marketing Accountability Standards Board (MASB) links marketing accountability to the financial contributions of marketing activities.

i.   Visit the homepage of the Marketing Accountability Standards Board (MASB) and review the Board's activities.

ii. Could these activities be applied in a digital context too?

iii. Try to find out whether there are similar boards that set out precisely what accountability means for digital marketing.

Standards and metrics are often stated as crucial for marketing accountability. Investments in marketing can only be justified if marketing as a discipline knows its contribution to the overall business. Marketers can predict future results, assess past activities, and allocate resources only if measurements and metrics are set that allow marketers to know their overall contribution (Stewart, 2009).

Marketing as a discipline is very good at measuring short-term outcomes (e.g. return to a direct mail campaign) but is less equipped to analyse long-term impacts (such as its contribution to brand equity) (Stewart, 2009). With the increased application of digital channels, this gap has widened further. Digital media has always come with the promise of more accountability as metrics and measurements are readily available. *Remember:* one key advantage of digital media is access to consumer data.

However, measuring short-term outcomes does not necessarily lead to accountability. Instead, with the high amount of data availability come questions about how this data is treated and protected. There seems to be growing concern among consumers, investors, businesses and the government about data privacy and data protection among marketing practitioners (Stewart, 2019). We will therefore review digital marketing accountability in detail in the next section.

Digital marketing accountability

In the previous section, we reviewed accountability in the overall marketing discipline. This part of the chapter will look into accountability specifically for the digital marketing discipline. Consider the channels that businesses have available today to reach and interact with their audience. With such interactions comes a lot of data that can track the performance of various campaigns in real time. With this ability to track performance comes pressure to be held accountable for the success of digital marketing campaigns.

Digital marketing activities need to be viewed first in terms of their contribution to general marketing outcomes and overall business strategy. If we consider these activities in light of MASB's earlier definition of marketing accountability, the concept of *digital marketing accountability* can be developed.

KEY TERM
Digital marketing accountability

Digital marketing accountability is the process that links metrics to digital marketing performance and general marketing outcomes and overall business growth. It allows digital marketers to specify how their strategy and campaigns have performed and overall contributed to marketing efforts.

There are different levels of accountability, and some digital marketing activities lend themselves to contributing to the return on investment (ROI) more than others. Figure 4.1 divides some digital marketing activities into whether they have established performance metrics and whether they contribute to digital marketing ROI.

As you can see in Figure 4.1, some digital marketing channels have better levels of accountability than others. For example, email marketing is relatively cheap, but once a business has a strong email list, the returns on investments can be very high. Email marketing still has one of the most comprehensive performance metrics available. While search engine optimization (SEO) takes longer to be implemented, website visitors are guaranteed once a business shows up high in Google's organic search results. Websites come with the ability to measure performance very quickly. On the other hand, mobile advertising provides relatively little data, making calculating the ROI challenging.

Digital marketing accountability is only one fraction of the digital world's accountability debate. The following section will discuss what accountability in the digital world entails.

Figure 4.1   Levels of digital marketing accountability

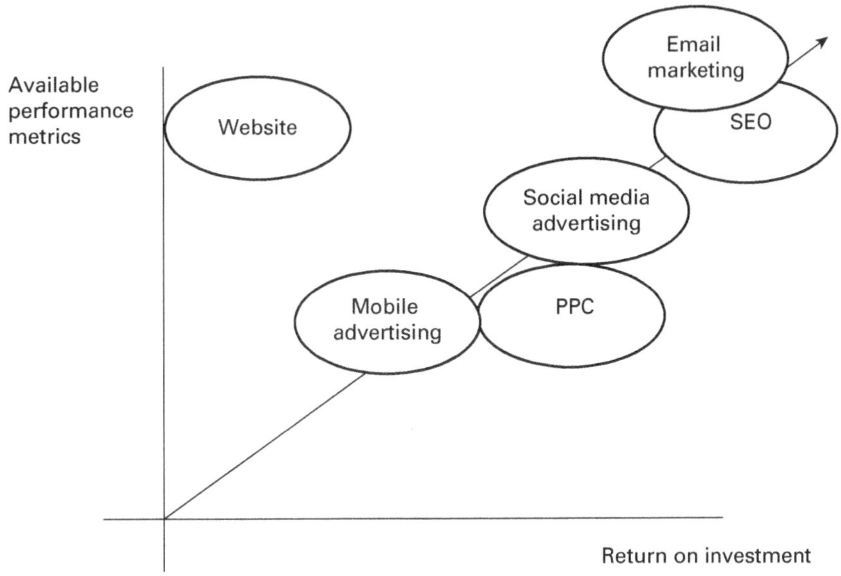

Available performance metrics

Email marketing

Website

SEO

Social media advertising

Mobile advertising

PPC

Return on investment

SOURCE Knight, 2022; some content based on Wishpond (nd)

Accountability in the digital world

The digital world has grown exponentially since access to the internet was introduced globally in the late 1990s. The last decade in particular has shown tremendous growth in user access and online activities. We spend a lot of time on the internet, making millions of transactions every minute. This time spent online poses new opportunities for businesses to reach and interact with new audiences.

Legislation and standards, however, have not developed fast enough to keep up with this rapid development in technology. The absence of clear guidelines unavoidably leads to people and businesses testing boundaries of what is appropriate. For example, the European Commission has accused Google of anti-competitive conduct in online advertising technology (European Commission, 2021). Some businesses themselves request such regulations and standards to be set (Zuckerberg, 2019). Mark Zuckerberg, the founder of Facebook, said new regulations are needed in four areas: harmful content, election integrity, privacy and data portability.

There will be a significant impact on the marketing industry when such legislation and rules are introduced. Stewart (2019) specifies four primary sources of concern regarding accountability in the digital world. He specifies that these are not all exclusive to digital technologies but play a crucial role:

1 **Privacy:** The right to privacy is one of the main concerns of the digital world. The amount of user data being collected is mostly unregulated. There are attempts

being made to protect users' data, such as the GDPR introduced by the European Union. However, due to the monopolist situation of the leading technology firms (such as Google, Facebook and Amazon), the data collected can draw a very clear picture of consumers. Stewart (2019) argues that protecting the users' privacy concerns ownership and control of personal information, and stronger regulations should be put in place to protect users.

2 **Fraud and inappropriate information:** Fraud and inappropriate information are easily published and shared in the digital world. With the digitalization of advertising comes a growing risk of fraud. The worldwide costs related to fraud in digital advertising were assessed to grow from $35 billion to $100 billion between 2018 and 2023 (Statista Research Department, 2021). Ad fraud can take many shapes, from click fraud, where fake ad impressions are generated, to 'ad stuffing' and serving hidden ad impressions (Hornby, 2016).

3 **Competition and marketing concentration:** The concentration of market power to a few leading players in the digital world has raised concerns in the past. Companies such as Meta, which owns Facebook, WhatsApp and Instagram, can collect and combine vast data on their consumers. Some countries have taken legal action to avoid such detailed consumer profiles from being established through the collected data on social media channels. The German competition regulator, Bundeskartellamt, has enforced limitations on how Facebook can process and combine its users' data and stipulated that users have to provide voluntary consent (Singer, 2019).

4 **Management of assets:** As part of the business, marketing usually produces several intangible assets such as brands and customer loyalty. These assets contribute to the business's overall success but are very difficult to quantify in terms of value. Future rules and regulations about marketing in the digital world have to recognize the role of intangible assets and their benefits to the consumer and the business (Stewart, 2019).

Activity 4.2

A lack of legislation and standards reduces businesses' accountability when operating in the digital world. Businesses and individuals take advantage of this lack of regulations and are testing how far they can go without being held accountable. In the 1950s there was a big scandal about fixing TV quizzes. The ins and outs of this scandal aren't too dissimilar from where we are today.

i.   Visit the Television Heaven website.

ii. Familiarize yourself with what happened in the quiz show scandals of the 1950s.

iii. Why do you think the networks thought they could get away with what they were doing?

iv. Do you believe they broke the law?

v. Where do you see parallels between the scandal of the 1950s and the issues we are facing today?

Accountability in the digital world describes both rights and responsibilities online. People would be held accountable for what they do in the real world, and the same should apply in the digital world. Unfortunately, the rapid development and novelty of the internet led to a problem for lawmakers not being able to catch up with regulations that clarify such rights and responsibilities. Growing concerns about a lack of accountability in the digital world have been raised among businesses, governments and consumers. There are three main groups online that we will review regarding accountability in the digital world:

- **Individuals:** We shop, search, message and share online, and with those transactions come responsibilities. If we cause any harm online, we need to be willing to face the consequences. Digital accountability for individuals means following generally accepted rules of behaviour and facing the consequences if you do not follow them. Such rules include some of the following:
  - Do not share any offensive or rude material.
  - Do not disguise your identity online.
  - Do not threaten or harm any other online users.
  - Don't be disrespectful towards others when voicing your opinion.
- **Government:** The government's digital accountability refers to the provision of easily accessible information about the government's actions. This refers to some of the following examples:
  - easily accessible information about how taxes are spent
  - transparency about how collected data is being used
  - ensuring safe storage and privacy of stored data
- **Businesses:** Businesses operate in several ways in the digital world. Accountability entails, therefore, a number of varying responsibilities for businesses. Some of those include:
  - treating the collected data of employees, customers and stakeholders respectfully
  - reviewing the use of digital technologies, so it does not harm society

o ensuring that digital transactions are safe

o preventing any third-party cyber attacks

All three actors – individuals, governments and businesses – must be accountable for their actions. Governments are starting to see the necessity to formalize accountability in the digital world in the form of lawful regulations. For example, the Digital Accountability and Transparency Act of 2014 was passed in the United States in 2014, and the Members of the European Parliament have adopted the Digital Services Act.

Activity 4.3

The Digital Services Act is an attempt by the European Commission to ensure a safe and accountable online environment.

i.   Visit the EU's website (European Commission, nd) and search for the article 'The Digital Services Act: Ensuring a safe and accountable online environment'.

ii. Review what the new rules according to the Act would mean for users, businesses and platforms.

iii. Do you think such an Act is necessary to ensure an accountable online environment?

Despite attempts by governments to formalize accountability in the digital world, the reality is that individuals, businesses and governments are currently still mainly being held accountable through self-regulation. One way businesses self-regulate their accountability is seen in the rise of corporate digital responsibility.

Corporate responsibility in the digital era

Businesses have widely applied the concept of *corporate social responsibility* since the 1970s (see also Chapter 24). It describes the idea that businesses exist due to public consent, so they have an obligation to contribute to the needs of society (*CSR Journal*, 2019).

KEY TERM
Corporate social responsibility (CSR)

Corporate social responsibility is a self-regulating business model that helps a company be socially accountable to itself, its stakeholders and the public.

SOURCE Fernando, 2022

Fernando (2022) explains that businesses that engage in CSR operate in ways that enhance society and the environment rather than contribute negatively to them. The business model of CSR has been contextualized to the digital world, coining the phrase *corporate digital responsibility* (see also Chapter 24). This concept, similar to CSR, is seen as a self-regulating business model that helps businesses to be held accountable to stakeholders and the public for actions in the digital world.

KEY TERM
Corporate digital responsibility (CDR)

Corporate digital responsibility is the set of shared values and norms guiding an organization's operations concerning four main digital technology and data processes. These processes are: creating technology and data capture; operation and decision-making; inspection and impact assessment; and refinement of technology and data.

SOURCE Lobschat et al, 2021

Some argue that corporate digital responsibility is, in fact, a subset of corporate social responsibility (Wade, 2020). More closely aligned to the definition of CSR, Wade (2020) explains CDR to be 'a set of practices and behaviours that help an organization use data and digital technologies in a way that is socially, economically, technologically and environmentally responsible'.

Despite this minor difference of opinion, CDR guides business in the responsible use of data. It aids in setting out standards for businesses to self-regulate their accountability. Chapter 24 will discuss CDR in further detail.

Unilever is at the forefront of implementing responsible behaviour in the digital space. In an attempt to combat digital advertising fraud, Unilever has created a network of Unilever Trusted Publishers. In collaboration with Unilever, this network of global, regional and local online publishers and platforms aims to transform online advertising into a more positive experience for the consumers online (Unilever, 2019).

Activity 4.4

You have now learnt about the term corporate digital responsibility. Unilever is a great advocate for ensuring responsible business practices.

i.   Visit Unilever's 'Planet & Society' web page.

ii. Try to find at least three CDR actions that Unilever seems to be taking.

iii. What do you reckon are the benefits for Unilever of taking part in CDR activities?

Summary

We have covered varying meanings of accountability in marketing. We started by reviewing general marketing accountability, regarding the marketing department as being held accountable for their spending and contribution to the overall business. We then discussed digital marketing accountability and covered how there are different levels of digital marketing accountability.

We then looked into accountability in the digital world, which dealt with customer privacy and data protection issues. We put this into the perspective of self-regulating business efforts without rules and regulations that guide accountability in the digital world. We introduced corporate digital responsibility as one of those self-regulating business models.

Chapter review

Reflective questions

Q1 What is the difference between marketing accountability and digital marketing accountability?

Q2 What are the four primary sources of concern for accountability in the digital world?

Q3 Who needs to be held accountable online and why?

Q4 What is corporate digital responsibility and how does it fit with corporate social responsibility?

Key learning points

- There are four primary sources of concern regarding accountability in the digital world: privacy, fraud and inappropriate information, competition and market concentration, and management of assets.

- There are three main groups online that have an interest in accountability in the digital world: individual users, businesses and the government.

- The importance of incorporating corporate digital responsibility into a business strategy.

References

CSR Journal (2019) A brief history of Corporate Social Responsibility in the US, 26 September, thecsrjournal.in/a-brief-history-of-corporate-social-responsibility-in-the-us/#:~:text= Although%20responsible%20companies%20had%20already,Social%20 Responsibilities%20of%20the%20Businessman (archived at https://perma.cc/BM4D-CLTU)

D&MA (2019) GDPR for marketers: Accountability, responsible marketing, dma.org.uk/ uploads/misc/new-gdpr-accountability.pdf (archived at https://perma.cc/863N-P7MR)

European Commission (2021) Antitrust: Commission opens investigation into possible anticompetitive conduct by Google in the online advertising technology sector, European Commission, 22 June, ec.europa.eu/commission/presscorner/detail/es/ip_21_3143 (archived at https://perma.cc/EWD8-DPQD)

European Commission (nd) The Digital Services Act: Ensuring a safe and accountable online environment, ec.europa.eu/info/strategy/priorities-2019-2024/europe-fit-digital-age/ digital-services-act-ensuring-safe-and-accountable-online-environment_en (archived at https://perma.cc/U4V8-6G8S)

Fernando, J (2022) Corporate social responsibility, Investopedia, 7 March, www. investopedia.com/terms/c/corp-social-responsibility.asp (archived at https://perma. cc/88LQ-4HAF)

Frankenfield, J (2020) General Data Protection Regulation (GDPR), Investopedia, 11 November, www.investopedia.com/terms/g/general-data-protection-regulation-gdpr. asp#:~:text=The%20General%20Data%20Protection%20Regulation%20(GDPR)%20 is%20a%20legal%20framework,the%20European%20Union%20(EU) (archived at https://perma.cc/E97W-BN6K)

Hornby, J (2016) Adland is failing to defeat digital fraud, *The Guardian*, 13 January, www. theguardian.com/media-network/2016/jan/13/johnny-hornby-online-digital-ad-fraud-advertising (archived at https://perma.cc/W4L5-RQGM)

Lobschat, L, Mueller, B, Eggers, F, Brandimarte, L, Diefenbach, S, Kroschke, M and Wirtz, J (2021) Corporate digital responsibility, *Journal of Business Research*, 122, 875–88

MASB (2016) Marketing accountability, Marketing Accountability Standards Board, October, marketing-dictionary.org/m/marketing-accountability/ (archived at https://perma.cc/ KNN7-CATH)

Singer, H (2019) Germany's competition agency cracks down on Facebook: But is antitrust the right tool for the job? *Forbes*, 18 March, www.forbes.com/sites/washingtonbytes/ 2019/03/18/germanys-competition-agency-cracks-down-on-facebook-but-is-antitrust-the-right-tool-for-the-job/?sh=3d974e24260e (archived at https://perma.cc/R7K6-PW53)

Statista Research Department (2021) Estimated costs of digital ad fraud worldwide from 2018 to 2023, Statista, 14 September, www.statista.com/statistics/677466/digital-ad-fraud-cost/ (archived at https://perma.cc/AQ92-6883)

Stewart, D W (2009) Marketing accountability: Linking marketing actions to financial results, *Journal of Business Research*, 62, 636–43

Stewart, D W (2019) The accountability crisis in advertising and marketing: Self-regulation and deeper metrics are needed to survive the digital age, *Journal of Advertising Research*, December, 385–90

Television Heaven (nd) televisionheaven.co.uk/tv-history/the-quiz-show-scandals-of-the-1950s (archived at https://perma.cc/RH53-D4ZE)

Unilever (2019) Unilever unveils next phase in clean-up of digital advertising with creation of Unilever Trusted Publishers, 28 March, www.unilever.com/news/press-and-media/ press-releases/2019/unilever-unveils-next-phase-in-clean-up-of-digital-advertising-with-creation-of-unilever-trusted-publishers/ (archived at https://perma.cc/GT5T-D6XE)

Unilever (nd) Planet and society, www.unilever.com/planet-and-society/ (archived at https:// perma.cc/7BDE-9X7F)

Wade, M (2020) Corporate responsibility in the digital era, *MIT Sloan Management Review*, 28 April, sloanreview.mit.edu/article/corporate-responsibility-in-the-digital-era/ (archived at https://perma.cc/EQ7X-EK69)

Waterson, J and Milmo, D (2021) Facebook whistleblower Frances Haugen calls for urgent external regulation, *The Guardian*, 25 October, www.theguardian.com/technology/2021/ oct/25/facebook-whistleblower-frances-haugen-calls-for-urgent-external-regulation (archived at https://perma.cc/PJ64-FTRZ)

Wishpond (nd) Which digital marketing channels offer the best ROI? blog.wishpond.com/ post/115675438234/best-marketing-roi (archived at https://perma.cc/TW5S-JZQF)

Zuckerberg, M (2019) Opinion: Mark Zuckerberg: The internet needs new rules. Let's start in these four areas, *The Washington Post*, 30 March, www.washingtonpost.com/opinions/ mark-zuckerberg-the-internet-needs-new-rules-lets-start-in-these-four-areas/2019/ 03/29/9e6f0504-521a-11e9-a3f7-78b7525a8d5f_story.html?noredirect=on (archived at https://perma.cc/8SA5-N2YV)

PART TWO
Researching the digital environment

The macro-environment

05

By the end of this chapter, you should be able to:

- explain the importance of monitoring the external macro-environment
- distinguish between the different forces that shape the macro-environment
- conduct a macro-environmental analysis
- elaborate on how forces in the macro-environment can impact businesses and digital marketing

Introduction

The macro-environment of a business refers to forces in the wider economy of a company. Forces in the macro-environment may present opportunities or pose threats to a business and are usually hard to control. For example, higher charges will occur for business loans if interest rates are raised nationally. Nevertheless, digital marketers need to monitor changes in the macro-environment before these become threats to the business.

The macro-environment consists of several forces such as political influences, cultural changes, innovations in technology, laws and economic development. The digital marketer has to be particularly informed about trends and innovations in technology to stay competitive. This involves turning macro-environmental forces into opportunities for businesses. A common framework to apply when analysing the *macro-environment* is the *PESTEL analysis*. PESTEL stands for political, economic, social/cultural, technological, environmental and legal forces.

This chapter will explain such forces in detail and discuss how these might impact businesses and digital marketing. You will find a template in Worksheet 1 in Additional Resources that you can use to conduct a macro-environmental analysis.

> **KEY TERM**
> Macro-environment
>
> The macro-environment refers to the set of conditions in the economy as a whole rather than in a particular sector or region. The state of the macro-environment affects business decisions on things such as spending, borrowing, and investing.
>
> **SOURCE** Khartit, 2021

Competitive advantage

Businesses that monitor and respond effectively to their macro environment can create differentiation and a *competitive advantage* that enables the company to survive and prosper. Reviewing the macro-environmental forces allows businesses to innovate better products and services and create advantages to perform better than their competitors.

> **KEY TERM**
> Competitive advantage
>
> Competitive advantage refers to factors that allow a company to produce goods or services better or more cheaply than its rivals. These factors allow the productive entity to generate more sales or superior margins compared to its market rivals. Competitive advantages are attributed to a variety of factors including cost structure, branding, the quality of product offerings, the distribution network, intellectual property and customer service.
>
> **SOURCE** Twin, 2021

As you can see from the key term definition, several attributes can result in businesses gaining a competitive advantage. These can be based on actual product features, such as the quality of the product. Alternatively, additional services such as overall customer service or an efficient distribution network can result in a competitive advantage. Take, for example, Amazon, the biggest marketplace in the world. Amazon's core strength is fast delivery times enabled through an extensive distribution network. Besides internal factors that can lead to competitive advantage, monitoring the macro-environment and reacting to changes is another way of ensuring a competitive edge. We will discuss critical macro-environmental factors in detail in the following section.

Activity 5.1

Apple has managed to sustain a competitive advantage for an extended period.

i. Visit Apple's website and review the products and services that Apple is offering.

ii. Based on Apple's products and services, what do you reckon aids their sustained competitive advantage?

Key macro-environment factors

Technology

Technological innovation has changed the way we live for generations. Just think of the mainstream adoption of television in the 1950s. People didn't have to rely on audio through radio any more but experienced a completely new visual way of entertainment. Such innovations usually had implications for businesses and marketers, as they provided new routes to reach and engage with customers. Advertisement could now include moving pictures and sound, which opened many opportunities for businesses.

   The difference between technological change then and today is the speed of developing new products and services. Take Facebook as an example. Not even 20 years ago, it started as a platform to connect students at one university with each other. In 2022, Facebook has almost 2.9 billion active monthly users (Statista, 2022). That means that more than one-third of the world's population is connected through a single platform. Around 6.2 billion people are estimated to own a smartphone subscription worldwide (Statista Research Department, 2022). Owning a smartphone means that customers can connect and shop wherever and whenever they want. As you can imagine, such innovation and adoption of digital technology have significant implications for marketers and consumers. Technological change can lead to opportunities for businesses by, for example, developing new products, creating new markets or changing the way we communicate. The following describes current trends and forces in digital technology of which marketers should be aware.

Artificial intelligence

Many of us think of robots when we hear the term 'artificial intelligence' (AI). While robots are certainly one form of AI, plenty of other applications are relevant to digital marketing. One of the core attributes of *artificial intelligence* is machine learning. Machine learning refers to the fact that computer programs can learn from and adapt to new data without the assistance of humans (Frankenfield, 2021).

> **KEY TERM**
> Artificial intelligence (AI)
>
> Artificial intelligence refers to the simulation of human intelligence in machines that are programmed to think like humans and mimic their actions. The term may also be applied to any machine that exhibits traits associated with a human mind such as learning and problem-solving.

AI will impact digital marketing by allowing better decision-making through rich data sets that recognize consumer trends. AI also will enable businesses to personalize their messages on a grand scale by generating unique data profiles. Amazon is driving 35 per cent of its total sales by suggesting real-time customized recommendations, created by combining past consumer behaviour and predictive algorithms (Rintanen, 2022).

Metaverse

Facebook's CEO Mark Zuckerberg announced in 2021 that the company will invest $10 billion in the development of the *metaverse*, the future of the internet. It is explained as a space where the physical and digital worlds come together (Milmo, 2021).

> **KEY TERM**
> Metaverse
>
> The metaverse is a space where digital representations of people – avatars – interact at work and play, meeting in their office, going to concerts and even trying on clothes.
>
> **SOURCE** Milmo, 2021

Large brands seem to be already considering how the metaverse could impact marketing opportunities, but nobody knows yet what that will look like. It needs to be noted that such a novel concept as the metaverse will have significant implications on how to reach and engage consumers. Interestingly, research has shown that 22 per cent of US respondents think that brands should advertise in the metaverse.

CASE STUDY   Meta

Facebook has rebranded itself as Meta and announced a substantial investment in the metaverse – a space where the physical and the digital world come together. While nobody knows yet exactly what the metaverse will look like, a lot of interest has already been noted. Interest seems to be soaring in Asia while both European and American users currently remain critical (Rintanen, 2022). Some 36 per cent of UK and 27 per cent of US respondents say they do not need the metaverse in their lives (Proulx, 2021).

Facebook has come under immense pressure from consumer groups, regulators and politicians worldwide to review its impact on users. With Meta owning popular social media channels such as Instagram and WhatsApp, more calls are being heard asking the tech giant to be limited in its monopolistic market power. Facebook's immense influence can be seen in its profits, mainly generated from harvesting users' data and selling this data to advertisers. Across all of its platforms, Facebook generated a net income of $29 billion in 2020 (Milmo, 2021).

Other issues surrounding the metaverse concern privacy, security and ethics. Data collected about consumers on social media platforms is already very rich in detail and allows for precise targeting. If you take a virtual space, collected data can go further by looking at the user's body language and other physiological responses (Milmo, 2021). This could have numerous implications, especially thinking about some of the younger users.

Meta is trying to develop the metaverse responsibly by investing money in organizations as well as academic institutions such as the Seoul National University and Women in Immersive Tech (Milmo, 2021). It remains to be seen whether the development of the metaverse will end as a digital marketer's heaven or a nightmare.

Questions

- Metaverse is a very innovative new way of coming together but also has some ethical questions to answer. What are your thoughts on the metaverse?
- Try to visualize how businesses could advertise in the metaverse.

Blockchain and cryptocurrencies

Other technological breakthroughs that potentially have significant implications for how we do business are blockchain technologies and cryptocurrencies. In very simple terms, a *blockchain* can be described as a peer-to-peer exchange that eliminates the need for a third party (Feeney, 2021). Blockchain technology has been crucial in the success of cryptocurrencies as it can facilitate a secure and decentralized record of transactions (Hayes, 2022).

> **KEY TERM**
> Blockchain
>
> A blockchain is a distributed database that is shared among the nodes of a computer network. As a database, a blockchain stores information electronically in digital format.
>
> **SOURCE** Hayes, 2022

The most common use for blockchain technology is as a ledger for transactions, even though different types of information can be stored on a blockchain. Blockchain technology is so relevant because it is used in a decentralized way. This means that rather than a single person or institution having control, all users collectively hold control (Hayes, 2022). This has been why blockchain technology has been so crucial to the success of *cryptocurrencies*. For example, Bitcoin is built on a blockchain and uses it as a means to transparently record a ledger of payments (Hayes, 2022).

> **KEY TERM**
> Cryptocurrencies
>
> A cryptocurrency is a digital or virtual currency that is secured by cryptography, which makes it nearly impossible to counterfeit or double-spend. Many cryptocurrencies are decentralized networks based on blockchain technology. A defining feature of cryptocurrencies is that they are generally not issued by any central authority, rendering them theoretically immune to government interference or manipulation.
>
> **SOURCE** Frankenfield, 2022a

Frankenfield (2022a) outlines the advantages of cryptocurrencies: money transfers are cheaper and faster than traditional currencies. Furthermore, as the system is decentralized it is less likely to collapse at a single point of failure. Disadvantages include price volatility and use in criminal activities.

There are numerous ways in which blockchain technology and cryptocurrencies are relevant to digital marketing. One key aspect of blockchain technology is that it can facilitate transactions without the need for a third party. This also applies to digital marketing activities and could change the way businesses and consumers interact (Feeney, 2021). For example, if you think of traditional advertising on social media channels, you usually have the advertiser, the social media platform and the consumer. Blockchain technology would allow businesses to directly market to the consumer without needing the social media platform. Advertisers would upload their advertisements to a blockchain, and the block-chain would make them available to its users (Wise Marketer, 2022). Blockchain allows companies to collect customer data and create individual consumer pro-files that are incorruptible which will help to create more targeted campaigns. Also, the more widely used blockchain technology and cryptocurrencies become, businesses will need to consider incorporating them into their marketing strate-gies in rewards or loyalty programmes (Wise Marketer, 2022).

Non-fungible tokens

Non-fungible tokens (NFTs) are digital assets representing a real-world object and are often bought and sold online using cryptocurrency (Conti, 2022). Similarly to cryptocurrency, NFTs are encoded with the same underlying software. NFT's live on the blockchain that functions as a ledger, and it keeps track of when the NFT was bought, how much it was bought for and how much it was sold for (Digital Marketer, 2021). So instead of keeping a receipt when you have purchased an NFT, that pur-chase goes on the blockchain.

One of the strong selling points of an NFT is that, contrary to most digital assets, NFTs have limited supply (Conti, 2022). It is common for digital assets to have an infinite supply which devalues their nature. On the contrary, creating scarcity around NFTs is one of their unique selling points. An NFT can be many different things, ranging from digital artwork to a domain name and an event ticket (Ethereum, 2022). One of the most famous examples of an NFT is the hugely popular YouTube video *Charlie Bit Me*, that sold as an NFT in 2021 for £500,000 (Evans, 2021).

Activity 5.2

Ethereum is a platform powered by blockchain technology, best known for its native cryptocurrency called Ether. Ethereum was second in market value only to Bitcoin as of January 2022 (Frankenfield, 2022b).

i.   Visit Ethereum.org, search for the page 'Non-fungible tokens (NFT)' and read the difference between 'An NFT internet' and 'The internet today'.

ii. Do you think that an NFT internet will be the future for the typical consumer?

iii. Take a look at the NFT examples to understand how broad the spectrum of NFT products is.

NFTs should be seen as products in the form of digital assets and require to be marketed as such. Digital Marketer (2021) recommends focusing on telling people why owning an NFT would be beneficial to the consumer and stresses three considerations when trying to market an NFT:

- understand your customer to see why they care about the NFT
- validate whether the customers are ready for NFTs – they should at least own cryptocurrency to be able to purchase an NFT
- if your customers understand NFTs and have the means to purchase, then determine what utility best aligns with your product

Social commerce

Have you ever bought your favourite brand directly on your social media channel? Then you aren't alone. *Social commerce* describes the process of selling products directly on social media and is a market projected to become a $605 billion market by 2027 (McLachlan, 2020). The complete customer journey from product discovery to the checkout process takes place on the social media platform.

KEY TERM
Social commerce

Social commerce uses networking websites such as Facebook, Instagram and Twitter as vehicles to promote and sell products and services. A social commerce campaign's success is measured by the degree to which consumers interact with the company's marketing through retweets, likes and shares.

SOURCE Dollarhide, 2022

Social commerce is executed slightly differently on several large social media channels. Burton (2021) outlines the social commerce offerings on the big platforms:

- **Facebook Shops:** On Facebook, brands can set up free Facebook Shops where users can complete purchases within the app or on the seller's website. Facebook Messenger can be used to communicate directly with brands.
- **Facebook Live Shopping:** Live Shopping Fridays let Facebook users see products in action, ask questions and make purchases all in real time.
- **Instagram shoppable posts:** These are linked to a Facebook Shop account. Sales are completed either in-app or on the brand's website.

- **Pinterest Product Pins:** These provide space for price and availability details and redirect to product landing pages.
- **Twitter Shop Module:** This allows select brands to showcase products at the top of Twitter business profiles. Users can scroll through a carousel of products on a brand's profile, and tap on individual products to read more and purchase without leaving the platform.

One of the most important features of social commerce is consumer interaction. According to Dollarhide (2022) several different tactics are employed by businesses that are successful in social commerce:

- encouraging users to provide their opinion in the form of voting for their favourite product
- using videos, 360-degree pictures and large graphics to attract viewer clicks
- stimulating consumer involvement with user-submitted photos and commentary
- using celebrities and influencers
- offering special deals to those who share the product on their feeds
- linking to the checkout

Most brands succeed by establishing some of these tactics in their social commerce. For example, whereas ASOS is very successful by using bold and large pictures, Burberry convinces its consumers using short product videos. J Crew puts consumer feedback at the forefront of its campaigns and Haiavanas encourages user-generated content by featuring consumers' pictures in their social commerce content (Barnhart, 2022).

Economy

The economic environment includes factors that potentially impact consumer spending and the overall economic climate. Marketers must be aware of economic developments to foresee spending patterns and communicate messages that resonate with consumers. If consumers have less disposable income due to a rise in living costs, marketers should focus on messages that stress value rather than luxury. We will review three main economic influences on the marketing environment.

Economic climate

Businesses need to closely monitor the economy of any given market, national or international, to understand consumers' purchasing power and spending patterns. The economic climate within a particular market will be influenced by figures such as *economic growth* and unemployment rates.

> **KEY TERM**
> Economic growth
>
> Economic growth is an increase in the production of economic goods and services, compared from one period of time to another.
>
> **SOURCE** Potters, 2021

There are several different ways in which economic growth can be generated. Potters (2021) outlines four different strategies for encouraging economic growth:

1 increase in capital goods (more tools equal more output)

2 technology improvement (better tools equal more output)

3 grow the labour force (more workers equal more output)

4 increase in human capital (better-skilled workers equal more output)

One way of looking at economic growth is to compare a person's income with the prices of goods and services that person wants. This would enable us to measure the options that a person's income represents (Roser, 2021). This is important for marketers to consider as it determines what consumers deem affordable. For example, if a person would have to work for two months to afford to buy a particular product, this effort would need to be reflected in the marketing strategy. Marketing mix decisions such as product pricing and promotions would need to consider that the average person would have to work for two months to afford the said product.

It is also essential to consider that it might take a person in the UK, for example, less time to work for the product they want than it would a person in India. Imagine you live in a country with minimal economic growth – say, with incomes that are ten times lower. This means that everything you want to buy would suddenly cost ten times more. So instead of paying £1 for a pint of milk, you would suddenly have to pay £10 for the same product. These changed prices would enormously impact what you could afford, and you would have to adjust your consumption choices (Roser, 2021).

Interest and exchange rates

Interest and exchange rates are essential to consider as they indicate the economic climate.

In very simple terms, an interest rate outlines how high the cost of borrowing is or how high the rewards for saving money are (Bank of England, 2022). If you want to borrow money, the interest rate would be shown as a percentage of how much more money you will have to pay back. The saving rate will determine how much money will be paid as a percentage of your savings if you are saving money. Consumers, as well as businesses, need to have an understanding of whether interest rates fall or rise.

High interest rates mean that fewer people would borrow money to purchase products. There is a rising trend of buying products and services using BNPL (buy now, pay later) schemes (Aratani, 2022). Many of these are impacted by interest rates, which means borrowing money would get more expensive if interest rates rose.

An exchange rate is the value of one currency compared to another currency. For example, how many British pounds does it take to buy a euro? The exchange rate is essential to consider as it can increase or decrease the price of products. For example, if a business produces televisions, the materials are often bought in different countries, and the televisions are produced in yet another country. If the exchange rate favours the business's home country, this would mean that it is cheaper to buy the materials and pay the labour to produce the products. If the exchange rate changes to become unfavourable for the home country, these aspects would become more expensive as a business would need more money for the same products and services.

Brexit and the European Union

Twenty-seven countries form the European Union (EU), an economic and political union. The EU is important to consider as an environmental force as it has substantial implications for marketers. Goods, capital, services and people can move freely between member states as the EU operates a single market (UK Government, 2022a).

The aims of the EU are of a societal and economic nature. Aims relating to societal prosperity deal with promoting peace, offering security, combating social exclusion and respecting culture. Some economic aims stress establishing an internal market, enhancing economic solidarity, establishing a monetary union, and achieving sustainable development based on balanced economic growth and price stability (European Union, 2022).

The single market means that products and services can move freely between Member States. This is particularly important for digital marketplaces as consumers aren't restricted from where they buy. No additional taxes would be charged for purchasing a product from a different Member State. Businesses with a strong e-commerce standing benefit from being able to cater to Europe as a whole rather than only their home market.

However, the EU is not without its challenges, with significant discrepancies between members' economic wealth and cultural differences need to be considered when planning digital marketing strategies.

The term Brexit refers to the decision made by the UK in 2016 to leave the EU. Leaving the EU has several implications for the UK according to Edgington (2020):

- There is no more freedom to work and live between the UK and the EU.
- British citizens now require a visa if they want to spend more than 90 days in an EU country.
- New checks are introduced at borders, such as safety checks and customs declarations.
- Businesses offering services, such as banking, architecture and accounting, will lose their automatic right of access to EU markets and will face some restrictions.
- There will no longer be automatic recognition of professional qualifications for people such as doctors, chefs and architects.

As you can imagine, some of these changes have severe implications for businesses in general and digital marketers in particular. The pool of potential employees has shrunk, and doing business with the EU has become more time-intensive and requires additional taxation and paperwork. Digital marketers are impacted in that the data protection of their consumers needs to be reviewed and ensured.

Activity 5.3

The UK government has outlined how Brexit rules apply to doing business with the EU.

i.   Visit the website on Brexit guidance (UK Government, 2022b).

ii.   Try to identify three rules that would have a direct impact (good or bad) on digital marketing.

iii. Try to come up with solutions of how negative impacts could be avoided.

Society and culture

We have covered how technological and economic forces may impact businesses and consumers. As you have previously seen, innovation in technology changes how a company can engage customers. Consumer income has implications on whether consumers choose to buy something or not. Other areas that require attention are societal and cultural forces. Cultural and societal shifts can significantly influence consumer behaviour and require close attention from companies. Such changes can happen relatively slowly, such as an ageing world population, or faster, such as consumer trends (e.g. veganism).

Demographics

Demographics refers to factors that describe a population and socioeconomic information. Monitoring these forces can be helpful for governments and companies.

KEY TERM
Demographics

Demographic analysis is the study of a population based on factors such as age, race and sex. Demographic data refers to socioeconomic information expressed statistically, including employment, education, income, marriage rates, birth and death rates, and more.

SOURCE Hayes, 2021

As described in Chapters 2 and 10, knowing your customers is essential when designing your digital marketing strategy. Dividing your market according to demographic and socioeconomic data is segmenting your market. Therefore, a business needs to know the demographic data of its consumers. A company's target market might consist of male consumers in their late 20s, who earn above-average income and are married with young children. Companies could look at the data and find out exactly how big their potential target audience is and where they could find them. The importance of monitoring the external environment for demographics is to be aware of changes. If we revisit our example, a change in demographics might be that men are getting married later. Hence, if the company were to continue to target married men, it would be unlikely to execute a successful digital marketing strategy.

Socioeconomic trends can have significant implications for businesses too. If you think of employment rates, companies must be aware if these are rising. During the 2020 Covid pandemic, many people were made redundant or put on furlough. This meant that a larger than usual part of the population had to do with less disposable income than previously. Successful companies would reflect such changes in their digital marketing strategy.

Ketter and Avraham (2021) found that such a shift in communication strategy was particularly prominent among tourism businesses. Many digital marketing strategies were observed that acknowledged social and cultural changes. These strategies were executed in different shapes and forms. The official Greek tourism promotor Discover Greece implemented a digital marketing campaign on YouTube called 'Greece from home'. This campaign featured Greek artists, cooks, musicians and sports personalities that posted short videos. The message was that while people could not visit Greece, they could still interact with the destination online (Ketter and Avraham, 2021).

Activity 5.4

Countries have executed different digital marketing campaigns in 2021 and 2022 to attract tourists after the Covid-19 pandemic.

i.   Visit the YouTube channel of #Love GREAT Britain, and search for the video 'We're Open – Know before you go' as well as New Zealand's tourism channel on YouTube #NewZealand: 100 per cent Pure New Zealand, and search for 'A journey of reflection'.

ii. Try to identify which social and cultural shifts these campaigns focus on.

iii. How do these campaigns differ, and where do you see similarities?

Another crucial demographic force to consider is age distribution across the world. A lot of the Western world is struggling with an ageing population. This means that fewer people are dying than are born. This has several implications for society, a main one being a shrinking workforce and insufficient funds to care for the elderly. By 2050, 1 in 6 people will be older than 65 years. This is almost double the 2019 figure when only 1 in 11 people was over 65 (United Nations, 2019).

The household structure is changing across the globe and needs to be considered by businesses. The traditionally depicted family structure of two straight, white, married parents with an average of two birth children does not reflect reality any more. Instead, family structures are much more diverse. Many more families have mixed cultural, ethnic or religious backgrounds, and with a rise in divorce rates, single parents and stepfamilies are much more common. Many countries now allow gay couples to marry, challenging traditional male/female parenting. Many successful companies reflect these societal changes in their advertising campaigns.

CASE STUDY   Starbucks

Starbucks has supported LGBT+ rights for a long time and often features same-sex couples in their advertising. In 2020 Starbucks launched a #whatsyourname campaign showing their support for transgender people (Starbucks, 2020). Starbucks openly supports same-sex marriage and is creating 'safe spaces' for their LGBT+ customers.

Most customers appreciate this consideration for a societal shift but Starbucks has reported that some governments are boycotting the business over their support of gay rights. Howard Schultz, CEO of Starbucks, has stated that he doesn't welcome customers or stockholders who are against same-sex marriage (British LGBT Awards, 2022).

Questions

- The above examples show how some companies openly support societal causes.
- What do you think might be the advantages and disadvantages for businesses doing so?

Cultural trends

We have discussed how demographic changes need to be monitored for businesses to understand their environment. An advantage of demographic forces is that they are relatively easy to measure and the data is readily available. For example, a business could easily identify the size of its target market if based on demographical data such as gender, age and family status. Cultural shifts and trends are much harder to quantify but are just as important to consider.

Cultural factors or forces refer to the values an individual or a group of individuals holds. These values are based on different habits and beliefs and are usually formed during upbringing. Family values highly impact individual values and differ tremendously across cultures.

KEY TERM
Cultural forces

Culture encompasses the set of beliefs, moral values, traditions, language and laws (or rules of behaviour) held in common by a nation, a community, or other defined group of people. Culturally determined characteristics include: the language spoken at home; religious observances; customs (including marriage customs that often accompany religious and other beliefs); acceptable gender roles and occupations; dietary practices; intellectual, artistic and leisure-time pursuits; and other aspects of behaviour.

SOURCE Trollope-Kumar and Last, 2022

As you can see from the definition, cultural forces contain a lot of different aspects. It is important to note that cultural forces do not only apply to a limited geographical area but are established through similar characteristics. For example, teenagers worldwide portray a similar consumer culture by wanting to spend on social media and purchasing the things they come across on those channels. So even though their religion and language might be different, they probably care about similar product offerings. Such smaller groups are part of a subculture formed through similar leisure-time pursuits.

There has been a growing trend to care about ethical consumption, especially among younger audiences. This form of consumption cares about fair trade, animal welfare, organic products and others.

Ethical consumption

Ethical consumption, which arises from *ethical consumer behaviour*, has existed for a long time but it is only in the last two decades that it seems to have caught mainstream attraction.

KEY TERM
Ethical consumer behaviour

Ethical consumer behaviour is decision-making, purchases and other consumption experiences that are affected by the consumer's ethical concerns.

SOURCE Bray et al, 2011

This definition is very general and includes several aspects of the consumer journey. Consumers can start to make ethical choices when deciding whether to buy a product at all. A trend that is growing in popularity is to stop any new purchases at all to reduce consumerism. In other words, consumers actively choose not to consume and instead purchase used products. Companies such as eBay and Vinted are examples of digital businesses that cater for this trend.

Boycotting products that do not follow ethical principles held by the consumer is another way of executing ethical consumerism at the very early stages of the buying process. On the flip side, consumers may decide to buy products that overlap their moral principles. Examples of such products might be fair trade coffee, products free of animal testing and sweatshop-free clothing.

Other consumption experiences might relate to online experiences where the ethical consumer might want to be assured of the business conducting ethical practices regarding data privacy.

Activity 5.5

Some companies put great emphasis on catering for the ethical consumer. The Ethical Consumer is a website rating brands and products according to ethical principles of people, politics, animals and the planet.

i. Visit the Ethicalconsumer.org website.

ii. Type your favourite brand in the search tab.

iii. Take a look at how ethical your favourite brand is.

Businesses need to be aware of cultural and demographic changes to cater to their customers' needs. Digital marketing strategies need to reflect cultural shifts and trends to feel relevant to a particular target audience. Holbrook (1987) introduced an approach known as 'advertising as a social mirror'. The argument is that advertising should reflect the values, attitudes and trends that already exist in society (Ketter and Avraham, 2021). The digital landscape has highlighted this need even further. This is due to more transparency in business practices and faster communication among consumers. Unethical business practices used to be more challenging for consumers to identify.

Environment

The physical environment is another macro-environmental force that needs to be considered by businesses. It describes the relationship between people and the environment. We have previously discussed ethical consumers, a group which would include consumers who care about brands and businesses that protect the environment.

Climate change

Climate change has been one of the most prominent topics dealing with protecting the environment over the past two decades.

KEY TERM
Climate change

Climate change refers to long-term shifts in temperatures and weather patterns. These shifts may be natural, such as through variations in the solar cycle. But since the 1800s, human activities have been the main drivers of climate change, primarily due to burning fossil fuels like coal, oil and gas.

SOURCE United Nations, 2022

There has been a lot of publicity about climate change, particularly since 2018 when Greta Thunberg, a 15-year-old Swedish schoolgirl, protested outside the Swedish Parliament and who has become a symbol of climate change for a whole generation. Since then, Greta has spoken at numerous climate change events and has initiated climate change protests worldwide (Kraemer, 2021).

The consequences of climate change are droughts, water scarcity, forest fires, declining biodiversity, flooding and melting polar ice (United Nations, 2022). These daunting consequences worry consumers, with 37 per cent of the world's population claiming that climate change is their main environmental concern (Lyons, 2019).

Businesses need to understand these concerns and communicate whether they are doing something about it. Some big brands are powerful in expressing their support for fighting climate change. Volvo is one car brand that actively participates in the global warming discussion and tries to educate its customers through its communication strategy. This includes, for example, publishing a children's book that covers global warming issues (Lyons, 2019).

Pollution

Businesses often face criticism for contributing to polluting our planet. Large-scale manufacturing processes, expensive waste disposal and lack of proper waste management are just some of the contributing factors. One of the main issues is the vast production of single-use plastic products. The figures are staggering; for example, half of all plastics ever manufactured have been made in the last 15 years (Parker, 2019). This number shows the problem of speed of production. Another significant issue is how long it takes for plastic to break down. Scientists estimate that a lot of plastic takes at least 400 years to dissolve (Parker, 2019).

Some of the primary problems of plastic pollution are:

- entangled marine species being injured or killed
- threat to food safety and quality through microplastics
- contribution to climate change

Many governments, especially in poorer countries, do not have the means or infrastructure to avoid plastic pollution. This is why there are many calls for businesses to contribute to the fight against plastic pollution. Some of the major global brands are already participating. For example, McDonald's has pledged to ensure 100 per cent of its packaging comes from renewable, recycled or certified sustainable sources by 2026 (Wentworth, 2018).

Recycling

One of the main challenges that companies face is their packaging. As we have seen, large brands such as McDonald's aim to improve their packaging to reduce its impact on the environment. Recycling describes the process of transforming waste into material that can be used again. Recycling is done to varying degrees in different countries and on a national level is guided by government waste collection schemes. For example, in England, waste that can be recycled is collected separately to waste that will end up in a landfill.

Businesses often show their support by taking part in recycling initiatives. These range from using recycled packaging (e.g. McDonald's) to producing actual products that are made from recycled material. H&M is among some of the fast-fashion brands that are already using 20 per cent recycled materials when producing their clothing (H&M Group, 2022). Other brands go even further and make their complete product from recycled material. The bag company Freitag started out by producing its bags from used truck tarps, discarded bicycle inner tubes and car seat belts (Freitag, 2022). While using recycled materials is no doubt something good to do, businesses need to be mindful not to overstate their involvement in such initiatives, as this might be seen as *greenwashing* (see also Chapters 12 and 24).

KEY TERM
Greenwashing

Greenwashing is the process of conveying a false impression or providing misleading information about how a company's products are more environmentally sound. Greenwashing is considered an unsubstantiated claim to deceive consumers into believing that a company's products are environmentally friendly. Created by Jay Westerveld in 1986, the term is used to describe companies' efforts to claim to be pro-sustainable to mislead consumers and cover up questionable environmental records.

SOURCE Kenton, 2022; Kopnina, 2019

Greenwashing is a real problem especially around recycling efforts as it is easy for companies to use some recycled materials and then overstate their efforts.

Activity 5.6

There are several reasons why businesses use recycled materials. Some companies do so to improve the planet, while others might want to reap the benefits of 'doing good' in the eyes of their customers.

i. Try to find three different brands that claim to use recycled materials.

ii.   Search their social media channels and websites for information about the usage of such materials.

iii. Does it seem like genuine attempts to save the environment or do you suspect greenwashing? If so, why?

Politics, laws and legal requirements

The internet is difficult to govern as it doesn't have borders like a country and is not run by one central governing body. However, there are some standard sets of rules that have to be followed in the cyberspace which are controlled by *internet governance*.

KEY TERM
Internet governance

Internet governance refers to the rules, policies, standards and practices that coordinate and shape global cyberspace.
SOURCE Internet Governance Project, 2022

Numerous actors together ensure internet governance. These range from the private sector to education groups and technical standards organizations to selected national governments. Several policy topics are covered by internet governance. These include, among others, cyber security, privacy and surveillance and digital trade (Internet Governance Project, 2022).

Besides internet governance, other political factors can also influence how we experience the internet. For example, the internet is more open in some countries than in other countries where a certain degree of censorship can be observed. Such censorship can be executed in various forms and for many different reasons. Censorship can be in place for religious reasons or to protect vulnerable audiences by stopping people from viewing pornographic sites. Other forms of internet censorship include blocking the distribution of political opinions (*The Guardian*, 2016).

The OpenNet Initiative (ONI) claim internet censorship and surveillance to be a growing global phenomenon and follow their mission to 'identify and document internet filtering and surveillance, and to promote and inform wider public dialogues about such practices' (OpenNet Initiative, nd). The initiative constantly reviews potential censorship in several countries and classifies the results based on four censorship categories:

- political: usually content opposing the current government
- social: usually content deemed offensive by society
- conflict security: usually content related to armed conflicts
- internet tools: usually tools that enable communication

The ONI then divides countries according to how severe the censorship is, ranging from 'No evidence of filtering' to 'Pervasive filtering'. For example, there is no evidence of filtering in any of those four categories in the UK (ONI United Kingdom, 2010). Compared to such an open internet, Iran came last in the openness ranking, with political, social and internet tools categories all pervasively filtered (*The Guardian*, 2016).

The more recent forms of censorship show that governments are less often fully banning complete websites and instead only putting temporary bans in place when perceived necessary, for example, around elections (*The Guardian*, 2016).

Internet censorship can impact businesses as some countries might be less available to enter than others, especially if products or services are deemed offensive or against the religious values of some governments.

Corporation tax and value-added tax on products are further examples of decisions made by politics that might impact businesses. These decisions affect the profitability of a business. If, for instance, the corporation would have to pay substantial corporation tax under the current government and a campaign promise of the opposing party includes the lowering of corporation tax, there would be a great incentive for the business to elect the opposing party. Furthermore, governments could change the national minimum wage, which would impact businesses if raised in terms of profits.

Finally, plenty of laws impact how businesses go about doing business and digital marketing online. These range from consumer protection acts to the General Data Protection Act and will be discussed in Chapter 25. A template for undertaking a macro-environmental analysis of digital marketing activities is provided in Worksheet 1 in the Additional Resources.

Summary

This chapter has discussed the external macro-environmental forces that can impact business in general and digital marketing decisions. These and many more forces require close observation by companies as they can become threats if left unacted. If recognized in time, these forces can also pose opportunities to businesses as they might provide a competitive edge.

We have put a lot of emphasis on the technological forces as these changes constantly and significantly impact digital marketing strategies. We have further reviewed economic forces as these can affect consumers' willingness to spend money. Societal changes require close attention from businesses as these can impact who to target. Demographic data helps understand how society is changing and is relatively easily available. Changes in consumer culture are even more important as they present new business opportunities if recognized in time. Ethical consumer behaviour is one such shift in a consumer culture where consumers care about how products are produced. Furthermore, we reviewed the physical environment and how things like pollution and climate change are forces that need to be considered when producing, packaging and marketing products and services. Finally, we have covered how politics can significantly influence how open the internet is and which parties actually 'govern' the internet.

Chapter review

Reflective questions

Q1 Why is it essential for a business to review its external macro-environment?

Q2 What are the technological forces that can impact a business?

Q3 Who is responsible for making decisions such as corporation tax, and how does that influence business decisions?

Q4 How can we gain access to review demographic data, and why is it essential?

Q5 Why is the physical environment essential for businesses to monitor even though not all products directly impact the environment?

Q6 Who sets rules and regulations for the internet, and who has to adhere to these rules?

Key learning points

- Companies need to pay close attention to technological forces to elaborate on which forces pose an opportunity or could develop into a threat to the business.
- Economic forces such as interest and exchange rates can significantly impact business costs and might be reflected in product pricing.
- Ethical consumer behaviour is a growing trend that is an umbrella term for consumer decision-making guided by their ethical concerns.

- The physical environment is essential to consider when reviewing the macro-environment of a business.

- Internet governance is a network of different players that ensure that specific rules and regulations are upheld.

References

Apple (nd) Home page, www.apple.com/uk (archived at https://perma.cc/7AGY-DXWB)

Aratani, L (2022) Buy now, pay later schemes are catching the eyes of consumers and of federal regulators, *The Guardian,* 27 January, www.theguardian.com/money/2022/jan/27/buy-now-pay-later-schemes-entice-consumers-spend-more (archived at https://perma.cc/K46H-X5ZD)

Bank of England (2022) What are interest rates? Bank of England, 17 March, www.bankofengland.co.uk/knowledgebank/what-are-interest-rates (archived at https://perma.cc/7K36-K4HV)

Barnhart, B (2022) Social commerce case studies: 16 awesome examples of social selling, Photoslurp, hi.photoslurp.com/blog/social-commerce-examples/ (archived at https://perma.cc/LW6V-BGZH)

Bray, J, Johns, N, and Kilburn, D (2011) An exploratory study into the factors impeding ethical consumption, *Journal of Business Ethics*, 98(4), 597–608

British LGBT Awards (2022) Top 10 LGBT+ brand or marketing campaigns of 2018, britishlgbtawards.com/top-10-lgbt-brand-or-marketing-campaigns-2018/ (archived at https://perma.cc/D6V7-DQYK)

Burton, S (2021) 5 genius social commerce examples you can learn from, SproutSocial, 28 October, sproutsocial.com/insights/social-commerce-examples/ (archived at https://perma.cc/TZL2-6F26)

Conti, R (2022) What is an NFT, *Forbes*, 16 February, www.forbes.com/uk/advisor/investing/nft-non-fungible-token/ (archived at https://perma.cc/5QXH-EJR4)

Digital Marketer (2021) What marketers need to know about NFTs, 17 December, www.digitalmarketer.com/blog/nft-marketing/ (archived at https://perma.cc/TX5L-DU3S)

Dollarhide, M (2022) Social commerce, Investopedia, 27 March, www.investopedia.com/terms/s/social-commerce.asp (archived at https://perma.cc/5TWC-GE2P)

Edgington, T (2020) Brexit: What are the key points of the deal? BBC, 30 December, www.bbc.co.uk/news/explainers-55180293 (archived at https://perma.cc/44GF-FM89)

Ethereum (2022) Non-fungible tokens (NFTs), Ethereum. ethereum.org/en/nft/ (archived at https://perma.cc/MD68-W4EY)

European Union (2022) Aims and Values, european-union.europa.eu/principles-countries-history/principles-and-values/aims-and-values_en (archived at https://perma.cc/HQG2-77WK)

Evans, A (2021) Charlie Bit Me NFT sale: Brothers to pay for university with auction money, BBC, 3 June, www.bbc.co.uk/news/newsbeat-57333990 (archived at https://perma.cc/XD4Z-NBBV)

Feeney, L (2021) Thinking inside the blockchain: Digital marketing 2.0, The Drum, 26 October, www.thedrum.com/opinion/2021/10/26/thinking-inside-the-blockchain-digital-marketing-20#:~:text=While%20still%20a%20comparatively%20fledgling,to%20go%20straight%20to%20source (archived at https://perma.cc/4M3R-FSL8)

Frankenfield, J (2021) Artificial Intelligence (AI), Investopedia, 8 March, www.investopedia.com/terms/a/artificial-intelligence-ai.asp (archived at https://perma.cc/6RUT-MDU5)

Frankenfield, J (2022a) Cryptocurrency, Investopedia, 11 January, www.investopedia.com/terms/c/cryptocurrency.asp (archived at https://perma.cc/GK7U-MCSE)

Frankenfield, J (2022b) Ethereum, Investopedia, 12 January. www.investopedia.com/terms/e/ethereum.asp (archived at https://perma.cc/JMJ6-PNAD)

Freitag (2022) Materials, www.freitag.ch/en/materials (archived at https://perma.cc/DQ8C-UWEL)

H&M Group (2022) Materials, hmgroup.com/sustainability/circular-and-climate-positive/materials/ (archived at https://perma.cc/9QPJ-9ZWE)

Hayes, A (2021) Demographics, Investopedia, 7 November, www.investopedia.com/terms/d/demographics.asp (archived at https://perma.cc/XXP8-92QC)

Hayes, A (2022) Blockchain explained, Investopedia, 5 March, www.investopedia.com/terms/b/blockchain.asp (archived at https://perma.cc/3BCR-6GV6)

Holbrook, M B (1987) Mirror, mirror, on the wall, what's unfair in the reflections on advertising? *The Journal of Marketing*, 51 (3), 95–103

Internet Governance Project (2022) What is internet governance? www.internetgovernance.org/what-is-internet-governance/ (archived at https://perma.cc/95HY-QM7B)

Kenton, K (2022) Greenwashing, Investopedia, 22 March, www.investopedia.com/terms/g/greenwashing.asp (archived at https://perma.cc/L28R-E25Q)

Ketter, E and Avraham, E (2021) #StayHome today so we can #TravelTomorrow: tourism destinations' digital marketing strategies during the Covid-19 pandemic, *Journal of Travel & Tourism Marketing*, 38(8), 819–32

Khartit, K (2021) Macro environment, Investopedia, 3 September, www.investopedia.com/terms/m/macro-environment.asp (archived at https://perma.cc/B6L6-B2EN)

Kopnina, H (2019) Green-washing or best case practices? Using circular economy and Cradle to Cradle case studies in business education, *Journal of Cleaner Production*, 219, 613–21

Kraemer, D (2021) Greta Thunberg: Who is the climate activist and what are her aims? BBC, 5 November, www.bbc.co.uk/news/world-europe-49918719 (archived at https://perma.cc/D4EZ-QCMA)

#Love GREAT Britain (2020) We're open – know before you go, YouTube, www.youtube.com/watch?v=TzdMaT9Thdk (archived at https://perma.cc/F8DH-YWQV)

Lyons, E (2019) It's time for the ad industry to address climate change, *Marketing Week*, 29 May, www.marketingweek.com/erin-lyons-ad-industry-address-climate-change/ (archived at https://perma.cc/GBS7-V7KY)

McLachlan, S (2020) What is social commerce and why should your brand care, 3 November, Hootsuite, blog.hootsuite.com/social-commerce/ (archived at https://perma.cc/N74F-PTZX)

Milmo, D (2021) Enter the metaverse: The digital future Mark Zuckerberg is steering us toward, *The Guardian*, 28 October, www.theguardian.com/technology/2021/oct/28/facebook-mark-zuckerberg-meta-metaverse (archived at https://perma.cc/SK2N-YK2B)

#NewZealand (2020) 100% Pure New Zealand. A journey of reflection, YouTube, www.youtube.com/watch?v=wEGshu0HTlc (archived at https://perma.cc/23VT-WJWX)

ONI United Kingdom (2010) United Kingdom, 18 December, opennet.net/sites/opennet.net/files/ONI_UnitedKingdom_2010.pdf (archived at https://perma.cc/LQB4-5WWZ)

OpenNet Initiative (nd) Home, opennet.net/ (archived at https://perma.cc/7TNR-GGSM)

Parker, L (2019) The world's plastic pollution crisis explained, *National Geographic*, 7 June, www.nationalgeographic.com/environment/article/plastic-pollution (archived at https://perma.cc/2RWE-8D5S)

Potters, C (2021) Economic growth, Investopedia, 1 January, www.investopedia.com/terms/e/economicgrowth.asp#:~:text=Economic%20growth%20is%20an%20increase%20in%20the%20production%20of%20goods,all%20contribute%20to%20economic%20growth (archived at https://perma.cc/SY72-FW65)

Proulx, M (2021) Consumers aren't ready for the metaverse yet,. Forrester, 21 September, www.forrester.com/blogs/consumers-arent-ready-for-the-metaverse-yet/ (archived at https://perma.cc/2YJL-WFSM)

Rintanen, R (2022) What are the key marketing technology trends for brands in 2022? The Drum, 9 February, www.thedrum.com/opinion/2022/02/09/what-are-the-key-marketing-technology-trends-brands-2022 (archived at https://perma.cc/5RFQ-GUY4)

Roser, M (2021) What is economic growth and why is it so important? Our World in Data, 13 May, ourworldindata.org/what-is-economic-growth (archived at https://perma.cc/TGM8-BWBK)

Starbucks (2020) What's your name, YouTube, www.youtube.com/watch?v=l-CjB1fr1zU (archived at https://perma.cc/R3N2-HTS8)

Statista (2022) Most popular social networks worldwide as of January 2022, ranked by number of monthly active users, www.statista.com/statistics/272014/global-social-networks-ranked-by-number-of-users/ (archived at https://perma.cc/83E2-AVLH)

Statista Research Department (2022) Number of smartphone subscriptions worldwide from 2016-2021, Statista, 22 August, www.statista.com/statistics/330695/number-of-smartphone-users-worldwide/ (archived at https://perma.cc/53ZC-PLEE)

The Ethical Consumer (nd) www.ethicalconsumer.org (archived at https://perma.cc/ZK4H-4MRQ)

The Guardian (2016) Battle for the internet, www.theguardian.com/technology/datablog/2012/apr/16/internet-censorship-country-list (archived at https://perma.cc/PBP5-74NN)

Twin, A (2021) Competitive advantage, Investopedia, 8 March, www.investopedia.com/terms/c/competitive_advantage.asp (archived at https://perma.cc/M2KC-LJXV)

Trollope-Kumar, K and Last, J (2022) Cultural forces, Encyclopedia.com, www.
encyclopedia.com/education/encyclopedias-almanacs-transcripts-and-maps/cultural-
factors (archived at https://perma.cc/WT2U-YXLX)

UK Government (2022a) Countries in the EU and EEA, www.gov.uk/eu-
eea#:~:text=The%20European%20Union%20(%20EU%20)%20is,and%20people%20
between%20member%20states (archived at https://perma.cc/SJL2-JJ3E)

UK Government (2022b) Brexit guidance, www.gov.uk/government/collections/brexit-
guidance (archived at https://perma.cc/4DMD-B55L)

United Nations (2019) World Population Prospects 2019: Highlights (ST/ESA/SER.A/423),
population.un.org/wpp/Publications/Files/WPP2019_Highlights.pdf (archived at https://
perma.cc/6YFX-P88E)

United Nations (2022) What is climate change? United Nations Climate Action, www.un.
org/en/climatechange/what-is-climate-change (archived at https://perma.cc/T844-F8QB)

Wentworth, A (2018) 5 companies leading the way to live plastic free, Climate Action, www.
climateaction.org/news/5-companies-leading-the-movement-to-go-plastic-free (archived at
https://perma.cc/T6Z6-J6JN)

Wise Marketer (2022) How crypto driven marketing will transform the industry, The
Wise Marketer, 1 February, thewisemarketer.com/cards-payments/how-crypto-driven-digital-
marketing-will-transform-the-industry/#:~:text=Crypto's%20Effects%20on%20Digital%20
Marketing&text=With%20blockchain%20advertising%2C%20advertisers%20
can,available%20to%20its%20platform%20users (archived at https://perma.cc/2Y2E-BKW2)

The micro-environment

06

By the end of this chapter, you should be able to:

- briefly outline the internal marketing environment
- explain the micro-environment and its relevance to business and digital marketing decisions
- distinguish between the micro- and macro-environment
- explain Porter's Five Forces
- elaborate on how digital technologies have impacted Porter's Five Forces analysis

Introduction

We have previously covered forces in the macro-environment of a business. Such forces can be trends and changes in the wider external environment of a company and require constant monitoring to evaluate when businesses might turn these into opportunities or when they might become threats.

Some forces that will affect a business are more closely connected to the company and require regular assessment. Such forces are part of the micro-environment surrounding businesses. It might help to think of the macro-environment as forces that do not have a direct, contractual relationship with the business and the micro-environment as players who directly interact with the business.

The micro-environment is formed by the company itself, its customers, suppliers, competitors and the general public. The company itself is often described as the internal marketing environment. All of these factors, both internal and micro-environment, usually directly influence day-to-day business decisions and can result in either strengths or weaknesses of a business. Digital technologies have greatly affected the way the micro-environment can be analysed. For example, shopping behaviour of consumer in an e-commerce setting provides rich data insights that allow companies to adapt their offerings quickly. This could include price adjustments, offering special promotions, discontinuing an unsuccessful product and many more strategies.

The internal marketing environment

The internal marketing environment is specific to the business itself. To analyse the strengths and weaknesses, one would look at physical resources such as machinery, inventory and raw materials. Such physical resources are essential when it comes to product development. From a digital marketing point of view, physical resources would relate to the owned media of a business. As discussed in Chapter 1, owned media refers to media that a business controls. This would be, for example, the website of a company. So, if you were to analyse the internal marketing environment, a well-designed website would be considered a strength. We will review what makes a well-designed website in Chapter 16.

In addition to physical resources, it is essential to review intangible assets. These are, for example, employee capabilities, brand value and customer lists. If we were to review these from a digital marketing point of view, a strength might be an extensive email customer list, while a weakness might be seen as the inability of staff to analyse email response data.

The internal marketing environment also consists of the current strategy and current management style. This would influence digital marketing if, for example, there were a lack of strategic support for digital marketing.

Activity 6.1

You have now learnt about the internal marketing environment.

i.   How important is the internal marketing environment to plan your digital marketing strategy?

ii. Try to list digital marketing assets by dividing them into physical resources and intangible assets.

iii. What do you reckon are the benefits of considering the internal marketing environment?

The micro-environment

In addition to the internal marketing environment, we need to consider the *micro-environment* of a business for decision-making and to identify the strengths and weaknesses of a business.

KEY TERM
Micro-environment

The micro-environment refers to the factors within a company that impact its ability to do business. Micro-environmental factors are specific to a company and can influence the operation of a company and management's ability to meet the business's goals. These factors include the company's suppliers, resellers, customers, and competition.

SOURCE Khartit, 2021

As you can see from the definition, there are several players that businesses need to factor in when it comes to daily decision-making. For example, think of the relationship between the business and its suppliers. If the supplier experiences delivery delays, the company will experience a product shortage. This will result in delays for the customers, and if this happens frequently will turn into a weakness of the business. Another example is the competition. A company will have to adjust prices if the competition offers similar products at lower prices.

The relationship between the players in the micro-environment has been greatly influenced by digital technologies and digital marketers have to take these changes into consideration. If we go back to the competitive prices example, digital channels allow a much quicker monitoring of competitor prices and adjustment of offered prices. So whereas competitors' pricing traditionally has often been reason for concern, it now offers several opportunities. Many businesses offer a 'price match guarantee', assuring the consumer that if they find the same product cheaper elsewhere, that price would be matched. This puts the responsibility of checking competitor prices onto the consumer and projects confidence of the business that they are offering competitive prices.

Several models help to analyse the micro-environment of a business. Porter's Five Forces is one of such commonly applied models that reviews the competitive landscape of an industry. We will first review the model in its traditional sense and then review how digital technologies impacted the model.

Porter's Five Forces

Michael E Porter first introduced his model of Five Forces that shape strategy in 1979 in the *Harvard Business Review*. The model looks at five forces that determine the state of competition in an industry (Figure 6.1). These forces are (Porter, 1979):

- the threat of new entrants
- the threat of substitute services or products

Figure 6.1   Porter's Five Forces

- the bargaining power of buyers
- the bargaining power of suppliers
- the intense rivalry of competitors

The idea is that once these forces have been reviewed and assessed, a company can make an informed decision on where its strengths and weaknesses lie and how best to deal with the competition.

Threat of new entrants

This force assesses the likelihood of other businesses entering your market. The ease of entering a new market depends on several factors. First, a company needs to consider the *barriers to entry* of this new market.

KEY TERM
Barriers to entry

Barriers to entry is an economics and business term describing factors that can prevent or impede newcomers into a market or industry sector, and so limit competition. These can include high start-up costs, regulatory hurdles, or other obstacles that prevent new competitors from easily entering a business sector.

SOURCE Hayes, 2022

Businesses need to assess the time and money it would take to enter a new market. For example, if a particular market requires a lot of specialist product knowledge that a company might not yet possess, the time and costs to enter this new market would be very high. The requirement of highly specialized knowledge means that the threat of new entrants would likely be low. Take the space industry as an example. Not many businesses could easily enter the space industry as it is currently based on decades of research that would be hard to imitate.

A low threat of entrants is good for businesses operating in that particular industry as it means there won't be a lot of competition.

The impact of digital technologies on the threat of new entrants

The internet has heightened the threat of new entries by reducing the barriers to entering a new market. Whereas businesses trying to sell something were required to have some brick-and-mortar outlet, e-commerce allows many companies to set up their shop without a physical store's financial and time commitments.

Also, the internet makes the copying of products and ideas much more accessible, raising the threat of new entrants further. For example, a business might see a successfully selling product online and can decide to offer a similar product.

Activity 6.2

The threat of new entrants has been raised through technology development by reducing barriers.

i. How has the development of the internet changed the airline industry?

ii. Think of the barriers that have existed to entering the airline industry and how these might have been affected by the development of the internet.

Threat of substitute services or products

This force describes the likelihood that products and services within a particular industry can be exchanged. For example, there is a very high threat of substitutes in the *fast-moving consumer goods* industry.

KEY TERM
Fast-moving consumer goods (FMCGs)

Fast-moving consumer goods are products that sell quickly at a relatively low cost. FMCGs have a short shelf life because of high consumer demand (e.g. soft drinks and confections) or because they are perishable (e.g. meat, dairy products and baked goods). These goods are purchased frequently, consumed rapidly, priced low, and sold in large quantities. They also have a high turnover when they're on the shelf at the store.

SOURCE Kenton, 2021a

It is very easy for consumers to switch between these products. For example, if your favourite branded cookies are sold out in the supermarket, you could easily take the supermarket's own branded cookies. Usually, the threat of substitute products or services can be reduced by making products unique.

The impact of digital technologies on the threat of substitute products or services

Digital technologies have resulted in a higher threat of substitute products or services as products and services are much more readily available online. The general market-place has become more easily accessible for consumers. If consumers don't find their preferred product on one website, the next business selling the same or a similar prod-uct is just one click away. Also, the internet has made comparing products much easier. Take, for example, insurance. It used to be very difficult to compare insurance quotes and often, consumers had to consult insurance brokers to get the best deal. Nowadays, comparison websites, also referred to as aggregators, such as Comparethemarket.com allow consumers to compare car insurance easily. This information availability means a very high threat of substitute services in the insurance industry.

Bargaining power of buyers

The bargaining power of buyers describes the strength of consumers in demanding better products, better customer service and/or lower prices. There are different rea-sons for when the bargaining power of buyers can be high. If you take a *business-to-business* (B2B) context, the bargaining power of buyers is usually higher than in the business-to-consumer market.

KEY TERM
Business-to-business

Business-to-business (B2B or B-to-B) is a form of transaction between businesses, such as one involving a manufacturer and wholesaler, or a wholesaler and a retailer, rather than between a company and individual consumer. Business-to-business stands in contrast to business-to-consumer (B2C) and business-to-government (B2G) transactions.

SOURCE Chen, 2020

This is simply because there are fewer buyers in the B2B context. Think, for example of a company that produces medical equipment such as incubators for new-borns. The buyers for this company's product would be very limited even if you were to serve a global market. In this scenario, the bargaining power of the buyers would be very high as they could demand better customer service or lower prices, given the dependency of the business on a small number of buyers. Besides the limited number of buyers, other factors can influence the bargaining power of buyers. These are the size of each customer, the difference between competitors, the ability to find substitutes and the cost of changing.

The impact of digital technologies on the bargaining power of buyers

Digital technologies and the internet have increased the bargaining power of buyers as consumers have a wider choice of products through e-commerce platforms. Also, the internet allows for much higher price transparency, meaning that consumers can compare prices easily. It is now easier than ever for consumers to change who they are buying from. Think, for example of when you purchase airline tickets. Consumers used to have to go to travel agents to book a flight and they had to trust that they were getting the best deal. Comparing prices would have taken a lot of leg work. Nowadays, prices can be compared in an instance. Because of this, companies are trying to make it harder for consumers to switch by offering additional services such as collecting frequent flyer awards.

Activity 6.3

i. Visit an airline and pretend to book a flight.

ii. Try to see which additional services you will be offered to 'lock you in' to purchase the flight with the chosen airline rather than switching to a rival.

iii. Do you think offering additional services effectively reduces the bargaining power of buyers?

Bargaining power of suppliers

The bargaining power of suppliers is the counterpart to the bargaining power of buyers and describes how much power lies with the *supply chain* of a business.

> **KEY TERM**
> Supply chain
>
> A supply chain is a network between a company and its suppliers to produce and distribute a specific product to the final buyer. This network includes different activities, people, entities, information and resources. The supply chain also represents the steps it takes to get the product or service from its original state to the customer.
>
> **SOURCE** Kenton, 2021b

If the bargaining power of the supplier is high, they can demand higher prices or greater order quantities. Suppliers can assert a higher bargaining power by reducing the availability of their products.

The bargaining power of the supplier depends on a number of factors. For example, the number of suppliers in the market is one key factor. Think back to our company that produces medical equipment. You would require highly specialized products such as optical lenses for microscopes for a lot of such equipment. There aren't very many suppliers of medical-grade optical lenses in the market. Hence the pressure that the supplier of these lenses could assert is likely to be high. Other factors impacting the bargaining power of suppliers are the uniqueness of service and product offered, the ability to substitute such services and products, and the cost it would take to change the supplier.

The impact of digital technologies on the bargaining power of suppliers

The internet had both positive and negative effects on the bargaining power of suppliers. Similarly to end-consumers, companies have a more comprehensive range of suppliers. The internet is allowing even smaller suppliers to have a presence, thus reducing the bargaining power of suppliers.

On the flip side, though, suppliers also have a larger market of businesses to work with, given the transparency and accessibility of the internet.

Rivalry among existing competitors/Intensity of industry rivalry

Another force of Porter's Five Forces analysis deals with the amount of competition within an industry. The more competitors there are within an industry that offer the same products or services, the more limited the company's power. The more rivalry there is within an industry, the less likely a business is to be able to charge higher prices.

The impact of digital technologies on the intensity of industry rivalry

Digital technologies and the internet have significantly increased the rivalry among competitors in many industries. One reason for this is the greater transparency of online products and services. Companies are sharing more information about their products than ever before, making it easier for the competition to offer similar products and deals. You might have noticed that many companies now offer a price matching guarantee whereby a company promises to match the lowest advertised price. This results from more extensive transparency online and aims to lock in the consumer to purchase with this particular business rather than the competition. Such techniques are aimed at limiting consumer switching.

PRACTITIONER INPUT
Lena Hochstrat

Lena Hochstrat is senior manager for Global Account Development at NielsenIQ. NielsenIQ is a leading information services company and is part of Nielsen, a global leader in audience insights, data and analytics.

Could you please tell us about the organization that you work for?

I work for NielsenIQ and we empower our customers around the world to make bold decisions and transform their business with trusted data, solutions and insights. Our products optimize the performance of consumer packaged goods (CPG) manufacturers and retail companies, bringing them closer to the communities they serve and helping to power their growth.

   Within Global Account Development at NIQ, I am leading the commercial strategy and sales of NielsenIQ's solutions for our key clients. The core responsibilities are to establish a strategic partnership where I engage and act upon the client's business priorities and challenges. With our available data, capabilities and insights I help them to achieve their strategic goals and ambitions.

Why is it essential for businesses to conduct market research? What can businesses gain from market research?

Market research empowers businesses to act and maximize their potential. For both consumer packaged goods retailers and manufacturers, business growth and competitive advantages are key to success. The CPG environment is fast moving: changing shopper trends and market dynamics challenge businesses every day. These developments often come with uncertainties.

Let us take 'sustainability' as an example. At first, smaller products and brands with organic and sustainable benefits enter the market, creating a niche. The market share of those products continues to grow, they become popular. Sales increase and start to compete with bigger brands. Manufacturers might start to wonder: How relevant are 'sustainable' products in my categories? What does 'sustainability' mean to our consumers? What do they look out for in the products they buy? How should we adjust our offering to profit from this trend? Many questions whose answers would help to understand the potential behind this trend. The only way to get to the bottom of it is to conduct market research and leverage the gained insights to make profound decisions.

What are the most common types of market research that your customers are benefiting from?

At NielsenIQ there are many practice areas serving the needs of different business questions. Our key area is Omnisales. We globally collect, process and analyse data from retailers, consumer panels, e-commerce platforms and more. This data enables the clients to understand and track the performance of their brands and identify opportunities and risks.

With NielsenIQ Advanced Analytics, we help our clients to understand the true impacts of their strategic decision-making. We leverage the data we collect within Omnisales and analyse the effectiveness and incrementality of in-store execution strategies, assortment and innovations.

Further practice areas are NielsenIQ Innovation Management where the potential of future innovation concepts or product changes is assessed. The methodology of consumer surveys including eye-tracking and neuroscience. With NielsenIQ Consumer Insights we offer survey-based solutions for several consumer and brand-related questions such as market and consumer segmentations, path to purchase, shopper and in-store analytics.

What are some of the questions that your customers have recently sought answers to through market research?

The ongoing inflation raises a high level of uncertainty. Private labels are growing in market shares leaving manufacturers with challenges on their brands to fight for market share. Hence critical business questions evolve. An example would be to understand the impact of price changes pressured by inflation. How do product sales develop when prices are increased? How do different promotion mechanics such as display, leaflet or in-store events drive sales? Our clients would like to understand how successfully they are driving brand growth in these challenging times. How may they balance out the raising competition of private label and increased interest in promotions caused by financial constraints of the consumers?

At NielsenIQ we have different approaches to address those questions. Analysing the development of price helps to understand how inflation has impacted the pricing structure across CPG categories. Diving deeper, we identify elasticities, assessing the impact of possible price increases and promotion tactics on our client's product that help them to build effective retail strategies.

How has the internet and digital channels impacted market research?

The rise of online is disrupting the course of the FMCG industry, and the pandemic has only served to accelerate the fragmentation. Over the course of the past few years, NielsenIQ has made significant and meaningful investments in the e-commerce space, so that our clients understand the deepest insights based on the broadest view of the e-commerce landscape and shopping behaviour. We aim to offer a blind-spot-free view on how products perform across all e-commerce channels, while also generating insights on shoppers and shopping behaviours so that our clients can elevate their performance, adapt and react to ever-changing market dynamics.

How important is Big Data for market research? Could you elaborate on how and which forms of Big Data you are using for the market research that you are offering?

The e-commerce landscape has grown everywhere – yet in very different ways across the globe. In the United States, for example, we're seeing extreme market fragmentation, whereas in Latin America we see large pure players. French consumers still favour click-and-collect while South Korea focuses on the digital wallet. The unique market dynamics require tailored approaches locally, which can create business challenges. We believe that an all-channel view is a critical component of a business strategy, and that granularity, accuracy and coverage should be equally measured for both e-commerce and brick-and-mortar stores to get the most complete view of the total market.

Summary

We have now covered how and why it is essential to review and monitor the internal marketing landscape and the micro-environment of a business. We have looked at the individual players within the micro-environment and clarified that the micro-environment is formed by those players who have a direct relationship with the business. These players usually impact the day-to-day decision-making of the company. We have reviewed Porter's Five Forces and looked into each of those forces in the context of digital technologies.

Chapter review

Reflective questions

Q1 What is meant by the internal marketing environment?

Q2 What are the five forces outlined in Porter's model, and why are they important to consider?

Q3 What is the micro-environment of a business, and how does it differ from the macro-environment?

Q4 How have digital technologies, particularly the internet, impacted Porter's Five Forces?

Key learning points

● The internal marketing environment is specific to the business itself.

● Micro-environmental factors are specific to a company and can influence the operation of a company and management's ability to meet the business's goals.

● Porter's Five Forces looks at the five forces that determine the state of competition in an industry. These forces are the threat of new entrants, the bargaining power of customers, the bargaining power of suppliers, the intense rivalry of competitors, and the threat of substitute services or products.

● The impact of digital technologies on Porter's Five Forces.

References

Chen, J (2020) Business-to-business (B2B), Investopedia, 28 May, www.investopedia.com/terms/b/btob.asp (archived at https://perma.cc/9BCW-WBR6)

Hayes, A (2022) What are barriers to entry, Investopedia, 8 January, www.investopedia.com/terms/b/barrierstoentry.asp#:~:text=Barriers%20to%20entry%20is%20an,easily%20entering%20a%20business%20sector (archived at https://perma.cc/K62D-8LKN)

Kenton, W (2021a) Fast-moving consumer goods industry, Investopedia, 6 December, www.investopedia.com/terms/f/fastmoving-consumer-goods-fmcg.asp (archived at https://perma.cc/PQ96-W9JE)

Kenton, W (2021b) Supply chain, Investopedia, 29 August, www.investopedia.com/terms/s/supplychain.asp (archived at https://perma.cc/G5A4-AZ57)

Khartit, K (2021) Macro environment, Investopedia, 3 September, www.investopedia.com/terms/m/macro-environment.asp (archived at https://perma.cc/YAT6-27LM)

Porter, M (1979) How competitive forces shape strategy, *Harvard Business Review*, March–April, 137–45

Market segmentation, targeting and positioning

07

By the end of this chapter, you should be able to:

- briefly outline the difference between market segmentation, targeting and positioning
- explain in detail why it is important to segment consumer markets including online consumer typologies
- distinguish between the different segmentation variables focusing on online behaviour
- explain the main four targeting strategies and how these apply in the digital context
- elaborate on why positioning a product or service is essential to its success.

Introduction

So far we have covered the environmental analyses for the macro- and micro-environment. In this chapter, we now move on to analysing the customers of a business. It is crucial for any business to understand who their consumers are. Once a market is broken down into smaller segments, a business has to decide which of these segments to target. Who to target can be influenced by several factors. Some of these factors would include consumers' buying power, the ability to reach that particular market segment, or the intensity of competition for that segment. After a segment has been chosen to be targeted, positioning the product in the mind of the consumer so it occupies a meaningful position is crucial for marketing success.

Digital technologies have impacted all three of the segmentation, targeting and positioning (STP) activities. The internet has allowed us to draw quite accurate pictures of consumers and it is essential to break down a market into smaller segments in order to serve those smaller segments effectively. With digital technologies we can target very specific segments via a number of different online channels. Positioning a product or service in the mind of the consumer can be much more effective using digital channels as there are plenty of routes to reach and engage with consumers.

Market segmentation

Segmenting consumer markets

It is impossible for any service or product to satisfy every single person. We all have different needs, wants and purchasing abilities. *Market segmentation* allows businesses to divide their markets into smaller submarkets that have common interests and features. By dividing the market, businesses can then form marketing communications to resonate with that particular part of the market.

KEY TERM
Market segmentation

Market segmentation is a marketing term that refers to aggregating prospective buyers into groups or segments with common needs and who respond similarly to a marketing action. Market segmentation enables companies to target different categories of consumers who perceive the full value of certain products and services differently from one another.

SOURCE Tarver, 2021

Businesses can divide a market into several segments in different ways. *Remember:* a segment should have similar interests and therefore similar requirements when it comes to serving them. Common consumer segmentation variables are behavioural, psychographic and demographic factors. In the online context, we also need to take characteristics into account that deal with online consumer behaviour. These characteristics are referred to as *webographics* or digital literacy (see also Chapter 10).

KEY TERM
Webographics

Webographics are those characteristics referring to online consumer behaviour. A consumer's webographic details include information on their knowledge of computers and the internet and how to navigate in digital spaces (also referred to as digital literacy).

SOURCE Garín and Perez Amaral, 2009

Consumer segmentation methods

As you have now learnt, market segmentation allows businesses to find those segments of the market that offer them a commercially viable opportunity to serve their customers' needs. Think of Patagonia, for example, an outdoor clothing brand that focuses on being a sustainable brand. According to an audience analysis in the United States, Patagonia's consumers are (Helixa Marketing, 2018):

- married men between 55 and 69 years
- likely to have an income over $100K
- likely to be found in cities close to mountain ranges
- interested in activities and organizations that support wildlife and the environment,
- actively reading media publications focused on outdoor sports and social responsibility.

This consumer analysis demonstrates how the company segments the overall consumer market into segments that they can serve effectively. Breaking down a consumer market into segments can be done according to a number of different variables. As you can see from the example, Patagonia applies segmentation variables such as demographics (e.g. age and marital status), psychographics (e.g. people who lead an outdoor lifestyle), and behavioural (e.g. media interest in social responsibility).

Activity 7.1

You have just learnt about one of the consumer segments that Patagonia is targeting.

i. Visit *Forbes* online and search for the article 'Outdoor clothing chain Patagonia starts selling online again after unusual decision to pause its e-commerce due to pandemic'.

ii. Do you think the shut-down of their e-commerce platform has been perceived well by their target audience?

iii. Do you think that if Patagonia were targeting a different segment, the implications of an e-commerce shutdown might have been different?

Figure 7.1 shows the segmentation variables that businesses can apply to divide their consumer market into smaller segments so that they can target them successfully with their communication strategy.

Online consumer typologies

It is essential to understand how consumers behave online when segmenting consumer markets, especially when designing digital marketing strategies and campaigns. If we consider Patagonia's consumer segment, the likelihood of this segment having access to both computers and the internet is very high given the affluent nature of the consumer segment. However, the higher age bracket of the segment might indicate how the internet is accessed. In 2019, 16- to 24-year-olds spent on average 4.1 hours

Figure 7.1   Consumer segmentation variables

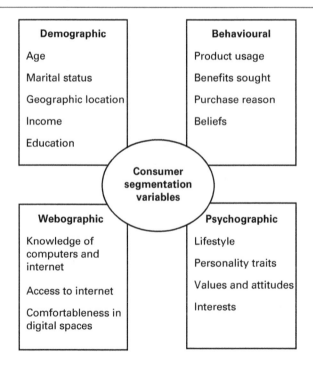

daily using the internet via a mobile phone. Compared to that, 55- to 64-year-olds only spent 1.42 hours online via a mobile phone (Johnson, 2021). Another major importance would be social media usage: in 2020, 88 per cent of 16- to 24-year-olds had their own social media profile, opposed to only 73 per cent of 55- to 64-year-olds (Statista Research Department, 2022).

There are numerous studies that have researched online consumer audiences and found that there is no single market segment, but instead subsegments of online shoppers with varying behavioural characteristics in terms of online shopping (Huseynov and Yildirim, 2019). For example Liu et al (2015) researched real e-commerce transactions of Chinese online consumers and found the following six different types of online consumers:

- economical purchasers
- active-star purchasers
- direct purchasers
- high-loyalty purchasers
- risk-averse purchasers
- credibility-first purchasers

Another example is a study by Huseynov and Yildirim (2017) who segmented real e-commerce transaction records of Turkish online customers and found five different types of consumer segments:

- opportunist customers
- transient customers
- need-based shoppers
- sceptical newcomers
- repetitive purchasers

Activity 7.2

We have now covered different segmentation variables that apply to online shopping behaviour.

i. Think of a situation where you last bought something online.

ii. Try to describe yourself as a segment covering all four categories of the consumer segmentation variables (demographic, behavioural, psychographic and webographics).

As you can imagine, these different consumer segments have strong implications on how companies should try to reach and engage with their consumers online. One way of depicting the webographics of a particular segment is to visualize the consumer as a persona. Consumer personas are fictitious representations of your intended target audience that resemble real people and will be discussed in detail in Chapter 10.

The benefits of market segmentation

There are many advantages associated with market segmentation. The main advantage is that of being able to serve the needs of customers with similar interests more effectively. This can be delivered through marketing communications by telling a story to one market segment and a similar story to another segment, but focusing on different attributes.

For example, Lego has different products for different age ranges. These differ between larger building blocks for over 1.5-year-olds to complex structures for over 18-year-olds. Lego also ensures it caters for different interest groups and often designs new toys based on current movies (e.g. Marvel superheroes, Harry Potter). Only having to serve a smaller segment of an overall consumer market means that communication strategies can be more specialized and focused exactly on what that particular segment is interested in.

Being able to better serve particular customer segments usually means more profits due to repeat purchasing and overall improved customer retention. Digital technologies allow for an easier breakdown of consumer segments. Digital channels also are very transparent in that they allow consumer journeys to be tracked, which can help when identifying market segments.

Dividing a consumer market into smaller segments is only the first step of the STP analysis. Once businesses have identified several segments, they need to decide which of these segments they want to service or, in other words, which of these segments they want to target.

Targeting

Once a business has researched their market and identified possible segments, they then need to assess which of those segments is most promising. This can depend on a number of things but usually companies need to evaluate how easily accessible the segment is and how likely it is to generate a profit for the business.

Think, for example, of an e-commerce business that sells traditional soap bars. This company might have identified a segment of women over the age of 70, living in rural areas with a keen interest in gardening. While this might be a segment interested in buying the soap, difficulties in accessing this segment due to a lack of digital literacy would mean that the business might target a different segment instead.

Businesses might identify several different segments in their consumer market but choose to target only a couple of those segments. Part of the target analysis is to determine how much demand there is.

A common set of six criteria is applied to segments to decide which of the identified segments a business should target (Kotler and Keller, 2012):

1 **Identifiable:** The buyers in your segments need to be identifiable in order for you to be able to serve them effectively.

2 **Substantial:** A segment needs to be of sufficient size to promise profits.

3 **Accessible:** A business needs to consider the accessibility of the segment, since if you cannot reach your audience, you cannot communicate with them.

4 **Stable:** A segment needs to be around for long enough to justify a tailored communication strategy.

5 **Differentiable:** Consumers in one segment need to have similar needs to those within the segment but different enough to those not part of the segment.

6 **Actionable:** This is almost the summarizing factor of all the previous ones. A business must be able to put their plan into action for the identified segment, otherwise they would need to choose an alternative.

Another major factor to consider when choosing which segment to target is the competition. A segment is more attractive if there is less competition.

Target market strategies

Once a business has decided which segment to target, it needs to decide on target market strategies. There are several different strategies of how consumers can be targeted. These differ according to how much of the marketing mix is adjusted based on the individual needs of the segment.

Fahy and Jobber (2015) outline the following four generic target marketing strategies:

- **Undifferentiated marketing:** If companies are unable to identify segments that are worth targeting, they might decide to have one marketing mix for the whole market. This means they send the same message to the whole market. There may be a number of reasons for this. It might be that none or just very few of the six criteria for successful segmentation can be identified (Kotler and Keller, 2012). So, for example, the identified segments might not be accessible, actionable or substantial enough to justify differing marketing strategies. The brand M&M's, which are multicoloured button-shaped chocolates, is a good example of undifferentiated marketing. The marketing message involves the same funny marketing communications that are aimed at the whole market.

- **Differentiated marketing:** If a business has identified segments that are worth targeting, a differentiated marketing strategy is applied to communicate with each of the segment. In this strategy, businesses try to appeal to the differences that are apparent between the segments. So it would try to appeal to the thing that makes one segment unique. Patagonia, the sustainable outdoor brand that we discussed earlier in the chapter, is a good example of differentiated marketing as it specifically communicates messages that appeal to their health-conscious, outdoorsy and sustainability-aware audience.

- **Focused marketing:** If the segmentation analysis shows that most of the segments do not seem to be very profitable and a company has limited resources, it might choose to focus on one narrow and specific segment of the market. The business would then have one marketing mix to sell a specific product to a specific customer group. The luxury car manufacturer Rolls Royce is a good example of focused marketing as they only offer a single product (luxury cars) to wealthy consumers.

- **Customized marketing:** If the segmentation analysis identifies that each individual customer is unique in their needs and wants, and it promises to be profitable to cater for these needs, customized marketing would be the strategy to choose. Here, instead of having different marketing mix decisions for individual segments, the messages are personalized for each individual consumer. Sometimes, this strategy is referred to as one-to-one marketing. A good example of customized marketing is Starbucks' mobile app. The buying rewards scheme is linked to the app and customers can order and customize their drinks via the app. By using purchasing history and location data, Starbucks can customize their offering to meet the needs of each individual customer.

Activity 7.3

We have now covered the four target market strategies of undifferentiated, differentiated, focused and customized marketing (Fahy and Jobber, 2015).

i.   Visit the Research-methodology.net website by BMR (Business Research Methodology) and search for the article 'Amazon Segmentation, Targeting and Positioning: widest range of target customer segment'.

ii. Familiarize yourself with Amazon's segmentation, targeting and positioning.

iii. Review the table the outlines that different segmentation factors that Amazon seems to be using.

iv. Which of the four target market strategies does Amazon seem to follow?

v. What are the advantages and disadvantages of following the chosen strategy?

The impact of digital technologies on target marketing strategies

Digital technologies have extended the ways in which businesses can target their audiences. In the following we are going to highlight how the main four targeting strategies can be impacted through the use of digital channels.

Undifferentiated marketing would traditionally employ mass media channels such as TV or print media to reach their audiences. This used to be sufficient when consumers had the choice between a manageable amount of television channels. With the advent of pay TV and streaming services, the choice of what to watch is almost limitless. With that came a fragmentation of the viewers which meant that undifferentiated marketing messages were more difficult to reach large audiences.

Developments in digital technologies have provided new avenues that enable undifferentiated marketing to reach their audiences. Take, for example, Google or other search engines. Consumers can be targeted when searching for specific keywords. Google allows for very specific targeting if a business requires it, but also allows a business to target anybody who searches for a particular product or service. So digital channels have not only provided new avenues for undifferentiated target marketing but also improved the message delivery.

Differentiated, *focused* and *customized marketing* have all been greatly impacted by digital technologies. The following list shows a few examples of how digital channels facilitate successful targeting strategies:

- targeting based on interests (e.g. social media ads being shown for products related to consumer interests such as sustainability, gardening, working out, etc)

- targeting through personalization of emails (e.g. sending email reminders for those who have not completed an e-commerce transaction)

- targeting through personalization of the shopping experience (e.g. allowing consumers to personalize their orders according to their own individual taste)

- targeting with the help of augmented-reality apps (e.g. seeing what products would look like before purchasing the product)

- targeting through custom video content (e.g. seeing product reviews tailored towards individual consumers)

- targeting through multiple channel exposure (e.g. repeating and reinforcing marketing messages via several digital touchpoints)

This list is by no means exhaustive but demonstrates just how much undifferentiated marketing (including focused and customized marketing) has benefited from the development of digital technologies. Once the market has been segmented and suitable segments identified, businesses need to consider how to position their product or service in the mind of the consumer.

Positioning

Product positioning is all about linking the benefits of a product or service to the consumer's needs. Businesses need to make a decision on where to position their product in the market.

KEY TERM
Product positioning

Product positioning describes the act of situating a product or service favourably in potential consumers' minds in relation to its competitors. It describes where a product or service fits into its market and what features make it unique.

SOURCE Qualtrics XM, 2022; Perez, 2021

There are a number of key advantages of product positioning. The following shows a list of some of the reasons why it is so important (Qualtrics XM, 2022):

- A well-positioned product will stand out from the rest.
- Customers will hear clearly positioned messages above the general noise of marketing.
- Consumers will buy what they know, like and trust.
- Justifying the product price is easier for well-positioned products.
- The product's story, content and marketing messages can be written from a position of authority.
- It informs creative visual design.

There are a number of different perspectives that businesses need to consider when planning their product positioning. First of all, understanding the needs and wants of the target audience is a priority. Second, a business wants to clearly distinguish their product or service from the competition and ensure that it cannot be easily copied or matched. Finally, a business has to review its own resources to ensure that it can deliver what it promises in the product positioning. One way of deciding where to position a product or service is with the help of positioning maps.

Positioning map

A positioning map should be based on values that matter to the target audience and can visualize where existing products and services are in the market. By comparing extant products and services, a business can identify gaps that they then decide to position their product in.

The positioning map in Figure 7.2 shows a number of competing high-street fashion brands. These are organized according to price points and their sustainability focus. A gap could be identified for brands with a strong sustainability in the mid-price segment.

There are various features that a company can choose on which to base their positioning. The following list highlights a few of those features (Haley, 2022):

- pricing
- quality
- differentiation
- convenience
- customer service
- user groups

Figure 7.2 Example of a positioning map of high-street fashion brands

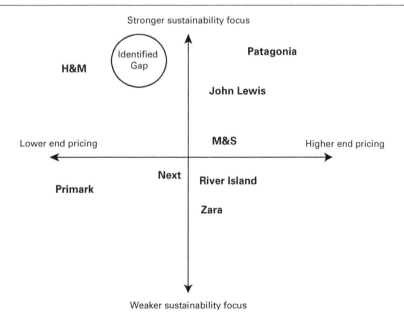

Activity 7.4

We have now learnt about the importance of choosing a position for a product or service in the mind of the consumer. Positioning maps can help to identify gaps where a product or service could be positioned.

i. Choose two features from the following list and pick an industry that you are interested in: pricing, quality, differentiation, convenience, customer service, user groups.

ii. Try to draw your own positioning map to identify where there might be a gap in the market.

Once a business has established how it wants to be positioned in the consumer's head and the competition has been reviewed, a positioning statement needs to be drafted.

Positioning statement

KEY TERM
Positioning statement

A positioning statement is an expression of how a given product, service or brand fills a particular consumer need in a way that its competitors don't. Positioning is the process of identifying an appropriate market niche for a product (or service or brand) and getting it established in that area.

SOURCE Wigmore, 2022

A *positioning statement* should be memorable, image enhancing and communicate the product's desired offering. Fahy and Jobber (2015) suggest that there are four key features of a successful positioning statement:

- clarity: idea must be perfectly clear and memorable
- consistency: break through the quantity of information
- credibility: differential advantage must be credible to a consumer
- competitiveness: differential advantage must have competitive edge

Answering the following questions before creating a positioning statement can help when designing a powerful statement (Haley, 2022; Patel, 2021):

- Who is your target audience?
- What is your product or service category?
- What is the greatest benefit of your product or service?
- What is the proof of that benefit?

Take, for example, Amazon's positioning statement: 'Our vision is to be the earth's most customer-centric company; to build a place where people can come to find and discover anything they might want to buy online.' It is perfectly *clear* what they are aiming to do (e.g. people can find anything they want); the message is *consistent* as it is simple to remember; given the size of Amazon, the statement is *credible*; and it seems *competitive*.

At times, a product needs to be repositioned, which can be due to changing customer preferences or segments becoming too small to be worth targeting. Repositioning can be based on either changing the target market or the product. The decision to reposition should not be taken lightly as there are risks involved when doing so as customers can be alienated.

CASE STUDY   Levi Strauss

Levi Strauss & Co (LS&Co) is a US apparel manufacturer and marketer that is very well known for its brand Levi's iconic denim jeans. They produce a wide range of tops, shorts, skirts, jackets, footwear and accessories but are most famous for their Levi's jeans.

By the year 2000, the jeans maker had been reporting a reduction in sales for six years.

One of the identified reasons for this was a move amongst consumers to buying trendier and less expensive clothes (Vrontis and Vronti, 2004). In an effort to overcome this problem, back in the early 2000s Levi's widened its target audience to include segments of younger customers (teenagers and young adults) by designing clothes that appealed to this segment (Vrontis and Vronti, 2004). They also entered the discount jeans market in 2004 in the United States, selling their Signature brand in Wal-Mart stores in America and were planning an extension of this discount brand into Europe (Vrontis and Vronti, 2004).

Now, almost 20 years later, Levi's seems to have different ideas for continuing their success. Levi's is one of the top-rated brands that care about sustainability (The Good Trade, 2022). LS&Co is steering towards a more circular economy focus by changing consumption patterns. The following initiatives show just some of their commitment (Levi Strauss & Co, 2020):

- introducing innovative denim using organic cotton and fibre spun from discarded denim

- increasing the use of cottonized hemp and recycled fibres across the product assortment
- global marketing messaging focusing on 'Buy Better – Wear Longer' to shift consumers' intentions
- launch of a buy-back and resale platform to extend their products' lives

These are just some of the initiatives that LS&Co is using to become a more sustainable brand. Overall, the brand says they are committed to using their scale, reach and platform to advocate for positive change, address overconsumption and drive towards a more sustainable, less resource-intensive apparel industry (Levi Strauss & Co, 2020).

LS&Co seems to be doing something right as they have reported a net income of $196 million in 2022 compared to $143 a year earlier and revenue rose by 22 per cent (Thomas, 2022). One of the reasons for the success is seen in direct-to-consumer sales through their website and brick-and-mortar stores which account for 39 per cent of total sales (compared to 36 per cent a year before) (Thomas, 2022). Direct-to-consumer sales can be more profitable, allows a brand to build stronger relationships with its customers and provides the ability to collect more consumer data.

Questions

a. Over the years, LS&Co has tried different STP strategies to stay competitive. Try to identify three different segments that Levi's currently aims to target with their famous denim jeans Levi's 501.

b. Read LS&Co's Sustainability Report on their website and draw a positioning map for the product based on the two factors of sustainable focus and price point, and compare the Levi's 501 jeans to competing products.

c. Try to come up with a positioning statement for the Levi's 501 jeans using their sustainability focus by completing the template in Worksheet 2 in Additional Resources.

Summary

In this chapter, we have covered the STP analysis: segmentation, targeting and positioning. You should now be able to distinguish between the three different parts of the STP analysis. Segmenting a market means to break the overall market into smaller segments to be able to serve these identified segments more profitably. After the market has been segmented, a business has to decide which of these segments are worth their while to target. Essential questions to ask here are whether the segment is large enough to provide a profit and different enough to justify a separate marketing mix. Once a target strategy has been chosen, the product or service needs to be positioned in the mind of the consumer which can be done with the help of a positioning statement.

Chapter review

Reflective questions

Q1 What is the difference between market segmentation, targeting and positioning?

Q2 Why is it important to segment consumer markets?

Q3 What are the different segmentation variables and why are those important to consider?

Q4 What are the main four targeting strategies?

Q5 Elaborate on why positioning a product or service is essential to its success.

Key learning points

- The difference between market segmentation, targeting and positioning.
- Segmenting consumer markets allows businesses to divide their markets into smaller submarkets that have common interests and features.
- There are several different strategies of how consumers can be targeted: differentiated, undifferentiated, focused and customized targeting strategies.
- Positioning a product is all about linking the benefits of a product or service to the consumer's needs.

References

Fahy, J and Jobber, D (2015) *Foundations of Marketing*, McGraw-Hill Education, Berkshire

Garín Muñoz, T and Perez Amaral, T (2009) Modeling the key determinants of online shopping in Spain, papers.ssrn.com/sol3/papers.cfm?abstract_id=1363999 (archived at https://perma.cc/NLS5-TBB4)

Haley (2022) Positioning in marketing: Definition, types, examples, benefits and how to, Mageplaza, 1 May, www.mageplaza.com/blog/positioning-in-marketing.html (archived at https://perma.cc/FMW8-HE9E)

Helixa Marketing (2018) Patagonia: US Audience Analysis, www.helixa.ai/blog/patagonia-audience-analysis (archived at https://perma.cc/AH2E-TMU5)

Huseynov, F and Yildirim, S O (2017) Behavioural segmentation analysis of online consumer audience in Turkey by using real e-commerce transaction data, *International Journal of Economics and Business Research*, 14, 12–28

Huseynov, F and Yildirim, S O (2019) Online consumer typologies and their shopping behaviors in b2c e-commerce platforms, Sage Open 9(2), doi.org/10.1177/2158244019854639

Johnson, J (2021) Average duration of daily internet usage worldwide as of 1st quarter 2019, by age group and device, Statista, 27 January, www.statista.com/statistics/416850/average-duration-of-internet-use-age-device/ (archived at https://perma.cc/EL2Z-YSDJ)

Kotler, P and Keller, K (2012) Marketing Management, 14th edn, Prentice Hall, Upper Saddle River, NJ

Levi Strauss & Co (2020) Sustainability Report, www.levistrauss.com/wp-content/uploads/2021/09/LSCo.-2020-Sustainability-Report.pdf (archived at https://perma.cc/E3L6-LMCK)

Liu, Y, Li, H, Peng, G, Lv, B and Zhang, C (2015) Online purchaser segmentation and promotion strategy selection: Evidence from Chinese e-commerce market, Annals of Operations Research, 233, 263–79

Moore, G (2014) Crossing the Chasm, 3rd edn, Harper Business

Patel, S (2021) A complete guide to successful brand positioning, Hubspot, 3 October, blog.hubspot.com/sales/brand-positioning-strategy#:~:text=For%20example%2C%20take%20a%20look,might%20want%20to%20buy%20online.%22 (archived at https://perma.cc/9BX9-7NGP)

Perez, Y (2021) Similarities between product differentiation and positioning, Investopedia, 29 October, www.investopedia.com/ask/answers/062415/what-are-similarities-between-product-differentiation-and-product-positioning.asp (archived at https://perma.cc/Y6RG-GQFS)

Qualtrics XM (2022) What is product positioning, www.qualtrics.com/uk/experience-management/product/product-positioning/?rid=ip&prevsite=au&newsite=uk&geo=GB&geomatch=uk (archived at https://perma.cc/VWN4-26EH)

Statista Research Department (2022) Social network profile ownership in the United Kingdom (UK) 2015-2020, by age group, 28 April, www.statista.com/statistics/271879/social-network-profile-creation-in-the-uk-by-age/ (archived at https://perma.cc/4GN6-U3VG)

Tarver, E (2021) Market Segmentation, Investopedia, 5 April, www.investopedia.com/terms/m/marketsegmentation.asp (archived at https://perma.cc/A7GH-66N7)

The Good Trade (2022) 35 ethical and sustainable clothing brands betting against Fast Fashion, www.thegoodtrade.com/features/fair-trade-clothing (archived at https://perma.cc/7SWE-ERG3)

Thomas, L (2022) Levi Strauss earnings top estimates as shoppers buy at higher prices, denim retailer reaffirms 2022 outlook, CNBC, 6 April, www.cnbc.com/2022/04/06/levi-strauss-co-levi-reports-q1-2022-earnings-beat.html (archived at https://perma.cc/8ETL-TLK7)

Vrontis, D and Vronti, P (2004) Levi Strauss: An international marketing investigation, Journal of Fashion Marketing and Management, 8(4), 389–98

Wigmore, I (2022) Positioning statement, Tech Target, www.techtarget.com/whatis/definition/positioning-statement#:~:text=A%20positioning%20statement%20is%20an,it%20established%20in%20that%20area (archived at https://perma.cc/WAY7-WUHV)

Big Data

08

By the end of this chapter, you should be able to:

- explain the importance of Big Data in informing marketing decisions
- outline how data has changed the role of marketing
- distinguish between the 3Vs of Big Data
- explain the main ways of how Big Data can be collected and applied

Introduction

In the previous chapter we started to learn about a very common marketing tool, the STP analysis. You have been introduced to the importance of breaking a market down into smaller subsegments that have similar needs and wants and can be targeted with a clear positioning statement. In our digital world, it is progressively important to understand those segments from a digital perspective. You have been introduced to segmentation variables such as webographics or digital literacy already and these are essential to consider as several interactions between businesses and consumers are taking place on digital channels such as e-commerce and social media. Some factors to consider are channel usage, media consumption, digital buying behaviour and many more. In order to serve segments most efficiently, data needs to be collected and analysed. Businesses have an array of different opportunities to collect data. For example, data is collected through businesses' websites, on analytical platforms, through publicly shared comments on social media and review sites or through third party analytical tools to name but a few. Technology allows for huge data availability and such data available in large quantity is often referred to as Big Data.

Big Data

As we have seen in the beginning of this book, marketing is all about identifying and anticipating customers' wants and needs. The digital context allows for a lot of data to be collected. With such opportunities to collect vast amounts of data also come problems. Leeflang et al (2014) confirm that the main challenge facing digital marketers involves data. It was found, based on a survey with more than 750 marketing executives, that there is a knowledge gap on how to use and analyse consumer data to compete effectively. *Big Data* is a term that covers techniques and systems that can make sense of larger volumes of data and has changed the role of marketing.

> **KEY TERM**
> Big Data
>
> Big Data refers to the large, diverse sets of information that grow at ever-increasing rates. It encompasses the volume of information, the velocity or speed at which it is created and collected, and the variety or scope of the data points being covered (known as the '3Vs' of Big Data). Big Data often comes from data mining and arrives in multiple formats.
>
> **SOURCE** Segal, 2022

Marketing in a data-driven digital world

In the world we live in today, the issue is not how data can be collected but what we do with the amount of data that can be collected. The role of marketing has changed due to the availability of data through digital technologies. Shah and Murthi (2021) stress that the use of data in the marketing discipline has evolved from being mainly about analysing advertisements to designing analytics-driven customer-centric campaigns. In other words, the scope and role of marketing grew with the increased application of data-driven marketing as per the following stages:

- **Creativity:** Data was mainly used to analyse the effectiveness of advertisements often in the form of consumer panels and survey data.
- **Relevancy:** The next stage allowed data to be used for understanding the customer better to present product and service solutions that put the customer at the heart of marketing.
- **Analytics capability:** This stage is where the use of Big Data started and with that the increased application of analytics.
- **Accountability:** This era describes the importance of holding marketing departments accountable for firm-level financial outcomes.
- **Technology:** Now transformative technologies like blockchain technology and the Internet of Things (IoT) (see Chapter 5) inform marketing practices.

Activity 8.1

You have just learnt about the importance of data in shaping the marketing discipline.

i.   Visit Explainity on YouTube (#explainitychannel) and search for the video 'Big Data explained'. In this video, the application of Big Data is explained using practical examples.

ii. Do you think the use of Big Data is essential for a successful digital marketing campaign?

iii. Do you think that the collection of Big Data is ethical from a consumer's point of view?

The 3Vs of Big Data

There are three main dimensions that describe opportunities and challenges of Big Data: volume, variety and velocity (Figure 8.1). These are expanding at an increasing rate on all three fronts.

Data volume

The data volume describes the amount of data that is available. One of the main reasons why it is possible to collect such huge amounts of data is the ever-decreasing costs of storing data. Think back to about 50 years ago when it took a server the size of a room to store only fractions of the data that can nowadays be stored in chips the size of a fingernail or in cloud services that don't require any physical storage at all.

In 2020, every single person generated around 1.7 megabytes of data per second with internet users generating about 2.5 quintillion bytes of data each day (Petrov, 2022). This amounted to around 44 zettabytes of data in 2020 which would mean that there are 40 times more bytes than there are stars in the observable universe (Desjardins, 2019).

The Statista Research Team (2022) predicts that by 2025, global data creation will grow to more than 180 zettabytes. Table 8.1 shows the relationships between data volumes.

Figure 8.1   Three main dimensions of Big Data

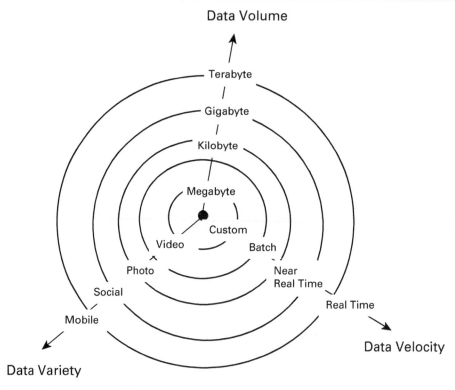

SOURCE Knight, 2022, adapted from Soubra, 2012

Table 8.1   Data storage scales

Abbreviation	Unit	Value	Size (in bytes)
b	bit	0 or 1	1/8 of a byte
B	byte	8 bits	1 byte
KB	kilobyte	1,000 bytes	1,000 bytes
MB	megabyte	$1,000^2$ bytes	1,000,000 bytes
GB	gigabyte	$1,000^3$ bytes	1,000,000,000 bytes
TB	terabyte	$1,000^4$ bytes	1,000,000,000,000 bytes
PB	petabyte	$1,000^5$ bytes	1,000,000,000,000,000 bytes
EB	exabyte	$1,000^6$ bytes	1,000,000,000,000,000,000 bytes
ZB	zettabyte	$1,000^7$ bytes	1,000,000,000,000,000,000,000 bytes
YB	yottabyte	$1,000^8$ bytes	1,000,000,000,000,000,000,000,000 bytes

Based on Desjardins, 2019

The following statistics show just how much data we as online users are producing (Wise, 2022):

- 1GB of data can create 350,000 emails
- Skype has 3 billion minutes of calls per day
- 5 billion Snapchat videos and photos are shared per day
- 333.2 billion emails are sent per day

CASE STUDY   Coca-Cola

We have just learnt about the unfathomable amount of data that is produced and collected every day. Businesses can use data to inform their marketing decisions. Those businesses that are doing well can utilize Big Data to understand how best to serve their customers.

The Coca-Cola Company is a US beverage corporation best known for its famous drink Coca-Cola. The Coca-Cola Company is the market leader in the beverage and refreshments category and acknowledges the use of Big Data as playing a major part in their success (Pathak, 2020). Coca-Cola has been recognized as one of the first businesses, outside of the IT industry, to talk about Big Data. In 2012, Coca-Cola's chief Big Data officer, Esat, Sezer said:

> Social media, mobile applications, cloud computing and e-commerce are combining to give companies like Coca-Cola an unprecedented toolset to change the way they approach IT. Behind all this, Big Data gives you the intelligence to cap it all off (Marr, 2017).

The following outlines some of the ways in which Coca-Cola utilizes Big Data to stay the market leader in a dynamic, fast-changing market (Pathak, 2020):

- **Identification of purchase patterns:** Purchasing behaviour differs greatly among consumers given the multinational markets that Coca-Cola is serving. With the help of Big Data analytics, purchase patterns are identified and products are launched according to what people of a specific region prefer.
- **Brand mentions and image searches:** Coca-Cola collects a vast amount of data by searching the web for its brand mentions and product images posted by consumers. They then show targeted ads to consumers on several channels.
- **Personalization through the collection of user information:** Big Data is collected that identifies crucial information of users. In 2015, they identified that their products were mentioned once every two seconds.

Questions

Coca-Cola utilized Big Data successfully in a number of ways.

a. Visit the YouTube video (Marr, 2019) to see how Coca-Cola uses data and experiments to drive business decisions. Can you imagine how such a consumer study would have worked prior to the availability of Big Data and machine learning?

b. Do you see any ethical issues with the amount of data that is collected by businesses?

Data velocity

Data velocity describes the second factor of Big Data and refers to the speed at which data is generated.

KEY TERM
Data velocity

Data velocity is the speed at which data is processed. This includes input such as the processing of social media posts and output such as the processing required to produce a report or execute a process.

SOURCE Spacey, 2017

There are different levels of data velocity depending on when the data is being processed. Spacey (2017) explains the following levels:

- **Real-time:** Data is being processed in real time meaning that it can respond to events as they occur (e.g. consumers will be accepted for a buy-now-pay-later credit card as soon as they apply for it online).

- **Near-real-time:** Data is being processed in almost real time but it cannot respond immediately (e.g. a comparison website can process your data for a few minutes and provide a number of different insurance options).

- **Batch:** Data is being processed when resources are available so data might not be analysed as it is being produced (e.g. social media brand mentionings might not be detected as they occur but with a delay).

- **Custom job:** Data is being processed only once or on an irregular schedule (e.g. a brand might be running a campaign and is only looking for a specific mentioning in social media posts).

Data variety

Big data comes in a lot of different shapes and forms and this *data variety* is one of the reasons why Big Data is indeed so big.

KEY TERM

Data variety

Big data comes from a great variety of sources and generally is one out of three types: structured, semi-structured and unstructured data. The variety in data types frequently requires distinct processing capabilities and specialist algorithms.

SOURCE Middelburg, 2019

Think of the data available to businesses. As you saw in the Coca-Cola example, they collected mentionings of the brand on social media channels but also reviewed images of their brand posted. These are already two different varieties of data: the written word vs a picture. If you add to this motion pictures in the form of videos, and audio files in the form of voice messages (e.g. podcasts), you can imagine how many different forms of processing capabilities are required.

It is no surprise that one of the main challenges of Big Data is the actual analysis of the data.

The application of Big Data

As you have seen in the third V of Big Data, the data can be split into two categories, structured and unstructured. If you think of *structured data*, think of data that is already owned by the company. This can be consumer data such as purchasing behaviour collected through loyalty schemes. Such structured data usually comes in the form of databases and spreadsheets and is opposed to *unstructured data* which is unorganized information that does not fall into a specific format (Segal, 2022). An example of unstructured data would be the information that businesses collect on social media channels. It is estimated that around 80–90 per cent of the data that is generated today is unstructured (Petrov, 2022).

The following is a list of different ways in which Big Data can be collected (Segal, 2022):

- publicly shared comments on social media networks and websites
- voluntarily gathered from personal electronics and apps

- through questionnaires
- product purchase history
- electronic check-ins
- smart device sensors which enable data collection in several different ways

---

Activity 8.2

We have reviewed several ways in which Big Data can be collected.

i.   Review the following options for Big Data collection and try to establish what type of methods would result in structured or unstructured data:

- publicly shared comments on social media networks and websites
- voluntarily gathered from personal electronics and apps
- through questionnaires
- product purchase history
- electronic check-ins
- smart device sensors which enable data collection in several different ways

ii. Establish the implications for businesses if the data collected is structured or unstructured.

iii. Explain in which context the results of the different data being collected can be applied.

As you can see from the list above there are many different ways in which Big Data can be collected. We have already reviewed some of the ways in which such collected data can be applied to improve decision-making. A very common application of Big Data is the analysis of consumer behaviour particularly with a focus on purchasing patterns. Particularly large, multinational businesses have to serve markets with different products and services to cater for all sorts of consumer preferences. Collecting large amounts of purchasing data and applying Big Data analytics can help to keep track of purchasing patterns and allow businesses to serve their products more effectively and efficiently. Such data is often collected in the form of structured data and is relatively easy to analyse.

Another common application of Big Data is that of analysing any brand mentions on social media. Such mentions can be collected in a lot of different formats, ranging from written comments to videos and images. As you can imagine, this collected data is unstructured and much more difficult to analyse. However, this is one of the most crucial applications of Big Data as it allows businesses to engage with their consumers. Such personalized engagement can be in the form of customer service in the case of a complaint or publishing customized advertisements.

These are just a few ways in which Big Data can be applied in marketing. A lot of other business departments are using Big Data. As Segal (2022) puts it:

> The goal of Big Data is to increase the speed at which products get to market, to reduce the amount of time and resources required to gain market adoption, target audiences, and to ensure customers remain satisfied.

It is easy to see how Big Data provides numerous opportunities for businesses and consumers alike. However, we also need to be aware of the risks and challenges that Big Data brings. The large amount of data that can be collected needs to be analysed and often it is difficult for businesses to decide which data is actually useful and what can be ignored. For example, 95 per cent of surveyed business state that managing unstructured data is a problem for their business (Petrov, 2022). Furthermore, one needs to consider the ethical side of data collection on the scale that it is currently collected. Consumer privacy and data protection need to be given great consideration given the rise of data being collected.

Summary

We have now learnt what Big Data is, how it can be collected and how it is applied. We have seen how the role of marketing has changed with the use of data. Big Data consists of 3Vs that describe data volume, velocity and variety. The sheer amount of data volume is only possible to collect through improved storage opportunities. The velocity describes the speed of the process by which the data can be processed. While some data can be processed in real time, other sets of data will only be processed on an irregular or needs-based basis. The variety of data that can be collected poses several challenges to the usability of data as a number of different processing abilities are required. Big Data is applied in a number of different contexts but ultimately has the goal to increase efficiency and effectiveness of serving customers.

Chapter review

Reflective questions

Q1 How does Big Data inform marketing decisions?

Q2 How has the role of marketing changed over the years with the increased availability of data?

Q3 What are the differences between data volume, data velocity and data variety?

Q4 How can Big Data be collected?

Q5 In which context can analysed Big Data be applied?

Key learning points

- Big data is a term that covers techniques and systems that can make sense of larger volumes of data and has changed the role of marketing.
- The scope and role of marketing grew with the increased application of data-driven marketing.
- The 3Vs of Big Data (volume, velocity and variety) describe opportunities and challenges of Big Data.
- A very common application of Big Data is the analysis of consumer behaviour particularly with a focus on purchasing patterns.

References

Desjardins, J (2019) How much data is generated each day? Visual Capitalist, 15 April, www.visualcapitalist.com/how-much-data-is-generated-each-day/ (archived at https://perma.cc/K8ES-U4VY)

Leeflang, P S H, Verhoef, P, Dahlström, P and Freundt, T (2014) Challenges and solutions for marketing in a digital era, *European Management Journal*, 32, 1–12

Marr, B (2017) The amazing ways Coca Cola uses artificial intelligence and Big Data to drive success, *Forbes*, 18 September, www.forbes.com/sites/bernardmarr/2017/09/18/the-amazing-ways-coca-cola-uses-artificial-intelligence-ai-and-big-data-to-drive-success/?sh=56f0ef6678d2 (archived at https://perma.cc/DQ5Z-LPHS)

Marr, B (2019) How Coca-Cola uses data and experiments to drive business decisions, YouTube, www.youtube.com/watch?v=b0ttUoL2pyY (archived at https://perma.cc/YFE9-PG2E)

Middelburg, J-W (2019) The 4 characteristics of Big Data, Enterprise Big Data Framework, www.bigdataframework.org/the-four-vs-of-big-data/ (archived at https://perma.cc/3SRN-HNPF)

Pathak, R (2020) How Coca-Cola uses technology to stay at the top? Analytic Steps, 24 October, www.analyticssteps.com/blogs/how-coca-cola-uses-technology-stay-top (archived at https://perma.cc/TU8H-5CUU)

Petrov, C (2022) 25+ impressive Big Data statistics for 2022, techjury, 26 April, techjury.net/blog/big-data-statistics/#gref (archived at https://perma.cc/CJ7H-BC2Q)

Segal, T (2022) Big Data, Investopedia, 28 March, www.investopedia.com/terms/b/big-data.asp (archived at https://perma.cc/FES7-NXCK)

Shah, D and Murthi, B (2021) Marketing in a data-driven digital world: Implications for the role and scope of marketing, *Journal of Business Research*, 125, 772–79

Soubra, D (2012) The 3Vs that define Big Data, Data Science Central, www.datasciencecentral.com/forum/topics/the-3vs-that-define-big-data (archived at https://perma.cc/V7ET-ABGN)

Spacey, J (2017) 5 Types of data velocity, Simplicable, 29 November, simplicable.com/new/data-velocity (archived at https://perma.cc/PL4R-5KNS)

Statista Research Team (2022) Volume of data/information created, captured, copied, and consumed worldwide from 2010 to 2020, with forecasts from 2021 to 2025, www.statista.com/statistics/871513/worldwide-data-created/ (archived at https://perma.cc/5FNC-6NVX)

Wise, J (2022) How much data is created every day in 2022? Earthweb, 29 May, earthweb.com/how-much-data-is-created-every-day/ (archived at https://perma.cc/KJ99-VYHA)

PART THREE
Online customer behaviour

Primary and secondary data sources

09

By the end of this chapter, you should be able to:

- distinguish between and briefly define primary and secondary data
- describe each source of data
- understand how data is gathered from each source
- explain in simple terms what the benefits and disadvantages are of each data collection source

Introduction

This chapter is the start of Part Three, where we will explore online consumer behaviour. More specifically, this chapter is focused on gaining insights from consumers via investigation of data sources. Collecting data allows marketers to learn more about their consumers and/or marketplace. Data can be collected by researchers in academic jobs, professional research companies or research teams within a business.

In this chapter we will learn about the different types of data sources, i.e. what they are, when they are useful, and a very brief overview of how to go about collecting data from them. As we are concerned with digital marketing, we will also take a closer look at some newer means of obtaining data from digital platforms, such as netnography and social listening.

Data can be either *qualitative* or *quantitative* in nature. Both approaches are valuable and add valid insights.

> **KEY TERM**
> Qualitative/quantitative data
>
> **Qualitative data:** Data involving understanding of the complexity, detail and context of the research subject, often consisting of texts, such as interview transcripts and field notes or audiovisual material.
>
> **Quantitative data:** Data that can be described numerically in terms of objects, variables and their values.
>
> **SOURCE** Hox and Boeije, 2005

Quantitative studies tend to draw from a larger number of participants to allow for analytical approaches such as statistical analysis. Qualitative studies draw from smaller numbers of participants, but involve in-depth probes into a research topic that also result in rich data. Researchers can also combine quantitative and qualitative studies, in which case the project uses a mixed methods approach.

Data can be collected from primary and secondary sources. *Note:* primary and secondary data can be either quantitative or qualitative. The difference between *primary data* and *secondary data* is described in the Key Term box.

> **KEY TERM**
> Primary/secondary data
>
> **Primary data:** Original data collected for a specific research goal.
>
> **Secondary data:** Data originally collected for a different purpose and reused for another research question.
>
> **SOURCE** Hox and Boeije, 2005

When you collect your own data, it is classified as primary. When you use a previously collected set of data (for example census data or a database full of consumer data), it is classified as secondary. As the definitions state, primary data tends to be more specific to your research goal as it involves asking questions specifically created for the project. Secondary data might not be as specific to your research goal, but it can still hold a lot of valuable information that can be beneficial in reaching your project goal.

Primary data

Sources of primary data

Surveys

Surveys are a quantitative method and usually involve gathering consumer responses via a questionnaire. These questionnaires are carefully developed and tested, often using previously validated scales and measures. Survey data is predominantly collected using electronic or digital questionnaires, where participants get sent a link. There are instances of people going around in marketplaces with surveys to be completed on clipboards or smart devices such as tablets, but this is more costly and time-consuming and often not as effective in recruiting willing participants. The survey data is processed and analysed using a range of methods. The methods range from basic descriptive analyses and comparisons to sophisticated statistical analysis and modelling.

Interviews

Interviews, a qualitative method, are transcribed dialogues where the researcher asks the participant a set of questions to gather their views and accounts of a phenomenon under investigation. Interviews can be structured or semi-structured and recorded using audio and/or visual means. The most common means of getting data from interviews is to read the transcripts (a typed copy of the conversation) and code them using methods such as thematic or narrative analysis. The codes from each interview are compared (both within the transcript and with other interviews' transcripts) and insights developed to answer the research question.

Focus groups

Focus groups (sometimes referred to as consumer panels in marketing practice) consist of a group of participants engaging in a conversation with the researcher or facilitator. Often with a list of topics or questions to cover, similar to an interview. Focus groups are often also analysed using the same methods as for interview analysis. However, focus groups can also add another interesting dimension when looking at the power dynamics and interactions within the participant group. Interviews and focus groups can be conducted in person or online.

Netnography

As mentioned above, we are inspecting online consumer behaviour. As marketplaces and consumer activity shifts online, so do data collection methods. With this in mind we look at the evolution of ethnography to *netnography*, which is quite useful for digital marketers.

> **KEY TERM**
> Netnography
>
> A qualitative research approach that adapts the traditional ethnographic techniques to the study of the 'net', which is the online communities, practices and cultures formed through computer-mediated communications.
>
> **SOURCE** Addeo et al, 2019

Netnography and ethnography involve observation of participants' behaviour in the research setting, taking field notes and documenting other things of interest (e.g. taking a photograph). In the case of netnography, participants' behaviour in digital spaces are observed and documented with, for example, the hyperlink to the website, community page or platform where they were observed. Screenshots, downloads and other things of interest make up the digital version of field notes. Netnography has been used in marketing and consumer research since the 1990s (Sandlin, 2007).

If you are interested in learning more about netnography, read Addeo et al (2019).

Social listening

Another means for digital marketers to collect online consumer behaviour is through *social listening*.

> **KEY TERM**
> Social listening
>
> Essentially, social media monitoring, documenting (or 'listening' to) consumer communications on social media platforms.
>
> **SOURCE** Reid and Duffy, 2018

Social listening usually involves both quantitative and qualitative analysis. The number of posts, mentions, hashtags, participants (profiles), etc are counted or quantified (for example, '30 per cent of consumers noted X as the thing they like the most about brand Y'). However, this does not give you the complete picture. The data also needs to be subjected to qualitative analysis, predominantly starting via sentiment analysis. This is needed because you need to determine whether consumer communications about the phenomenon being studied are negative, positive or neutral. For example, you might have 500 comments on a brand post or use of a specific hashtag, but that does not tell you what is being said or the nature of consumers' responses.

Reid and Duffy (2018) take things a step further and argue for a combination of netnography and social listening to allow marketers to cope with the sheer volume of data they have access to in digital spaces like social media platforms. They call this combination *netnographic sensibility*.

KEY TERM
Netnographic sensibility

An approach that marries netnography and social listening practices, enabling richness and depth in data obtained from mass consumer realities.

SOURCE Reid and Duffy, 2018

Activity 9.1

In a group, spend some time searching for journal articles.

 i. Using your library resources or Google Scholar, search for digital marketing or consumer studies that use different methods:

  – surveys

  – interviews

  – focus groups

  – netnography

  – social listening

 ii. Discuss the differences in using each of these methods as documented in the papers.

iii. Did you find any other interesting methods or combination of methods? Why were they interesting?

iv. Present your thoughts to the class for a wider group discussion.

Benefits of primary data

- gives you specific data gathered with your research goal in mind
- you own the data (no need for copyright and permissions to use)
- easy access to your data

Disadvantages of primary data

- time-consuming
- expensive

Secondary data

Sources of secondary data

Government reports and statistics

Government reports and statistics are valuable and useful sources of secondary data that provide an overview of the population (or large parts thereof) and the city, region or country. Depending on what information you need, it might be useful to search for reports or statistics from specific departments within the government. For example, in the UK the Department of the Environment, Food and Rural Affairs would have data on the outdoor environments that serve your marketplace or target consumer, and Office for National Statistics (UK census bureau) would have the census data and their subsequent reports and statistics on the population's demographics.

Industry associations

Government bodies are not the only ones who do regular studies about the marketplaces. Industry associations often have their own data sets and reports that are written by specialists in the industry for the benefit of members and practitioners within the same field (Table 9.1). Depending on the market you serve, there may be national or international associations that can be of value to you as a secondary source.

Table 9.1   Industry associations

Advertising Association	adassoc.org.uk/
WARC	www.warc.com/Welcome
Data & Marketing Association UK	dma.org.uk/
IAB Europe	iabeurope.eu/
The Federation of European Data and Marketing	www.fedma.org/
Association of National Advertisers	www.ana.net/

Market research reports

There are also numerous market research reports from big firms, niche market research companies or even marketing agencies. Depending on the nature of the enquiry, these can usually provide overviews of, for example, consumer trends for the year, changes in media consumption or consumer spending in categories. These studies and reports are updated frequently, giving you recent data to work with. Often you will find global/international and national research reports from big firms that require a change of search terms and website (e.g. Nielsen in Table 9.2).

Trade publications and awards

Trade publications and awards are good sources of inspiration and information, particularly in terms of trade specific insights or case studies of successful and creative campaigns. For a good example, visit Trendhunter's website (Trendhunter, 2022).

Table 9.2   Market research companies

Company	Contact	Comment
Research and Markets	www.researchandmarkets.com/	
Market Research Reports	www.marketresearchreports.com	
Nielsen	*Global* global.nielsen.com/ *Denmark* www.nielsen.com/dk/da/	
Statista	www.statista.com/	(not everything is free, but could have an institution subscription)
Mintel	store.mintel.com/	(not free, but could have an institution subscription)
PricewaterhouseCoopers	www.pwc.com/gx/en/research-insights.html	
Ernst and Young Insights	www.ey.com/en_gl/insights	
American Marketing Association	www.ama.org/topics/market-research/	

CASE STUDY   D&AD

The D&AD is a non-profit association that hosts a global annual competition for the best in design and advertising. They have a number of interesting categories and winning case studies that result in a rich database of great marketing campaigns. One of their categories is focused on the future impact of the campaign or concept.

One such example is the S-Park campaign that won a D&AD Future Impact Pencil award for environment and sustainability in 2019. In short, the concept revolves around an innovation in bicycles and bicycle racks in Amsterdam that allows consumers to contribute to the generation of renewable energy whenever they use their bicycles. Given that the Netherlands is a country with a lot of cyclists, the idea has a lot of potential.

Question

Go and read the case study, including visual and video portrayals, by visiting D&AD's website (D&AD, 2019).

Activity 9.2

In your groups, spend some time researching more examples of award-winning campaigns.

i.   Can you come up with a similar campaign for one of your favourite brands?

ii. What could the environmental or social impact be of your idea?

iii. Would this be costly for your brand?

iv. Would it generate positive consumer responses (such as loyalty and increased sales)?

Company websites

Company websites provide information straight from the source. Some websites include information on the company and/or their consumers. If the company is big enough you can often find copies of their quarterly or annual reports and news about their activities on the website. Some companies also include some consumer sentiments (although these would hardly be the negative ones). Websites are a good place to start a brand or marketing audit of a company.

Benefits of secondary data

- less expensive than primary data
- less time-consuming than primary data

Disadvantages of secondary data

- can be difficult to access data
- permission to use data
- interpreting other people's data

Activity 9.3

In your groups, search for examples of sustainable campaigns (in the form of detailed case studies including objectives, results, etc).

i.　Did they conduct market research?

ii.　Did they use primary or secondary data?

iii.　Which insights from sources did they use to inform their strategy and campaign development?

iv.　Discuss with the class.

Summary

Primary and secondary data sources offer marketers valuable avenues to understanding consumers and their behaviour in the marketplace. For online consumer behaviour data you can still use the tried and tested methods such as surveys or interviews. However, new methods such as netnography and social listening allow marketers to access, process and develop insights about consumers in online environments in a more effective manner. There are a lot of secondary sources out there that can serve as starting points for market research or as valuable sources of information.

Chapter review

Reflective questions

Q1　Why is it necessary to conduct primary research?

Q2　What can you get from primary research that you cannot find from secondary sources?

Q3　Where can I find secondary data?

Q4　What do I need to keep in mind in terms of ethical and responsible data use, for primary and secondary sources?

Key learning points

- Primary data is your own, original data and secondary data is previously collected data for another project.

- There are a variety of primary and secondary sources that allow improved knowledge and understanding of consumers and marketplaces, including digital spaces.

- While primary sources offer specific data related to the project, the process is expensive and time-consuming.

- While secondary sources might not be 100 per cent relevant in terms of data for the project, the process is a lot less expensive and the data is ready for use.

References

Addeo, F, Paoli, A D, Esposito, M and Bolcato, M Y (2019) Doing social research on online communities: The benefits of netnography, *Athens Journal Of Social Sciences*, 7(1), 9–38 D&AD (2019) S-Park, www.dandad.org/awards/professional/2019/future/232266/s-park/ (archived at https://perma.cc/2BF7-J4RL)

Hox, J J and Boeije, H R (2005) Data collection, primary versus secondary, dspace.library. uu.nl/bitstream/handle/1874/23634/hox_05_data+collection,primary+versus+secondary. pdf?sequence=1 (archived at https://perma.cc/A2S5-4DCF)

Reid, E and Duffy, K (2018) A netnographic sensibility: Developing the netnographic/social listening boundaries, *Journal of Marketing Management*, 34(3–4), 263–86

Sandlin, J A (2007) Netnography as a consumer education research tool, *International Journal of Consumer Studies*, 31(3), 288–94

Trendhunter (2022) Create the future, Trendhunter, www.trendhunter.com/ (archived at https://perma.cc/VK8P-3PQH)

The digital consumer

10

By the end of this chapter, you should be able to:

- briefly define what a digital consumer is
- understand how to create a digital consumer persona
- describe what user-generated content is
- explain in simple terms what a prosumer is

Introduction

By now we have introduced the key concepts to get you started with the basics of digital marketing. We have also looked at doing research in the digital environment and where to find data sources. This means that we can now move on to the main actor in the online environment: the digital consumer. In this chapter we will examine consumer behaviour in digital marketplaces. We introduce consumer personas and learn how to develop them in line with market and target group research and the marketing objectives. Lastly, we introduce the empowered consumer, exploring key concepts emerging from digital consumer behaviour such as the prosumer and user-generated content.

Consumer behaviour

History

Simply, consumer behaviour is how consumers behave in the marketplace. Consumer behaviour is a well-established area of marketing research that has been around for decades. Insights from consumer behaviour are very handy, because they are used to develop marketing campaigns and materials. The more we understand about consumers, their needs and subsequent behaviour, the better our marketing and communication strategies can be.

Physical marketplace behaviours

Consumer behaviour in physical marketplaces takes many forms, ranging from general movement through brick-and-mortar stores or marketplace high streets, purchases, and interactions with others and with marketing materials. Companies are interested in consumer behaviour because it gives them insights into effectively engaging with their clientele. In a retail environment, for example, companies monitor how many consumers visit their stores (also known as monitoring foot traffic), which aisles are visited the most, which products are the most popular, which promotional activities work the best, etc.

Digital marketplace behaviours

In digital marketplaces it is a bit more difficult to measure consumer behaviour, as consumers are not physically present when engaging with the company or its products and services. Digital marketplace behaviour requires several other measuring and evaluation tactics, which will be discussed in detail in Part Five of this book.

However, before we get into the measuring and evaluation of consumer behaviour in digital marketplaces, it is worth introducing the types of digital marketplaces and a couple of key behavioural concepts we find in contemporary societies.

Types of digital marketplaces

Digital marketplaces exist in many different forms, and can basically be any digital platform companies and consumers engage in. We will look at three main types of digital marketplaces.

Digital storefronts

We start with digital versions of the companies' stores. Usually the company website serves as the digital version of the store window or storefront. The digital storefront attracts consumers with the familiar brand identity (logo, slogan, colours, images, celebrity endorsements, etc) and displays of the products and services offered by the company. Just like temporary window displays, *microsites* and *pop-up windows* showcase the companies' promotions or competitions.

KEY TERM
Microsite/pop-up window

Microsite: A brand-specific page within a website that is created and visible for the duration of a specific promotion, competition or event. Usually deactivated when the event ends.

Pop-up window: As the name implies, a window that pops onto your screen when you visit a website or certain page on a website; for example a spring promotion offering 15 per cent off on all floral fashions.

The microsites or pop-up windows are temporary digital storefronts, dedicated to that specific marketing campaign or offer. A lot of websites, whether on computers or mobile devices, usually contain an e-commerce component. Having this *electronic commerce* capability allows consumers to purchase directly from the website (see also Chapter 16).

KEY TERM
Electronic commerce (e-commerce)

The term electronic commerce refers to a business model that allows companies and individuals to buy and sell goods and services over the internet. E-commerce operates in four major market segments including business-to-business, business-to-consumer, consumer-to-consumer and consumer-to-business. It can be conducted over computers, tablets, smartphones and other smart devices. Nearly every imaginable product and service is available through e-commerce transactions, including books, music, plane tickets, and financial services such as stock investing and online banking.

SOURCE Bloomenthal, 2021

Of course, if digital marketplaces can be any digital platform companies and consumers engage in, that means that social media channels can also essentially function as digital storefronts. In a way, they do, especially if there are dedicated company pages (e.g. Facebook and Instagram business pages). The companies' profiles on social media channels are also branded, linking the social media channels to the brand via links to the website, in-store promotions and other engagement opportunities. See Chapter 17 for more details on digital marketing and social media channels.

There are two interesting consumer behaviour concepts that have emerged from this ability to interact with brands, browse and shop on a wide range of digital storefronts, namely *webrooming* and *showrooming*.

> **KEY TERM**
> Webrooming
>
> Consumers first search for information about the product or service online and then go to purchase their selection offline, in the physical marketplace.
>
> **SOURCE** Flavián et al, 2020

> **KEY TERM**
> Showrooming
>
> Consumers first search for information about the product or service offline and then go to purchase their selection online, in the digital marketplace.
>
> **SOURCE** Gensler et al, 2017

New digital technologies, such as augmented and virtual reality, allow companies to build webrooming and showrooming capabilities into their digital consumption experiences. These digital consumer behaviours are now commonplace (Flavián et al, 2020). Consumers can now try on virtual jewellery (e.g. Fenton) and glasses (e.g. Warby Parker) through filters on smartphones or websites. You can even design a whole room online; for example, selecting and swopping Ikea furniture until you find the right combination to match your style.

Digital high streets and malls

As developments in artificial intelligence (see Key Term in Chapter 5) and metaverses (see Key Term in Chapter 5) grow, digital marketplaces develop with them. We are seeing whole high streets, and even malls, going online. Due to the Covid-19 pandemic and the worldwide lockdowns, the decline of physical high streets has increased rapidly. Big brands such as Debenhams are moving entirely online.

> **Activity 10.1**
>
> According to the BBC (2022) there were over 6,000 fewer physical stores in the UK after the first half of 2020. Chesterfield Council in the UK, for example, has an initiative to support local high-street businesses to build their online presence,

offering web hosting, digital specialists and other digitizing support to ensure they don't go out of business.

i. Visit the East Midlands Chamber's web page about the Chesterfield Digital High Street.

ii. Consider the benefits and disadvantages of having both physical and digital stores. What are the cost, staffing and consumer service implications?

Advergaming

Of course, the new technological developments and marketplaces moving into digital spaces means that new opportunities for creative and clever marketing are opening up. One such avenue is in marketing in metaverses and gaming platforms. Metaverses originate from virtual games, more specifically in 'massively multiplayer online role play games' (MMORPGs) (Bourlakis et al, 2009, 137). It is estimated that over 3,243 million people worldwide are active gamers online (Clement, 2021). Marketers are also operating in these alternative realities. By adding e-commerce capabilities to metaverses, companies convert these virtual worlds into digital marketplaces.

Two key avenues of digital marketing in these spaces are *in-game advertising* and *advergaming*, where consumers can engage with the marketing to get rewards such as in-game currency.

KEY TERM
In-game advertising

In-game advertising (or IGA) is advertising in games, e.g. through pop-up windows, digital banners and backgrounds, popular in mobile and console gaming.

SOURCE Herrewijn and Poels, 2014

Advergaming can take two forms:

- partnerships between brands and gaming platforms, e.g. Mercedes-Benz and Nintendo Switch in Mario Kart 8 (Gaudiosi, 2015)
- partnerships between two brands, e.g. Coca-Cola and McDonald's collaboration for the Crabs and Penguins game (Herrewijn and Poels, 2014)

> **KEY TERM**
> Advergaming
>
> Combining advertising and gaming. When companies embed brand-related advertising into interactive digital games as a means to increase consumer engagement.
>
> **SOURCE** De Pelsmacker et al, 2012

Through these forms of marketing, companies are able to engage with consumers in gaming environments. Often these forms of advertising drive consumers to the brand website and social media (see Chapter 11, The Customer Journey).

As we saw with the examples above, metaverses are starting to move beyond gaming environments and companies are starting to explore ways to embed their digital marketing in these new digital marketplaces (see the sections on cryptocurrency and blockchain in Chapter 5).

Creating customer personas

Target market research

As mentioned at the start of the chapter, the more we know about consumer behaviour, the better our chances of developing effective marketing strategies. However, there is a lot to investigate, and a lot of variables to consider when trying to gather information about consumers. As we saw in Chapter 2, marketing strategies often involve one or a couple of specific consumer groups, subsegments of the whole population. That is why consumer behaviour research often takes the form of target market research. In other words, research about the specific consumer groups you want to target with your marketing strategy.

A useful way to convert consumer behaviour data into insights about your target audience is to create a consumer persona. Consumer personas tell us a lot about our target audience's consumer behaviour and how we can engage with them in the marketplace, whether offline or online. Consumer personas typically include your target audience's consumer characteristics: details about their demographics, geography, psychographics, *webographics*, lifestyle choices, etc (see also Chapter 7). The consumer characteristics of our target audience govern their consumption behaviour.

Webographics

KEY TERM
Webographics

Webographics are those characteristics referring to online consumer behaviour. A consumer's webographic details include information on their knowledge of computers and the internet and how to navigate in digital spaces (also referred to as digital literacy).

SOURCE Garín and Perez Amaral, 2009

This digital literacy covers a range of variables such as:

- how to find a brand online
- how to search for something on a website
- how to buy a product from an online shop
- ability to make online payments
- ability to engage with social media posts
- ability to engage with sponsored advertisements

Other related insights that could be useful to have are:

- your target audience's preference in channels they use (e.g. preferring Instagram or TikTok to websites or emails)
- when they are most active online (e.g. commute or bedtime scrollers)
- their online consumption activity (which products are actually bought, but this knowledge is usually limited to the brand itself due to data protection – see Part Six).

Combining digital consumer behaviour or webographic information with your other target audience insights (from demographics, geographics and psychographics) allows you to put it all together into a profile. These profiles are typically known as 'consumer personas' and are usually textual and/or visual representations that offer a summary of the key characteristics of your target audience.

Consumer personas are fictitious representations of your intended target audience that resemble real people. In other words, they are fictional embodiments of your ideal consumer from the target audience with a name, job, address, hobbies, interests, car, music, leisure activities, personality, etc. These personas give you and your team an overview of who your target audience is and how to engage with them via your marketing strategy and campaign(s).

There are many different categories and labels you can include in creating your consumer persona. Some companies prefer to categorize according to income, others according to personality, others according to product category, others according to ethnicity, and others according to age. The list and combinations are endless. What you include depends on your industry, your brand (for example specific values or product categories), details you need about your intended target audience and ultimately what you are trying to achieve with your marketing strategy.

Two things to remember:

- Consumer personas should not be based on one real consumer, but rather a combination of multiple characteristics found in the data about your target audience (i.e. from multiple consumers in the target audience).

- Consumer personas can and should change as your brand grows and marketplaces change. Often those macro- and micro-environment changes you learnt about in Chapters 5 and 6 impact revision or even addition of target audiences, e.g. having a vegan target audience is becoming more and more necessary for food brands.

There is no specific rule for the number of consumer personas you should have for your brand, but the general consensus is that it makes sense to have one for each of your target audiences. If your company has five main target audiences, you should have five consumer personas. For example, a clothing brand selling sports clothing would perhaps have five main target audiences (runners, swimmers, dancers, cyclists and gym goers) that each become a consumer persona based on type of products required/sports participating in. Others might want to be more specific; for example, an outdoor clothing brand might wish to segment along the lines of type of adventure and combine activity level with age and family life cycle, e.g. snowy mountain climbers (extreme level, 20–30, no family) or leisure campers (low level, 30–45, young family). The more (useful) information the better. Some even create quotes or draw from consumer data about experiences with the brand to create a more well-rounded picture.

A frequently used method to establish what you need to include in your persona is to find the answers to these basic questions, as supplied by SurveyMonkey (2022):

1 What are your audience's basic demographics? (Age, gender identity, race, income, marital status, etc)

2 What is your audience's educational background? (High school diploma, some college, college graduate)

3 Where do they work? (Industry, job title, level entry, intermediate, management)

4 Describe a typical day in their life. (Daily tasks, influences on their decisions)

5 What are their goals, values, aspirations? (What do they want? What is stopping them from achieving their goals?)

6   Where do they research or shop online? (Google, Amazon, etc)

7   What are their questions/concerns about your product/service? (Price, quality, value, warranty, etc)

8   How do they prefer interaction? (Phone, email, live chat)

9   Which times would be best for them to engage with and respond to your content?

10   When are they available to spend the time to speak with you?

Once you have all of the information you want to include in your consumer personas it is a good idea to summarize the key points into an easy-to-use format. Usually this means creating a table or figure that includes all of the key characteristics of your target audience as represented by your fictional character. There are many free templates available (see Persona Templates box).

EXAMPLE
Persona templates

Mockplus (2022) presents a couple of persona examples. You can view them by visiting Mockplus's website. Under the Learn tab, click on blog. On the blog page, search for 'User persona template' and click on the result titled '20 Best User Persona Templates & Examples for Free Download in 2020'. These serve as good inspiration for what to include and what these visual summaries look like.

Some of the examples are also available for free download, but require some design skills and software. If you do not have access to design software, there are free online editors that can build your skills and confidence in creating your own consumer personas.

Question

One such website is Canva (2022). Visit the website, create a free profile and explore.

Activity 10.2

i.   Pick a brand or product you would like to market.

ii.   Decide who your key target audience is and create a persona. You can use Hubspot's handy persona generator tool. Visit their website (Hubspot, 2022) and search for 'persona generator' to find the link.

iii.   Add at least one new section each for personality, hobbies and interests.

Activity 10.3

Use Worksheet 2 in the Additional Resources to develop a customer persona by filling in the template.

The empowered consumer

Due to technological developments such as social media platforms, consumers have more power in managing their engagements in digital marketplaces (Vollero and Valentini, 2021). In fact, Vollero and Valentini identify three different types of power consumer have in digital marketplaces:

- **Information-based power:** Consumers are able to quickly access multiple online information sources for free to inform their consumption choices, which reduces companies' influence on their consumption behaviour.

- **Participation-based power:** Consumers are able to dictate their involvement on social media, creating networks of power based on the content they create, share, like, comment on, etc.

- **Community-based power:** Groups of like-minded consumers can form consumer or brand communities that have a significant impact on marketing activities and the success of a product, service or company. These communities can share or recommend their consumption activities to others, thereby promoting the brands they support (or damage brand reputations and sales when they boycott brands and dissuade people from buying from them).

The forms of consumer power through social media use are increasing so much that companies are forced to engage with consumers across multiple platforms via company and user-generated content (Vollero and Valentini, 2021).

User-generated content

The most definitive consumer behaviour resulting from consumer engagement in digital spaces is *user-generated content* (commonly referred to as UGC).

KEY TERM
User-generated content (UGC)

User-generated content (also known as consumer-generated content) is original, brand-specific content created by customers and published on social media or other channels. UGC comes in many forms, including images, videos, reviews, a testimonial, or even a podcast.

SOURCE Beveridge, 2022

Prosumer

Another key consumer behaviour concept that has become more popular (and more possible due to digital environments) is that of the *prosumer*.

KEY TERM
Prosumer

Combining producer and consumer, a prosumer is 'a person that creates goods, services or experiences for his own use or satisfaction, rather than for sale or exchange'.

SOURCE Toffler, 1980

Originally this type of consumption was viewed primarily as consumers' customization of products or services to suit their own needs (Seran and Izvercian, 2014). However, as mentioned above, due to technological developments this has changed:

> Prosumption on the internet has increasingly occurred through user-generated content on what has become known as Web 2.0 (in Web 1.0, such as AOL or Yahoo, content is generated by the producer, leaving little room for prosumption). Web 2.0 includes the social web with sites such as Facebook and Twitter, the blogosphere, Wikipedia, content-sharing sites such as Flickr and You Tube, and much else where users not only consume but also produce content.
>
> Ritzer et al, 2012, 385

Consumers are now key to producing shared meanings of brands (Ritzer et al, 2012). Consumers consume and produce content about the brand online, without being paid. Through their prosumer activities consumers have a significant role in co-creating value for brands (Payne et al, 2008).

UGC contributes to the development of consumers to prosumers. UG can be helpful or destructive to brands, depending on the nature of the content the consumer is producing and distributing to their networks and beyond. Read more about consumers' impact on the marketplace in Chapter 12 (through responsible consumer behaviour) and Chapter 13 (responsible consumer behaviour on an international level via digital channels).

Summary

This chapter introduced you to the main actors in the online environment, the digital consumer. We examined consumer behaviour in digital marketplaces, specifically looking at how this differs across platforms. We discussed consumer personas and how to develop them, using insights derived from market and target group research. We also discussed how digital marketplaces, and specifically user content generation and access to information, is empowering the consumer and changing the way they consume and their impact on brands.

Chapter review

Reflective questions

Q1 How do consumers engage with brands online?

Q2 Why should companies invest in digital marketing?

Q3 Should companies exist online and offline?

Q4 What is the impact of UGC on consumer–brand relationships?

Key learning points

- Informed digital consumer personas are essential for digital marketing strategies.
- A digital consumer is empowered by information and their ability to influence consumption behaviour.
- User-generated content has changed the way companies do digital marketing.
- Consumers are involved in the co-creation of brand meanings.

References

Angelides, M C and Agius, H (eds) (2014) *Handbook of Digital Games,* John Wiley & Sons, London

BBC (2022) Store closures at lowest level for seven years, BBC News, www.bbc.com/news/business-62632353 (archived at https://perma.cc/WK8E-EZ6N)

Beveridge, C (2022) What is user-generated content and why is it important, Hootsuite, 13 January, blog.hootsuite.com/user-generated-content-ugc/#What_is_user-generated_content (archived at https://perma.cc/RGD4-YVWG)

Bloomenthal, A (2021) E-commerce defined, Investopedia, 16 September, www.investopedia.com/terms/e/ecommerce.asp (archived at https://perma.cc/8PZJ-JJWF)

Bourlakis, M, Papagiannidis, S and Li, F (2009) Retail spatial evolution: Paving the way from traditional to metaverse retailing, *Electronic Commerce Research*, 9(1), 135–48

Canva (2022) Home page, www.canva.com/

Chesterfield Digital High Street, East Midlands Chambers, www.emc-dnl.co.uk/chesterfield-digital-high-street/ (archived at https://perma.cc/9SPL-V4VY)

Clement, J (2021) Number of video gamers worldwide in 2021, by region (in millions), Statista, 27 July, www.statista.com/statistics/293304/number-video-gamers/ (archived at https://perma.cc/N5U3-AU7R)

De Pelsmacker, P and Neijens, P C (2012) New advertising formats: How persuasion knowledge affects consumer responses, *Journal of Marketing Communications*, 18(1), 1–4

Flavián, C, Gurrea, R and Orus, C (2020) Combining channels to make smart purchases: The role of webrooming and showrooming, *Journal of Retailing and Consumer Services*, doi.org/10.1016/j.jretconser.2019.101923

Garín Muñoz, T and Perez Amaral, T (2009) Modeling the Key Determinants of Online Shopping in Spain, papers.ssrn.com/sol3/papers.cfm?abstract_id=1363999 (archived at https://perma.cc/DSA5-DWLZ)

Gaudiosi, J (2015) Why Mercedes-Benz is targeting Nintendo gamers, fortune.com/2015/12/15/mercedes-benz-targets-nintendo-fans/ (archived at https://perma.cc/47HQ-DDK6)

Gensler, S, Neslin, S A and Verhoef, P C (2017) The showrooming phenomenon: it's more than just about price, *Journal of Interactive Marketing*, www.sciencedirect.com/science/article/pii/S1094996817300142

Haugtvedt, CP, Machleit, KA and Yalch, R (eds) (2005) *Online Consumer Psychology: Understanding and influencing consumer behavior in the virtual world*, Taylor & Francis Group, Mahwah

Herrewijn, L and Poels, K (2014) Rated A for advertising: A critical reflection on in-game advertising in *Handbook of Digital Games*, eds M C Angelides and H Agius, 305–35, John Wiley & Sons, London

Hubspot (2022) Make my persona, www.hubspot.com/make-my-persona (archived at https://perma.cc/RL4V-RZVS)

Mockplus (2020) 20 best user persona templates and examples for free download in 2020, Mockplus, 20 October, www.mockplus.com/blog/post/user-persona-template (archived at https://perma.cc/UZ7C-N9XQ)

Payne, A F, Storbacka, K and Frow, P (2008) Managing the co-creation of value, *Journal of the Academy of Marketing Science*, 36 (1), 83–96

Ritzer, G, Dean, P and Jurgenson, N (2012) The coming of age of the prosumer, *American Behavioral Scientist*, 56 (4), 379–98

Seran, S and Izvercian, M (2014) Prosumer engagement in innovation strategies: The prosumer creativity and focus model, *Management Decision*, 52 (10), 1968–980

Surveymonkey (2022) Using customer personas to build successful products and campaigns, Surveymonkey, www.surveymonkey.com/market-research/resources/using-customer-personas/ (archived at https://perma.cc/5UJH-K6ZT)

Toffler, A (1980) *The Third Wave,* William Morrow, New York, NY

Vollero, A and Valentini, C (2021) Social media and consumer power: Opportunities and challenges for digital marketing activities, in *Contemporary Issues in Digital Marketing*, Routledge, London, 105–15

Customer journey and experiences

11

By the end of this chapter, you should be able to:

- briefly define what a customer journey is and what it includes
- describe what a touchpoint is with examples
- understand how to map a customer journey using key marketing research insights
- explain in simple terms what customer relationship management and customer experience management has to do with customer journeys

Introduction

In the previous chapter we developed a foundational understanding of digital consumers and their behaviour in online environments. We also learnt how to create a consumer persona to help develop the digital marketing strategy. The next step in building the strategy is to plan the customer journey. In this chapter we take a closer look at the customer journey and how to create one that aligns to your digital marketing strategy and related objectives. We will unpack customer journeys, inspecting key concepts such as touchpoints and the different phases and stages that make up this useful marketing strategy tool. We will have a brief overview of the types of customer journeys you get and a media consumption phenomenon that impacts on your customer journey mapping. Lastly, we will discuss key concepts related to customer journeys and how they aid customer relationship management.

The customer journey

From need to purchase

A customer journey, as the name implies, is essentially the route a customer follows from awareness of the need for a product or service to actually buying it. The company is concerned with their interactions (or ***touchpoints***) with the consumer and how they can influence the consumers' decision-making and ultimately win their custom and brand loyalty.

Touchpoints

KEY TERM
Touchpoint

A touchpoint is a point of interaction between the company and its customers. It takes the form of, for example, brand-specific social media advertisements, emails or in-store customer service encounters.

SOURCE Dhebar, 2013

When do these touchpoints occur?

Customer journeys can be physical or digital (most journeys today include touchpoints in both environments). There are many different variations of customer journeys, each one looks different, depending on the consumer segment, the product, the brand, their communication channels, etc. You also have to consider which touchpoints to include, in what order and what will be communicated in each of these touchpoints. The company uses the information gathered through their market and marketing research to create a potential customer journey for their customer persona. Thus, they use what they now know about their marketplace, their micro- and macro-environment, their targeted consumer group and specifically their consumption habits and media channel selection to map a typical journey to buying something from the brand.

The customer journey is typically tailored for each target audience or consumer group the company seeks to interact with. So, an outdoor clothing company with two main target audiences would, for example, visualize what a customer journey would look like for a young, tech-savvy, adventure-loving bachelor who spends a lot of time outdoors and on Instagram and Pinterest. Will this customer have a journey that includes touchpoints on these social media channels and other interesting and creative ways to interact with the ideal consumer, e.g. an article in a newsletter about mountain-climbing or a digital banner on websites devoted to outdoor adventure places'? For their second consumer group – a young family that also loves the outdoors – they might consider how their journey would differ. They might prefer camping sites with playgrounds and pools for toddlers. Would these customers use the same social media channels? At different times, or follow different adventure profiles than the first consumer group? Would they visit the same websites? Are there other opportunities to interact with them in the marketplace?

Customer journey mapping

The customer journey is usually a visual representation of the process the customer follows from awareness to advocacy for the brand (Court et al, 2009; Følstad and Kvale, 2018). This visual representation process is referred to as 'customer journey mapping' (CJM). CJM is a strategic marketing tool that helps companies to understand their target audiences' needs and behaviours (Crosier and Handford, 2012).

CJM is done systematically, using phases – each with its own important part to play in creating a positive consumption experience. According to Dhebar (2013) the customer journey is typically divided into three phases: pre-purchase, purchase and post-purchase (see Figure 11.1).

Phases

Pre-purchase phase

As you can see in Figure 11.1, the pre-purchase phase is focused on the problem or need that should be satisfied. The consumer experiences problem awareness, analyses the problem and after some research selects a possible solution (Dhebar, 2013). It is in this phase that marketers attempt to create awareness of their brand and their products or services that can help in fulfilling this need. This is done through strategic marketing with awareness- and interest-generating objectives. Touchpoints can be anything that gains consumer attention and increases awareness and engagement, i.e. advertising, events, peer recommendations, etc.

Purchase phase

The purchase phase naturally contains the act of purchasing the product or service from the brand to fulfil the need. Here the customer service and customer experience at the point of purchase is really important. (Any engagement with the consumer can also be considered a touchpoint; it is not just the physical or digital marketing materials that the consumer is exposed to.)

Post-purchase phase

After the purchase the consumer enters the post-purchase phase, which contains key touchpoints on their customer journey that impact on their overall experience with the brand or company. These key touchpoints are related to the product and/or service of the item purchased. These key touchpoints are normally:

- the speed of delivery
- use or usability of the product or service
- supplements or additional value
- maintenance and disposal

Figure 11.1   Adaptation of customer touchpoint schematic

SOURCE Dhebar, 2013

The whole customer journey is dependent on good customer relationship and experience management (see customer relationship management later in this chapter), but
this becomes key in the last phase to ensure the experience with the brand continues
after the purchase and can lead to potential returning customers.

Note: marketers are more involved with developing and maintaining touchpoints
related to marketing activity, but they should be aware of other touchpoints (such as
distribution logistics) when developing a customer journey map or anything related
to customer experience management.

Lemon and Verhoef (2016) developed the customer touchpoint schematic further
by turning it into a model on which to base other customer journeys. As you can see
in Figure 11.2, they propose that previous experience, current customer experience
and future experience all make up a customer journey. A customer journey should
consider all brand engagements to keep customers returning.

These authors depict the behaviours in Figure 11.2 to show development in consumer behaviours as they go through the customer journey:

> need recognition > consideration > search > choice > ordering > payment > consumption >
> usage > engagement > service requests

The behaviours identified by Lemon and Verhoef (2016) correspond to the three
phases of the customer journey developed by Court et al (2009), according to whom
the customer journey consists of five key stages of behaviour: awareness, consideration, conversion, loyalty and advocacy.

Most CJM models opt for the five key stages in combination with the three phases
to serve as a basic structure for mapping a customer journey. When developing the
customer journey, marketers strategically organize touchpoints along this route to
optimize the customer experience and build a strong relationship to get them to become loyal customers and even advocates of the brand.

Although customer journeys are useful for placing yourself in the shoes of your
consumer, it is worth noting that things are not always as simple as creating a journey

Figure 11.2 Customer journeys

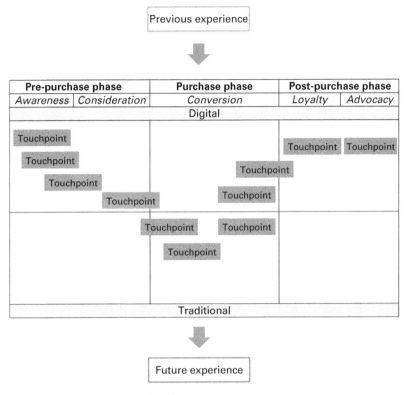

Based on Court et al, 2009; Lemon and Verhoef, 2016

that goes from point A to point B. Often consumers can move between phases or stages, get distracted by other things (responsibilities or competitors for example) or even deviate from the hypothetical route envisaged by the marketer (see Consumer Behaviour in Chapter 10). Using CJM is a time-consuming exercise and should be done when necessary and not just for the sake of doing it. Here are a couple of benefits and disadvantages of CJM to consider when deciding whether your digital marketing strategy warrants a CJM exercise.

Benefits of CJM

- provides insights into the ways brands can interact with potential consumers
- provides insights into the ways brands can build better relationships with their existing consumers
- identifies frustration points or weaknesses in the digital marketing strategy and consumer experience

Disadvantages of CJM

- costly and time-consuming because it requires insights into market and consumer research (for example, competitor activities, target audience needs, preferences and media consumption behaviour)
- can lead to feelings of annoyance and spamming when consumers are bombarded with aggressive journeys/strategies with too many touchpoints

---

Activity 11.1

i. In Google, search online for the phrase 'customer journey map'.

ii. Explore all the examples provided in the images of the search results.

iii. Can you identify touchpoints you did not know about?

iv. Is there a particular example you like? Why? Is it creative, easy to use or very detailed?

v. Discuss the benefits and advantages of your example in class.

Activity 11.2

Try your hand at customer journey mapping. Let's put this into practice by mapping a basic customer journey. Follow these key steps:

i. Choose any brand, have a look at their products and/or services and pick one to market.

ii. Make a list of all of their marketing communication channels, for example, website, Facebook page, newsletter, stores, etc.

iii. Create a basic persona for a new or existing target consumer group (think about your usual journey to purchase a product and keep in mind how your route differs when you know a brand or when you are looking for something completely new and unfamiliar to you).

iv. Using the template (Worksheet 3) create a customer journey map with touchpoints and frustration points for your target audience. (Remember, asking for peer recommendations and reading reviews also counts as touchpoints or frustration points.)

Types of customer journeys

Wolny and Charoensuksai (2014) categorize customer journeys into three types: impulsive, balanced and considered. These types depend on the problem and the type of product or service needed to solve it. As you can see from the Key Term boxes, they differ in their typical touchpoint collection and order, which means the customer journey will be different. Yet another consideration to take into account when developing a customer journey.

Impulsive journeys

Journeys characterized by a quick or impulsive decision that does not require a lot of mental effort, for example buying a bar of chocolate. Consumers are easily influenced by their mood, new product display, etc, and do not spend a lot of time searching for information (Wolny and Charoensuksai, 2014).

Balanced journeys

Balanced journeys require a bit more thinking and often stem from recommendations by influential peers such as parents, partners and friends, or opinion leaders such as influencers and celebrities. As the decision to purchase is greatly influenced by the recommendation, this journey typically also does not include major searching (especially for alternatives), for example when eating at a particular restaurant or buying a certain cosmetic product (Wolny and Charoensuksai, 2014).

Considered journeys

Considered journeys include an extended pre-search. The pre-search is characterized by intensive gathering of information from multiple sources, including product reviews, news articles, recommendations, etc. This type of journey involves a lot of mental effort and is typically associated with expensive, special and specialist purchases, for example buying a coffee machine (Wolny and Charoensuksai, 2014).

Note: some balanced journeys can turn into considered journeys for particular consumer groups, for example, someone with allergies or a personal vegan-only cosmetic policy may need to do more extensive research before deciding to purchase. Knowing the values, beliefs and needs of your consumer persona comes in really handy here.

Customer experience

Customer experience management (CEM)

The exact origin of the customer journey is hard to pinpoint, but whether from marketing, service encounters or design disciplines, the key function is to view the consumption decision-making process of the consumer (awareness to advocacy) from the consumer's perspective. Viewing the journey from the consumer's perspective allows companies to establish, maintain and improve the *customer experience.*

KEY TERM

Customer experience

A multidimensional construct focusing on a customer's cognitive, emotional, behavioural, sensorial and social responses to a firm's offerings during the customer's entire purchase journey.

SOURCE Lemon and Verhoef, 2016

Customer experience management forms a big part of customer journeys. When the marketing team is equipped with the customer journey map they can monitor how well (or badly) the brand is doing from the customers' perspective. Within this customer experience management, the team should be particularly concerned with frustration points (touchpoints that went bad or even a lack of touchpoint altogether).

KEY TERM

Customer experience management (CEM)

The process of strategically managing a customer's entire experience with a product or a company.

SOURCE Smilansky, 2009

Frustration points

Mapping a customer journey requires a critical review of the customers' experience with the brand from point A to point B. Within the customer journey there will be multiple touchpoints. When evaluating the customer journey (either in testing and development of a journey before going to market or after receiving feedback from actual customers' experiences and journeys with the brand) it is useful to identify potential *frustration points* for consumers.

KEY TERM
Frustration points

Frustration points are interactions that can create a bad brand experience for the consumer, causing them to abandon the journey, either temporarily or permanently.

When you have identified frustration points it is a good idea to evaluate what went wrong, i.e. is a particular advertisement causing offence, is a link broken or a check-out process on the website really slow? The company should attempt to fix or remove the frustration points to decrease the likelihood of losing customers, both old and new. If the frustration point is not addressed, this can lead to journey abandonment or shopping cart abandonment (leaving an item in a digital shopping cart without purchasing it).

When consumers have gone through the customer journey it is useful to consider their previous and future experiences. Consumers compare their experiences and use their opinions to repeat purchases, stay loyal to the brand and recommend it to their peers (good experience) OR to never buy from the brand again, move to a competitor and dissuade peers from buying from the brand (bad experience). Brands can seek to get information from consumers via feedback to inform future consumption experiences and to improve frustration points.

A customer experience concept that goes hand-in-hand with CJM is *customer relationship management*.

Customer relationship management (CRM)

KEY TERM
Customer relationship management

A marketing strategy that uses customer knowledge to effectively and efficiently sell products and services, while maintaining relationships with customers to improve satisfaction and loyalty.

SOURCE Wali and Wright, 2016

Companies often use CRM tools or systems to help them manage the customer experience, for example a digital database that automatically sorts consumers according to a variety of categories that the company finds useful for managing customer experiences. Some of these categories can include: the types of products purchased, frequency, subscriptions, loyalty club members, new customers, returning customers, complaints, returns, etc.

CRM systems include (Javalgi et al, 2006):

- websites
- call centres
- CRM software with consumer databases
- customer service and support initiatives
- loyalty programmes

How digital consumption has changed how consumers use media

Digital marketplaces have changed how consumers interact with brands. How consumers search for information or 'get to know' brands have changed. Consumers use the internet and their various digital devices to inform themselves and shape their consumer journey (Silva et al, 2020). Modern consumers are media multitaskers (Marsden, 2013). Consumers use multiple channels and touchpoints at any stage of the customer journey.

Consumers interact differently with brands because of (Swaminathan et al, 2020):

- rise of digitally native brands
- easy access to information and products via digital and mobile channels
- broad availability of smart, connected devices

This means that companies have had to adapt. Two key concepts that have emerged and are being used as starting points for more intricate customer journey mapping are *media meshing* and *media stacking*.

Media meshing

> **KEY TERM**
> Media meshing/stacking
>
> **Media meshing**: Using multiple devices simultaneously to enhance a media experience e.g. interacting or communicating on a smartphone about TV content being viewed. Characterized by a constant search for complementary information, different perspectives and even emotional fulfilment – a means of gaining attention across media.
>
> **Media stacking**: Consuming unrelated media across various channels/devices at the same time e.g. chatting on messenger, streaming series on television, and shopping online.
>
> **SOURCE** Marsden, 2013; Luck and Klaehn, 2007

As digital marketplaces become more and more advanced (see Digital Marketplace Behaviours in Chapter 10), customer journeys will have to become more fluid, customer relationship management more responsive or even proactive to retain consumers and impact on their consumption decision-making process.

Summary

Customer journey mapping is a time-consuming yet rewarding part of developing a digital marketing strategy. It allows the company to map the intended target audience or consumer persona along a detailed route towards purchasing from the brand. CJM leads the consumer from initial discovery to advocacy of the brand in fulfilling their specific need. CJM requires use of insights from market, marketing and consumer research to enable the company to develop a relevant journey that adds to the customer experience. Customer experience and customer relationship management lie at the heart of the CJM strategy. Changing consumer behaviour and media usage presents a challenge for companies in making the customer journey less linear and more fluid. Constant feedback from customers, proactive and reactive CRM is required to make sure the CJM works for both consumer and company.

Chapter review

Reflective questions

Q1 Why are customer journeys useful for marketing strategies?

Q2 How are customer journeys tailored for consumer segments?

Q3 Would all customer journeys be the same? How would they differ?

Q4 Would customer journeys always go from point A to B without any detours?

Key learning points

- A customer journey is a target consumer group's typical route to purchase from a brand.
- Customer journeys include various touchpoint such as email, website, recommendations and customer services in-store.
- You need insights from marketing research to be able to map customer journeys.
- Customer relationship management and customer experience management form an integral part of positive customer journeys that lead to brand loyalty and advocacy.

References

Court, D, Elzinga, D, Mulder, S and Vetvik, O J (2009) The consumer decision journey, *McKinsey Quarterly*, 1 June, www.mckinsey.com/business-functions/marketing-and-sales/our-insights/the-consumer-decision-journey (archived at https://perma.cc/8Y2K-23F6)

Crosier, A and Handford, A (2012) Customer journey mapping as an advocacy tool for disabled people: a case study, *Social Marketing Quarterly*, 18 (1), 67–76

Dhebar, A (2013) Toward a compelling customer touchpoint architecture, *Business Horizons*, 56 (2), 199–205

Følstad, A and Kvale, K (2018) Customer journeys: A systematic literature review, *Journal of Service Theory and Practice*, 28 (2), 196–227

Javalgi, R R G, Martin, C L and Young, R B (2006) Marketing research, market orientation and customer relationship management: A framework and implications for service providers, *Journal of Services Marketing*, 20 (1), 12–23

Lemon, K N and Verhoef, P C (2016) Understanding customer experience throughout the customer journey, *Journal of Marketing*, 80 (6), 69–96

Luck, E and Klaehn, M (2007) Digital clutter: Relevance of new media to gen Y, in *Australia And New Zealand Marketing Academy 2007 Conference Proceedings and Refereed Papers*, 1423–429, eprints.qut.edu.au/13095/ (archived at https://perma.cc/B3Y4-3CG2)

Marsden, P (2013) Speed summary: Media meshing vs media stacking (Ofcom report 2013), Digital Wellbeing, 19 August, digitalwellbeing.org/speed-summary-media-meshing-vs-media-stacking-ofcom-report-2013/ (archived at https://perma.cc/X4ST-FRVW)

Silva, S C, Paulo, D and Anel, S (2020) Multichannel versus omnichannel: A price-segmented comparison from the fashion industry, *International Journal of Retail and Distribution Management*, 48 (4), 417–20

Smilansky, S (2009) *Experiential Marketing: A practical guide to interactive brand experiences,* Kogan Page, London

Swaminathan, V, Sorescu, A, Steenkamp, J E M, Clayton, T, O'Guinn, G and Schmitt, B (2020) Branding in a hyperconnected world: Refocusing theories and rethinking boundaries, *Journal of Marketing,* journals.sagepub.com/doi/full/10.1177/0022242919899905 (archived at https://perma.cc/FKA2-NJWF)

Wali, A F and Wright, L T (2016) Customer relationship management and service quality: Influences in higher education, *Journal of Customer Behaviour*, 15 (1), 67–79

Wolny, J and Charoensuksai, N (2014) Mapping customer journeys in multichannel decision-making, *Journal of Direct, Data and Digital Marketing Practice*, 15 (4), 31726

Socially responsible consumer behaviour

12

By the end of this chapter, you should be able to:

- briefly define what socially responsible consumer behaviour is
- understand motivations driving consumers' actions and responses to sustainability initiatives
- understand the difference between boycotting and buycotting
- explain in simple terms what greenwashing and woke-washing mean
- describe key concepts: triple bottom line, circular economy and sharing economy

Introduction

In this chapter we take what we've learnt about consumers and digital marketplaces thus far and consider them alongside contemporary issues in socially responsible consumer behaviour. We explore what motivates responsible or sustainable behaviour in consumers – both environmentally and socially. We also compare this to the impact on businesses and their marketers via introductions to the triple bottom line, and new business models such as the circular and sharing economy. Lastly, we reflect on the implications for digital marketing.

Socially responsible consumer behaviour

There are many definitions of sustainability, and it is a hard concept to pin down as it is constantly evolving. The most frequently used definitions state that it is actions to meet the needs of our current generation without destroying future generations' chances to fulfil their needs via irreparable damage (Fletcher, 2008; Hu et al, 2019; Trudel, 2020).

Consumers and their consumption behaviour is directly linked to good or bad sustainability, depending on the conscious choices made by consumers (Trudel, 2020). There is a growing awareness and motivation among consumers to be more responsible in what they buy, use and recycle, with most consumers opting to support brands with a social feature such as environmental protection initiatives or enforcing basic human rights (Han and Stoel, 2017). Hence the term *socially responsible consumer behaviour*.

KEY TERM
Socially responsible consumer behaviour

The broadest definition of socially responsible consumer behaviour is that consumer behaviour which 'takes into account diverse ethical matters such as environmental protection, employment and human rights support, and community support'.

SOURCE Han and Stoel 2017

While the group of consumers motivated by consuming sustainably is growing, consumers' expectation of business behaving with social responsibility when it comes to their personal information is more widespread (see Part Six for more information). Social responsibility of businesses in terms of digital marketing is embodied through ethical use of consumers' data, not breaching their privacy, and responsible use of technologies such as algorithms and artificial intelligence. Apart from the more straightforward digitally responsible use of consumer data and ethical application of technologies, brands are also held more accountable online. When digital marketing campaigns appear online they are no longer confined to the intended target audiences and marketplaces. These campaigns can travel the world in a matter of seconds. This means that any campaign that is offensive or misleading can gather a viral swell of negative responses worldwide, which can damage the brand financially and reputationally.

EXAMPLE
Misleading campaigns

- The YouTube advertisement by Pepsi with Kendall Jenner trivialized the #BlackLivesMatter movement and the deep-rooted tensions and trauma from race-related protests, causing outrage on social media and forcing the brand to pull the campaign after only 24 hours (Victor, 2017).

- Burger King's 'Women belong in the kitchen' tweet tainted a well-meaning campaign about gender disparity for International Women's Day, resulting in negative global response and reputational damage, with accusations of using a sexist sentence for clickbait (Denham, 2021).

Questions

a. Search for the Pepsi and Burger King examples.

b. Gain an understanding of just how badly digital marketing campaigns can go wrong.

c. What implications did this have for the companies?

While the examples above are related to social issues, the same goes for digital marketing campaigns about brands' environmentally friendly products, services and initiatives. With the scrutiny of global audiences, digital marketers need to ensure their strategies and campaigns are informed, authentic and sensitive to potentially controversial interpretations.

Communicating about sustainability

Socially responsible consumers do their research and are also more critical and cynical of sustainability claims, which has a big impact on how marketers communicate. Subsequently, there is a growing body of research and business practices being developed around these consumers, making it possible to integrate the responsible drive and sustainability communication in marketing strategies. Han and Stoel (2017) provide a number of valuable recommendations for marketing strategies to target socially responsible consumers and promote sustainable consumption. They found that marketing strategies should appeal to consumers':

- social norms
- moral norms
- self-identity
- environmental consciousness

Nevertheless, communicating about sustainability is not without its problems. Corporate responsibility communications have increased dramatically and become crucial to business in answering stakeholder demands for transparency (Frostenson et al, 2011). However, Frostenson et al (2011), for example, in their study of the 206 largest retail companies in Sweden, found that this increased drive for professional corporate responsibility communication does not always factor in communicating to consumers as an integral stakeholder group. Sustainability communication scholars note that responsible businesses need to engage with their different stakeholders – including consumers – about sustainability issues on a regular basis, going beyond just talking about their corporate social responsibility actions (Crane and Glozer, 2016). Communicating about these sustainability issues can be via specific campaigns, informative web pages about modifications in products or services, business reports and other engagement initiatives via traditional and digital communication channels (Crane and Glozer, 2016).

Barriers to effective communication

However, communicating or marketing sustainability is easier said than done. There are additional things to consider when developing a marketing strategy that includes these aspects. Some of these barriers to effectively reaching consumers marketers face today are:

- noise
- consumer scepticism (see Customer Motivations section later in this chapter)
- lack of widespread consumer access to digital devices, power and data in developing marketplaces (see Chapter 13)
- misrepresentation and other challenges for communicating in diversity (see Chapter 13)

Operating in busy, data-rich and constantly changing marketplaces is already difficult for marketers. A lot of research, strategy and campaign development go into each communication initiative to cut through the clutter or noise to make your campaign stand out from the rest. Lately a lot of campaigns aim to add a sustainable angle (varying on the sustainability spectrum depending on the company and the intended audience) to overcome the noise barrier. However, this is not always enough. White et al (2019) developed the SHIFT framework, suggesting that the way to encourage consumers to behave more socially responsibly is to integrate social influence, habit formation, individual self, feelings and cognition and tangibility in marketing messages.

Belz and Peattie (2009) identify a need for marketers to have a better understanding of what motivates consumers and the challenges they have that are encouraging or preventing them from consuming sustainably. Thus, we will take a closer look at some consumer motivation concepts that can help us understand why consumers take part in sustainability initiatives.

Consumer motivations and attitudes

There are a number of prominent consumer responses and critiques that brands can come across when engaging in corporate social responsibility, sustainability marketing or socially responsibility marketing. These are largely influenced by consumers' motivations and beliefs.

Maslow's hierarchy of needs

You cannot talk about motivations without considering Maslow's Hierarchy of Needs (1970), a theory often used in the study of consumer behaviour. The hierarchy works on the principle that people need to have basic physiological needs satisfied first, for example having food, shelter, clothing and water (Maslow, 1970). Then more abstract levels of need can be pursued. After physiological needs, in ascending order, Maslow lists:

- safety needs (security, employment, resources, health, property)
- love and belonging (friendship, family, intimacy)
- esteem (respect, status, recognition)
- self-actualization (desire to be more)

If a consumer needs to satisfy a lower level need, communicating about things higher up in the hierarchy can be perceived as noise that is filtered out. It should be noted that needs are dependent on the marketplace consumers find themselves in and significantly influences the way they behave (yet another reason market and target audience research is crucial for effective marketing strategies).

Cui et al (2021) applied Maslow's hierarchy to the sale of electric vehicles, testing consumer motivations to make the sustainable change in their car purchases. They found that environmental concern serves as a big motivation for choosing electronic vehicles in the Chinese market. However, price consciousness, social influence, self-esteem and openness to experience were also motivational factors. Consumers that were in need of food and shelter tended to be more price conscious, which indicates that high prices serve as a barrier to purchase in this marketplace (Cui et al, 2021).

Environmental awareness

Another means of distinguishing between target audiences and how to communicate to them about sustainability is to assess whether they are *high environmentally conscious* or *low environmentally conscious* consumers (Grebmer and Diefenbach, 2020).

KEY TERM
High/low environmentally conscious consumers

High environmentally conscious (HEC): consumers have a lot of knowledge and awareness about sustainability practices and are willing to pay more to support companies that contribute to environmental sustainability. However, they are also more sceptical of the communicative efforts to convey this company environmental information.

Low environmentally conscious (LEC): consumers have less knowledge about environmental sustainability, and are less concerned with the facts and figures behind companies' sustainability initiatives – but that does not necessarily mean that they are less willing to consume sustainably. Just that they might not want to think about their choices too much.

SOURCE Grebmer and Diefenbach, 2020

There are a number of key differences in the approach to LEC or HEC consumers, as demonstrated in the definitions and Table 12.1.

Table 12.1   Key differences in the approach to LEC and HEC consumers

High environmentally conscious consumers	Low environmentally conscious consumers
More likely to read detailed information about the environmental activities of the company to assess their credibility	Less likely to read detailed information about the environmental activities of the company to assess their credibility
Text-based communication elements reduces scepticism	Text-based communication elements do not reduce scepticism (might be related to line above)
Non-verbal and visual communication elements increases scepticism	Non-verbal and visual communication elements decreases scepticism
Highly perceptible to greenwashing	Less perceptible to greenwashing
More receptive of substantial information via a specific information channel e.g. product text	More receptive of peripheral, easy-to-understand information channels e.g. conceptual motifs

Summative table based on information from Grebmer and Diefenbach, 2020

EXAMPLE

McKinsey and Company

McKinsey and Company (Heineke et al, 2021) did research on the changes to consumers' modes of transport. They found that in 2021 over 70 per cent of consumers would opt for more sustainable transport such as bicycles or electronic scooters for their daily commute.

Task

Read the full article by searching for 'Why micromobility is here to stay' on McKinsey's website (Heineke et al, 2021).

Activity 12.1

In groups, take another look at the McKinsey example and pick either LEC or HEC consumers. You have a client – a bicycle brand – who wants to sell to a new group of students just starting university.

i. How would you communicate to them the sustainable processes the business employs?

ii. How would you communicate the value of micromobility for the environment?

iii. Would you use an informational approach with a lot of facts and figures or a more conceptual approach? Why?

Green consumers

Young et al (2010) note that businesses should promote sustainable consumption by prompting their consumers to become environmental citizens that think about their attitudes and motivations for consuming in the first place. They characterize sustainable consumers with an environmental motivation as 'green consumers' – another more specifically environmentally conscious consumers group. These green consumers primarily consider environmental factors when shopping as they fit their personal values of doing good for the environment. Interestingly, Young et al also found that these green consumers do not completely discard people and profit in their choices, but also consider things such as:

- brand strength
- culture

- demographic characteristics
- finance
- habit
- lack of information
- lifestyles
- personalities
- trade-offs between different ethical factors

Buycotting and boycotting

Politically motivated consumerism concepts (Neilson, 2010), *boycotting* and *buy-cotting* are essentially ways in which consumers practise socially responsible behaviour and demand compliance from businesses in behaving ethically (in the world and with the use of their private information). In other words, consumers use their buying power to make a statement and influence action, informing brands of their requirement to be accountable, as consumers can have a significant impact on their success in the marketplace. According to Lee and Yoon (2020), 'Values-driven brand activism is on the rise as consumers vote with their wallets supporting companies and brands that operate with a set of values that are working as authentic forces for good.'

KEY TERM
Buycottting/boycotting

Buycotting: Purposely supporting businesses deemed to do something good, by actively buying and spreading favourable reviews.

Boycotting: Purposely refusing to support businesses deemed to do something wrong, by not buying or spreading favourable reviews.

SOURCE Neilson, 2010

Weber Shandwick (2018) conducted a study with 2,000 consumer activists in the UK and United States to get a better understanding of why and how brands are boycotted or buycotted. They found that 90 per cent have boycotted and 65 per cent buycotted a brand.

Through their actions boycotters hope to influence brands to do better, by (Weber Shandwick, 2018):

- changing the way they do business (36 per cent)
- harm the company's reputation (35 per cent)
- get complaints noticed (20 per cent)
- harm sales (18 per cent)
- get an apology (15 per cent)
- discourage new employees (6 per cent)
- support competitors (6 per cent)
- replace brand leadership (5 per cent)
- hurt employee morale (3 per cent)
- start viral social media (2 per cent)
- get personal attention on social media (2 per cent)

Buycotters, on the other hand, attempt to (Weber Shandwick 2018):

- help the company's reputation (48 per cent)
- help sales (27 per cent)
- change the way they do business (19 per cent)
- improve employee morale (13 per cent)
- get support noticed (12 per cent)
- hurt competitors (7 per cent)
- force competitor apology (6 per cent)
- start viral social media (5 per cent)
- replace brand leadership (4 per cent)
- encourage new employees (4 per cent)
- and get personal attention (2 per cent)

Some of the buycotter actions are also skewed towards hurting an offending brand, for example forcing competitor apologies. Overall, this study shows the impact of consumer power in increasing or decreasing reputation, loyalty and profits in their consumption behaviour. Given that consumers invest more money in sustainable products, and believe in the brands and products or services they consume, the fall-out from any form of wrong-doing (such as greenwashing or woke-washing – see later in this chapter) could potentially be even more disastrous for companies. The detailed report with more results can be found listed in the References at the end of this chapter.

Consumer scepticism

> ## KEY TERM
> Consumer scepticism
>
> Consumer scepticism is when consumers do not believe claim(s) about pro-environmental or pro-social performance in marketing communications.
>
> **SOURCE** Sindhuri et al, 2017

As consumers become increasingly aware of the potential socially responsible impacts of their purchases, products labelled as 'eco-friendly', 'organic' or 'sustainable' have become more popular than ever (Schmuck et al, 2018). While these strategies are a meaningful way of engaging with socially responsible consumers, if not done correctly, this can cause *consumer scepticism*. The more actively involved in social responsibility consumption, the more sceptical the consumer becomes (Do Paço and Reis, 2012).

CASE STUDY   The Attenborough effect

Sir David Attenborough is a well-known public figure in the environmental conservation field. As the narrator and presenter of countless nature documentaries, he has sparked a social consciousness among consumers known as #TheAttenboroughEffect (Glenday, 2020). This effect attributes an increased awareness of the detrimental impact our daily lives have on the planet. However, this awareness is yet to translate into decisive action by businesses, causing more and more consumer scepticism (Glenday, 2020).

A survey of 2,264 internet users conducted by GlobalWebIndex (2020) found that shifting consumer awareness is increasing pressures on big brands and their stances on sustainability (Glenday, 2020):

- 49 per cent believe climate change pledges are empty promises to appease public concern
- 65 per cent are unaware of big sustainability pledges made by big companies
- 43 per cent believe these pledges to be achievable
- 29 per cent believe these pledges to be unrealistic and unobtainable

These results not only indicate that consumers think brands should do more to be sustainable apart from making empty, unachievable pledges; it also shows a need for more substantial sustainability marketing to communicate about those initiatives that are successful in making a difference.

Greenwashing

Greenwashing is when brands make claims about their efforts to be eco-friendly or sustainable which are misleading about the real impact or benefit of a product, service or production process, are based on unsubstantiated claims, or even distract from real problems that are not pro-environmental at all (see also Chapters 5 and 24). This is a deliberate action, and consumer and public responses are usually negative and damaging to company bottom lines.

KEY TERM
Greenwashing

Greenwashing is the process of conveying a false impression or providing misleading information about how a company's products are more environmentally sound. Greenwashing is considered an unsubstantiated claim to deceive consumers into believing that a company's products are environmentally friendly. Created by Jay Westerveld in 1986, the term is used to describe companies' efforts to claim to be pro-sustainable to mislead consumers and cover up questionable environmental records.

SOURCE Kenton, 2022; Kopnina, 2019

As there is such an abundance of information and potential audiences on the internet, businesses are at increased risk of getting negative responses to marketing efforts or sustainability initiatives. This increased risk requires careful planning that is informed by research and not embellishing on the impact or nature of green or sustainable initiatives. The next case study describes how things went wrong for H&M, which resulted in a lot of bad press and viral online conversations and memes about the brand and their greenwashing (whether intentional or not).

CASE STUDY   H&M

H&M participated in 'World Recycling Week' to promote their 'recycle-your-cheap-clothes-and-get-money-off-more-cheap-clothes project' initiative. Unfortunately, this fast-fashion company's global campaign coincided with Fashion Revolution Week.

In an effort to raise consumer awareness, Fashion Revolution (a not-for-profit environmental campaigning organization) asks retailers to tell the truth about textile ethics, workplace conditions, and pushes policymakers to introduce transparent supply chains and better conditions for garment workers around the world. Their Fashion Revolution Week serves as a reminder of the Rana Plaza disaster in Bangladesh in 2013, where over 1,100 people lost their lives and 2,500 were injured in a disastrous factory accident.

In the wake of H&M's ill-timed campaign, Fashion Revolution accused the company of greenwashing, stating that even though the brand claims to be environmentally friendly through the use of organic cotton materials, this only constitutes a minimal percentage of all of their clothing, which are all still manufactured in sweatshop conditions in Bangladesh making their sustainability efforts miniscule and irrelevant and deliberately misleading to consumers.

Thus, instead of a strategic contribution to consumer awareness and touting their brand's sustainable practices, the campaign resulted in widespread condemnation and accusations of greenwashing from environmental journalists and fashion publications.

What this case study also highlights is that even though environmental, green and sustainable marketing communications seem to be more pro-environmental in their focus, the social impact on human rights and well-being also plays a big part in determining socially responsible behaviour.

SOURCE Outi Les Pyy, 2019

Woke-washing

Consumers are not only demanding socio-environmental initiatives by brands, they are also concerned with their socio-political stances (Vredenburg et al, 2020). Hence the birth of *woke-washing*. This is a concept that is similar in approach to green-washing, but based on critiques of misleading claims of advancing social justice initiatives, by empty pledges for brand activism that are detached from the brand's values and practices (Sobande, 2019; Vredenburg et al, 2020). Consumer responses to deemed woke-washing are just as quick and damaging as greenwashing allegations, especially considering the hype negative conversations online can cause when going viral.

KEY TERM
Woke-washing

Woke-washing is when brands potentially mislead consumers via their claims about pro-social initiatives, which has a damaging impact on their brand equity and potential for enacting social change.

SOURCE Vredenburg et al, 2020

Vredenburg et al (2020) developed a useful typology to measure the authenticity of brands' engagements with socio-political causes. This typology offers four quadrants in which to position brands to avoid accusations of woke-washing, namely: absence of brand activism, silent brand activism, authentic brand activism and inauthentic brand activism. Table 12.2 provides more details on considerations for developing marketing strategies for addressing pro-social activities by the brand.

Vredenburg et al (2020) also note that the level of compatibility between the brand, the socio-political cause they address and the values and beliefs of their intended target audience play a role in negative or positive consumer responses, again reinforcing the need to know the customers you want to engage with.

Sobande (2019) conducted a review of prominent brands' efforts to market their socio-political stances, where she found that brands' 'woke' marketing strategies often include well-intentioned but ill-advised misuse of famous black women (e.g. Serena Williams in Gatorade and Nike advertisements). These representations can result in increased consumer scepticism and eventually accusations of woke-washing.

Table 12.2   Authenticity of brands' engagement with socio-political causes

Silent brand activism	Authentic brand activism
• low activism levels in messaging	• high activism levels in messaging
• high engagement with pro-social corporate practice	• high engagement with pro-social corporate practice
• clear communication of pro-social brand purpose and values	• clear communication of pro-social brand purpose and values
• potential to be perceived as authentic brand activism	• framing and pursuing solutions to social problems
Absence of brand activism	**Inauthentic brand activism**
• low activism levels in messaging	• high activism levels in messaging
• low engagement with pro-social corporate practice	• low engagement with pro-social corporate practice
• no communication of pro-social brand purpose and values	• no communication of pro-social brand purpose and values
• opportunity to pursue authentic brand activism	• deliberately misleading and opportunistic decoupling of message from actions (perceived as woke-washing)

Based on typology of brand activism Vredenburg et al, 2020

Activity 12.2

i.   Can you think of a brand that has been accused of greenwashing or woke-washing?

ii. Try searching online if one doesn't come to mind.

iii. Discuss in groups:

   – Why were they accused?

   – How did they respond?

   – Did they change any of their business or communication practices as a result?

Pro-sustainability business strategies

As a result of the growing pressure or demand from consumers for companies to do better, a couple of pro-sustainability business strategies have been developed and are used when marketers develop socially responsible marketing campaigns. Geissdoerfer et al (2017) remark on the increasing urgency of adopting more pro-sustainability strategies, based on a three-fold impact of humans on the Earth. This urgency becomes evident when you investigate environmental problems (such as pollution, resource depletion and biodiversity loss), societal problems (such as poor working conditions, social vulnerability and widespread inequality and inequity) and economic problems (such as deregulated markets, financial instability and supply risk) (Geissdoerfer et al, 2017).

Triple bottom line

A well-known and widely used business model to motivate adoption of socially responsible business practices is the triple bottom line. The triple bottom line is a model that demonstrates where business objectives meet consumer and planet needs (Elkington, 1997). The basis of the model is three Ps: profit, planet and people (Figure 12.1). The school of thought (and strategic action) around the triple bottom line is that businesses need to address all three in order to be successful today. Business cannot only pursue profits; they are being held accountable by all their stakeholders in terms of responsible business and actions that do not damage the environment or society.

There are studies that develop this concept further, for example in weighing up the possibilities for different stakeholder groups. Richardson (2019) adapted it to determine where business should focus in terms of their practices, corporate social

Figure 12.1   Triple bottom line

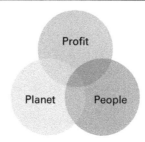

SOURCE Based on Elkington, 1997

Figure 12.2   Triple bottom line stakeholder positions

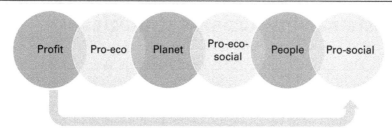

SOURCE Based on Richardson, 2019

responsibility initiatives and, ultimately, their marketing strategies for communicating about their sustainability (Figure 12.2). He discusses the sustainable stakeholder,
developing a spectrum of sorts with different stakeholder positions that dictate the
focus businesses should take:

- purely **profit**-driven stakeholders
- **pro-eco** stakeholders that fall between profit and planet, that are eco-aware and
  light to medium in their behaviour
- **planet**-driven stakeholders as dark green, eco-warriors
- **pro-eco-social** stakeholders that are interested in fair trade and positive impacts
  on people and planet
- **people**-driven stakeholders as those concerned with social well-being
- **pro-social** stakeholders focused on investments with a positive impact on people

Richardson (2019) also specifically considers what this implies for sustainable consumers as a stakeholder group. He notes the impact of their position on this spectrum
for decision-making and subsequent consumer behaviour, noting their willingness to
spend more now to secure a better future.

Circular economy

The concept of the *circular economy* is reliant on reuse, repurposing or recycling products (creating a circular product life cycle with multiple uses and a responsible disposal method when it reaches the end of use).

KEY TERM
Circular economy

A recent approach to waste and resource management that promotes waste and resource cycling as an alternative to single-use practices.

SOURCE Stewart and Niero, 2018

Based on a systematic review of a number of corporate sustainability reports, circular economy has not yet been widely adopted in companies' sustainability strategies, even though the concept has environmental, resource and economic benefits (Stewart and Niero, 2018). However, this approach can be very beneficial for companies in terms of sourcing operations efficiency, end-of-life initiatives for products, innovative solutions to product designs, innovative business models and partnerships with consumers and partners to be more socially responsible (Stewart and Niero, 2018).

Testa et al (2020) state that the transition towards a circular economy is a crucial issue to pursue a more sustainable development. 'Beyond companies' adoption of the circular economy approach, they found that consumers' engagement in this approach is also crucial to its success and that companies need to provide the information (for example on packaging) to influence increased socially responsible consumption habits.

Sharing economy

KEY TERM
Sharing economy

An umbrella term for business and consumption practices that are based on sharing underutilized resources (e.g. goods, services and spaces) for free or for a fee, typically enabled by online platforms and peer communities.

SOURCE Guyader and Piscicelli, 2019

Sharing economy is a new concept that significantly alters consumer views about ownership and use of a number of products and services. The sharing economy model has seen significant growth with the development of digital platforms and a growing consciousness about socially responsible consumption behaviour. Renting an electronic car to get around a big city instead of buying and owning your own is a good example of an increasingly widely adopted sharing economy business model. The sharing economy approach necessitates business model diversification (Guyader and Piscicelli, 2019). The Vinted case (see box) offers an example of an innovative integration of digital platforms, fashion and consumers' willingness to engage in socially responsible consumption behaviour which afforded the business a lot of success.

EXAMPLE
Vinted

Vinted successfully engages consumers in both circular economy behaviour and a sharing economy model. They operate as an online retailer in numerous countries such as the United Kingdom, Germany, France, Austria, Czech Republic, Poland, Lithuania and the United States (Vinted, 2022).

The company operates in the second-hand fashion market and works on the premise of selling or swapping your second-hand clothing with consumers (a combination of prosumer and C2C strategies – see Chapter 10). The second-hand fashion market was worth £14 billion in 2019, and was set to grow 11 per cent annually to reach £25 billion in 2021 (Hu et al, 2019). Buying second-hand clothing is a socially responsible consumption action, as these clothing items are re-used (Hu et al, 2019).

Summary

In this chapter we took an in-depth look at socially responsible consumer behaviour. We explored what motivates responsible or sustainable behaviour in consumers – both environmentally and socially – and how misleading or ill-prepared content can cause a global online consumer response that can be quite damaging for the brand. We compared that to consumer attitudes and responses to sustainability marketing and how their expectations for business to operate ethically are dictated through their responses. We also compared this to the impact on businesses and their marketers via recommendations for authentic strategies that reduce scepticism and effectively communicate brand activism efforts. We also briefly explored recent pro-sustainability business approaches that were developed and are growing as an answer to this increasing pressure from consumers to conduct socially responsible business.

Chapter review

Reflective questions

Q1 How can brands engage with consumers and other marketplace actors to promote socially responsible behaviour?

Q2 Why are consumers sometimes sceptical about brands' socio-environmental or socio-political initiatives?

Q3 How can brands develop authentic marketing campaigns to reduce this scepticism?

Q4 What do new pro-sustainability business models such as circular and sharing economy mean for brands in the future?

Key learning points

- Socially responsible consumer behaviour can be defined as actions to meet the needs of our current generation without destroying future generations' chances to fulfil their needs via irreparably damage (Fletcher, 2008; Hu et al, 2019; Trudel, 2020).

- Consumer motivations and beliefs, such as Maslow's Hierarchy of Needs, high or low environmental consciousness, and consumer scepticism, have a big impact on their behaviour.

- Greenwashing is deliberately misleading and/or unsubstantiated information to inflate the sustainability of a company's initiatives, processes, products or services.

- Woke-washing is deliberately misleading about the company's pro-social sustainability by communicating social justice stances that are disconnected from any real company values and actions.

- The triple bottom line is concerned with pursuing healthy growth for planet (environment), people (social) and profit (economic) sustainably.

- Circular economy is an approach to products that aims to extend their lifespan through reuse, repurposing or recycling.

- Sharing economy is a business model that operates on revised ideas about ownership, allowing consumers to temporarily own, use or share products and services.

References

Belz, F M and Peattie, K (2009) *Sustainability Marketing: A global perspective,* Wiley and Sons, UK

Crane, A and Glozer, S (2016) Researching corporate social responsibility communication: Themes, opportunities and challenges, *Journal of Management Studies,* 53(7), 1223–252

Cui, L, Wang, Y, Chen, W, Wen, W and Han, M S (2021) Predicting determinants of consumers' purchase motivation for electric vehicles: An application of Maslow's hierarchy of needs model, *Energy Policy,* doi.org/10.1016/j.enpol.2021.112167

Denham, H (2021) Burger King sparks uproar with 'Women belong in the kitchen' tweet, ad on International Women's Day, www.washingtonpost.com/business/2021/03/08/burger-king-tweet-women/ (archived at https://perma.cc/6N5N-PPJU)

Do Paço, A M F and Reis, R (2012) Factors affecting scepticism toward green advertising, *Journal of Advertising,* 41(4), 147–55

Elkington, J (1997) *Cannibals with forks. The triple bottom line of 21st century,* Capstone, Oxford

Fletcher, K (2008) *Sustainable fashion and textiles: Design journeys,* Earth Scan, London

Frostenson, M, Helin, S and Sandström, J (2011) Organizing corporate responsibility communication through filtration: A study of web communication patterns in Swedish retail, *Journal of Business Ethics,* 100(1), 31–43

Gardetti, M A and Muthu, S S (2018) *Sustainable luxury: Cases on circular economy and entrepreneurship,* Springer, London

Geissdoerfer, M, Savaget, P, Bocken, N M and Hultink, E J (2017) The circular economy: A new sustainability paradigm? *Journal of Cleaner Production,* 143, 757–68

Glenday, J (2020) Sceptical consumers are not convinced by big brand environmental pledges, The Drum, 27 February, www.thedrum.com/news/2020/02/27/sceptical-consumers-are-not-convinced-big-brand-environmental-pledges (archived at https://perma.cc/V4V7-GGUY)

GlobalWebIndex (2020) Social, www.gwi.com/hubfs (archived at https://perma.cc/R2Y9-43ZM)

Grebmer, C and Diefenbach, S (2020) The challenges of green marketing communication: Effective communication to environmentally conscious but sceptical consumers. *Designs,* 4(3), 25

Guyader, H and Piscicelli, L (2019) Business model diversification in the sharing economy: The case of GoMore, *Journal of Cleaner Production,* 215, 1059–69

Han, T I and Stoel, L (2017) Explaining socially responsible consumer behavior: A meta-analytic review of theory of planned behavior, *Journal of International Consumer Marketing,* 29(2), 91–103

Heineke, K, Kloss, B, Rupalla, F and Scurtu, D (2021) Why micromobility is here to stay, McKinsey Insights, www.mckinsey.com/industries/automotive-and-assembly/our-insights/why-micromobility-is-here-to-stay (archived at https://perma.cc/SFL8-GVJQ)

Hu, S, Henninger, C E, Boardman, R and Ryding, D (2019) Challenging current fashion business models: Entrepreneurship through access-based consumption in the second-hand luxury garment sector within a circular economy, in *Sustainable Luxury: cases on circular economy and entrepreneurship,* 39–54, eds M A Gardetti and S S Muthu, Springer, Singapore

Kenton, K (2022) Greenwashing, Investopedia, 22 March, www.investopedia.com/terms/g/greenwashing.asp (archived at https://perma.cc/UN3E-T5GX)

Kopnina, H (2019) Green-washing or best case practices? Using circular economy and Cradle to Cradle case studies in business education, *Journal of Cleaner Production*, 219, 613–21

Kumar, V, Rahman, Z, Kazmi, A A and Goyal, P (2012) Evolution of sustainability as marketing strategy: Beginning of new era, *Procedia-Social and Behavioral Sciences,* 37, 482–89

Lee, M and Yoon, H J (2020) When brand activism advertising campaign goes viral: An analysis of Always #LikeAGirl video networks on YouTube, *International Journal of Advanced Culture Technology*, 8(2), 146–58

Maslow, A (1970) *Motivation and Personality*, Harper and Row, New York

Neilson, L A (2010) Boycott or buycott? Understanding political consumerism, *Journal of Consumer Behaviour,* 9(3), 214–27

Outi Les Pyy (2019) H&M is the Donald Trump of Recycle Week, outilespyy.com/hm-is-the-donald-trump-of-recycle-week/ (archived at https://perma.cc/R7A8-9CP7)

Richardson, N (2019) *Sustainable Marketing Planning,* Routledge, London

Schmuck, D, Matthes, J and Naderer, B (2018) Misleading consumers with green advertising? An affect–reason–involvement account of greenwashing effects in environmental advertising, *Journal of Advertising*, 47(2), 127–45

Sindhuri, P, Julianna, P, Timo, O, Friederike, V and Werner, W (2017) The effect of consumer scepticism on the perceived value of a sustainable hotel booking, *Journal of Tourism and Hospitality*, 6(5), 7

Sobande, F (2019) Woke-washing: 'Intersectional' femvertising and branding 'woke' bravery, *European Journal of Marketing*, 54 (11), 2723–745

Stewart, R and Niero, M (2018) Circular economy in corporate sustainability strategies: A review of corporate sustainability reports in the fast-moving consumer goods sector, *Business Strategy and the Environment*, 27(7), 1005–022

Testa, F, Iovino, R and Iraldo, F (2020) The circular economy and consumer behaviour: The mediating role of information seeking in buying circular packaging, *Business Strategy and the Environment*, 29(8), 3435–448

Trudel, R (2020) Sustainable consumer behavior, *Consumer Psychology Review*, 2(1), 85–96

Vredenburg, J, Kapitan, S, Spry, A and Kemper, J A (2020) Brands taking a stand: Authentic brand activism or woke washing? *Journal of Public Policy & Marketing*, 39(4), 444–60

Victor, D (2017) Pepsi Pulls Ad Accused of Trivializing Black Lives Matter, www.nytimes.com/2017/04/05/business/kendall-jenner-pepsi-ad.html (archived at https://perma.cc/WZC4-FTFG)

Vinted (2022) Vinted, www.vinted.co.uk/ (archived at https://perma.cc/P4RC-QMKE)

Weber Shandwick (2018) *Battle of the Wallets: The changing landscape of consumer activism report*, Weber Shandwick, www.webershandwick.com/wp-content/uploads/2018/05/Battle_of_the_Wallets.pdf (archived at https://perma.cc/9PSE-AHTJ)

White, K, Habib, R and Hardisty, D J (2019) How to SHIFT consumer behaviors to be more sustainable: A literature review and guiding framework, *Journal of Marketing*, 83(3), 22–49

Young, W, Hwang, K, McDonald, S and Oates, C J (2010) Sustainable consumption: green consumer behaviour when purchasing products. Sustainable development, 18(1), 20–31

Global consumer behaviour on digital channels

13

By the end of this chapter, you should be able to:

- explain in simple terms what motivates consumers to consume on digital channels
- briefly describe why international consumer behaviour is of concern to businesses
- distinguish between standardization and adaptation
- understand the implications of irresponsible global marketing strategies

Introduction

In this chapter we expand our horizons even further, attempting to understand consumers and how to address them on a global scale. We explore consumer motivations for engaging in virtual spaces, whether for convenience, education, leisure, etc. Using these motivations, we also review how consumer behaviour differs across generations. We also inspect global and local marketing strategies and the impact of digital, sustainability and consumers on their development. We conclude the chapter with a practitioner interview, getting insights into an international company's efforts to understand consumer behaviour on a global scale via digital technology that informs their clients' marketing strategies.

Consumer motivations for going digital

In 2022 there were approximately 4.7 billion internet users around the world, which equates to about 60 per cent of the global population being active on digital platforms (Euromonitor, 2022a). As detailed in Table 13.1, consumers have a lot of

Table 13.1   Consumer motivations for going digital

Convenience	<ul><li>access</li><li>variety</li><li>delivery to your door</li></ul>
Current affairs	
Scarce or specialist	
Leisure	<ul><li>gaming</li><li>streaming</li></ul>
Educational	
Social	<ul><li>social media channels</li><li>chatrooms/forums</li><li>online communities</li></ul>

motivations for consuming on digital platforms, providing convenient methods to shop, access to current affairs, scarce or specialist products or services, leisure activities, educational opportunities and opportunities for social interaction.

As has been illustrated throughout this part of the book, target audiences are important, often resulting in segmentation to increase efficacy and results of marketing strategies. However, as we have also seen, there are multiple ways to segment consumers. There are also overlapping (or even contradictory) motivations behind consumers' values, beliefs, motivations and actions. In Chapter 12 we focused on socially responsible consumer behaviour for marketers interested in sustainable marketing strategies. Many of the values attributed to sustainability change from generation to generation, because of differences in generational lived experiences of social, political, cultural and environmental events (Strutton et al, 2011). Technology also impacts greatly on each generation's motivations and behaviour in online environments (Calvo-Porral and Pesqueira-Sanchez, 2020).

Thus, there is a body of research that studies generational behaviour among consumers. Strutton et al (2011), for example, conducted research on the different motivations and manners of engagement on electronic word-of-mouth between Millennials and Generation X. They found no significant difference between the generations' lack of likelihood of passing on viral content, but found Millennials are more engaged on social media than Generation X. Calvo-Porral and Pesqueira-Sanchez found that Millennials are motivated to engage online for entertainment and pleasure, while Generation X are more motivated to satisfy utilitarian and information needs. Younger generations (Millennials and younger) are *digital natives*, while older generations are *digital immigrants*. Calvo-Porral and Pesqueira-Sanchez also found that these digital natives tend to exhibit more socially responsible consciousness.

KEY TERM
Digital natives/immigrants

Digital natives: People who grew up with technology, used to having technology integrated into their daily lives and everyday activities.

Digital immigrants: People who did not grow up during the age of digital technology, but rather had to adapt to it.

SOURCE Calvo-Porral and Pesqueira-Sanchez, 2019

Activity 13.1
Consider motivations for going digital.

i. Based on the discussion above about generational differences in digital consumer behaviour, have a think about how and why consumers of different ages behave on digital channels.

ii. Pick at least two of the following for comparison and discussion with the class:

- baby boomers
- Generation X
- Millennials
- Generation Z
- Generation Alpha

Global and international marketing

With 4.7 billion internet users around the world, avoiding reputational damage is increasingly difficult. Richardson (2019) found a number of socially responsible consumer expectations that are impacting on global and international marketing strategies:

- levels of environmental awareness
- shifting consumer values
- demand for less pollution
- greater regulation by government
- demand for, and availability of, information on environmental issues
- opportunities to develop ways to protect the natural environment, animal rights and endangered species

Table 13.2   Global marketing strategy benefits and disadvantages

Advantages	Disadvantages
• Economies of scale in production and distribution • Lower marketing costs • Power and scope • Consistency in brand image • Ability to leverage good ideas quickly and efficiently • Uniformity of marketing practices	• Differences in consumer needs, wants, usage patterns for products • Differences in consumer response to branding elements • Differences in consumer response to marketing mix elements • Differences in brand and product development and the competitive environment • Differences in the legal environment • Differences in administrative procedures

Based on Keller and Swaminathan, 2019

Global brands derive at least 50 per cent of their revenue outside their domestic market and a lot of their growth is derived from global markets, such as Apple, Google, Coca-Cola and Microsoft (Keller and Swaminathan, 2019). As seen in Table 13.2. there are a number of benefits and strategies related to global marketing strategies.

Standardization or adaptation

A fundamental decision when developing marketing for new, international marketplaces is opting for either a *standardization* or an *adaptation* approach. This decision is applied across the marketing mix, for example in deciding which marketing channels to use, how to distribute the budget, customizing a social media post, advertisement or email to the local context, or sticking to the international marketing campaign and message. This differentiating decision is rooted in a philosophical debate:

1 treat the world as a single global economy and cater to global consumer culture as everyone is exposed to the same globalized communications (De Mooij, 2019)

2 treat every marketplace as a unique space, due to increasing (awareness and acknowledgement of) diversity and a drive for more inclusive practices for marginalized groups (Demangeot et al, 2015)

KEY TERM
Standardization

The same marketing strategy (including communication materials, concepts, etc) is applied across the marketing mix to all markets.

SOURCE Rao-Nicholson and Khan, 2017

Those who advocate a standardized approach to the marketing mix argue that standardized products provide a consistent global or international brand image (De Mooij, 2019).

The key factors influencing adoption of this strategy are:

- less costly
- increasing similarities in consumer demand
- more similarities across markets and less identifiable consumer segments

---

KEY TERM
Adaptation

The marketing strategy (including communication materials, concepts, marketing mix, etc) is adapted to the marketplace in which it is to be implemented.

SOURCE Rao-Nicholson and Khan, 2017

The key drivers include:

- product and service usage varies across cultures
- differences in government regulations can influence the decision too
- differing consumer behaviour patterns depending on different needs, climates, etc
- intra-national cultural diversity should also be considered

The motivations underpinning international and global marketing strategies range from pure sales-oriented goals to more socially responsible objectives (see section on Triple Bottom Line in Chapter 12). However, it may not be a simple either/or dilemma (Vrontis et al, 2009), which means that a lot of global or international companies combine variations of the two for optimal impact. Entering new markets involves multiple strategic decisions and market research is essential (even if your company is purely digital). Within the standardization vs adaptation approach organizations need be wary of the ethical implications of their strategy too (see Part Six: Legal and Ethical Considerations).

Activity 13.2

i.   Choose a global or international brand.

ii. Find a campaign that they implemented in their home or local marketplace.

iii. Find a campaign that they implemented in an international or foreign marketplace.

iv. Is it the same campaign?

v. If so, did they adapt the campaign in any way? How?

vi. Present your analysis to the class and discuss the different strategies employed by different brands.

The fresh mindset

The work by Strizhakova, Coulter and Price (2021) on the *fresh mindset* demonstrates just how complicated a decision standardization vs adaptation can be for global and international marketing strategy development.

KEY TERM
Fresh mindset

A belief that people can make a new start, get a new beginning, and chart a new course in life, regardless of past or present circumstances.

SOURCE Strizhakova et al, 2021

The fresh mindset is a concept originally developed based on the US marketplace and was found to have a tremendous impact on consumers' behaviour (Price et al, 2018). According to Strizhakova et al (2021) the fresh mindset scale indicates that there is a link between this mindset and consumers' global and personal beliefs, particularly for pro-sustainability companies seeking to effectively engage responsible consumers, and they go on to provide some recommendations for integrating the theory into global and international marketing strategies:

- Using the fresh mindset scale, determine if consumers possess a strong or weak fresh start mindset.
- Stronger fresh start mindset consumers are more receptive to pro-sustainability messaging.
- Pair the fresh start mindset consumer characteristic with social media use, travel and religion when developing customer personas.
- Integrate 'fresh start metaphors'.

Global consumer trends

Apart from the increasing demand for more socially responsible business practices and products, there are also other global consumer trends that should be taken into consideration when developing global and international marketing strategies.

There are a lot of research companies that do annual studies with detailed reports on consumer behaviour trends, which provide a good overview of the international consumer. More recent studies, like the one by Euromonitor (2022b), usually include some aspects of digital consumer behaviour trends too. Paired with broader global consumer mindsets and needs, these secondary data sources offer valuable insights for developing global and international marketing strategies.

CASE STUDY   Global consumer trends for 2022

1 backup planners

2 climate changes

3 digital seniors

4 financial aficionados

5 the great life refresh

6 the metaverse moment

7 pursuit of preloved

8 rural urbanites

9 self-love seekers

10 the socialization paradox

SOURCE Euromonitor, 2022b

At a glance, you notice a couple of prominent concepts that reiterate the consumer behaviour materials, theories and concepts introduced in this book. There are indicators that pro-environmental sustainability (2,7,8) pro-social sustainability (3,9,10) pro-economic sustainability (1,4,7), and expanding digital horizons (3,6,10) are significant factors that impact consumer behaviour on a global scale.

Another observation is that a lot of these trends rely on the notion of the empowered consumer, using their own beliefs and actions to be socially responsible in physical and digital spaces.

Activity 13.3

i. Read the *Global Consumer Trends 2022* report by Euromonitor (2022b).

ii. As a group, draw some more nuanced conclusions on one or more of the global consumer trends:

- What impact would this trend have on businesses?
- What impact would this trend have on marketing campaigns?

However, you cannot rely only on these type of reports. They should always be compared to the market research done about the specific marketplaces your business or client will be operating in. It is also a good idea to possess some understanding about the global sustainability issues digital marketers face.

Global issues for digital marketing

Due to the advances in digital technologies and connectivity via the internet, new access-based business models became a global phenomenon (Hu et al, 2019). However, this is not without issues, particularly from a social responsibility perspective.

Digital inequality

Digital inequality is a global issue, not limited to but more prevalent in poorer countries. One pertinent issue related to this inequality is the impact of digital poverty. Lack of access to technological devices and/or internet connectivity causes digital exclusion and can have a significant impact on where and how digital marketing campaigns can be delivered or engaged with.

Digital poverty is not just an issue faced in emerging economies. According to Coleman (2021), 9 per cent of households with children in the UK did not have access to digital devices such as laptops or tablets; 4 per cent only had access to a smartphone; and 2 per cent had no internet at all. Without access to a computer or stable, constant internet access during the Covid-19 pandemic, these children's education was severely disrupted as they were not able to attend school digitally to continue their education.

Something that is more prevalent in emerging economies is infrastructure challenges. In, Pakistan, for example, consumers are experiencing forced power outages for 8–12 hours in urban areas and 18 hours a day in rural areas (Valasai et al, 2017). Another challenge that causes digital poverty is expensive data costs. For example, in South Africa mobile companies were forced to reduce their data tariffs by 30–50 per cent in 2020, but this still remains too expensive for a large proportion of the population (Chinembiri, 2020).

Another issue with a direct impact on digital marketing strategies is differing levels of digital literacy or digital skills. Earlier in this chapter we talked about digital natives vs digital immigrants, where we touched upon generational differences in terms of motivations to engage on digital channels. However, to elaborate the concept a bit further, people without a native knowledge of digital channels or who do not possess the digital skills to operate complex digital platforms are excluded from a lot of contemporary, digital marketing campaigns. For example, scanning a QR code to gain access to information is quite exclusionary for people who do not possess the necessary digital skills to complete the action (or even own a smartphone). This might not seem like a big problem, but what if your digital campaign includes vital information such as locations for medical services or the only means of ordering food at a restaurant is via a non-user-friendly mobile application?

Social inequalities

Several nations are currently experiencing a rise in intercultural tensions (Demangeot et al, 2019), which is partly due to worsening inequalities. Marketers can play a key role in the marketplace as agents for social change (Vorster et al, 2020). Although marketers cannot solve infrastructure and poverty barriers, they can be more responsible in the strategies they develop and implement, for example in having non-digital alternatives for those lacking access to digital devices or skills to complete an action or contact the company.

Language also becomes a barrier for global and international marketing campaigns on the internet if alternative language options are not considered and integrated from the start. Although new technologies are making automatic captioning and translation easier to do, these services are still not perfect, which provides people who do not understand the language (or who have visual or hearing impairments) with the wrong information or even no means to understand the message at all.

Apart from digital barriers, there are also other social inequalities that reduce the impact of digital marketing and positive consumer responses. Frequently these are as a result of uninformed or insensitive marketing practices such as:

- exclusion from marketplaces due to lack of representation (via campaigns and in products or services that answer to specific consumer needs, e.g. Halal products in the supermarket)
- misrepresentation of consumer groups via insensitive and disrespectful portrayals such as stereotypes
- discriminatory actions such as different ethnicity-based price points for the same product
- deliberate woke-washing (see Chapter 12)

While it is a challenge to operate with social responsibility in contemporary, diverse marketplaces, not doing so can have significantly negative consequences for marketers and their brands (Kipnis et al, 2013) and can even impact on the sustainability of marketing as a profession (Vorster et al, 2020). Kipnis et al (2021) note that marketers should adopt a diversity-and-inclusion-engaged marketing (DIEM) approach that promotes consumer well-being to maintain the relevance of the profession. The DIEM approach also requires marketers to reduce inequalities in marketplaces through socially responsible marketing strategies (Kipnis et al, 2021) that do not intentionally exclude or harm any consumer group.

Activity 13.4

There are many examples of marketing campaigns that got into trouble for being disrespectful, which resulted in negative consumer responses.

i. Can you find an example?

ii. In your group, investigate the campaign and discuss the following questions:

- What was the consumer or global response?
- What did they do wrong?
- Did they do anything to repair the damage to their reputation? To their customer relationships?

PRACTITIONER INPUT
Melissa Coetzee

We conclude the chapter with an industry interview with Melissa Coetzee, Behavioural Analyst at Fatti Solutions. This interview offers insights into the data they gather and analyse to provide their companies with behavioural insights and recommendations for new digital marketing strategies. We get a look behind the scenes at work they do to help clients get to know their customers locally and on a global scale.

Fatti Solutions: Background information on the company

Fatti is a leading analytics company that is driven by a dynamic, passionate and innovative team. The highly specialized team has more than 100 years of combined experience providing Fatti with a solid track record in designing, configuring, customizing, developing and deploying innovative real-time location services (RTLS) and intelligent behavioural analytics. Fatti installs, manages, supports and actively monitors world-class, affordable Wi-Fi networks in public areas as a key foundation in 'feeding' landlords' behavioural insights based on their unique visitors.

Apart from analysing the behaviour of shoppers within multiple shopping centres in various countries, we have the ability to conduct out-of-mall proximity studies that monitor the change in behaviour and activity in each mall's catchment area. These studies include information on the primary, secondary and tertiary areas (from which mall visits originate) and lists: the top competitors in each area, rental insights, demographics, psychographics, crime information, property transactions, the difference in tenant mix and social media analysis findings.

Utilizing various data sources, the main objective of Fatti is to structure an 'action strategy' based on relevant behavioural insights, which will not only add qualitative value in key decision-making but also help monetize the commercial network for additional non-GLA (gross lettable area) income.

In conclusion, Fatti thrives on building a library of insights – enabling our clients to access a wealth of information by simply asking questions. We do not believe in dumping our clients with a mass of data, but rather we assess, sort, dissect, analyse and feed them with insights that drive an action strategy.

Which countries do you operate in?

The Fatti Solution has been implemented in over 60 locations, locally and globally. The majority of our clients are located in South Africa. Some of the major international deployments include countries such as Mauritius, Cyprus and Namibia.

Who is your typical client?

Fatti specializes in shopping centres where landlords and tenants are our typical clients. However, Fatti also operates across multiple sectors or verticals spanning many sectors of business, including stadiums, large warehouses, ocean liners, universities and airports.

What do you do for them?

Behavioural Location Analytics is a tool that enables the tracking of visitor journeys throughout a physical area. It is not a snapshot of behaviour at one point in time, but rather continuous real-time monitoring of approximately 70 per cent of all individual visitors. Digital online companies make use of behavioural data in order to monitor website clicks, churn rates, returning visitors, etc. Fatti has made it possible to implement the same concept in the physical world by means of Wi-Fi, enabling decision-makers to eliminate the guesswork and allow for operational and marketing activities to be measured. Fatti provides confidential behaviour analytics to landlords and tenants.

Developments in international marketing

Would you say digital marketing has changed marketing? If so, in what way?

The internet has generally transformed the marketing world for the past decade. It has liberalized the way businesses market and advertise their products. There was a time when print, radio, television, magazines and events dominated the marketing industry. Now with the new digital age, the traditional forms of marketing are taking a back seat. In the new digital world, millions of people spend a maximum of their time online on a number of digital platforms.

Marketers will always look for new ways and strategies to reach their target audiences and get the best results out of marketing strategies. However, it is always important to keep the different age groups with their preferences and habits in mind. Generation X and Millennials are most likely to benefit from digital marketing, via social media marketing (due to their active and online presence on social media platforms) and mobile marketing.

Fatti does not do physical marketing inside shopping centres or public spaces. However, Fatti offers a platform on the venue's Wi-Fi captive portal for marketers to make use of digital marketing to engage with visitors and to advertise any products or services on this platform. Fatti also assists marketing teams in making the right decisions and targeting the right consumers with their marketing campaigns.

Comparative reflections on international consumers

Would you say consumers are more sustainability conscious and more environmentally conscious?	
Local marketplace, South Africa	*International marketplaces, e.g. Mauritius and Cyprus*
Yes, however attitudes towards the environment and being more sustainable vary across generations, countries and industries.	While attitudes towards sustainability and being environmentally friendly vary between generations, they also vary across countries.
People in South Africa would like to be more sustainable and environmentally conscious. However, it often comes with a price. For example, if you go to buy groceries and you have a choice of whether you will take the plastic bag (0.60 cents) or the paper bag (Rand 1.40) people tend to go for the 'cheaper' option.	In some developed economies, it has become the convention and policy to be more environmentally conscious.

(continued)

(Continued)

Generation Z are more aware of being sustainable and environmentally friendly and they would shift their purchasing habits towards being more sustainable.

Now that younger generations are almost set in this behaviour, other generations such as Millennials and Generation X are becoming a force to reckon with by also portraying the traits of their younger generation.

Would you say the way consumers shop has changed in the last five years? In what way(s)?

Most definitely. We have seen across the Fatti portfolio that shopper behaviour had a forced change since lockdown.

'Shopability' is a Fatti word for a consumer's motivation to shop. For quite some time consumers were used to only frequenting one or maybe two stores per visit to the mall (for essential items only). According to scientists, it takes on average more than two months (66 days to be exact) before new behaviour becomes habit. Therefore, companies could encourage consumers to enter more than one store and to also dwell around in the mall.

Consumers have also become mindful of their purchases, from fashion to groceries. The fundamental economic strain that people experience also contributes to a change in shopper behaviour. For example, people (perhaps families) used to go to the movies, have dinner and visit a couple of stores per outing. Whereas now people may not be able to afford such outings any more, and now perhaps only the parents will go to the movies and go straight home afterwards.

The rise of e-commerce also plays a role in the way consumers shop, especially since Covid-19 in SA specifically. For example, you can now buy groceries online and get it delivered within the same day, something that was not widely offered in SA before the pandemic.

The same trends that Fatti has seen in South African malls, were also visible at the international malls in the Fatti portflio. Some of these countries' restrictions lasted longer than those in SA. Not only did consumers frequent fewer stores per journey, but spent less time inside the mall and spent less money.

(continued)

(Continued)

'Convenience shopping' has also changed consumer behaviour. Convenience in the sense of not only being a convenience store where you park in front of the grocery store and run in, but also convenience in the sense that shopping malls provide shoppers with necessary mall information, such as mall maps, digital maps, social media presence, and online communication.

How does that impact marketing and what you do?

Fatti works closely with mall marketing managers. Thereby providing the marketing teams with actual data to assist in making strategic decisions based on facts and trends rather than assumptions about consumer behaviour in the malls. These decisions vary from: choosing the right trading hours for shopping centres, marketing and event campaigns, necessary billboards inside and outside the mall, engaging with customers to determine their needs and wants or even assisting with in-store location and placements.

Marketers need to be aware of what is happening with society as well as the environment in order to understand what consumers want and what their shopping behaviour looks like to be able to develop more effective marketing strategies.

Summary

We explored different consumer motivations for engaging in virtual spaces, such as convenience, education, leisure, etc. Using these motivations, we also reviewed how consumer behaviour differs across generations. We investigated the benefits and disadvantages of global and international marketing strategies. Building on that we delved into decisions marketers face when developing these strategies, including standardization vs adaptation, fresh mindset and changing global consumer needs. We also took a look at issues digital marketers face on a global scale in terms of inequalities and the role marketers play in making these worse or improving them. We concluded the chapter with a practitioner interview, with valuable insights into international marketers' efforts to engage with consumers despite rapidly changing behaviour patterns.

Chapter review

Reflective questions

Q1 How do consumer motivations impact on digital marketing strategies?

Q2 Why should marketers be concerned with global or international consumer responses beyond the market they operate in?

Q3 Why is it important to do market and target audience research when developing marketing strategies?

Q4 What can marketers do to reduce digital and social inequalities?

Key learning points

- Consumers can have multiple motivations to engage with brands on digital channels such as convenience, education and interaction.

- Digital channels expose businesses to international consumers, making them susceptible to international responses and demands for accountability.

- Brands need to hold understanding about the marketplaces they operate in to determine when they should adapt their marketing strategies to the local marketplace or when it is acceptable to implement a standardized strategy.

- As brands expand into other international environments (and are exposed to international consumer groups even if they are not) there can be dire financial consequences if they employ irresponsible global marketing strategies.

References

Calvo-Porral, C and Pesqueira-Sanchez, R (2020) Generational differences in technology behaviour: Comparing Millennials and Generation X, *Kybernetes*, 49 (11), 2755–72

Chinembiri, T (2020) Despite reduction in mobile data tariffs, data still expensive in South Africa, AfricaPortal, 25 June, www.africaportal.org/publications/despite-reduction-mobile-data-tariffs-data-still-expensive-south-africa/ (archived at https://perma.cc/HQ78-RRJA)

Coleman, V (2021) Digital divide in UK Education during Covid-19 pandemic: Literature review, Cambridge Assessment, www.cambridgeassessment.org.uk/Images/628843-digital-divide-in-uk-education-during-covid-19-pandemic-literature-review.pdf (archived at https://perma.cc/F8WQ-Y6AM)

Demangeot, C, Broderick, A J and Craig, C S (2015) Multicultural marketplaces, *International Marketing Review*, 32(2), 118–40

Demangeot, C, Kipnis, E, Pullig, C, Cross, S N, Emontspool, J, Galalae, C, Grier, S A, Rosenbaum, M S and Best, S F (2019) Constructing a bridge to multicultural marketplace well-being: A consumer-centered framework for marketer action, *Journal of Business Research*, 100, 339–53

De Mooij, M (2019) Fairy tales of global consumer culture in a polarizing world, *International Marketing Review*, 36(4), 581–85

Euromonitor (2022a) *Euromonitor Top Five Global Consumer Trends 2022*, Euromonitor, go.euromonitor.com/rs/805-KOK-719/images/Top%20Five%20Digital%20 Consumer%20Trends%20in%202022.pdf?mkt_tok=ODA1LUtPSy03MTkAAAGFTjCk XX0sMhShM1aMf-eNf3JqdQBjfWyF2FbjxX9QprNuPEzIuoDhyk2BpNDjcmBGvSsMO fXkQd2noB-M17BFpKs-L5P_k-Ngt7uwqXkPJkSZhNZh (archived at https://perma.cc/ AM63-5TZY)

Euromonitor (2022b) *Euromonitor Top 10 Global Consumer Trends 2022*, Euromonitor, go.euromonitor.com/rs/805-KOK-719/images/wpGCT22EN-v1.1.pdf?mkt_tok=ODA1LUtPSy 03MTkAAAGFTje7iKJIloxzAlAWcQ_jrbTFvjLkrpaMBdDQ90-pg_cX4IvRE1voAN8HJSe EI0PBI6aAu8MSFtqqeFBgcgXWgF4zXeOvc-fs_4YMUvF8AFbM_Dlk (archived at https:// perma.cc/G6TW-CWDM)

Fatti Location (2022) Home page, www.fattilocation.com/ (archived at https://perma.cc/ RZS7-S5KC)

Gardetti, M A and Muthu, S S (2018) *Sustainable Luxury: Cases on circular economy and entrepreneurship,* Springer, London

Hu, S, Henninger, C E, Boardman, R and Ryding, D (2019) Challenging current fashion business models: Entrepreneurship through access-based consumption in the second-hand luxury garment sector within a circular economy, in *Sustainable Luxury: Cases on circular economy and entrepreneurship,* 39-54, eds M A Gardetti and S S Muthu Springer, Singapore,

Keller, K L and Swaminathan, V (2019) *Strategic Brand Management: Building, measuring, and managing brand equity,* Global Edition, Pearson Education

Kipnis, E, Broderick, A J, Demangeot, C, Adkins, N R, Ferguson, N S, Henderson, G R, Johnson, G, Mandiberg, J M, Mueller, R D, Pullig, C and Roy, A (2013) Branding beyond prejudice: Navigating multicultural marketplaces for consumer well-being, *Journal of Business Research*, 66(8), 1186–194

Kipnis, E , Demangeot, C, Pullig, C, Cross, S N, Cui, C C, Galalae, C, Kearney, S, Licsandru, T C, Mari, C, Ruiz, V M, Swanepoel, S, Vorster, L and Williams, J R (2021) Institutionalizing diversity-and-inclusion-engaged marketing for multicultural marketplace well-being, *Journal of Public Policy & Marketing*, 40(2), 143–64

Price, L L, Coulter, R A, Strizhakova, Y and Schultz, A E (2018) The fresh start mindset: Transforming consumers' lives, *Journal of Consumer Research*, 45(1), 21–48

Rao-Nicholson, R and Khan, Z (2017) Standardization versus adaptation of global marketing strategies in emerging market cross-border acquisitions, *International Marketing Review,* 34 (1), 138–58

Richardson, N (2019) *Sustainable Marketing Planning,* Routledge, London

Strizhakova, Y, Coulter, R A and Price, L L (2021) The fresh start mindset: A cross-national investigation and implications for environmentally friendly global brands, *Journal of International Marketing*, 29(4), 45–61

Strutton, D, Taylor, D G and Thompson, K (2011) Investigating generational differences in e-WOM behaviours: For advertising purposes, does X= Y? *International Journal of Advertising*, 30(4), 559–86

Valasai, G D, Uqaili, M A, Memon, H R, Samoo, S R, Mirjat, N H and Harijan, K (2017) Overcoming electricity crisis in Pakistan: A review of sustainable electricity options, *Renewable and Sustainable Energy Reviews*, 72, 734–45

Vorster, L, Kipnis, E, Bebek, G and Demangeot, C (2020) Brokering intercultural relations in the rainbow nation: Introducing intercultural marketing, *Journal of Macromarketing*, 40(1), 51–72

Vrontis, D, Thrassou, A and Lamprianou, I (2009) International marketing adaptation versus standardisation of multinational companies, *International Marketing Review*, 26(4/5), 477–500

PART FOUR
Implementation of a digital strategy

Objective setting   14

By the end of this chapter, you should be able to:

- explain the purpose of setting objectives to implement a successful digital marketing plan
- outline how considering the customer journey is a good starting point for setting objectives
- distinguish between the five aspects of setting SMART objectives
- criticize the SMART acronym and present alternative ways of writing objectives

Introduction

In this part of the book, we will discuss the implementation of a digital marketing plan. We will start by looking into the art of setting realistic objectives and reviewing the marketing mix for the digital work. We will then learn about digital tools and techniques by covering essential topics such as user experience (UX) when designing websites and the increasing fact of automation in the digital marketing environment.

This part of the book will explore the various digital channels available when implementing a digital marketing plan. Every digital marketing plan requires setting goals to visualize what it is trying to achieve. While setting objectives might sound relatively straightforward, there are essential aspects to remember to ensure that realistic objectives have been developed. We will explore how to do so in the coming chapter.

Purpose of objective setting

Every digital marketing plan should have a clear set of goals of what it is trying to achieve. Setting out clear goals is essential for implementing a business's mission and vision. Such business goals need to be broken down for different departments, and within the departments, they usually refer to different timeframes. Goals can be described as objectives.

A common differentiation is between long-term strategic and shorter-term operational objectives. When implementing a digital marketing plan, objectives are usually set on two levels:

- a strategic digital marketing level: containing a general direction of where the digital marketing department is heading; usually longer term
- a tactical, operational level for digital marketing campaigns: outlining exactly which digital technologies to employ; usually set for the shortest time frame

In Chapter 2, Figure 2.2 (Hierarchy of Business Objectives) describes how different levels of objectives fit into the overall business and marketing planning process. Generally, setting objectives can help in the following ways:

- establish exactly what a business wants to achieve
- clarify what a successful outcome would be
- develop a clear purpose
- manage time effectively
- allow progress to be evaluated

Activity 14.1

You have just learnt about the importance of setting goals for your digital marketing plan.

i. Consider both levels of a digital marketing department, the strategic and the operational level.

ii. Try to draft one goal for each level. Think about what you want to achieve.

Difference between goals and objectives

Often goals and objectives are used interchangeably. This means that when you set the direction for your business, you establish goals that you aim to achieve. However, some authors clearly distinguish between objectives and goals and claim that using the terms interchangeably can cause confusion (MacLeod, 2012). The authors clearly distinguish between broader business goals and objectives but agree that sub-goals can be compared to objectives. Table 14.1 highlights the differences between goals and objectives according to MacLeod (2012).

Table 14.1   Differences between goals and objectives

GOALS	OBJECTIVES
Broad in scope	Narrower in scope
General	Specific
Intangible	Tangible
Qualitative	Quantitative
Abstract	Concrete
End result	Required steps
Hard to validate	Easy to validate
Longer term	Shorter term

Consideration of the consumer journey

One of the main challenges when setting digital marketing objectives is that there are so many different options. Writing good objectives is all about being clear and concise. It is often worth considering at which point your consumer has reached in the consumer journey to determine clear objectives.

In Chapter 11, you learnt about the different phases of the customer journey. Identifying which part of the customer journey the consumer is in helps set objectives for a digital marketing activity. During the pre-purchase phase, the consumer might be becoming aware of a problem or need that they can potentially solve by purchasing something (Dhebar, 2013). We want them to be aware of our product during this stage and consider it an option to fulfil their need. Suitable objectives for this stage would include the creation of awareness and aid in the evaluation process that the consumer is going through. In digital marketing strategy, awareness and consideration are about audience reach. For example:

> We aim to reach 300k new followers on Twitter by the end of the financial quarter.

The second phase in the customer journey is the actual purchase (Dhebar, 2013). This phase is all about the actual purchase of a product. Suitable objectives would contain conversion sales ambitions:

> We aim to convert 20 per cent of our website visitors to purchase a product from our e-commerce platform within the next six months.

The final stage is the post-purchase stage which describes the stage after a transaction (Dhebar, 2013). The post-purchase phase is crucial as it determines whether the consumer will become a loyal customer. During this stage of the consumer journey, objectives would usually deal with customer retention. In digital marketing terms, this relates to the engagement of the consumer, such as:

> We aim to get 50 per cent more comments for our posts on the company's Facebook channel.

The above shows one way of setting objectives based on the customer's position in the customer journey. Other strategies help when setting objectives, one commonly applied model is that of the SMART acronym.

SMART objectives

Today, many marketers are using the term SMART, referring to an acronym that describes how to set goals. It seems generally accepted that a US consultant called George T Doran first published a paper in 1981 referring to the SMART way to write objectives (Doran, 1981). While the acronym SMART does not have a definitive definition, and some of the words within the acronym vary on the person using them, it originally stood for the following criteria (Haughey, 2014):

- specific: target a specific area for improvement
- measurable: quantify, or at least suggest, an indicator of progress
- assignable: specify who will do it
- realistic: state what results can realistically be achieved given available resources
- time-related: specify when the result can be achieved

Some of the words within the acronym vary. For example, assignable is often applied as 'achievable' or 'attainable', whether the goals are actually achievable based on the available means. Chen (2015) defines an achievable objective as one that can be reasonably met with existing resources.

This acronym does not mean that every goal or objective specifies all five aspects of the SMART acronym, but one should consider these when setting them.

There are several reasons why the acronym is as popular today as it was more than 40 years ago when it was first introduced. It is a very simple tool that helps set clear and precise goals, avoiding vague language. It is easy to remember and does not require prior knowledge or expertise. However, critics say that goals established with the SMART acronym lack flexibility (Haughey, 2014).

Activity 14.2

You have now been introduced to the SMART acronym for writing clear goals and objectives.

i. Revisit the objectives you wrote down earlier in this chapter.

ii. Try to evaluate whether your objectives would pass the SMART test by establishing whether your objectives are indeed specific, measurable, assignable, realistic and time related.

Challenging SMART objectives

As with every model or theory, staying critical in its application is important. The SMART acronym for setting objectives has been around since 1981, and there is hardly any company that has not applied it in some shape or form. However, just because it is one of the most common models, it does not mean that it comes without criticism. For example, Bjerke and Renger (2017) criticize the aim to simultaneously fulfil all of the five aspects of the SMART acronym. They review the application of SMART objectives and have concluded that often crucial data is missing when setting objectives that are meant to be SMART. They find that in their context of setting objectives for planning programmes, the three aspects of specific, measurable and realistic objectives were relatively easy to apply (Bjerke and Renger, 2017). However, further research needed to be done within the programme's context to ensure achievable and timely objectives. Therefore, they suggested a multiple-step approach to setting objectives to ensure that all SMART criteria are satisfied.

Another critique of SMART objectives relates to not being ambitious enough (Murphy, 2015). Murphy criticizes the fact that setting achievable and realistic goals stops businesses from taking risks and pursuing greatness. He paraphrases Jeff Bezos, Amazon's CEO, as saying to his employees, 'Exercise new muscles, never mind how uncomfortable and awkward-feeling those first steps might be' rather than saying to them 'pursue goals that you're already equipped to handle'.

To follow the steps of successful companies such as Amazon, Google, Meta and Apple, businesses should not set achievable and realistic objectives but instead focus on how they can equip their staff with the skills needed to meet even ambitious and risky objectives (Murphy, 2015). Trevor (2015) agrees that SMART objectives inhibit change and limit organizations to remain as they are performing in the present. They advise businesses to follow goals that encourage companies to stretch themselves to aim for the impossible, as proposed by Collins and Porras (1994), who introduced the idea of **BHAGs** (Big Hairy Audacious Goals).

> ## KEY TERM
> BHAG
>
> A true BHAG is clear and compelling, serves as a unifying focal point of effort, and acts as a clear catalyst for team spirit. It has a clear finish line, so the organization can know when it has achieved the goal; people like to shoot for finish lines.
>
> **SOURCE** Collins and Porras, 1994

Trevor (2015) describes the following as examples (albeit they are rather dated) of BHAGs:

Organize the world's information and make it universally accessible and useful (Google).

A computer on every desk and in every home (Microsoft).

While there are some critical voices around using the SMART acronym to set business objectives, there is a reason it is still commonly applied. These reasons include its simplicity and adaptability to varying contexts.

Summary

You have reviewed how to set objectives for a digital marketing plan to be successful. We have looked at the purpose of setting objectives and how considering the consumer journey can help when setting specific objectives. We have introduced the meaning of SMART objectives and how those can be applied in a digital marketing context. We have outlined critical voices around the SMART way of setting objectives and presented alternative approaches.

Chapter review

Reflective questions

Q1 What is the purpose of setting objectives to implement a successful digital marketing plan?

Q2 Why do you need to consider the customer journey when setting objectives?

Q3 What are the five aspects of setting SMART objectives?

Q4 How would you criticize the SMART acronym?

Q5 What are alternative ways of writing objectives?

Key learning points

- The purpose of setting objectives to implement a successful digital marketing plan.
- Consideration of the customer journey when setting objectives.
- The five aspects of setting SMART objectives.
- Criticism of the SMART acronym.

References

Bjerke, M B and Renger, R (2017) Being smart about writing SMART objectives, *Evaluation and Program Planning*, 61, 125–27

Chen, H T (2015) *Practical program evaluation: Theory-driven evaluation and the integrated evaluation perspective*, 2nd ed,, Sage, Thousand Oaks, CA

Collins, J and Porras, J (1994) Built to last: Successful habits of visionary companies, Harper Business

Dhebar, A (2013) Toward a compelling customer touchpoint architecture, *Business Horizons*, 56 (2), 199–205

Doran, G T (1981) There's a SMART way to write management's goals and objectives, *Management Review*, 70(11), 35–36

Haughey, D (2014) A brief history of SMART goals, Project Smart, 13 December, www.projectsmart.co.uk/smart-goals/brief-history-of-smart-goals.php (archived at https://perma.cc/3YZR-ZKBY)

MacLeod, L (2012) Making SMART goals smarter, *Physician Executive*, 38(2), 68–72

Murphy, M (2015) 'SMART' goals can sometimes be dumb, *Forbes*, 8 January, www.forbes.com/sites/markmurphy/2015/01/08/smart-goals-can-sometimes-be-dumb/?sh=7a5a5f58718e (archived at https://perma.cc/TM5J-RZLT)

Trevor, W (2015) Are SMART objectives really that clever? LinkedIn, 22 February, www.linkedin.com/pulse/smart-objectives-really-clever-will (archived at https://perma.cc/Z3L4-NAUH)

Marketing mix for 15 the digital world

By the end of this chapter, you should be able to:

- distinguish between the 4Ps and 7Ps of marketing
- explain the seven individual elements of the marketing mix
- outline how the marketing mix needs to be adjusted to fit the digital world

Introduction

This chapter deals with the impact of technology on the marketing mix. We have introduced the 4Ps of marketing in Chapter 1. As a reminder, the 4Ps are also referred to as the marketing mix and are commonly applied to aid decision-making when marketing products and services. The rise of the internet and other technologies such as smartphones has opened up many new ways to communicate with consumers and generally added new options for marketers. This chapter will review the main 4Ps of the marketing mix and elaborate on how these have to be adjusted for the digital world. We will also extend our discussion to include a further three Ps (people, processes and physical environment) as these are commonly applied when drafting a marketing mix to include services rather than just tangible products.

The marketing mix

There are several different *marketing mix* definitions. We have highlighted a few early definitions below:

A marketing mix is a combination of all of the factors at the command of a marketing manager to satisfy the target market (McCarthy, 1964).

A marketing mix contains the controllable variables that an organization can co-ordinate to satisfy its target market (McCarthy and Perreault, 1987).

A marketing mix is the set of controllable marketing variables that the firm blends to produce the response it wants in the target market (Kotler and Armstrong, 1989).

These definitions have a common theme in that they talk about controllable factors that need to be adjusted to fit the target audience. If you recall from Chapter 7, the target market is formed from smaller segments identified as worth pursuing. If we now look at a more recent definition of the marketing mix, the definition has not changed very much.

KEY TERM
Marketing mix

The marketing mix is the set of tactical marketing tools – product, price, promotion and place – that the firm blends to produce the response it wants in the target market.

SOURCE Kotler and Armstrong, 2014

We need to consider two things, even though the definitions do not seem to have changed much over the past 40 years. The marketing mix is still one of the leading models that help marketers decide how to market their services and products to their target audience.

First of all, and this addition happened a while ago, we need to consider the importance of adding further Ps to the mix to understand better how to market services. And secondly, and probably more importantly, given the addition of the digital world to marketing decisions, we need to know how to adjust the marketing mix accordingly.

The extended marketing mix: the 7Ps of digital marketing

In the second half of the 20th century (particularly in the United States), the service sector dominated employment and value-added shares. This period was termed the 'service economy' (Witt and Gross, 2020). In simpler terms, this meant that, rather than people working in manufacturing and buying pure goods (e.g. cars), more people were working in the service industry and purchasing services (e.g. going on holiday).

Far more than in the manufacturing sector, the delivery and purchasing of services is a 'people' economy. Think, for example, of a visit to the hairdresser vs purchasing a hair product such as shampoo. When you want to buy a shampoo, you go to the store, pick a shampoo based on your preference and pay for the shampoo at the checkout. The checkout might be the only interaction you have with a person. Today, self-checkout machines even eliminate that contact. Now consider a visit to the hairdresser. You are getting your hair washed by a person, another person might be cutting your hair, and you will likely receive a blow-dry from a third person at the end of the visit.

The difference between these two scenarios is that the product purchase (e.g. the shampoo) is likely to be the same every time you buy the product. There is no significant variability when purchasing products. However, the service is unlikely to be the same on different occasions as human beings are involved. The hairdresser might be having a great day. This might translate into them being quite chatty and doing a great job cutting your hair. The next time, the same hairdresser might have a bad day. They might not feel like talking and might be doing a poor job on your haircut. Even though it would be the same setting and even the same hairdresser, your experience might be completely different as we are only human. So, the service provider's behaviour can have a direct influence on the quality of the service you are receiving.

Activity 15.1

You have just learnt about the difference between buying a product and receiving a service provision. Think of the traditional marketing mix of product, price, promotion and place.

i. Try to make marketing mix decisions for the product (e.g. shampoo) you were buying.

ii. Think of product decisions such as what makes the product special, how you would promote the product, where people could buy the product and how much you would charge for the product.

iii. Try to do the same for the service encounter (e.g. visiting a hairdresser).

iv. Try to identify how you could plan for the involvement of people in both the provision and receiving of the service.

In 1981, marketing scholars Mary J Bitner and Bernhard H Booms highlighted that the 4Ps are ill-equipped to deal with the involvement of people in the service industry. To solve the issue, they came up with the extended marketing mix, also referred to as the 7Ps model or the Services Marketing Mix (Booms and Bittner, 1981). This marketing mix extends the original one by three additional Ps: people, physical processes and process (Figure 15.1).

Figure 15.1   The extended marketing mix

Product

The product element of the marketing mix describes the product a company is selling. It establishes the main benefits of a product or service to the consumer. There are several aspects that this part of the marketing mix relates to – some of the following form the product category:

- product quality
- product features
- packaging
- branding

Digital technologies have impacted products in several ways. First, the digital world has allowed entirely new products to be invented. One such example would be streaming platforms such as Netflix and Amazon Prime. Let's review the product features listed above to see the influence digital technologies have on the product category.

Product quality

Technologies influence the quality of products in several ways. There is the school of thought that through wider choice and comparison opportunities on the internet, product quality has improved overall. This would mean that the products we are buying today are generally better. The idea is that consumers can easily compare products and find alternatives if they want to.

The other side of the argument is that the internet has heightened consumer demands for new products. For example, the lifespan of a smartphone today is minimal compared to a landline telephone from the 1990s.

The jury on product quality in the digital world is still out. However, let us view product qualities individually, such as usability, usefulness, longevity and reliability. It is possible to see how some of these aspects (e.g. usefulness and usability of products) have improved with digital technologies as customers can be better understood, and technologies have improved the way products can be made (Littlefield and Harrison, 2015). Yet other parts of product quality (e.g. longevity and reliability) have decreased with the internet.

Product features

With improved technologies came more product features. So this part of the product has been impacted by technologies. Now let's take a look at the digital environment to see how far it needs to be adjusted to cater to these feature-rich products. Horrigan (2008) found that 43 per cent of respondents who searched the internet before buying a mobile phone would get a product with more features than they initially set out to purchase. This can also be supported by websites that sell additional services. It is common practice among many industries to offer **add-on sales** to the primary product.

KEY TERM
Add-on sale

An add-on sale refers to an ancillary item sold to a buyer of a primary product or service. Depending on the business, add-on sales may represent a source of significant revenues and profits to a company. An add-on sale is generally suggested by the salesperson once the buyer has made a firm decision to buy the core product or service. It is sometimes known as 'upselling'.

SOURCE Kenton, 2021a

Packaging

Technologies have impacted packaging in several ways. New technologies such as robotics, smart packaging and 3D printing (Benadi, 2018) have all changed the way products are packaged today. If we look at packaging from a digital marketing point of view, there are numerous impacts. 'Unboxing' is a trend that started in 2006 when the first video was posted that showed a video blogger (vlogger) unpacking a product. Today, YouTube has specific channels dedicated to unboxing, with more than 14 million subscribers (Smithers, 2019). From a digital marketing point of view, this means that packaging decisions need to bear this trend in mind. Packaging should be designed to allow the vlogger to unwrap the product in several steps to tell a story that ends in a 'WOW' moment when finally the product is revealed, allowing the viewers to be engaged through the process (Smithers, 2019).

Activity 15.2

We have discussed various ways in which digital technologies have impacted the product. Unboxing is a trend that started in the early 2000s.

i. Visit YouTube's most successful unboxing channel 'Unbox Therapy' with more than 18 million subscribers.

ii. Take a look at the different products that the vlogger is unboxing.

iii. Can you think of an offline equivalent where such unboxing might have a similar effect?

iv. How important do you think the packaging is for a product's success?

Another impact of the digital world on packaging is personalization. Many individual businesses have set up their e-commerce store and require packaging that can be personalized to meet the individual consumer needs. However, even large corperations use personalized packaging to provide a personalized service. For example, L'Oréal is offering a direct-to-consumer hair colouring product with a personalized greeting message and product labels (Smithers, 2019).

Branding

Branding is one of the most critical aspects of the product category of the marketing mix. This is because brands are often one of the most valuable business assets. Often, brands are confused with recognizable company messages such as logos or slogans, but these are mainly tactics that help communicate a *brand*.

KEY TERM
Brand

Brand refers to a business and marketing concept that helps people identify a particular company, product or individual. Brands are intangible, which means you cannot touch or see them. They help shape people's perceptions of companies, their products or individuals. Brands commonly use identifying markers to help create brand identities within the marketplace. They provide enormous value to the company or individual, giving them a competitive edge over others in the same industry. Many entities seek legal protection for their brands by obtaining trademarks.

SOURCE Kenton, 2021b

There are several ways in which a brand can be communicated by branding a business online. Digital marketing activities need to extend brand values to the online sphere. For example, online brand assets such as distinctive brand names, images and symbols need to be designed so that they are recognizable to the consumer. Consumers have to ensure that the brand heritage and brand identity are consistent across digital channels and the offline world.

Wang and Chen (2021) find that in the luxury brand industry, social media advertising only leads to positive brand evaluation when it is based on cultural aspects such as the company's history, heritage, values and beliefs.

Another consideration for businesses is to carefully manage their brand identity on social media to ensure no discrepancy exists between the brand's desirable online brand identity and the actual brand identity prevailing in the consumers' minds (Wang and Chen, 2021).

Place

Place describes the location where the product is available for the consumer. Products can be made available to consumers via several locations and digital channels have contributed to extending these options. A business needs to decide whether to sell its products directly, through retail or wholesale outlets, via direct selling or through the internet.

The internet has impacted where we buy our products in many forms, some of which include:

- retail
- wholesale
- direct selling
- multichannel
- peer-to-peer

A business needs to decide where to sell goods and services. Most of the companies that sell products or services to consumers are considered to be retailers. These might produce their own goods or purchase goods from manufacturers. Buying from manu-facturers can be either direct or through a wholesaler. Wholesaling is usually described as a sale to a business or institutional customer. Before the internet, the options of getting a product to a consumer were relatively limited. This could be done through a retailer, direct sales techniques (e.g. door-to-door sales), or mail ordering (e.g. catalogue businesses in the 80s and 90s).

Activity 15.3

You have been introduced to several places where consumers could purchase products before the internet.

i.   Imagine you are looking to buy your next vacuum cleaner.

ii. What are the different options for you offline to purchase a vacuum cleaner?

iii. Now also look into the online places you could visit to purchase a new vacuum cleaner.

iv. How have the additional online marketplaces impacted your choice?

Digital technologies have impacted the number of channels where consumers can purchase goods and services and have also allowed for new business models to appear. For example, manufacturers can now sell their goods directly to consumers. This means they can potentially leave the retailer or wholesaler out altogether, partaking in the direct-to-consumer business model. This can be profitable as the manufacturer does not have to pay any profit margins. For example, Rajasekharan (2020) reports a jump in sales margins from 38 to 62 per cent for US manufacturing firms engaged in direct-to-consumer vs wholesale sales.

Peer-to-peer selling is another new form of utilizing the internet to find a different place to sell products. Online marketplaces such as Etsy allow individual producers or artists to sell their (often personalized) products to end-consumers.

A business needs to decide where to sell its products, and that decision should not be taken lightly. While it might seem tempting to sell directly to the consumers, there are risks involved that are usually mitigated by going through a retailing system. Services offered by the retailers to wholesalers and manufacturers include the following:

- offering access to a large consumer base
- buying large quantities, avoiding the need for individual sales
- investing in consumer knowledge
- offering after-sales services

Promotion

Promotion techniques describe the promotional options available to businesses to communicate product and service features to an audience. Promotion includes the different efforts a company makes to encourage consumer choice of its products and services.

Promotion can include several different promotional activities, often referred to as the promotional mix and varying activities which include:

- advertising
- sales promotion
- endorsements
- competitions
- direct mail
- exhibitions
- public relations

Promotional activities have numerous new digital channels to work with. For example, advertising used to be seen through mass media such as television or print magazines. The digital landscape has made highly targeted advertising on different platforms possible. For example, display advertisements on websites can be highly targeted based on someone's interest or previous shopping behaviour. Some companies only exist to offer sales promotions. For example, Groupon or Wowcher offer sales promotions for numerous products and services from third parties.

The varying promotional techniques will be covered in detail in Chapters 16, 17 and 18 but Table 15.1 demonstrates how those activities listed above as part of the promotional mix can be implemented on digital channels.

Table 15.1   The promotional mix applied to the digital world

Promotional mix	Application to the digital world
Advertising	Targeted ads on social media, pay-per-click ads on search engines, display ads
Sales promotion	Online loyalty schemes, vouchers, cash-back offers
Endorsements	Influencer marketing, electronic word-of-mouth, product reviews, podcasts
Competitions	Gamification techniques on social media and other websites
Direct mail	Email newsletters
Exhibitions	Virtual exhibitions, webinars
Public relations	Viral marketing, influencer marketing, PR via numerous online channels

Price

Price is the only element of the marketing mix that generates revenue – rather than incurring costs, which all of the other elements do. The price refers to the amount of money businesses can charge for a product. It is crucial to set the right price to generate a profit.

To know which price is the right price, businesses need to conduct a demand analysis to establish how much demand in the market there is for the product or service. Successful companies have a clear understanding of their consumers' willingness to pay. One also needs to consider that prices indicate the product's position in the market compared to the competition (Allen, 2020). The role of promotional activities is to ensure that consumers are willing to pay the price for a product charged by a business.

There are some traditional pricing strategies available to a business:.

- penetration pricing
- price skimming
- premium pricing
- competitive pricing
- psychological pricing

Penetration pricing

Penetration pricing relates to offering cheap pricing when introducing a product to the market. Once product awareness is established, higher prices can be charged.

KEY TERM
Penetration pricing

Penetration pricing is a marketing strategy businesses use to attract customers to a new product or service by offering a lower price during its initial offering. The lower price helps a new product or service penetrate the market and attract customers away from competitors. Market penetration pricing relies on using low prices initially to make a wide number of customers aware of a new product.

SOURCE Kenton, 2021c

Penetration pricing is very common among online businesses, especially those offering subscription business models. This way, consumers can feel confident to 'try' a product/service first before paying a lot of money for it.

Price skimming

Skimming is almost the opposite of penetration pricing. With this strategy, businesses charge high prices when a new product is first introduced to the market. The idea is that if the product is unique and innovative enough, consumers are less price-sensitive and willing to pay a premium (Kenton, 2021c). Prices are usually lowered once the novelty has worn off.

Premium pricing

KEY TERM
Premium pricing

Premium pricing is a strategy that involves tactically pricing your company's product higher than your immediate competition. The purpose of pricing your product at a premium is to cultivate a sense in the market of your product being just that bit higher in quality than the rest. It works best alongside a coordinated marketing strategy designed to enhance that perception. Premium pricing is closely related to the strategy of price skimming. However, unlike skimming, it involves setting prices high and keeping them there.

SOURCE Campbell, 2020

Both price skimming and *premium pricing* strategies are often applied in the digital world as there are a lot of entirely new products that people are willing to pay money for. Think of some of the purely digital products discussed in Chapter 5. For example, NFTs – non-fungible tokens – are digital assets representing a real-world object. Due to their limited supply, people are willing to pay a lot of money for NFTs (Conti, 2022). One of the most famous examples of an NFT is the hugely popular YouTube video *Charlie Bit Me*, which sold as an NFT in 2021 for £500,000 (Evans, 2021).

Competitive pricing

KEY TERM
Competitive pricing

Competitive pricing is selecting strategic price points to best take advantage of a product- or service-based market relative to the competition. This pricing method is used more often by businesses selling similar products since services can vary from company to company while the attributes of a product remain similar. This type of pricing strategy is generally used once a price for a product or service has reached a level of equilibrium, which occurs when a product has been on the market for a long time, and there are many substitutes for the product.

SOURCE Khartit, 2020

The digital world has influenced *competitive pricing* strategies in many ways. Price transparency, comparison sites and enhanced consumer knowledge make price comparison much more accessible than before the internet.

Psychological pricing

Psychological pricing is a marketing strategy that sets prices in a way that they appeal to consumers' emotional side. Examples of psychological pricing would include setting a price of £9.99 rather than £10.00. There is only a 1p difference among those prices but the brain thinks it is getting a better deal as the price looks closer to £9.00 than £10.00. This is called charm pricing (Collins, 2021).

Other standard psychological pricing techniques include the omission of small-value denominations, so instead of showing the price as £10.00, the price is displayed as £10 as the mind thinks it looks cheaper. Some stores even remove the currency sign as this makes people think they are spending less (Collins, 2021). Another common tactic is to display the recommended retail price (RRP) to give the consumers something to compare against.

Technology has a significant impact on pricing strategies. For example, pricing strategies such as competitive pricing are much quicker to be implemented and adjusted given online price transparency. Also, prices can be modified quickly should they not receive the expected response. Before the internet, mail order companies would print different prices on different catalogues to see what consumers were willing to pay (Collins, 2021). Nowadays, split testing when setting prices is common practice.

Activity 15.4

You have now been introduced to several different pricing strategies. There are several websites that let you allow to compare prices. Priceable is a supermarket price comparison website that allows you to compare different product prices.

i.   Visit the Priceable website and search for a product of your choice.

ii. Which of the following pricing strategies does your product follow: penetration, skimming, premium, psychological or competitive pricing?

iii. Who could these comparison sites be helpful to besides the consumer?

We have discussed traditional pricing strategies and how these have to be adjusted to fit the digital world. In addition to considering how traditional pricing has been impacted, there is a plethora of new pricing methods enabled through new technologies, particularly the internet. We started to look at digital business models in Chapter 2. The following list highlights some digital pricing/business models that were not available in their current form before the internet and demonstrates just how much the internet has created new opportunities for businesses (Cuofano, 2022):

- **Free** (also hidden-revenue or ad-supported model): Companies such as Facebook and Google offer their product for free and generate money differently (e.g. by selling advertising).
- **Freemium:** Commonly used online, essential services are offered for free, but a paid version is available for additional benefits (e.g. no adverts, more extensive storage, etc).
- **Subscription:** A widespread business model whereby consumers pay a monthly fee to subscribe to a service. A significant advantage of this business model is a guaranteed stream of income.

Other innovative pricing strategies that seemed to be commonplace online are:

- **Pay what you want:** The term pay what you want (PWYW) describes a pricing strategy that puts the consumer in charge of how much they want to pay for a product or service (GoCardless, 2022). There are a number of reasons why companies might choose to adopt this approach. Cultural institutions such as the Metropolitan Museum of Art in New York City have applied PWYW for decades, ensuring an inclusive approach to their pricing – everybody can come. Some for-profit organizations use this concept to demonstrate high confidence in their product quality (GoCardless, 2022).
- **Buy now, pay later:** Buy now, pay later (BNPL) is a type of short-term financing that allows consumers to make purchases and pay for them at a future date, often interest-free. Also referred to as 'point-of-sale' instalment (Lake, 2022). BNPL is particularly popular among younger consumers who shop online as they offer flexibility and let the user try products first without fully committing to buying them.

Price discrimination

We have just learnt about the different options for pricing products. Pricing strategies need to be adapted to fit the online context. One significant advantage of the online marketplace is price transparency, meaning that it is easier for both businesses and consumers to evaluate and compare prices. One major issue with online pricing strategies concerns *price discrimination.*

KEY TERM
Price discrimination

Price discrimination is a selling strategy that charges customers different prices for the same product or service based on what the seller thinks they can get the customer to agree to. In pure price discrimination, the seller charges each customer the maximum price they will pay. In more common forms of price discrimination, the seller places customers in groups based on specific attributes and charges each group a different price.

SOURCE Twin, 2022

Price discrimination does not necessarily have to be something bad, and in many cases, it can benefit the consumer. For example, if you book your holiday well in advance, you usually get a better deal than when you book only a few weeks before going. The tour operator is still taking part in price discrimination as it charges a different price for the same product. According to Twin (2022), three conditions need to be met for price discrimination to occur:

- First, the company needs to have sufficient market power.
- Second, it has to identify differences in demand based on different conditions or customer segments.
- Third, the firm must have the ability to protect its product from being resold by one consumer group to another.

While discrimination pricing does not need to be something bad and is not illegal, ethical questions need to be addressed. One reason it is possible to charge consumers different prices is because of the data that can be (involuntarily) collected when consumers shop online. So, theoretically, a business can charge consumers different prices depending on whether they would classify them as price-sensitive. Such classification can result from data being collected through cookies and is called 'personalized pricing', which is part of price discrimination (Zuiderveen Borgesius and Poort, 2017). Would you say that being charged a different price for the same product based on your purchasing history would be fair or unethical?

The office supply store Staples.com was found to be charging people in different areas different prices based on IP address (Valentino-Devries et al, 2012). Another example was identified by Mikians et al (2013), who found numerous online shops that charged different prices for customers from different regions. Another company that has been in the news for charging different prices in different countries is Spotify. Singer (2014) found that the same subscription to Spotify costs around $18.42 in Denmark compared to \$4.61 in Malaysia. Waldfogel (2020, p 612) has analysed Spotify's cross-country price discrimination and has come up with the following conclusions:

- Price discrimination increases overall welfare.
- Price discrimination increases world revenue for Spotify by about 6 per cent relative to a world uniform price.
- Price discrimination increases Spotify's EU revenue by about 1 per cent relative to an EU uniform price.
- Price discrimination benefits consumers in lower-income countries while reducing consumer surplus in higher-income countries.

These conclusions sound relatively positive, but we need to consider how ethical the approach to price discrimination is.

Questions

a. Visit the IPdigIT website (Wicklow et al, 2020) and read Waldfogel (2020) to see how Spotify charges different prices around the globe.

b. Do you think it is fair that different prices are charged in different countries?

c. How do you feel about personalized pricing in general?

People

People is the first addition to the original 4Ps of marketing and refers to the people who work for a business. This includes management, salespeople, customer service personnel and other members of staff. People are crucial when they are consumer-facing, be that in person, through online chat, via social media or via the call centre (Allen, 2020). The issue with people as part of the service or product provision is that they can be inconsistent and unreliable. Yet, with the proper training and development of skills, people can provide an opportunity for a business to differentiate itself from the competition.

There are several ways in which the role of people has been impacted through technology and needs to be adapted to fit the digital world.

Customer service

Digital technologies have massively impacted the face of customer service provision. Most businesses see technological advances as advantageous to their business operations. However, critical voices highlight a concern that people who provide customer service are being replaced by technology. Professionals stress that technologies are only helping customer-facing staff to do their job more efficiently rather than replacing them (Redbord, 2020).

The most common change in customer service provision through technology has been seen in the form of live chats and social media interactions with consumers. Generally, technology has helped increase the speed and efficiency of providing customer service. This is because databases can hold more detailed information about customers, informing personalized service provisions.

The following are some of the main changes in customer service provision through the application of technologies (Redbord, 2020):

- real-time messaging to communicate with consumers
- customer service decisions are more data-driven
- social media will become a standard customer service tool
- self-service will become an absolute necessity

Rayport et al (2005) suggest that businesses should review their customer service to determine whether any of the following options would optimize service provision better:

- **Substitution:** Deploying people in place of machines or machines in place of people (e.g. an e-ticketing kiosk in place of a counter agent at an airport).
- **Complementarity:** Deploying people in collaboration with machines or machines in collaboration with people (e.g. an employee using a Wi-Fi-enabled handheld device to facilitate easy rental car returns).
- **Displacement:** Outsourcing or 'off-shoring' machines or labour (e.g. a fast-food chain centralizing drive-through order-taking in a remote call centre).

Corporate culture

The company's *corporate culture* is another facet of the people element of the marketing mix.

KEY TERM
Corporate culture

Corporate culture refers to the beliefs and behaviours that determine how a company's employees and management interact and handle outside business transactions. Often, corporate culture is implied, not expressly defined, and develops organically over time from the cumulative traits of the people the company hires.

A company's culture will be reflected in its dress code, business hours, office setup, employee benefits, turnover, hiring decisions, treatment of clients, client satisfaction, and every other aspect of operations.

SOURCE Tarver, 2021

As you can see from the explanation, the corporate culture is nothing tangible. It is something that develops over time. If you think of young start-up businesses, they usually have a very relaxed company culture, with no strict dress code and often flat hierarchies, which means no great distance between management and employees. By contrast, other, often more traditional, businesses have stricter rules regarding what employees should be wearing, which hours they need to be in the office, and how management personnel may be addressed.

The internet has almost acted as a magnifying glass in the sense that corporate culture is no longer something restricted to people inside of the business. Over the past few years, numerous cases have come to light where employees described their business environment as very negative. Companies compete for the best employees on the market, and projecting a desirable corporate culture to the outside world is one way of getting those. The internet and social media have provided a platform to do so.

Founders/management

Besides employees, the founders or management of a company are just as important to consider when making marketing mix decisions. You might have noticed that large technology firms in particular are consciously putting their founders into the spotlight and almost act as the face of the company. If you think of Facebook/Meta you are likely to have heard of Mark Zuckerberg. The same holds for Elon Musk, CEO of Tesla Motors, and Jeff Bezos, executive chairman of Amazon.

Even before the internet and social media, people would have been familiar with these names. Newspapers would have written about them. However, the amount of information that we are exposed to nowadays makes it easier for businesses to publish what they want the public to see.

Having a single face seen as leading or managing can be positive as it demonstrates the longevity and continued leadership of a business. Yet, it can also come with risks. For example, when Steve Jobs, founder of Apple, passed away, the company's future was uncertain as so much faith has been put in him to continue the success story.

Processes

Processes as an element of the marketing mix establish the procedures businesses have in place to deliver products and/or services to the consumer. Well-established processes allow for efficient business transactions by ensuring the same standard of service delivery to the consumer.

Most businesses had to adjust their processes when accessing the digital world. If you take the original marketing mix of product, price, promotion and place, all of these elements had certain processes before entering the digital market.

For example, a business such as Domino's Pizza used to take only in-store or telephone orders. The process would have involved a consumer calling to order a pizza. The pizza would then be baked in-store and delivered via a courier. The price would have been set and communicated in-store and on leaflets. Promotion would have taken place on mass media, billboards and mail flyers. Now think of how these processes would have had to be adjusted to fit the digital marketplace. The product itself stays the same, except that the personalization of the pizza has been made much more manageable. Everything else has changed. Consumers mostly order pizza online, so the company had to structure those incoming orders. There are many more opportunities to communicate the price via online channels. The company now must ensure to put processes in place to charge prices similar to or lower than the competition as consumers can easily compare prices online. While offline promotion used to be a relatively static exercise (once the advert was designed, it did not change much), online marketing allows many more promotional avenues. Again processes need to be put in place that ensure consistent and successful execution of promotional activities.

Processes also deal with service recovery in the case of complaints. Technology has made such service recovery processes greatly more efficient.

The customer journey outlines different touchpoints where businesses should have reliable processes in place (see Chapter 11 for a detailed account of the customer journey).

Physical evidence

The final element of the 7Ps of marketing describes physical evidence, referring to everything the consumer sees when interacting with a business. In an offline context, for example for a restaurant, this refers to the layout and design of the restaurant but also includes staff uniforms and the menus. The physical evidence is meant to help the consumer assess the quality of a place.

The physical evidence relates to the user experience on a business's website in an online context. The user experience includes variables such as ease of use, loading speed, availability and performance. This will be discussed in detail in Chapter 16.

Summary

In this chapter we have outlined how the marketing mix helps businesses to set a clear strategy on how they will provide services/goods to their customers. We have established how with the rise of the service economy the original 4Ps marketing mix has been extended to the 7Ps marketing mix. The original marketing mix dealt with the product, its pricing decisions, its promotional activities and the place the product could be bought. The extension to the marketing mix reflects the needs of services as products. People, processes and physical evidence have been added into the mix. We have reviewed in detail how digital technologies have impacted the individual elements.

Chapter review

Reflective questions

Q1 What is the difference between the 4Ps and 7Ps of marketing?

Q2 Why has the marketing mix been extended from four to seven Ps?

Q3 What are the seven elements of the marketing mix?

Q4 How do businesses need to adjust their marketing mix to fit the digital world?

Key learning points

- The 4Ps have been extended to the 7Ps to be better equipped to deal with the service industry.
- This marketing mix extends the original one of product, price, promotion and place to include additional three Ps: people, physical processes and process.
- The marketing mix has to be adjusted to fit the digital world.

References

Allen, A (2020) Understanding the 7Ps of the Marketing Mix, Oxford College of Marketing, 8 October, blog.oxfordcollegeofmarketing.com/2020/10/08/understanding-the-7ps-of-the-marketing-mix/ (archived at https://perma.cc/D5SD-GSNH)

Benadi, D (2018) Four technology trends transforming packaging, Raconteur, 1 August, www.raconteur.net/packaging/technology-transforming-packaging/ (archived at https://perma.cc/85XC-KGY4)

Booms, B and Bitner, M, (1981) *Marketing Strategies and Organizational Structures for Service Firms Marketing of Services*, 47–51, American Marketing Association, Chicago, IL

Campbell, P (2020) Complete guide to premium pricing, Profit Well, 6 May, www.profitwell.com/recur/all/premium-pricing (archived at https://perma.cc/LZN7-G9YN)

Collins, A (2021) Psychological pricing: What your prices really say to your customers, Shopify, 16 November, www.shopify.co.uk/blog/psychological-pricing (archived at https://perma.cc/5FSC-ZJAA)

Conti, R (2022) What is an NFT, *Forbes*, 16 February, www.forbes.com/uk/advisor/investing/nft-non-fungible-token/ (archived at https://perma.cc/GCZ4-4TUB)

Cuofano, G (2022) Digital business models map, FourweekMBA, fourweekmba.com/digital-business-models/ (archived at https://perma.cc/V6A8-PK8M)

GoCardless (2022) Pay what you want pricing, April 2022, gocardless.com/en-us/guides/posts/can-your-business-succeed-using-a-pay-what-you-want-model/ (archived at https://perma.cc/2EF8-8JQN)

Evans, A (2021) *Charlie Bit Me* NFT sale: Brothers to pay for university with auction money, BBC, 3 June, www.bbc.co.uk/news/newsbeat-57333990 (archived at https://perma.cc/6TV2-HEHH)

Horrigan, J (2008) Online shopping, PEW Internet and American Life Project, 13 February, www.pewresearch.org/internet/2008/2/13/online-shopping-2/ (archived at https://perma.cc/P3TY-Q2WV)

Kenton, W (2021a) Add-on sale, Investopedia, 3 June, www.investopedia.com/terms/a/add-on-sales.asp#:~:text=What%20Is%20an%20Add%2DOn,and%20profits%20to%20a%20company (archived at https://perma.cc/V7GL-MBZ4)

Kenton, W (2021b) Types of brands and how to create a successful brand identity, Investopedia, 24 March, www.investopedia.com/terms/b/brand.asp (archived at https://perma.cc/6JAZ-XSC6)

Kenton, W (2021c) Penetration pricing, Investopedia, 2 October, www.investopedia.com/terms/p/penetration-pricing.asp (archived at https://perma.cc/A4TZ-97V8)

Khartit, K (2020) Competitive pricing, Investopedia, 30 July, www.investopedia.com/terms/c/competitive-pricing.asp (archived at https://perma.cc/9NG7-EKBU)

Kotler, P and Armstrong, G (1989) *Principles of Marketing*, 4th edn, Prentice-Hall, Englewood Cliffs, NJ

Kotler, P and Armstrong, G (2014) *Principles of Marketing*, 15th edn, Pearson, Harlow, UK

Lake, R (2022) Buy now, pay later, Investopedia, 7 February, www.investopedia.com/buy-now-pay-later-5182291 (archived at https://perma.cc/N835-KFV5)

Littlefield, M and Harrison, R (2015) Leveraging the Internet of Things to improve product quality: What you need to know, LNS Research, 19 October, www.lnsresearch.com/research-library/research-articles/leveraging-the-internet-of-things-to-improve-product-quality-what-you-need-to-know (archived at https://perma.cc/6M3L-F4E6)

McCarthy, E J (1964) *Basic Marketing*, Richard D Irwin, Homewood, IL

McCarthy, EJ and Perreault, W D Jr (1987) *Basic Marketing*, 9th edn, Richard D Irwin, Homewood, IL

Mikians, J, Gyarmati, L, Erramilli, V and Laoutaris, N (2013) Crowd-assisted search for price discrimination in e-commerce: First results, in *Proceedings of the Ninth ACM Conference on Emerging Networking Experiments and Technologies*, 1–6

Rajasekharan, M (2020) Cutting out the middle man: Suppliers adopt direct-to-consumers, Supply Chain Brain, 17 August, www.supplychainbrain.com/blogs/1-think-tank/post/31754-cutting-out-the-middleman-suppliers-adopt-the-direct-to-consumer-model (archived at https://perma.cc/UQ6X-SVNG)

Rayport, J, Jaworski, B and Kyung, E (2005) Best face forward: Improving companies' service interfaces with customers, *Journal of Interactive Marketing*, 19(4), 67–80

Redbord, M (2020) 14 ways technology will affect the future of customer service, Hubspot, 10 December, blog.hubspot.com/service/customer-service-technology (archived at https://perma.cc/5BJG-E6U7)

Singer, M (2014) Spotify International Pricing Index, mts.io/2014/05/07/spotify-pricing-index/ (archived at https://perma.cc/L2KZ-GEAS)

Smithers (2019) Five ways packaging can make an impact on social media, www.smithers.com/en-gb/resources/2019/nov/how-packaging-can-make-an-impact-on-social-media (archived at https://perma.cc/8PQJ-JBKV)

Tarver, E (2021) Corporate culture, Investopedia, 2 September, www.investopedia.com/terms/c/corporate-culture.asp (archived at https://perma.cc/NP83-KLBD)

Twin, A (2022) What is price discrimination and how does it work? Investopedia, 7 February, www.investopedia.com/terms/p/price_discrimination.asp (archived at https://perma.cc/TAV9-69Z3)

Valentino-Devries, J, Singer-Vine, J and Soltani, A (2012) Websites vary prices, deals based on users' information, *Wall Street Journal*, 23 December, online.wsj.com/article/SB10001424127887323777204578189391813881534.html (archived at https://perma.cc/2HP9-99UE)

Waldfogel, J (2020) The welfare effects of Spotify's crosscountry price discrimination, *Review of Industrial Organization*, 56, 593–613

Wang, Y and Chen, H (2021) Self-presentation and interactivity: Luxury branding on social media, *Journal of Product & Brand Management,* 30(5), 656–70

Wicklow, M, Bellflamme, P and Peitz, M (2020) Who pays what on Spotify? IPdigIT, www.ipdigit.eu/2020/05/who-pays-what-on-spotify/ (archived at https://perma.cc/S8YB-2TQ8)

Witt, U and Gross, C (2020) The rise of the 'service economy' in the second half of the twentieth century and its energetic contingencies, *Journal of Evolutionary Economics*, 30, 231–46

Zuiderveen Borgesius, F and Poort, J (2017) Online price discrimination and EU data privacy law, *Journal of Consumer Policy*, 40, 347–66

Digital tools, techniques and technology

16

By the end of this chapter, you should be able to:

- explain the importance of user experience design
- outline success factors for website design
- explain good practice in e-commerce
- criticize marketing automation

Introduction

As part of implementing a digital strategy, we have learnt how to set objectives and how the digital marketing mix is adjusted to be a suitable tool in the digital world. This chapter will focus on digital tools, techniques and technology that can assist the digital marketing strategy implementation. Having a functioning website that puts the user experience at the forefront of its design can aid customer acquisition as well as retention. We will review essential factors for such a website. Also, we will look into how a website can enable the commercial aspect of e-commerce. Additionally, we will learn about the importance of user experience (UX) when designing websites.

The second part of this chapter focuses on automation in the digital world and how it can be applied during the digital marketing strategy implementation phase. Automation is one of those areas in the digital space that businesses feel less confident about and it is important to learn how it can actually help. Marketing automation includes elements such as automatic email responses, social media posts and ad campaigns, but is used frequently in customer service too, for example in the form of chatbots.

Website design

A *corporate website* is one of the first things that consumers see when they want to know more about a business.

KEY TERM
Corporate website

A corporate, or institutional, website is an internet site which presents a company, an institution or an organization to all its audiences and not only to its customers or users. Thus, the corporate site is classically distinguished from the commercial site intended only for customers or users. On the content side, the corporate site endeavours to promote the company (its history, values, commitments, purpose, governance, human resources policy, etc) and not directly its products or solutions.

SOURCE We Are Com, 2020

As you can see from the definition traditionally there is a distinction between a corporate site and a commercial (usually e-commerce) site. However, with the rise of e-commerce, a lot of corporate websites implemented a commercial aspect so the lines between a corporate and a commercial site are slightly blurry. In this chapter we will focus on both, the corporate site and the commercial aspect.

When the internet first started becoming accessible to the masses, businesses had to design websites to be found online. Those early websites used to look very different to the websites we see today. Websites in the early 1990s used to be about publishing information about businesses. Before the internet, such information would have been found in companies' brochures.

It was also about collecting information about consumers through online enquiry forms and providing consumer service by, for example, publishing frequently asked questions (FAQs). However, websites today do not resemble those early websites at all and their functionality has also grown tremendously. Today's websites are all about interaction with the consumer, enabling transactions, and providing comprehensive self-service to the consumer. With the development of websites, the role that the website visitor is playing has also changed. From being a relatively passive consumer, the website user today plays an integral part in the website experience.

Activity 16.1

You have just learnt about the difference between website design in the early 1990s and today. In digital terminology, the web has passed through the stages of Web 1.0 to Web 4.0 (see Chapter 1).

i.   Please visit Elton Boocock's YouTube channel (Boocock, 2014) and search for the video 'Web 1.0, 2.0, 3.0 and Beyond – Information and Interaction'.

ii. How has the role of the consumer changed during that time?

iii. Consider how the design of websites will have changed.

User experience design

The user should be key when designing any successful website. One formalized term that is frequently used when considering website design is *user experience* design.

KEY TERM
User experience

User experience design is the process design teams use to create products that provide meaningful and relevant experiences to users. This involves the design of the entire process of acquiring and integrating the product, including aspects of branding, design, usability and function.

SOURCE Interaction Design Foundation, 2020

The important features of UX for website design are branding, design, usability and function. The Interaction Design Foundation (2020) refers to the Why, What and How of UX, the individual aspects of which are illustrated in Figure 16.1.

The Why includes questions such as what motivates the user to use the website and what are their values and views. In Chapters 7 and 10 we discussed the use of personas, fictional representations of a target audience. Personas can help businesses visualize the Why. The What covers functionality and features of website design. The How covers accessibility and aesthetics. Later in this chapter we will discuss the success factors of website design and all these elements will be discussed.

Figure 16.1   The why, what and how of UX design

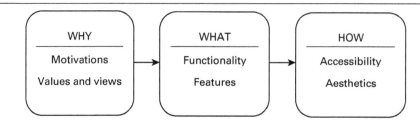

SOURCE Knight, 2022

It is important to note that creating a successful website design should be centred around the principles of *human–computer interaction (HCI)* and covers several different disciplines.

KEY TERM
Human–computer interaction (HCI)

HCI (human–computer interaction) is the study of how people interact with computers and to what extent computers are or are not developed for successful interaction with human beings.

SOURCE TechTarget, 2005

Some factors of human–computer interaction are the different ways of learning and keeping knowledge of users, cultural and national differences as well as user preferences. HCI is one consideration of user design (UX) but further disciplines need to be included for UX to create successful websites that are user-centred. Some of these disciplines include information architecture (IA), visual design, web analytics and user research among others.

Morville (2004) notes that, for any user experience to be meaningful and valuable, the information provided must be:

- useful: content should be original and fulfil a need
- usable: site must be easy to use
- desirable: image, identity, brand and other design elements are used to evoke emotion and appreciation
- findable: content needs to be navigable and locatable onsite and offsite
- accessible: content needs to be accessible to people with disabilities
- credible: users must trust and believe what you tell them

Success factors for website design

When designing websites, there are several aspects that need to be taken into consideration.

Korgaonkar et al (2009) questioned 349 web designers and developers and confirmed the following eight critical factors in successful website development. These can be divided into those benefiting the user and those focused on the business:

User-focused

1 entertainment and visual appeal

2 reliability

3 personalization

4 information quality

5 user empowerment

6 privacy/security

Business focused

7 cost reductions attained

8 back-end processes enabled

These success factors contain a number of different subsets that businesses should consider when designing their corporate as well as their commercial websites. We will now cover the most essential success factors in more detail.

Entertainment and visual appeal

The affective and aesthetics aspect is crucial in successful website design. Websites have to cut through a lot of noise online and need to find a way of standing out from the competition. Designing a website in such a way that it is pleasing for the consumer can be one way of drawing the visitor into the site to experience its usability. The visual appeal of website design is relatively subjective – meaning different visitors might find different designs appealing. Yet there are some guidelines that can help to design a website in a way that is aesthetically pleasing. According to Henderson (2022) a visually pleasing website has a good layout and displays clear graphics with colours and fonts that complement each other, with a balanced use of images and videos. A website should be clean and simple without too many distracting features that confuse the viewer and take away from the main purpose of the site (Henderson, 2022).

A very common way to introduce an element of entertainment to a website is by using gamification techniques. *Gamification* can provide entertainment on a website and makes it fun to explore for the visitor.

KEY TERM
Gamification

Gamification is the application of game design elements and game principles in non-game contexts. It can also be defined as a set of activities and processes to solve problems by using or applying the characteristics of game elements.

SOURCE Walter, 2022

The visual appeal and entertainment of a website is critical to both corporate and commercial websites.

Activity 16.2

Innocent Drinks is a company famous for its smoothies and juices and is well known for its playful attitude to marketing.

i.   Visit Innocent Drinks' website.

ii. Do you perceive the website to be visually appealing? If so why, or alternatively why not?

iii. Do you find the website entertaining and fun to explore?

iv. Can you find any gamification features on the website?

Reliability

From the user's point of view, the overall reliability of the website is crucial as it must allow the user error-free transactions. This is particularly crucial in an e-commerce context. If errors occur there are suggestions on how these should be presented from a website design point of view. Nielsen (1994/2020) has established general principles for interaction website design. Two out of those 10 principles deal with errors:

- 'Error prevention': Principle 5 states that good error messages are important, but the best designs carefully prevent problems from occurring in the first place.

- 'Recognize, diagnose and recover from errors': Principle 9 states that error messages should be expressed in plain language (no error codes), precisely indicate the problem, and constructively suggest a solution.

Another aspect of the reliability success factor identified by Korgaonkar et al (2009) deals with websites being supported by trained personnel. This refers to the provision of consumer support. This means that even if errors occur, which can happen, somebody needs to be available to recover those errors and ensure a positive user experience.

Personalization

Personalized features are extremely important in the e-commerce context and general website success. We discussed earlier the change that websites went through, starting out as merely digitalized brochure providing information about businesses and developing into interactive platforms that entertain the user.

The personalization of websites comes with its own set of challenges. In order for personalization to occur, businesses need to be able to collect information about their consumers. Only when having that information can they offer a personalized experience. Gouthier et al (2022) stress that consumers have two alternatives when shopping online. They either accept the disclosure of their data to receive certain benefits, such as personalized offers and communication, or they reject it and therefore would not receive those benefits.

With consumers agreeing to share their personal data comes an expectation for better products and further personalization. For example, companies must offer incentives for consumers to want to share their data to receive one-to-one marketing (Peppers and Rogers, 2000). The term personalized marketing is often used interchangeably with individual marketing or *one-to-one marketing*.

KEY TERM
One-to-one marketing

One-to-one (or 1:1) marketing is a strategy that emphasizes having an individualized experience with customers. One-to-one marketing campaigns can be 'a segment of one': instead of having to segment consumers into a group and send them all the same message, businesses can now deliver marketing material that appears unique to the individual. This can be done using a CRM (customer relationship management) system to reach out to an individual, sending them a personalized email, serving programmatic content through a marketing automation tool, or using video.

SOURCE Otalvaro, 2019

Information quality and information architecture

Information quality is rated very high when it comes to success factors for websites. When you think of information quality, quality refers to the following items (Korgaonkar et al, 2009):

- the website provides objective information
- the website helps users research products and services
- the information presented on the website is fair and accurate

In order to ensure that consumers perceive the information provided on a website as high quality, they need to be able to find that information. One way of ensuring good findability of information is *information architecture* as it aims to help people find what they are looking for. It is a way of mapping out online surroundings in a way that would be comparable to architectural drawings in the real/offline world.

> **KEY TERM**
> Information architecture
>
> We define information architecture as:
>
> **A.** The structural design of shared information environments.
>
> **B.** The art and science of organizing and labelling websites, intranets, online communities and software to support usability and findability.
>
> **C.** An emerging community of practice focused on bringing principles of design and architecture to the digital landscape.
>
> **SOURCE** Information Architecture Institute, 2013

The information architecture describes the underlying organization of a website and is essential when creating a good user experience (UX). Constructing the information architecture is one step of the UX design process. UX will be discussed later in this chapter in more detail.

The content structure of a website depends on the user requirements and can therefore differ a lot between, for example, an e-commerce store and a corporate blog (Fitzgerald, 2020) (see Figure 16.2).

Figure 16.2   Information architecture example for an e-commerce clothing store

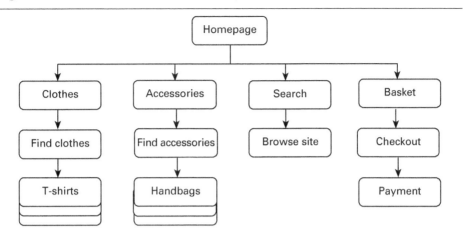

User empowerment

User empowerment can have different meanings in website design. Korgaonkar et al (2009, p. 49) referred to user empowerment as the website user being able to control the following:

- opportunities for interaction
- how fast to go through the website
- order and/or sequence of information access

Ladner (2015) sees the importance of user empowerment to design websites in a way that 'users of the technology are empowered to solve their own accessibility problems'. He claims achieving this can be done by following two school of thought: Human-Centred Design, and Design for User Empowerment. He refers to the six principles of human-centred design as outlined by the ISO standard ISO 9241-210:2010 as follows:

- The design is based upon an explicit understanding of users, tasks and environments.
- Users are involved throughout design and development.
- The design is driven and refined by user-centred evaluation.
- The process is iterative.
- The design addresses the whole user experience.
- The design team includes multidisciplinary skills and perspectives.

Ladner (2015) postulates that design for user empowerment should involve users even more closely. He states that users should develop the project, design the requirements and features, develop the prototypes, test the prototypes, and analyse the results of testing to refine the design. He states that it is especially important for users with disabilities to be involved to ensure design for user empowerment.

Nielsen (1994/2020) agrees on the importance of putting users in control. In his *10 Usability Heuristics for User Interface Design*, Nielsen lists 'user control and freedom' at no 3. He states that website design needs to enable users to undo an action or back out of a process easily to allow users to remain in control of the system. This is important as users often perform actions by mistake.

Activity 16.3

We have now discussed some features of good website design. Creating a visually stimulating experience for the user is one of the key success factors. We have also learnt about empowering the user in website design and how especially including users with a disability can ensure inclusive design.

i.   Please visit a website that you perceive to be visually pleasing and write down a few bullet points of what makes your chosen website visually stimulating.

ii. Now visit Toptal.com website and type the URL of your chosen website into the box. Leave the colour filter as it is. Now you can view your favourite website through the eyes of a colour-blind person.

iii. Is it still as visually pleasing? Are there any problems with readability?

Privacy/security

Addressing privacy and security concerns of users is essential when designing successful websites. It is important for website designers and developers to know current marketing privacy laws as those directly impact what is and what isn't allowed and will ultimately impact the end result of the finished website. There are a number of laws that are important to consider and we will review the main legal requirements for digital marketing in Chapter 25.

One of the biggest laws that ensures the protection of users' privacy and security is the General Data Protection Regulation (GDPR). There are many more laws that define the individual's rights to their personal data and set mechanisms for how their rights would be protected and enforced (Daniels, 2020).

When designing websites it is not just about avoiding fees or legal measures for non-compliance. It is actually about following consumer demand for more privacy and security online. Korgaonkar et al (2009, p. 49) find that consumers care about websites having adequate security features, ensuring that data is encrypted and also that they are safe when conducting transactions. Also, Daniels (2020) highlights that 82 per cent of Americans surveyed are concerned about the security of their online data and nearly 80 per cent are very or somewhat worried about how companies use the data they collect about them.

As discussed in the section on personalization in this chapter, there is a trade-off that consumers will have to make. This trade-off includes how much to protect one's privacy while still enjoying the benefits of personalized communication.

Today, minimizing the collection of data is perceived to be best practice among web designers and the following are some of the points that should be prioritized (Daniels, 2020):

- minimize and pseudonymize data collection to protect data privacy
- capture consent
- integrate security measures to protect data
- identify where privacy and data sharing notices need to be introduced
- implement just-in-time notices to provide consumers transparency and build trust
- give users the opportunity to manage their personal data

We have now covered success factors for website design from the user's perspective. We will now move on to two success factors from the business's point of view.

Cost reductions

From both the corporate and the commercial point of view, successful website design must deliver cost savings, when compared to not having the website at all. Such cost savings can come from several areas, and usually, websites should reduce costs in the following areas: administration, information processing, customer support and marketing (Korgaonkar et al, 2009). For example, a corporate website should make it easier to deliver swift customer support through automated emails, chatbots and/or live chats. Most of these cost reductions can be achieved through marketing automation, and the automated marketing tools available will be discussed later in this chapter.

Back-end processes

So far, we have mainly referred to the front-end of website design – the part of the website that is visible to the consumer. Front-end web design deals with the look and feel of a website including its functionality. However, a lot of work is going on when using a website that is invisible to the user but essential for the website to function. *Back-end web development* ensures that people can use websites without any issues.

KEY TERM
Back-end web development

Back-end development is the work that goes into managing web application logic on the server side of things. It's an essential part of web design because it makes sure your site works on all platforms (e.g. Mac, Windows, Linux) and allows people to use it without any issue.

SOURCE Benitez, 2021

In Korgaonkar et al's (2009) research, the back-end processes refer to the following aspects.

- the website facilitates shipment tracing for the company
- the website facilitates billing functions for the company
- the website facilitates electronic auditing for the company

So these back-end processes are all about how the work for the business can be more efficient. Yet, there are more things to consider when developing the back-end of a website. Benitez (2021) highlights the following responsibilities of web developers:

- **Write highly efficient code:** After establishing business requirements, back-end web developers need to write code that meets those requirements using an appropriate coding language (Table 16.1).

- **Build and maintain the system architecture:** The code written by the back-end developer needs to be translated into a website that front-end users can easily engage with. An example of such a back-end process development that is essential to front-end users is the payment-processing system.

- **Network security and protection:** The back-end developer needs to put security measures into place to ensure the right protection to avoid data theft.

We have now discussed in detail the various success factors that makes a good website. Most of these are applicable to both corporate websites as well as e-commerce websites. However, in the following section we will review e-commerce individually to stress some important differences.

Table 16.1 Back-end development languages

Programming language	Description	Application
Java	An object-oriented language that allows you to reuse the code in other programs	Netflix, Uber, Google Earth and Tinder
Ruby on Rails (RoR)	A language that uses a model-view-controller (MVC) architecture for stability and predictability. It allows you to easily modify the code or add new features to your site or app	Airbnb, Slideshare, Goodreads, Groupon and Kickstarter
Python	Python is one of the most commonly used programming languages in the world. Aside from website development, it also figures in network programming, artificial intelligence (AI) and machine learning (ML)	Spotify, Dropbox, Google, Reddit and Instagram
PHP	Responsible for server-side scripting for collecting data, producing dynamic page content, communicating with the database to fetch data to return to the browser, and more	Facebook, Wikipedia, Tumblr, MailChimp and Flickr

Based on Benitez, 2021; Techslang, nd

E-commerce

Electronic commerce (e-commerce) is transactions enabled through electronic devices (see also Chapter 10). The uptake of e-commerce has grown tremendously since the Covid-19 pandemic began in 2020. In the United States, e-commerce sales increased by 50.5 per cent between 2019 and 2021 (Goldberg, 2022).

KEY TERM
Electronic commerce (e-commerce)

The term e-commerce refers to a business model that allows companies and individuals to buy and sell goods and services over the internet. E-commerce operates in four major market segments including business-to-business, business-to-consumer, consumer-to-consumer and consumer-to-business. It can be conducted over computers, tablets, smartphones and other smart devices. Nearly every imaginable product and service is available through e-commerce transactions, including books, music, plane tickets, and financial services such as stock investing and online banking.

SOURCE Bloomenthal, 2021

Online value proposition

With the big increase of e-commerce, businesses see opportunities to reach their audience via new channels. However, the competitive intensity in the online marketplace requires businesses to clearly distinguish their offering from the competition. One way of doing so is to set an online *value proposition* strategy. An online value proposition is an extension of the value proposition that answers the simple question of why should a consumer buy your product.

KEY TERM
Value proposition

A value proposition refers to the value a company promises to deliver to customers should they choose to buy their product. A value proposition is part of a company's overall marketing strategy. The value proposition provides a declaration of intent or a statement that introduces a company's brand to consumers by telling them what the company stands for, how it operates and why it deserves their business.

A value proposition can be presented as a business or marketing statement that a company uses to summarize why a consumer should buy a product or use a service. This statement, if worded compellingly, convinces a potential consumer that one particular product or service the company offers will add more value or better solve a problem for them than other similar offerings will.

SOURCE Twin, 2022

Every business needs to consider what their value proposition is. It helps to guide a business and the consumer by clearly establishing why a consumer should choose products and/or services of that particular business. In an online context, the same rules apply. Businesses need to ensure that they convince their buyers why they should buy from them. As established earlier, the online marketplace is an extremely crowded one and a compelling online value proposition is a way to stand out from the competition.

The online value proposition should echo the overall value proposition but should extend this by clearly stating the benefits for the consumer in conducting e-commerce on your website. The online value proposition can be explicitly stated on the website, for example on a permanent visual or on a pop up banner (potentially time-restricted during a campaign only). Potential online values could include some of the following:

- free shipping
- free returns
- multiple return options (in-store, postal, pick-up, etc)
- amount of brands/products to choose from
- price-matching the competition
- try before you buy
- discounts for particular segments (e.g. students get 10 per cent discount)
- exclusivity (e.g. only available here!)

Activity 16.4

We have covered why it is important to consider an online value proposition to distinguish one product offering from another in an e-commerce context.

i. Please visit three websites that you frequently use when purchasing products or services.

ii. Try to find the online value proposition for each of those websites.

iii. Are they included in the following list?

- free shipping
- free returns
- multiple return options (in-store, postal, pick-up, etc.)
- amount of brands/products to choose from
- price-matching the competition
- try before you buy
- discounts for particular segments
- exclusivity

iv. Did you come across any further online value proposition techniques that are not covered in the list above?

Besides creating a compelling online value proposition, there are some best practices in the e-commerce world that seem to be commonly applied on successful e-commerce sites. The following checklist is created based on current best practice Khan (2022) and future trends Huynh (2021) among e-commerce practitioners.

18 best practices for e-commerce websites

- ✓ use big and clear images/360 degrees view
- ✓ use demonstration videos
- ✓ review options for augmented reality
- ✓ add a prominent call-to-action
- ✓ ensure easy navigation between pages
- ✓ create urgency by applying the scarcity principle
- ✓ ensure clear pricing
- ✓ display logos/badges to instil trust
- ✓ use real customer reviews
- ✓ have a stock meter and keep it updated
- ✓ write clear product descriptions using the language of your target audience
- ✓ help users to find similar products on your site to allow for upselling/cross-selling
- ✓ outline clear shipping and returns policy
- ✓ enable live chat and/or chatbots for 24/7 customer support
- ✓ review your website's speed
- ✓ offer diverse payment methods
- ✓ offer subscription and loyalty programmes
- ✓ offer personalized product recommendations

Worksheet 5 in the Additional Resources provides help in checking corporate and commercial websites according to best practices.

Marketing automation

One of the main benefits of using digital technologies in marketing is their efficiency to reach large audiences with relatively personalized messages. However, technology is changing ever so quickly and as a result, opportunities for both businesses and consumers arise. This results in an online marketplace that is constantly changing. Consumers have the option to consume media on many different channels and with different levels of involvement.

Biegel (2009) cautioned that consumers are unpredictable and changing consumer behaviour results in challenges to optimize marketing effectiveness. He highlights some of the factors that increase the complexity of the digital commercial world (Biegel, 2009):

- **Media mix optimization:** the allocation of resources across marketing channels, with special attention paid to combinations and sequencing of media selection.

- **Product life cycle compression:** the rate at which products are introduced, marketed and replaced.

- **Privacy rules and regulations:** laws and non-regulated 'best practices' that must be applied to direct and digital marketing initiatives in order to protect consumer data and rights.

- **Corporate governance:** increased requirements for tracking and reporting, driven by internal demands for accountability and external legislation

- **Resource constraints:** heightened economic pressures have hindered the availability of internal resources, forcing management to effectively 'do more' with the same or fewer resources (primarily staff).

- **Globalization:** marketing that was predominantly local in practice in the past has become global – facilitated by the internet and subsequently the ability to interact in real time – creating the need for standardized marketing messaging and content across geographies, suppliers and marketing channels.

As a response to these challenges, marketers are looking for ways to create efficiency in marketing operations that can be achieved through *marketing automation.*

KEY TERM
Marketing automation

The utilization of marketing technology solutions to automate marketing processes including (though not limited to) planning, budgeting, segmentation, database management, analytics, creative execution, asset management, campaign execution, lead management and reporting. These marketing technologies are a combination of software, networks and hardware that allow the inputs, processing and outputs of marketing and business information and content.

SOURCE Biegel, 2009

As with any technology that can potentially replace the interactions between two humans, care needs to be taken to offer a great customer experience. Marketing automation can be applied across the customer life cycle but needs to be carefully managed in order to benefit businesses in three ways, through the creation of personalized workflows, streamlined processes and integrated data analytics (Hubspot, nd). This automation is enabled through software that can track all of the data points when consumers are in touch with a business. These would be impossible to track manually.

There are many tools in the field of marketing automation and the goal is to create a more precise personalization of content to individual customers. Marketing automation is particularly helpful when driving engagement of consumers as it allows for a constant exchange between the business and the consumer without the need for 'real' staff to enable those conversations. Examples of marketing automation applications include (Patel, 2022):

- artificial intelligence (AI) in the form of chatbots that aid in the automation of delivering or collecting information to customers
- automated email delivery that can be customized in terms of timing, quantity, subject matter, triggering and content
- complete abandoned e-commerce purchases with the help of software that sends out follow-up messages to those who have not completed a purchase
- social media automation that ranges from replying to comments, stories and even direct messaging
- automated social media ad campaigns with cross-device and cross-platform retargeting capabilities
- automated in-bound calls with voice-based marketing automation
- automated landing pages based on consumers' interests

As you can see in these examples, marketing automation allows for efficient and effective ways to communicate with consumers. This has advantages for both the business and the consumer. As discussed, businesses require fewer resources to provide the consumer with an individual, personalized support system.

There are many benefits for the consumer (Hubspot, nd). From advertising on social media or receiving emails, marketing automation allows for the consumer to see information that is only relevant to them. Also, marketing automation software allows front-line employees to provide more appropriate help by relying on behavioural data stored in CRM systems. Finally, consumers will be able to get the same experience on different channels. This is enabled as data is collected, stored and used in the marketing automation software to offer services such as pre-filled order forms, targeted emails and personalized customer service (Hubspot, nd).

There are some serious drawbacks to consider, however, as marketing automation can be costly, requires some technical knowledge and can result in too frequent communication with customers leading to disinterest from the consumers' side.

Summary

In this chapter, we have outlined differences between a corporate website and a commercial website. We have reviewed the importance of user experience (UX) design, putting the user at the heart of website design. We have established the Why, What and How of UX. We have further learnt critical success factors for website design, divided into benefits for the consumer and benefits to the business. We have reviewed the difference between front-end and back-end design from a web-development point of view. While most of the success factors for website design can be applied to both corporate and commercial websites, we have looked into the specific case of e-commerce in further detail. The final part of the chapter dealt with marketing automation and outlined how market automation software can help to make the digital communication with consumers more effective and efficient.

Chapter review

Reflective questions

Q1 What is the difference between a corporate and e-commerce website?

Q2 Why is it important to put the user at the heart of website design?

Q3 What are the success factors for website design?

Q4 How does the back-end of web development differ to the front-end?

Q5 What are good practices in e-commerce?

Q6 Where and how can businesses apply marketing automation?

Key learning points

- The user should be key when designing any successful website and one formalized term that is frequently used when considering website design is user experience (UX) design.

- There are some success factors for website design such as entertainment and visual appeal, personalization and reliability.
- Besides creating a compelling online value proposition, using big, clear images, real customer reviews and demonstration videos are some of the factors for successful e-commerce sites.

References

Benitez, J (2021) What is front-end and back-end web development, L Form, 19 October, lform.com/blog/post/what-is-front-end-and-back-end-web-development/#:~:text=Back%2Dend%20development%20is%20the,use%20it%20without%20any%20issues (archived at https://perma.cc/2SPR-AHE9)

Biegel, B (2009) The current view and outlook for the future of marketing automation, *Journal of Data, Direct and Digital Marketing Practices*, 10, 201–13

Bloomenthal, A (2021) E-commerce defined, Investopedia, 16 September, www.investopedia.com/terms/e/ecommerce.asp (archived at https://perma.cc/4XMT-AJ6W)

Boocock, E (2014) YouTube, www.youtube.com/channel/UCjVrBXPI0KV_UhUFSFvzehQ (archived at https://perma.cc/X7P6-F83C)

Daniels, J (2020) Everything you need to know about websites and privacy laws, Squarespace, 30 October, www.webdesignerdepot.com/2020/10/everything-you-need-to-know-about-websites-and-privacy-laws/ (archived at https://perma.cc/YS3U-4W3P)

Fitzgerald, A (2020) What is information architecture and why does it matter, Hubspot, 26 November, blog.hubspot.com/website/information-architecture (archived at https://perma.cc/NNB5-7SN8)

Goldberg, J (2022) E-Commerce sales grew 50% to $879 Billion during the pandemic, *Forbes*, 18 February, www.forbes.com/sites/jasongoldberg/2022/02/18/e-commerce-sales-grew-50-to-870-billion-during-the-pandemic/?sh=673bc5b94e83 (archived at https://perma.cc/3SSU-KZ4V)

Gouthier, M, Nennstiel, C, Kern, N and Wendel, L (2022) The more the better? Data disclosure between the conflicting priorities of privacy concerns, information sensitivity and personalization in e-commerce, *Journal of Business Research*, 148, 174–89

Henderson, P (2022) Creating aesthetically pleasing websites: 5 elements to consider, Hiilite, 2 May, hiilite.com/creating-aesthetically-pleasing-websites/?utm_source=rss&utm_medium=rss&utm_campaign=creating-aesthetically-pleasing-websites (archived at https://perma.cc/U8M3-5M58)

Hubspot (nd) How does marketing automation work? www.hubspot.com/products/marketing/marketing-automation-information (archived at https://perma.cc/8C24-Y35T)

Huynh, T (2021) 15 top e-commerce trends for 2022, Miva, 11 December, blog.miva.com/ecommerce-trends-2022 (archived at https://perma.cc/K44X-2PM6)

Information Architecture Institute (2013) What is information architecture, 2013, www.iainstitute.org/sites/default/files/what_is_ia.pdf (archived at https://perma.cc/ DQ3V-UVTB)

Interaction Design Foundation (2020) User experience (UX) design, www.interaction-design. org/literature/topics/ux-design#:~:text=User%20experience%20(UX)%20design%20 is,%2C%20design%2C%20usability%20and%20function (archived at https://perma.cc/ VMS3-GV8X)

Khan, S (2022) E-commerce product page best practices in 2022, VWO, 4 February, vwo. com/blog/ecommerce-product-page-design/ (archived at https://perma.cc/UV7C-EQDU)

Kritzuk, N (2018) Why companies risk losing customers by not reciprocating on shared data: Rebuilding the data sharing economy in a consumer-driven world, *Journal of Advertising Research*, 58(4), 394–98

Korgaonkar, P, O'Leary, B and Silverblatt, R (2009) Critical factors to successful website development: Opinions of website designers and developers, *International Journal of E-Business Research*, 5(4), 39–54

Ladner, R (2015) Design for user empowerment, IX Interactions, 2 March, interactions.acm. org/archive/view/march-april-2015/design-for-user-empowerment (archived at https:// perma.cc/N6YV-87UR)

Morville, P (2004) User experience design, Semantic Studios, 21 June, semanticstudios.com/ user_experience_design/ (archived at https://perma.cc/2A45-J7RQ)

Nielsen, J (1994/2020) 10 usability heuristics for user interface design, Nielsen Norman Group, 15 November, www.nngroup.com/articles/ten-usability-heuristics/#poster (archived at https://perma.cc/Q8H9-YKYM)

Otalvaro, A (2019) What is one-to-one Marketing: Examples, definitions and more, Vedia, 2 July, www.vedia.ai/blog/one-to-one-marketing-definition/ (archived at https://perma.cc/ Z4W2-3T8P)

Patel, N (2022) Marketing automation: What is it, examples and tools, neilpatel.com/blog/ marketing-automation-tools/ (archived at https://perma.cc/6DTU-JSGT)

Peppers, D and Rogers, M (2000) Papers: Build a one-to-one learning relationship with your customers, *Interactive Marketing*, 1(3), 243–50

Techslang (nd) What is backend development, www.techslang.com/definition/what-is-backend-development/ (archived at https://perma.cc/77JW-LUFT)

TechTarget (2005) HCI (human-computer-interaction), www.techtarget.com/ searchsoftwarequality/definition/HCI-human-computer-interaction (archived at https:// perma.cc/4DFW-7CH4)

Toptal (nd) Colourblind web page filter, www.toptal.com/designers/colorfilter (archived at https://perma.cc/S4VU-GUGE)

Twin, A (2022) Value proposition, Investopedia, 10 March, www.investopedia.com/terms/v/ valueproposition.asp (archived at https://perma.cc/YN36-6AD5)

Walter, Z (2022) What is gamification, Gamify, www.gamify.com/what-is-gamification (archived at https://perma.cc/9AUN-GB8B)

WeAreCom (2020) Corporate website, www.wearecom.fr/en/dictionnaire/corporate-site/#:~:text=Corporate%20website,to%20its%20customers%20or%20users (archived at https://perma.cc/6ABT-QX65)

Social media marketing channels and concepts

17

By the end of this chapter, you should be able to:

- Understand the importance of social media channels for digital marketing campaigns
- Elaborate on how content marketing and influencer marketing are important concepts of social media marketing.
- Evaluate the advantages and disadvantages of the different social media channels and concepts.

Introduction

When implementing a digital marketing strategy, objectives need to be set, the digital marketing mix needs to be adjusted, and digital tools, techniques and technology implemented to assist the digital marketing strategy execution. In this chapter, we will review social media marketing channels including the use of content and influencer marketing.

Social media marketing

Social media has allowed both consumers and businesses to find new ways of communicating with each other. With over 4.5 billion social media users in the world, the opportunities to connect seem endless (Dollarhide, 2021). Consumers are using social media channels to chat with each other, learn about new products and share content they deem interesting or relevant to others.

Obar and Wildman (2015, p745) reviewed numerous definitions of social media and came up with the following commonalities among those definitions:

- User-generated content is the lifeblood of social media.
- Individuals and groups create user-specific profiles for a site or app designed and maintained by a social media service.
- Social media services facilitate the development of social networks online by connecting a profile with those of other individuals and/or groups.

The two main aspects of social media seem to be the importance of user-generated content as well as connectivity between the users. Li et al (2021) establish that social media has changed the marketplace in three fundamental ways:

1 Social media allows businesses and customers to connect in ways that have not been possible in the past.

2 Social media has changed how firms and customers interact and influence each other.

3 The amount of data created through social media has made it progressively possible for businesses to improve the management of customer relationships and enable informed decision-making in business.

If we take those ways in which social media has changed the marketplace we need to consider *social media marketing* to understand how those changes to the marketplace can be strategically managed.

KEY TERM
Social media marketing

Social media marketing is a form of digital marketing that uses social networking platforms to increase brand and product exposure and to cultivate relationships with consumers.

SOURCE Digital Marketing Institute, nd

The key term definition shows that the aim of social media marketing is two-fold. First of all, it is aimed at amplifying brand exposure. This means that businesses use social media channels to highlight their products and brands. This is important as research shows that particularly younger age groups are using social media channels to discover new brands, research products and listen to comments on social media channels to influence their product choice (GWI, 2022).

Secondly, social media marketing is all about building relationships with consumers. There are a number of different channels that count towards social media and can be utilized for social media marketing strategies:

- social networks
- blogs
- micro-blogs
- forums
- social media bookmarking
- wikis
- customer ratings sites
- online video websites
- digital photo websites

Activity 17.1

You have now been introduced to social media and social media marketing.

i. Please visit Erik Qualman's YouTube channel (aka Equalman) and watch his video titled 'Digital Transformation Video by Erik Qualman'.

ii. Can you divide these trends into the two aims of social media: increasing brand exposure and building relationships with consumers?

iii. Are there any figures that you find particularly surprising, and if so why?

Social media marketing process

Executing a social media marketing campaign requires research and planning. Too often businesses set up profiles on various social media channels and platforms without having a clear idea of what they want to post and how they want to represent themselves. There is also a lack of knowledge about what kind of customers (if any) are present on those chosen platforms. This results in a scattered picture of businesses on several social media channels with infrequent, often unfitting posts that do not utilize the advantages that social media marketing has to offer.

While some of the terminologies differ depending on the source, there are generally six main steps recommended to follow when executing a successful social media campaign (Figure 17.1).

Figure 17.1 Social media marketing process

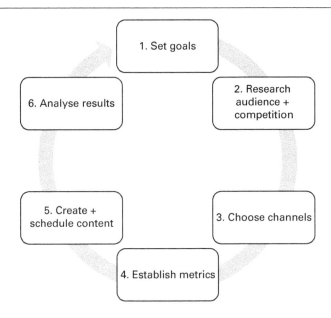

1. Set goals/objectives (What do you want to achieve?)

The first step of the process is to set *social media goals* to understand what the social media marketing campaign actually aims to achieve. Goals should be kept realistic to ensure that the social media marketing strategy is both reasonable and affordable (Barnhart, 2021).

> **KEY TERM**
> Social media goal
>
> A social media goal is a statement about what you want to achieve with a specific social marketing tactic or your whole social strategy. Good social media goals align with broader business objectives. Examples of common social media goals include generating leads, driving traffic to a website or online store, or getting more followers.
>
> **SOURCE** Sides, 2022

Goals for social media marketing campaigns vary greatly from company to company. Research shows the following top social media marketing goals for businesses (Barnhart, 2020):

- increase brand awareness
- sales/lead generation

- increase community engagement
- grow brand's audience
- increase web traffic

Li et al (2021) divide strategic social media objectives into four distinct strategies, depending on what the business aims to achieve:

- **Social commerce strategy:** where the goal is to promote and sell with a one-way interaction from the business.
- **Social content strategy:** where the goal is to connect and collaborate with a firm-initiated two-way interaction.
- **Social monitoring strategy:** where the goal is to listen and learn with a customer-initiated two-way interaction.
- **Social customer relationship management strategy:** where the goal is to empower and engage through a collaborative interaction between the business and the consumer.

The categorization suggested by Li et al (2021) helps to keep goals realistic as businesses can review the depths of customer interactions. Setting goals is essential as goals hold the social media marketing execution accountable, guide budgets and encourage businesses to pay attention to the data (Barnhart, 2020).

2. Research audience and competition (Who are you targeting and what is the competition doing?)

It is essential for any successful social media marketing campaign to research its target audience as well as review what the competition is doing on social media platforms. One main advantage of digital technologies is the availability of data, and most of the information businesses need to research the targeted audience is readily available online. Some of the following aspects should be reviewed in order to get an idea about the intended audiences' behaviour on social media:

- recognizing which channels the target audience is using
- establishing the style and tone that the targeted audience prefers (e.g. formal vs non-formal)
- reviewing the demographic of the target audience
- researching influencers in the targeted social media space

It is useful to understand that different platforms attract different audiences. For example, both Facebook and YouTube are lucrative places for advertising due to their high-earning user base (Barnhart, 2021). LinkedIn's users are highly educated making it a good channel for in-depth industry-specific content.

Activity 17.2

We have looked into the importance of researching the intended target audience for a social media marketing campaign.

i. Search for the brand 'Innocent Smoothies' on Facebook and read their posts and comments made in response by users.

ii. Try to establish the style and tone that the brand is using on Facebook.

iii. Could they use the same style and tone on another social media platform?

iv. What demographic do you think is being targeted and why?

Businesses also need to look into what the competition is doing on social media platforms. This allows businesses to see where the competition can be found and what they seem to be doing well. It might also help to understand what is expected in an industry (Baker, 2022). There are two opportunities once the competition has been reviewed: either try to enter the same space; or serve an underutilized social media channel neglected by the competition.

3. Decide which channels to use (Where do you find your audience and which channels are best fit to achieve your goals?)

One of the most important decisions to make in any social media marketing strategy is to decide which channel to share the content on. Doing the first two steps of the social media marketing process allows for an informed choice. The chosen channels must allow a business to achieve the set goals and the targeted audience must be present. For example, if a business tried to increase brand awareness among middle-aged male customers, Pinterest would not be a wise choice as women vastly outnumber men on Pinterest (Barnhart, 2021).

Zhu and Chen (2015) divide social media channels into content- and profile-based. They classify profile-based social media as the individual member being the focal point and establish that connections are mainly made because users are interested in the user behind the profile. On content-based social media, on the other hand, users make connections because they like the content of certain profiles. Examples of profile-based social media are Facebook, Twitter and WhatsApp and content-based social media channels are seen as Instagram, Pinterest and YouTube (Zhu and Chen, 2015). There are some considerations to make when choosing the right social media platform relevant to their goals:

- Consider the audience with regard to demographics including location and on which platform they might be users.

- Think about how the business fits onto the chosen platform in terms of style and tone.

- Decide who will be the voice of the business and how the business will respond to negative comments.

Please see the Additional Supporting Resources online for an overview of some of the most common social media platforms including user figures, audience, the industry impact (B2C = business to consumer; B2B = business-to-business) and what the platform is best utilized for (UG = user-generated content).

4. Establish metrics and KPIs

Social media marketing strategies have to be data-driven to establish whether the set goals have been achieved. Metrics and *key performance indicators* (KPI) provide information about how the chosen social media channels are performing. They also highlight areas that require improvement (Carmicheal, 2022). KPIs are relevant to overall business strategy but should also be applied to the social media context. Digital KPIs and metrics are discussed in detail in Chapter 20. In the following section, we will highlight those metrics particularly relevant to social media marketing.

KEY TERM
Key performance indicators (KPIs)

Key performance indicators refer to a set of quantifiable measurements used to gauge a company's overall long-term performance. KPIs specifically help determine a company's strategic, financial and operational achievements, especially compared to those of other businesses within the same sector.

SOURCE Twin, 2022

Most social media channels offer their own analytics to review. For example, Facebook has an Insights tab, Twitter offers Twitter Analytics, and on other platforms such as Instagram and Pinterest businesses need to set up a business account before accessing data (Chen, 2021).

The following are some of the most relevant metrics and KPIs for social media marketing campaigns.

Engagement   Engagement is essential to measure in order to understand how well a business is perceived by its audience and how willing the audience is to interact

(Baker, 2022). Engaged users interact with brands on social media through 'likes', comments and social sharing (Chen, 2021). Carmicheal (2022) describes social media engagement as 'the total number of likes, comments, shares and general interactions a piece of content or social media account receives relative to the size of the audience'.

The following formula can be used to measure the overall engagement rate of a social media account (Carmicheal, 2022):

Engagement Rate = Number of Engagements / Number of Followers × 100

Other crucial engagement indicators relate to organic mentions such as @example if these are not promoted or paid for by the social media platform (Chen, 2021).

Activity 17.3

You have now been introduced to how engagement can be measured on social media channels.

i.   Scroll through your Instagram feed and look for commercial messages.

ii. Try to find one that has many likes, shares, saves and comments and one that has very few likes, shares, saves and comments. Both posts do not need to be from the same brand.

iii. Can you identify the reasons why one post seems to have resulted in high engagement and the other one did not?

Reach   Reach is a metric that describes the number of unique users who saw a post (Barnhart, 2021). It is essential to differentiate between *impressions* and *reach* according to Chen (2021).

KEY TERM
Impressions/reach

Impressions: are how many times a post shows up in someone's timeline.

Reach: is the potential unique viewers a post could have (usually your follower count plus accounts that shared the post's follower counts).

Both reach and impressions are relevant metrics as they allow a business to evaluate how different types of content are resonating with an audience across different platforms (Carmicheal, 2022).

Other metrics that help determine reach are (Chen, 2021):

- follower count
- post reach
- web traffic
- *share of voice*

KEY TERM
Share of voice (SOV)

Share of voice establishes how much online visibility a company has compared to its competitors. SOV does not come readily available in native analytics. Instead, companies need to decide on keywords, hashtags or categories on which it wants to focus. For example, if a company wants to see its SOV around topics related to coffee, it would compile a list of hashtags and keywords to look at. Then information needs to be gathered on how often the brand is mentioned with these words compared to the total number of times the key terms are mentioned overall.

Hashtag performance   Knowing which hashtags have been most used and associated with the company can help influence the content going forward (Barnhart, 2021).

Clicks   The number of clicks on social media content or a business account is important to track as it helps to understand consumer behaviour.

Sentiment   Sentiment describes how users react to social media content, a brand or hashtag (Baker, 2022). There are various tools online to determine how users and consumers are talking about a brand or campaign.

5. Create and schedule engaging content

Businesses need to post content in social media marketing campaigns that stands out and engages their audience to follow, like and/or share (Baker, 2022). Some of the following recommendations can help when creating engaging content (Baker, 2022):

- conducting market research helps to understand audience needs, wants and interests
- reviewing what seems to be working for the competition can spark ideas

- taking advantage of unique features (e.g. live streaming) of social media platforms can help with innovative ways to engage consumers
- reposting customer's content and encouraging hashtag usage can engage consumers
- reviewing trends on different social media platforms and joining in can lead to engaged consumers

It is important to follow the same style and tone when creating content as it helps consumers to recognize a brand. Consistent and recognizable content can be created while posting different formats such as memes, product photos and even user-generated content by, for example, sticking to a defined colour scheme (Barnhart, 2021). Creating engaging content is crucial for successful social media marketing campaigns and we will cover content marketing as a separate digital asset later on in this chapter.

Scheduling social media content is an easy way to ensure that content is shared as planned and at times that are most suitable to engage the consumer. There are plenty of social media management solution tools on the market that let companies prepare and schedule posts in advance.

The frequency of posting content varies a great deal between brands, industries and platforms. General recommendations state that it should depend on when a brand/company has something relevant to say. Baker (2022) states that posting content should be about quality rather than quantity. McLachlan (2021) conducted research on the optimum posting frequency per platform and suggests the following:

- on Instagram, post between 3 and 7 times per week
- on Facebook, post between 1 and 2 times a day
- on Twitter, post between 1 and 5 tweets a day
- on LinkedIn, post between 1 and 5 times a day

The best time to post also varies greatly between industry and platform but there are some general guidelines on when to post that can be particularly helpful when a business is starting out. After a while, each business should review its own posting schedule and change it from time to time to see which times seem most suitable for its target audience. Barnhart (2021) warns that companies should be available to respond to comments or queries after something has been posted so one consideration for when to post is whether someone will be available to respond. Cooper (2021) analysed 30,000 social media posts and found days and times that universally get more engagement:

- the best time to post on Facebook is 8.00 am to 12.00 pm on Tuesdays and Thursdays
- the best time to post on Instagram is 11.00 am on Wednesdays

- the best time to post on Twitter is 8.00 am on Mondays and Thursdays
- the best time to post on LinkedIn is 9.00 am on Tuesdays and Wednesdays

6. Analyse results

The final step of any social media marketing campaign and strategy should be the analysis of what is working and what is not working. These results should inform how you adapt and adjust your next campaign. Barnhart (2021) suggests being reactive in the short term to get the most out of running campaigns and then proactively using the collected data to inform the next campaign. Measuring whether social media marketing efforts are actually helping to achieve the set goals requires the tracking of all posts on every channel. This can be done by reviewing *social media metrics.*

> **KEY TERM**
> Social media metrics
>
> Social media metrics are data related to the success of your posts and your impact on your audience and customers on various platforms. These metrics may include data about your level of engagement, likes, follows, shares, and all other interactions on each platform.
>
> **SOURCE** Baker, 2022

Following the suggested six steps can help to create a successful social media marketing strategy. One of the main measures of success is how well a campaign managed to engage its users. Engagement of users often includes the willingness of consumers to share particular content. Chen et al (2011) find that consumers' choices and consumer behaviour are influenced by online social interactions. Li et al (2021) agree that researchers have realized the relevancy of social media in affecting consumer decisions for a long time. Social media channels are particularly useful in reaching and engaging a large number of people in a relatively short period of time when content is shared frequently and goes 'viral'.

Viral marketing

Businesses are keen for their content posted on social media to reach large audiences. One of the advantages of social media is that content can easily and quickly be shared with a large number of users through the use of *viral marketing*. This is not only cost-efficient for businesses but also allows them to reach target audiences rapidly.

KEY TERM
Viral marketing

Viral marketing seeks to spread information about a product or service from person to person by word of mouth or sharing via the internet or email. The goal of viral marketing is to inspire individuals to share a marketing message to friends, family, and other individuals to create exponential growth in the number of its recipients.

SOURCE Kagan, 2022

Many social media marketing campaigns aim to create viral campaigns as they can increase reach and their customer base. However, there is very limited research on exactly how viral content can be created.

Tellis et al (2019) tested factors that influence sharing behaviour on a number of different platforms. They found that positive emotions of amusement, excitement, inspiration and warmth positively affect sharing and that drama elements such as surprise, plot and characters, including babies, animals and celebrities, arouse emotions. Another finding is that people are more likely to share moderately long ads (1.2 to 1.7 minutes) compared to very long or very short ads (Tellis et al, 2019). The things that seem to prevent sharing have been found to be the prominent placement of brand names and ads whose content is very strongly information focused.

Activity 17.4

We have now covered viral marketing and how important it is to social media marketing success.

i.   Try to remember the last time that you shared a commercial post on either Instagram or Facebook.

ii. Now try to remember roughly at what time (morning, midday or evening) you shared that post.

iii. Compare when you shared the post with the suggestions of Cooper (2021) of when content should be shared in order to most successfully engage consumers. The best times to post are:

   – 8.00 am to 12.00 pm on Tuesdays and Thursdays on Facebook

   – 11.00 am on Wednesdays on Instagram

iv. Did your sharing behaviour fit within the suggested time slot?

v.   If not, why do you think that could be?

vi. Can you think of reasons why you shared that particular post?

Theories underpinning social media marketing

The use of social media in a marketing context is relatively new compared to more established marketing communication techniques such as television or billboard advertising. Compared to the first billboard advertising (as we know it today) from 1889 social media marketing is in its infancy (Chappel, 2022).

Despite or maybe even because of its relative novelty, it is essential to understand some of the theories underpinning social media usage. In the following section, we will review some of the most relevant theories that have been applied in a social media marketing context.

Uses and gratification theory

The uses and gratification (U&G) theory was established in the late 1940s with the aim to understand how individuals use media to fulfil their needs and wants (Hossain et al, 2019). The theory postulates that users know their needs, motivations and expectations of the media, leading to media choice and gratification. This theory has extensively been applied to understand the reasons for individuals' use of different social networking sites.

Papacharissi and Mendelson (2011) examined motivations for the use of Facebook, applying U&G, and found the following nine motives:

- habitual pastime
- relaxing entertainment
- for expressive information sharing
- as a source of cool and new trends
- escape
- professional advancement
- companionship
- new friendships
- social interaction

Another study that applied U&G in the social media marketing context is that by De Oliveira and Huertas (2015). It suggested that subjective norms, social identity, group norms, entertainment and interpersonal interconnectivity positively impact user satisfaction on Facebook.

These research examples show how well the uses and gratification theory can be applied to understand drivers and motivations for consumers' social media behaviour. This is essential to businesses as it allows a deeper understanding of the target audience.

Social exchange theory

The social exchange theory (SET) was first introduced in 1964 by Peter Blau with the aim of understanding social structures. This understanding was based on the analysis of social processes that influence the relations between individuals and groups (Blau, 1986). The theory 'describes the behaviour during long- and short-term relationships where tangible (i.e. money) and intangible resources (i.e. social support) are exchanged' (Wang et al, 2022). The theory argues that over time social exchanges are made between people creating trust, affection and loyalty (Blau, 1986). It further states that individuals take part in an internal analysis to determine costs vs benefits before engaging in any social exchanges (Thaichon et al, 2018).

This is essential for a social media marketing context as the application of this theory could aid businesses to understand how such positive outcomes might be achieved by building a relationship with customers on digital channels. Ferm and Thaichon (2021) apply SET to determine social media drivers and their influence on attitudinal loyalty. They found that there are demographics as well as behavioural and perceptual differences among consumers that need to be taken into consideration.

Itani et al (2020) apply SET to determine whether a seller's relationship efforts encourage the buyer to share their market intelligence based on the concept of reciprocity. Simply put, the researchers tried to identify whether consumers give back if they feel as if they have received something. They found that the use of social media does enhance the competitive information collection abilities of the seller, meaning the consumer is more likely to share information with the seller.

Advantages and disadvantages of social media marketing

We have presented a lot of information about social media marketing in this part of the chapter, ranging from defining social media marketing to outlining six steps that help when setting up a social media campaign. We have reviewed how different channels work better for different target audiences. Viral marketing is an important part of social media marketing and finally, theories underpin how social media usage can be explained. In summary, we have listed the advantages and disadvantages of social media marketing from the company's viewpoint partly based on Davis (2022).

Table 17.1 Advantages and disadvantages of social media marketing

Advantages	Disadvantages
• Improved customer relationships	• Time-consuming
• Higher customer satisfaction	• Requirement of skilled knowledge base
• Helps to engage with consumers	• Exposed to competition
• Improved brand awareness	• Uncontrolled (negative) feedback
• Improved consumer knowledge	• High maintenance
• Cost-effective	• Possible slow return on investment
• Reach large audiences	
• In-bound traffic building	

Davis, 2022

PRACTITIONER INPUT
Ross Middleham (2)

Ross Middleham is Creative Lead for the UK's Meteorological Office (the Met Office), the home of weather and climate science.

Would you introduce the organization that you are working for?

The Met Office is funded by Government to provide a national weather service for all citizens of the UK. A critical part of this remit is to equip them with information to take appropriate decisions/actions to stay safe, particularly during severe weather.

I oversee design, video and social media production, setting the direction for our social channels and ensuring we publish timely and engaging content. I deliver positive creative leadership and clear brand direction by visibly encouraging future thinking and championing a culture of creativity. I work to empower the creation of consistent, accessible, high-quality interactions across all Met Office products and services.

How important is multichannel/omnichannel marketing for your digital marketing campaigns?

Tailoring our content across multiple channels is crucial. At the Met Office we operate much like a newsroom or content publisher. We have two meetings a day to agree key messages to make sure we are telling a consistent story across all our content, regardless of platform.

In February 2022, three named storms (Dudley, Eunice, Franklin) affected the UK within a week – an unprecedented event with two rare red warnings issued. Our objective during this crisis was to fulfil our remit as detailed, using social media channels. Quantifiably, we wanted to increase followers by 80k across channels.

As a turnaround time/resources were stretched, we needed clear focus areas to achieve the maximum reach, impact and engagement. We built on the success of previous formats, leveraging our relationships with partners/channels, choosing innovative ways to reach audiences, tailored by channel. Building on our progress on TikTok, this was an important way to reach a younger demographic. We made a series of presenter-led, quick forecasts, designed to grab attention, encouraging comments/sharing. We contacted TikTok, who featured #stormeunice on their home tab and promoted our content.

The implementation period began six days before the first storm was due using our longer-form, YouTube formats, providing a generic weather overview and talking around what was to come. We set hashtags on Twitter to centre conversations around our authoritative advice. We ran a dynamic 'One Minute Brief', working in real time, setting a creative challenge which went live as we issued the red warning.

This provided over 230 creative responses promoting our information to diverse audiences, with a number being featured in the creative press.

We partnered with RNLI on Twitter Spaces, knowing that Twitter was pushing this feature, allowing us to provide real-time safety updates/advice, along with direct user engagement. We contacted Twitter who featured our Spaces in the Spotlight tab. We created a schedule for going live across channels, knowing this is where we would get the most engagement and watch time, creating longer-form content discussing uncertainty/impacts. YouTube featured our live feed on their homepage driving views/subscribers, resulting in the biggest views ever of our channel in one day.

One main advantage of digital media is the ability to create a two-way dialogue with your audience. Do you see that as important for your organization and the success of your digital marketing campaigns?

Creating a conversation around your content is really important. To help, content that triggers an emotion is normally a good starting point. Around the storms we set hashtags on Twitter to centre conversations around our authoritative advice. It was important for us to lead the conversations and be seen as the go-to source, not only to help us reach more people but also to help combat disinformation.

We had lots of engagement on all content and it was important that we gave people the opportunity to ask us questions. Our first Facebook Live of the storm week had over 1.1k comments. Our final (on Friday) had over 2.6k comments, over 75k views and 1.8k likes/loves. When the live feature was first released, we used to be very formal and newsroom like with our content, but lockdown and the rise of other platforms, like TikTok, have changed that. We now find that a presenter-led, more informal approach brings us more engagement. People see the more serious side of the presenters in front of the weather map across a lot of our other content, and we find that live feeds provide the chance to show a friendlier, human side.

We do different types of live feed across our platforms to make each feel like it's a unique offering. For example, on Facebook we might have a presenter in front of screens, showing the weather charts. On TikTok we tend to have the presenter outside talking to their phone, and on Instagram we have invited guests to join conversations. Calling out names and comments is the key to making the audience feel involved – playing on the thrill of waiting to be name-checked. Physically responding in the comments is also great for the algorithms, as it highlights engagement on the lives is high.

Twitter Spaces also now provides us the opportunity to have real-time engagement with people. We have used this format to not only invite other trusted partners to speak with us, but also to allow members of the public to join and have their say. This makes for an engaging listen, with a variety of voices and opinions.

Do you actively encourage the opportunity for consumers to talk with each other in your digital marketing campaigns?

Perhaps unexpectedly, at the Met Office we also have a team called the 'Weather Desk' who monitor social media around the clock. They will respond to questions and queries on Twitter. In fact if you tweet us for a forecast, we aim to reply within 20 minutes, letting you know what you can expect in your area. Weather can be a highly emotive subject and the subject of accuracy is often at the centre of it. By using the Weather Desk team, along with tools like Brandwatch, we're able to identify and get us involved at the heart of any conversations around weather and climate.

We find that we have pockets of highly engaged weather and climate enthusiasts. For example, on YouTube we have people who regularly comment and have conversations with others in the comments. We also have a very active Press Office team who work with the media to make sure our accurate messaging and content is published. They drive the stories and set the news agenda, countering fake news, rife in the weather sector. To help with this, we increasingly have highlighted uncertainty in our various formats. Most notably we do this in our popular '10-day trend' YouTube video, where the presenter talks through the various models to give an indication of the longer-term forecasts. We find by arming our followers with the information, they help to self-police any negativity on our social channels.

One area we are exploring, but resource constrains us slightly, is around either starting or becoming more involved in Facebook Groups. This feature shows no sign of dwindling in popularity, and can be a useful way to get your content into already highly engaged communities.

What is typical data that you would be collecting to evaluate whether a campaign has been successful?

Regarding the February storms, our key objective was to make people aware of the storm impacts and take appropriate action. We use a range of methods to help evaluate whether activity has been successful. Those things range from public perception surveys through to using Google and in-app analytics to measure reach and engagement of specific content. We also use a social media management tool called Falcon, which is part of the Brandwatch suite, and allows us to run reports per channel and also do real-time social listening.

In this case, our public surveys show that the average awareness for storms is 87 per cent. Awareness of the warnings for Storms Dudley/Eunice scored much higher with 97 per cent and 98 per cent. This was coupled with 87 per cent of people surveyed saying they took action with four out of five people changing their travel plans/staying in.

Our aim was to convert our increased reach gaining an extra 80k followers – we exceeded this with an extra 125.5k followers. Our biggest riser was TikTok with 47k new followers. In the space of 9 days (14–22 February), we received 5.4 million video views. Two videos had over 1.4/1.5 million views respectively. We generated over 300 new followers from three lives, with over 13k viewers/12k likes.

We successfully drove the social news agenda partnering with TikTok, Twitter and YouTube to feature and endorse our content as the authoritative voice during this crisis countering fake news. We were able to capture anecdotal evidence in the comments of our posts to show that people were aware of and understood our warnings and were taking appropriate action to stay safe.

It is worth noting that getting useful, actionable insights is hard. It is easy to become distracted by large vanity metrics, but the real value comes from looking at how well specific content types are behaving over a period of time. For example, looking at drop-off rates on Facebook videos can help you make improvements around retention rates. By analysing some of our formats we recognized the need to start our content with the key messages, rather than bringing them in 10 seconds in, by which time a high proportion of our audience had stopped watching. Setting a baseline and then tracking a few improvements can be much more manageable than trying to tackle everything at once.

Content marketing

Content marketing is probably the single most important part of any social media marketing campaign. In order for social media marketing to be successful, content needs to be relevant, interesting and engaging to consumers. However, creating relevant content goes beyond social media marketing, and should be a consideration in its own right as a part of a successful digital marketing strategy.

KEY TERM
Content marketing

Content marketing is a strategic marketing approach focused on creating and distributing valuable, relevant and consistent content to attract and retain a clearly defined audience – and, ultimately, to drive profitable customer action.

SOURCE Content Marketing Institute, 2022

As you can see from the definition, content marketing is all about creating content that is relevant to its audience with the aim to create profitable customer action. The internet has allowed for content marketing to reach new levels in terms of how created content can be presented and consumed. However, the idea of content marketing is much older than the internet. Neil Patel (nd) argues that Marvel Comics had already perfected the art of content marketing in the 1980s when they published stories centred around superheroes. Only two months after publishing the first comic book, about 20 per cent of their target audience (boys between 5 and 12 years) owned two or more toys present in the comic book (Neil Patel, nd).

The example shows that the content in the comics was deemed to be valuable by consumers, who reacted by wanting to own something directly related to that content. The key factor in content marketing is to create content that consumers value. This makes it a very subjective form of marketing as one consumer might find a piece of content highly valuable whereas another recipient might not receive any value from it (Steimle, 2014).

Three main takeaways from Rowley (2008) are that content is contextual, can easily be reproduced and can be 'repackaged' to fit different audiences.

Activity 17.5

You have now learnt what content marketing is and we have covered some of its challenges.

i. Please visit the Content Marketing Institute's YouTube channel (CMWorld) and watch the video titled 'How Red Bull turned their content marketing into a media company'.

ii. How has content marketing helped Red Bull to become such a successful brand? What seem to be the benefits of content marketing?

iii. Can you think of challenges that Red Bull might have encountered through content marketing?

Mixing different forms of content

There are many different forms of content that digital marketers can choose from when creating a content marketing strategy. Businesses need to consider what type of content promotes their business and brand effectively. The Content Marketing Institute recommends the following steps for running successful content marketing operations (Rose, 2016):

- **Purpose and goals:** Why you are creating content and what value it will provide.
- **Audience:** For whom you are creating content and how they will benefit.
- **Story:** What specific, unique and valuable ideas you will build your content assets around.
- **Process:** How you will structure and manage your operations to activate your plans.

- **Measurement:** How you will gauge performance and continually optimize your efforts.

One of the essential questions to ask yourself as a content marketer is why content is created and what value it will provide. Are you planning on entertaining your audience or convincing them to buy something? If we take the Marvel Comic example from earlier, the books were meant to entertain the audience, and the purchasing of merchandise was a natural reaction from the consumer. If we take content such as testimonials or customer reviews published by a business, the goal of convincing the audience to purchase the product is much more upfront.

There are endless formats of content such as branded videos, webinars, blogs, memes and podcasts. The content varies in its main purpose. For example, while branded videos are good for entertainment, webinars are better suited to educate an audience. For a complete overview of content marketing types and their purposes see the additional online material.

Some types of content have been around for a while as they have proven a good way to create value and others, e.g. *internet memes*, are relatively new.

KEY TERM
Internet memes

An internet meme is an activity, concept, catchphrase or piece of media that gains popularity and spreads rapidly via the internet. An internet meme is often helped along by social networking sites and blogs that post and repost popular memes and, in doing so, reinforce the popularity of the memes.

SOURCE Techopedia, 2020

As opposed to internet memes, white papers and case studies have long been used to present relevant information to consumers. However, the way content is consumed online is changing and as such businesses need to be aware of trends and changes among their target audience to be best equipped to deliver valuable content. Content used to be very text-heavy, especially in the early days of the internet, with many businesses having blogs to share relevant information with their target audience. However, today many prefer visual content such as pictures and videos.

The following content trends have been identified for 2022 (Barnhart, 2021):

- **Stories and time-sensitive content:** this type of content helps to remain relevant and is becoming popular among consumers.
- **Short-form video:** this type of content is highly engaging.
- **Content relevant to certain causes:** content that covers relevant themes such as sustainability efforts helps to personalize a brand.

There are some general rules that aim to help digital marketers to get the balance right in terms of what type of content to post. Pack (2017) outlines the 4-1-1 and 70-20-10 Rules. The 4-1-1 Rule states that for every six pieces of content created by a business, four of those should be entertaining and new to the audience, one piece of content can be a soft promotion (e.g. news relevant to the business) and one piece of content can be hard promotion (e.g. including a call to action to buy something).

The 70-20-10 Rule is similar in that it guides businesses to focus 70 per cent of their content on adding value to their audience, 20 per cent of the content can be from others (e.g. tagging an article about someone else to get content) and 10 per cent of the content can contain hard promotional content (Pack, 2017).

These rules are just very basic guidelines on how to structure your content in terms of which purpose your content serves. Constantly creating content that is relevant and entertaining to an audience is very difficult to even the most well-resourced content marketing team let alone small and medium-sized enterprises that have less time and budget available. One widely practised way of producing content is that of content curation.

Content curation

Content curation is a valuable way for content marketers to produce valuable content to share with their audience. It is helpful to think of what a museum curator does in order to understand content curation. Think of a museum curator who selects the art pieces to include and arrange in an exhibit. The curators do not create any of the art themselves but do know their audience, so they choose pieces that they know will create a valuable experience for the audience (Gynn, 2022).

Essentially, it is the same with *content curation*. While content marketers do not come up with the content themselves, they arrange content created by others in a way that suits their target audience.

KEY TERM
Content curation

Content curation is the process of finding and collecting online content and presenting the best pieces in a structured way. Unlike content marketing, curation does not involve creating your own content. Instead, you are researching and sharing information created by other people that your audience will appreciate and respond to. Like all other aspects of marketing, content curation adds value to your brand and creates lasting relationships with your customers.

SOURCE Big Commerce, nd

There are different ways in which content can be curated and delivered to an audience. The overarching goal should be to provide information to a target audience that eliminates the need for them to research related topics elsewhere (Big Commerce, nd). This could be curated content shared in the form of an email newsletter, sharing on social media or creating blog posts. For example, some businesses publish 'Best of' blog posts wherein they curate articles over a specific period of time and then publish those on a specific day of the week or month (Big Commerce, nd). Ann Gynn from the Content Marketing Institute recommends the following innovative ways to curate content (Gynn, 2022):

1 Offer a list of relevant reading, listening or viewing.

2 Write an original article by tailoring others' content for your audience.

3 Simplify social threads.

4 Bring together multiple sources.

5 Go deep on a topic.

6 Make something new from something you already created.

Digital marketers agree that there are many benefits to content curation but also warn that there are pitfalls to consider. Content curators must always credit their sources and avoid passing off curated content as something original (Martin, 2022). If done correctly, the following list highlights some of the benefits of content curation (Gynn, 2022; Armitage, 2021; Martin 2022):

- adds value to an audience by finding content and preparing it to fulfil the specific needs of that audience
- builds trust with your audience by only presenting content relevant to them
- creates perception as a thought leader/go-to resource for a specific topic
- enables creation of more content with less effort
- saves time
- helps search engine optimization through link building

Activity 17.6

You have now learnt about content curation and about the different forms in which content can be curated.

i. Search for Porsche on Instagram and try to find content that seems to be curated.

ii. *Remember:* curated content is not produced by the business itself but is shared from someone else.

iii. What value do you see in the posts that Porsche is sharing that are not originally created by the company?

User-generated content (UGC)

One main way in which numerous brands are curating their content is by using ***user-generated content*** in the form of images, videos, testimonials and other social media content. UGC is a powerful way to demonstrate to consumers that there is a relationship between the brand and the user. It also shows that a business is listening to what consumers have to say and as such values their opinion.

KEY TERM
User-generated content

User-generated content (also known as UGC or consumer-generated content) is original, brand-specific content created by customers and published on social media or other channels. UGC comes in many forms, including images, videos, reviews, a testimonial, or even a podcast.

SOURCE Beveridge, 2022

There are several reasons why it is important for content marketers to take UGC on board and aim to make it part of their content marketing strategy. A study of more than 1,000 online shoppers revealed the following key findings that demonstrate the importance and relevancy of UGC (TurnTo Networks, 2017):

- Nearly a quarter of female shoppers consider UGC to be the most influential marketing tool.
- Shoppers under 30 report a greater influence of UGC in purchasing decisions vs older respondents. Of those aged 18 to 29, 97 per cent report UGC has an extreme influence.
- Nearly two-thirds of shoppers believe UGC creates a more authentic shopping experience.
- Nearly three-quarters say UGC increases their purchasing confidence.
- Nearly two-thirds report UGC encourages them to engage with brands.

The above figures demonstrate the huge importance for businesses of using UGC in their content marketing. You can see direct influences of UGC on purchasing decisions, the authenticity of a shopping experience, higher purchasing confidence and encouragement to be engaged with a brand. Beveridge (2022) agrees that authenticity is one of the key factors of user-generated content as people ultimately trust other people rather than brands. Benefits of using UCG according to Beveridge (2022) are seen as taking authenticity to the next level, being adaptable and flexible and acting as a trsut signal.

Mazouri (2021) cautions that businesses and content marketers need to be mindful of crediting the creator of the content. This includes asking permission and receiving the user's consent before sharing any content. Another critical success factor includes knowing which platform works best for what type of UGC.

Consumers' motivation to share

There are various research studies into users' motivation and drivers to generate and share content. For example, an early and widely cited study by Daugherty et al (2008) find that the creation of UGC helps consumers minimize their self-doubts and feel a sense of community as well as connect with others and feel important. A more recent study supports those findings that consumers contribute to UGC out of a desire for social connections and interaction (Yesiloglu et al, 2021). A further motive identified in the same recent study has been identified as enjoyment.

Advantages and disadvantages of content marketing

We have now covered content marketing as well as content curation and user-generated content. Table 17.2 summarizes the advantages and disadvantages of content marketing.

Table 17.2   Advantages and disadvantages of content marketing

Advantages	Disadvantages
• Building awareness	• Difficult to produce and find good content
• Creating preference	
• Wider reach at lower costs	• Can have hidden costs
• Increase sales	• Time-consuming
• Cost savings	• Results can take time to show
• Chances of virality	• Skill requirement
• Becoming reliable source of information	

Knight, 2022, based on Content Marketing Institute, 2022; Marketo, 2014; Leonard, 2022; Grow Traffic, nd

Influencer marketing

The previous part of this chapter covered content marketing which includes the use of user-generated content. A related form of marketing is *influencer marketing* as influencers are still often perceived as conventional users, as opposed to celebrities. Influencer marketing is a three-way relationship between a brand/business, the consumer and an influencer.

KEY TERM
Influencer marketing

Influencer marketing is a type of social media marketing that uses endorsements and product mentions from influencers – individuals who have a dedicated social following and are viewed as experts within their niche.

SOURCE Chen, 2020

Influencer marketing has grown in its relevancy as part of digital marketing strategies and it is difficult to find a major brand that is not using influencer marketing to some extent. The influencer market grew from $1.7 billion in 2016 to $9.7 billion in 2020 and is projected to reach $16.4 billion in 2022 (Santora, 2022a). This growth is explained as due partially to the pandemic and people spending even more time online, as well as the growing popularity of short video formats on platforms such as TikTok, Facebook and YouTube (Santora, 2022a).

Influencers can be celebrities but the majority of influencers are not celebrities in the traditional sense. This is for a good reason, as the majority of consumers prefer to follow influencers who look and act like 'normal' people rather than celebrities (Santora, 2022a). A statistic confirms this fact by establishing that 70 per cent of teenagers trust influencers more than traditional celebrities (Digital Marketing Institute, 2021). Geyser (2022a) defines an influencer as being someone who has:

- the power to affect the purchasing decisions of others because of his or her authority, knowledge, position or relationship with his or her audience
- a following in a distinct niche, with whom he or she actively engages. The size of the following depends on the size of his/her topic of the niche

An influencer does not have to be a celebrity but has to come with an engaged audience in order to be perceived as an influencer. There are many benefits associated with influencer marketing, listed below based on recommendations from Iyer (2022):

- **Building trust and credibility:** Influencers establish trust and credibility by building relationships with their followers over time. Such relationships are mostly based on the influencer sharing useful content with its audience. The audience will engage with said content, get inspired and trust recommendations made by the influencer. If this relationship is lasting and the consumer respects recommendations from the influencer, the follower will also be influenced by commercial product recommendations.

- **Enhancing brand awareness:** Influencer marketing allows a brand to be exposed to a large, engaged audience that would otherwise take immense time and resources to build.

- **Reaching the right audience:** One common problem of advertising is that it often reaches the wrong audience. A survey run by Trustmary found in 2022 that 80 per cent of content marketing is targeted at the wrong target audience (Trustmary, 2022). Influencer marketing prevents this mistake as influencers will be able to share specific characteristics about their followers which businesses can use.

- **Growing business, traffic, and revenues:** Most marketers agree that the return on investment when using influencer marketing is better than most other digital marketing tactics. Jacinda Santora from the Influencer Marketing Hub states that on average brands can earn \$5.78 for every dollar spent on influencer marketing (Santora, 2022a).

CASE STUDY   Gymshark

You have now been introduced to influencer marketing and its benefits to businesses. There are plenty of successful influencer marketing campaign examples and one such example has been the #gymshark66 challenge.

This challenge was introduced by Gymshark and the successful campaign asked its followers to change their lives and form a new healthy habit in 66 days. Gymshark published the following rules on their website (Gymshark, 2021):

1. Start #gymshark66 Whenever You're Ready: seriously, whenever you're ready. January 1st? Well, it'd be rude not to. 3.00 am on October 2nd? You might regret it in the morning, but go on then. Whenever you decide to start your journey, our family will be there to support you.

2. Decide on three rules: this is your challenge to change. Decide on three rules that you want to stick to during the 66 days. This could be as simple as: drinking more water, doing one workout a week, and for the night-owls among us, going to sleep before the clock strikes midnight.

3. Share your journey: this one isn't mandatory, but, during your 66-day challenge, we urge you to share your journey with the world. From workouts and progress pictures to paintings and new recipe creations – we want to see it all via the hashtag #Gymshark66.

One of the success factors of the campaign was the engagement of users over an extended period of time. Gymshark partnered with influencers that have a strong presence on TikTok, and #gymshark66 achieved 241.3 million views on TikTok alongside almost 750,000 posts on Instagram (Zheng, 2021).

Gymshark made use of influencers in two ways. First, it used influencers to spread the #gymshark66 campaign. Second, Gymshark used Instagram's IGTV for a 'Stories of the 66' video series. Here individuals shared their experience of changing to healthier habits in 66 days (Zheng, 2021).

Questions

a. Visit Gymshark's YouTube site and watch the video posted in 2020, 'How to change your life in 66 days' (Gymshark 66).

b. Now look for the #gymshark66 on Instagram

c. How important has the use of influencers been to the success of this campaign?

d. Can you identify which of the benefits associated with influencer marketing Gymshark will have received with this campaign?

Influencer marketing process

As with any marketing strategy, influencer marketing should be carefully planned and executed in order to reap the rewards. In the following section, we will discuss five steps to consider when planning an influencer marketing campaign (Chen, 2020; Haenlein et al, 2020; Iyer, 2022) (see Figure 17.2).

Figure 17.2   Influencer marketing process

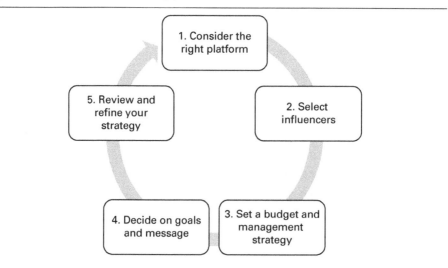

1. Consider the right platform

2. Select influencers

3. Set a budget and management strategy

4. Decide on goals and message

5. Review and refine your strategy

1. Platform choice

Different platforms lend themselves to influencer marketing better than others. Some of the aspects to consider when choosing the right channel for a campaign are audience characteristics, content format and platform usage (Haenlein et al, 2020). For example, younger populations are more sceptical towards traditional advertising and are therefore better audiences for influencer marketing. Younger audiences can be found on Instagram and TikTok rather than Facebook and Twitter (Haenlein et al, 2020). Furthermore, Twitter is very text-heavy compared to the rich content format of Instagram and TikTok, making those channels more usable for influencer marketing.

Finally, businesses should consider why consumers are using different platforms. In 2020, the average person has 8.4 different accounts (Santora, 2022a). While some platforms share similarities, the user will be interested in different content when visiting their Instagram profile as opposed to their LinkedIn profile. For example, Facebook is primarily a tool to stay in touch with friends and family while Twitter is used as a news source (Haenlein et al, 2020). Santora (2022a) highlights the importance of creating a cross-channel approach to influencer marketing ensuring that consumers are exposed to influencers across channels.

In order to generate relevant content, brands should work with influencers who specialize in each channel (Santora, 2022a). It is important to remember that influencers can be anywhere, and unlike celebrities, it is mainly their large followings that make them influential. As Werner Geyser from the Influencer Marketing Hub puts it: 'An influencer can be a popular fashion photographer on Instagram, or a well-read cybersecurity blogger who tweets, or a respected marketing executive on LinkedIn' (Geyser, 2022a).

2. Influencer selection

The choice of influencer depends on available budget as influencer fees vary greatly depending on the platform and the influencers' following. Influencers are traditionally based on follower count, e.g. (Geyser, 2022b):

- nano-influencers: 1,000–10,000 followers
- micro-influencers: 10,000–50,000 followers
- mid-tier influencers: 50,000–500,000 followers
- macro-influencers: 500,000–1,000,000 followers
- mega-influencers and celebrities: 1,000,000+ followers

Businesses need to make a choice on what type of influencer works best to reach their goals. This choice will be influenced by budget constraints as compensation between influencers varies greatly. Fees are based on some of the following facts (Geyser, 2022b):

- the influencers' reach and engagement
- the channel they use
- how many posts are wanted and if they include things like images, videos and audio
- how much effort it will require from the influencer
- where the ad will be promoted/cross-posted
- agency fees (if the influencer is with an influencer marketing agency)

Businesses need to ensure that the influencer has high engagement rates. These rates do not necessarily correspond to follower numbers. An influencer might have a huge following but a very low engagement rate. This would mean that many followers passively follow the account without actually engaging with it. This means that the level of influence from the influencer is lower.

It is also crucial to find influencers whose audience matches the brand's target audience to ensure that the influencer is actually influencing the right kind of people (Santora, 2022b). Please see the Additional Supporting Resources for further information about influencer earnings per post made.

Ultimately, each business needs to conduct its own research to determine which influencer seems best suited to reach its campaign goals.

Dada (2017) stresses that an influencer should have a combination of the following three factors which determine the influence potential of an individual:

- reach: the ability to deliver a message to a large number of people
- contextual credibility: the level of trust and authority given by the audience based on the influencer's perceived knowledge and expertise on a specific topic
- salesmanship: the presence and communications style that gives the influencer the ability to understand and embrace a particular point of view

3. Budget and management strategy

Influencer marketing is harder to automate than other campaigns and requires careful monitoring and following up. This is partially due to the fact that often multiple partnerships need to be balanced, and cultivating each relationship is important (Chen, 2020). At times, some influencers might not be as diligent with the posting as agreed, and monitoring those relationships takes effort.

Setting a budget is part of this stage too. Whereas we have established that the ROI of influencer marketing campaigns is often very high, having a budget in mind and sticking to it is essential in order for costs to stay under control. While it is important to monitor influencer posting, Haenlein et al (2020) advise that brands should avoid managing influencers too closely as excessive control can diminish creativity. Instead, they recommend that content should be approved before publication and creative briefings should be used to agree on crucial execution points.

4. Goals and messages

Marketers have to ensure that their business goals align with goals achievable through influencer marketing. As discussed in the second step (Influencer Selection), some platforms are better at achieving certain goals than others. Also, ensuring that both the influencer and their audience are fit to achieve the set business goals is essential for success.

Some of the most common goals when using influencer marketing are elevating brand awareness and increasing sales (Chen, 2020). However, goals should be defined more narrowly to be truly effective. For example, a business might decide to increase a specific customer group such as a younger demographic (Chen, 2020).

Another consideration is how the influencer should convey the brand's message. There are many different types of influencer marketing campaigns that can be utilized. Bhat (2018) lists the following types:

- **Host giveaways:** The influencer asks the audience to do things such as share or like a post, comment or tag their friends for the chance to win something. This strategy is effective for growing social actions such as follows, likes, shares, retweets and comments.

- **Social media takeover:** The influencer partners with a brand and is allowed to post their own content. This strategy is useful to increase brand exposure and offer new content to an audience.

- **Sponsored social media content:** The influencer produces and promotes social media content. This strategy is great for enhanced brand exposure.

- **Gifts/product seeding:** The influencer receives free gifts and is expected to talk about their experience with those products with their followers. The aim is publicity as well as increasing sales.

- **Sponsored blog posts:** The influencer writes a blog post about a brand (either exclusive or while discussing other products too). This strategy aims to increase the visibility of a product.

- **Brand ambassador programmes:** The influencer shares and promotes images, posts, videos and articles relating to a brand on an ongoing basis. This strategy aims to increase sales and visibility of a product.

- **Affiliate marketing:** The influencer receives a small commission on sales that are generated based on their content that is promoting a brand. The aim is to increase reach.

5. Revision of strategy

Businesses need to monitor the success of an influencer campaign by clearly establishing key performance indicators (KPIs). KPIs for an influencer campaign could
include the use of specific hashtags, affiliate discount codes or monitoring direct results such as *tracking links/URLs* from influencer campaigns (Iyer, 2022).

KEY TERM
Tracking link/URL

A tracking URL is a special URL (uniform resource locator) used for the purpose of
tracking certain elements when a link is clicked on. Tracking URLs are used in paid
advertising and to trace where visitors to your website are coming from. Tracking
URLs share important metrics such as the search engine your visitors came from, the
keywords the users searched for, and which of your calls to action got a response.

SOURCE Stamoulis, nd

Activity 17.7

You have now learnt about influencer marketing. One trend in influencer marketing is
the use of computer-generated imagery (CGI), and a particular example of such an
influencer is Lil Miquela who has more than three million Instagram followers and
has partnered with brands such as Prada and Diesel (Iyer, 2022).

i. Search Lil Miquela on Instagram and scroll through her feed.

ii. Try to identify posts where Lil Miquela has partnered with brands.

iii. Can you identify which of the influencer campaign types published by Bhat (2018)
she has taken part in?

iv. Visit the *Forbes* website and search for the article called 'The problematic fakery
of Lil Miquela explained – An exploration of virtual influencers realness' from 17
November 2020.

v. What are your thoughts on CGI influencers?

Ethical issues in influencer marketing

There are legal requirements for influencers to disclose if any of their content is commercially sponsored e.g. if they receive money or free products for making a post.

However, often sponsored posts are still difficult to identify as they are often positioned in organic, user-generated content (Evans et al, 2017). Younger audiences in particular might be persuaded by influencer marketing without being aware of the commercial intent behind those posts.

Ye et al (2021) established two sub-themes of ethics in influencer marketing that require attention. The first theme concerns the lack of an ethical framework to guide the influencer industry. Wellman et al (2020) examined influencer marketing in the travel industry and found that while it may seem that ethical frameworks are lacking, the influencer industry appears to set its own ethical guidelines. These are established around authenticity, which includes being true to one's self and the brand that the influencer is representing, as well as being true to one's audience (Wellman et al, 2020).

The second theme deals with the effectiveness of sponsorship disclosure. Ye et al (2021) establish that studies seem to have inconsistent findings on whether the disclosure of sponsorship influences consumer behaviour. For example, some results show a negative impact of advertising disclosure on consumers' credibility perception and purchase intention (Evans et al, 2017), while other studies found that products with clear disclosure messages can also lead to higher levels of purchase intention (Kay et al, 2020). These contrary findings demonstrate the need for further understanding of the effect of disclosure on consumer behaviour.

Haenlein et al (2020) suggest that brands using influencer marketing should ensure that paid collaborations are transparent to audiences to avoid any ambiguity and to ensure legal compliance with the law.

Another ethical problem can arise when influencers raise negative publicity which in turn can be transferred to the brand sponsoring the influencer. Suggestions on how businesses can safeguard against this include the incorporation of exit clauses and applying penalty details in case of negative publicity (Haenlein et al, 2020).

We have now covered influencer marketing by first explaining the term, then covering the five steps of the influencer marketing process in detail, and highlighting the ethical issues that might arise when using influencer marketing. In Table 17.3 we have summarized the advantages and disadvantages of influencer marketing.

Table 17.3   Advantages and disadvantages of influencer marketing

Advantages	Disadvantages
• Building trust and credibility	• Can be expensive
• Enhancing brand awareness	• Choice of influencer requires a lot of research
• Reaching the right audience	
• Growing business, traffic and revenues	• Requires a lot of monitoring
	• Lack of control
• Extending reach	• Lack of ethical framework

Knight, 2022; Iyer, 2022

Summary

In this chapter, we have reviewed social media channels and how these can be utilised to engage consumers. As part of social media marketing, we have discussed the importance of viral marketing. Relevant content usually underpins any successful social media marketing strategy which is why we covered content marketing in great detail. We have reviewed the importance of user-generated content as part of a content strategy. We have then reviewed influencer marketing as a channel and critically reviewed ethical issues that can be arising when using influencers to promote a product or service.

Chapter review

Reflective questions

Q1 Why is social media marketing an important part of a successful digital marketing strategy?

Q2 What do businesses need to consider when working together with influencers?

Q3 Why is it worth it for a business to invest in a sound content marketing strategy?

Key learning points

- Importance of social media marketing
- Understanding influencer marketing and its potential drawbacks
- Execution of a sound content marketing strategy.

Digital marketing channels and platforms 18

By the end of this chapter, you should be able to:

- differentiate between digital marketing channels and platforms
- evaluate the advantages and disadvantages of the different digital marketing channels
- provide justification for the suitability of digital channels

Introduction

In this chapter, we will review several digital marketing channels and platforms that can be utilised when deciding on specific marketing communications. Different channels have unique advantages and disadvantages that need to be considered when evaluating the suitability of each channel. It is essential for businesses to ensure that the chosen digital channel can achieve the objectives set in the digital marketing plan. In this chapter, we will review the most common digital marketing channels, covering affiliate marketing, search engine and display advertising, mobile and email marketing.

Affiliate marketing

In the previous section, we briefly covered affiliate marketing as part of the different influencer marketing campaign strategies. We will now elaborate further on what *affiliate marketing* is, why it is relevant and what pitfalls and challenges marketers might encounter.

> **KEY TERM**
> Affiliate marketing
>
> Affiliate marketing is an advertising model in which a company compensates third-party publishers to generate traffic or leads to the company's products and services. The third-party publishers are affiliates, and the commission fee incentivizes them to find ways to promote the company.
>
> **SOURCE** Frankenfield, 2022

Affiliate marketing is a marketing programme in which the act of selling products and services is outsourced to many different people across a network. Affiliate marketing seems to be here to stay; in the United States alone, affiliate marketing spending increased from $5.4 billion to $8.2 billion in 2022 (Guttmann, 2019). It is estimated that 81 per cent of brands around the world have affiliate programmes (Mileva, 2022).

Duffy (2005) explained affiliate marketing in simple terms. Picture, for example, a business that has many products to sell and does so without any affiliates. This would mean the business would have to have some sort of media platform where all of the products are described, orders can be made and payments can be processed. It would then have to try to gain customers' interest with a number of different marketing activities. Without the use of affiliates, all of these activities are solely at the risk of the business.

If we now look at affiliate marketing, the affiliate does not help to set up the platform on which to sell products, nor does it help with handling the shipment or payment. What the affiliate helps with is the gaining of interest through a number of marketing activities. This relationship is beneficial to both the business and the affiliate. The business shares its risk with another party and the affiliate does not need to produce, store or handle any products and instead only focuses on what it does best – promoting products. If done successfully, a business pays the affiliate a commission.

Affiliate marketing includes three different parties: the seller, the affiliate and the consumer (18.1). The seller can be an individual entrepreneur or a large corporation and is a vendor, a brand, (e-commerce) merchant, retailer or purely a product creator (Big Commerce, nd). If, for example, an e-commerce merchant wants to extend its reach to new consumers, it may hire an affiliate.

The affiliate, also known as the publisher or advertiser, can be an individual or company and often owns a large network either in the form of owning several websites or email lists (Frankenfield, 2022). Another form of owning a network as an affiliate is by having a large following on social media channels. The affiliate then

Figure 18.1   The affiliate marketing model

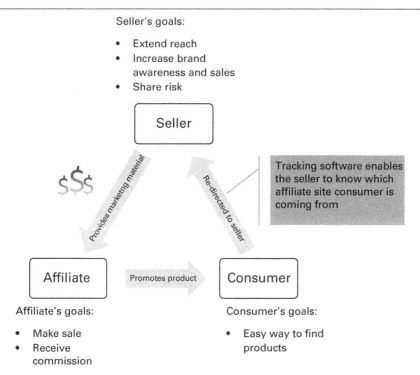

promotes the products that the e-commerce merchant is trying to sell. The promotion can be leveraged on different marketing channels (Frankenfield, 2022; Big Commerce, nd) through:

- running banner ads and contextual affiliate links
- posting links on websites and blogs
- sending emails to network
- social media mentionings and reviews (mainly through influencers)
- paid search-focused microsites

Finally, the consumer is the third party involved in the affiliate marketing model, as there are no sales and no commission without the consumer. Users who click on any of the content promoted by the affiliate are then redirected to the e-commerce site. Tracking software traces exactly which affiliate link users have clicked on before having been redirected to the seller's site. If the user makes a purchase from the e-commerce site, the affiliate receives a commission.

Activity 18.1

You have now been introduced to how affiliate marketing works. BuzzFeed is a New York-based digital media company known for viral news and entertainment stories (Frankenfield, 2022).

i. Visit BuzzFeed.com and click on the shopping tab.

ii. As you will be able to see, many of the suggested products are clearly labelled as containing affiliate content.

iii. How do you perceive the shopping experience on an affiliate site such as BuzzFeed?

iv. Can you think of affiliate marketing websites that are less obvious?

Commission and payment methods

Affiliates get paid based on a commission which can range from less than 1 per cent to 20 per cent or more. The commission percentage varies depending on the product and level of referral volume (Frankenfield, 2022). Traditionally, affiliates are compensated when a desired action, for example, a sale, is completed. The following show some of the traditional commission-based payment models for affiliates (Lattuca, 2018; Big Commerce, nd):

- **Cost-per-acquisition (CPA):** Fulfilment of a sale. In this standard form of payment, the merchant pays the affiliate a percentage of the sale price of the product after the consumer purchases the product as a result of affiliate marketing strategies (Big Commerce, nd).

- **Cost-per-lead (CPL):** Completion of a registration form, subscription to newsletter, etc. Pay-per-lead affiliate marketing programmes compensate the affiliate based on the conversion of leads. The affiliate must persuade the consumer to visit the merchant's website and complete the desired action – whether it's filling out a contact form, signing up for a trial of a product, subscribing to a newsletter or downloading software or files (Big Commerce, nd).

- **Pay-per-click (PPC):** Fixed rate based on banner/creative clicks. PPC programmes focus on incentivizing the affiliate to redirect consumers from their marketing platform to the merchant's website. The affiliate is paid based on the increase in web traffic. There are two common concepts in PPC (Big Commerce, nd):

- **CPA (cost-per-acquisition):** With this model, the affiliate gets paid each time the seller or retailer acquires a lead, which is when an affiliate link takes the customer to the merchant's online store and they take an action, such as subscribing to an email list or filling out a 'Contact Us' form.

- **EPC (earnings-per-click):** This is the measure for the average earnings per 100 clicks for all affiliates in a retailer's affiliate programme.

Lattuca (2018) highlights that payment methods will need to be adjusted given the ever more complex consumer journeys spanning across several channels and multiple devices. New and different affiliate payment models need to reward not only conversion but also other forms of engagement. Examples of new payment models should include cross-device tracking as well as first-time vs repeat purchase behaviour, suggests Lattuca (2018).

Affiliate tracking

Affiliate marketing and the corresponding payment structure work with the use of cookies. There are several different uses for cookies on the internet as well as different forms of cookies. The most common *cookie* type used in affiliate marketing is called first-party cookie (Gardener, 2020) instead of third-party cookies (Hughes, 2021).

KEY TERM
Cookie

A cookie is information that a website puts on a user's computer. Cookies store limited information from a web browser session on a given website that can then be retrieved in the future. They are also sometimes referred to as browser cookies, web cookies or internet cookies. Cookies can be accessed by the browser user, the site a user is on or by a third party that might use the information for different purposes. Common use cases for cookies include session management, personalization and tracking.

SOURCE Kerner, nd

There are multiple types of cookies that run in modern web browsers. Different types of cookies have specific use cases to enable certain capabilities:

- **First-party cookies:** Also known as SameSite cookies, the cookie and information it contains is restricted to the same site on which it was set.

- **Third-party cookies:** These cookies are not restricted to the initial site where the cookie was created. They enable entities other than the original site to access them for user tracking and personalization purposes (Kerner, nd).

In practical terms, cookies are dropped on a browser on which the consumer is reading content from the affiliate. The consumer then clicks through to the seller to make a purchase and the dropped cookie tracks the user's click-through journey (Gardener, 2020). The cookie allows the seller to recognize the affiliate. Gardener (2020) stresses that 'affiliate marketing is typically data light and does not track consumer's buying behaviour'.

Types of affiliate marketing

There are three different types of affiliate marketing, classified according to the involvement and relationship between the affiliate and the product to be sold (Frankenfield, 2022; Big Commerce, nd):

- **Unattached affiliate marketing:** This is the most uninvolved form of affiliate marketing where the affiliate has no connection to the product or service they are promoting. The affiliate does not have any expertise in the product. Often, unattached affiliates will run affiliate marketing in the form of pay-per-click campaigns.

- **Related affiliate marketing:** In this form of affiliate marketing, the affiliate has some sort of relationship with the product or service they are promoting. The affiliate may not use the product or service but they have some influence in the product category. For example, a fitness blogger might be affiliated with a protein shake that they are not using themselves but their followers might perceive the affiliate to have expertise in the area of fitness and therefore trusts the recommendation.

- **Involved affiliate marketing:** An involved affiliate is closely connected and involved with the product or service they are promoting. The affiliate will have used the product and therefore gains authority to make claims about its use. This form of affiliate marketing takes longer to establish but often pays off in the long run. For example, a brand ambassador for Gymshark recommends a new pair of workout leggings to their audience.

Advantages and disadvantages of affiliate marketing

We have mainly covered the advantages of affiliate marketing, of which there are many. For example, both the seller as well as the affiliate have a mutually beneficial relationship. It is relatively low-cost advertising with limited risk as the seller only has to pay the affiliate for converted customers.

However, it is also essential to highlight that affiliate marketing also has its risks and challenges. We have talked about the need to constantly monitor the affiliate as one drawback already. Back in the day, problems with affiliate marketing mostly had to do with fraud in the form of fake clicks and impressions. However, advancements in technology as well as stricter terms and conditions have solved this issue to a great extent (Frankenfield, 2022).

One of the main drawbacks of affiliate marketing is the lack of control. If the affiliate is involved in a scandal and they have been closely linked to the seller's brand, the damage can have a negative effect on the brand. Finding the right affiliate to work with can also pose a challenge as there are many different options out there. Another aspect surrounding the lack of control concerns the location of where the seller's products will be found online. For example, the seller's product might be found next to information that the seller does not agree with. This can be particularly the case for unattached affiliate marketing through banner ads or other pay-per-click campaigns.

Table 18.1　Advantages and disadvantages of affiliate marketing

Advantages	Disadvantages
• Reaching a broader audience	• Potentially subject to fraud
• Better accounting of qualified leads	• Less creative control
• Low-cost advertising (as pay-per-performance)	• Less control of placement of product information
• Diversify risk	• Difficult to find the right affiliate
	• May damage brand reputation

Search engine marketing (SEO and paid search)

KEY TERM
Search engine marketing

Search engine marketing (SEM) is an online marketing strategy that aims to increase the online visibility of a website in the search engine results pages (SERPs).

SEM intersects with search engine optimization (SEO), as it can include strategies like rewriting the content of a website and its architecture to achieve higher rankings. However, search engine marketing generally refers to paid search or pay-per-click (PPC).

SOURCE Lyons, 2022

In theory, search engine marketing refers to both search engine optimization and paid search results. However, in practice, most practitioners refer to search engine marketing as paid search results and pay-per-click campaigns. We will start by covering *search engine optimization (SEO)*, as SEO is one of the digital strategies that any company should aim to improve.

Search engine optimization

It is important for businesses to appear high in search engine results such as Google, Bing or Yahoo! One statistic shows that 75 per cent of internet users never scroll past the first page of search results (Kagan, 2016).

KEY TERM
Search engine optimization (SEO)

Search engine optimization is the art and science of getting pages to rank higher in search engines such as Google. Because search is one of the main ways in which people discover content online, ranking higher in search engines can lead to an increase in traffic to a website.

In Google and other search engines, the results page often features paid ads at the top of the page, followed by the regular results or what search marketers call the 'organic search results'. Traffic that comes via SEO is often referred to as 'organic search traffic' to differentiate it from traffic that comes through paid search. Paid search is often referred to as search engine marketing (SEM) or pay-per-click (PPC).

SOURCE Optimizely, nd

The key term definition is important as it clearly states that SEO is only about organic search results. Organic search is part of in-bound marketing with the aim of increasing website traffic (Leist, 2021). Besides the increase in website traffic, there are a number of benefits associated with search engine optimization (Muthoni, 2021):

- increased credibility: a website that ranks highly on search engine results is usually seen as high quality and trustworthy
- relatively low cost: SEO does not cost anything in the traditional sense unlike other marketing strategies such as pay-per-click
- maximizes pay-per-click campaigns: SEO can be used to maximize PPC campaigns
- increased competitive advantage: those companies that appear higher on search engine result pages are often perceived as market leaders
- increase reach: search results are visible to anyone, not just a defined target audience
- improves user engagement: an optimized website with useful content that matches a search will likely bring in quality in-bound traffic

---

Activity 18.2

You have now been introduced to search engine optimization.

i. Visit Google's YouTube channel and watch the video 'How Google Search Works (in 5 minutes)'.

ii. The video provides a brief introduction to how search engines perform their searches.

iii. Try to summarize the reasons why a business might not appear high in search engine results.

iv. Can you think of ways to solve this?

There are three main metrics that are evaluated to determine how a site should be ranked based on the perceived quality of such a website (Optimizely, nd):

- **Links:** Links from other websites are crucial when evaluating the ranking of a site on SERPs. Essentially, a link is perceived as a vote of confidence from other websites, since website owners are unlikely to link to other sites that are of poor quality. Search engines perceive sites with links from many other sites as having authority. (Called 'PageRank' in Google, this is especially the case if the sites that are linking to them are themselves authoritative.)

- **Content:** Search engines are also interested in the content of a web page to ensure it would be relevant for any given search query.
- **Page structure:** Web pages are written in HTML and how the HTML code is structured can impact a search engine's ability to evaluate a page.

The Digital Marketing Institute (2019) divides search engine optimization activities into three core *optimization components*: technical, on-page and off-page optimization.

KEY TERM
Optimization components

Technical optimization: The process of completing activities on a website that are designed to improve SEO but are not related to content. It often happens behind the scenes.

On-page optimization: The process of ensuring the content on a website is relevant and provides a great user experience. It includes targeting the right keywords within the content and can be done through a content management system.

Off-page optimization: The process of enhancing a website's search engine rankings through activities outside of the site. This is largely driven by back-end links, which help to build the site's reputation.

Technical optimization

Technical search engine optimization involves the ways in which a website can be improved so that search engines can crawl, index and render it successfully (Indig, 2022). Technical optimization is important as, no matter how appealing the content of your website, if search engines cannot successfully browse a website and index it, the site will not show up on the search engine results pages.

Examples of technical SEO would be designing a website in an orderly structure recognized by search engines as well as ensuring that every page of a website functions as it should (Indig, 2022).

On-page optimization

There are a number of different areas of a website that can be optimized such as keywords, content, title tags (also known as page title) and alt tags (image description), headers and URLs. The better these sections of a website align with what users are searching for, the better a website will rank on search engine results.

Imagine you are searching for a store that delivers flowers near you. A website will be optimized with regard to on-page optimization if the URL contains something related to delivering flowers, e.g. 'www.fastflowerdelivery.com', if the headers and page titles clearly communicate the option to have flowers delivered, and if pictures showing flowers on the website are clearly described as such.

The content of a website is crucial for SEO, as search engines prefer websites with relevant and up-to-date content. Content includes a broad mix of text, videos, graphics which is why content marketing is essential for SEO.

Another crucial aspect of on-page optimization is keyword research. Keyword research describes the process of finding the search terms or phrases that potential customers are commonly using. There are plenty of tools online that help with keyword research. Keyword research should not just be done online but also offline. Customer surveys can help to identify common search terms for your product or product category as well as brainstorming within an organization.

It is important not just to focus on single keywords as 70 per cent of searches use long-tail keywords which are highly specific 3+ word phrases (Bushery, nd). For example, very few people would search for the general term 'Flower delivery'; it is much more realistic that people would search for something like 'cheap flower delivery near me'.

Off-page optimization

Search engines like to rank websites highly that have several authoritative sites linking back to them. Imagine, for example, a construction company that has done some work for a city council. If this city council links to the construction company's website when reporting about the successfully completed building works, that would be considered a high-quality in-bound link for the business. Other in-bound links that would be considered of high quality could be from blogs or social media accounts with a lot of followers. This is where influencer marketing might become an interesting aspect of SEO. Inbound links considered by search engines as lower quality would be directory links or broken links.

Advantages and disadvantages of search engine optimization

Search engine optimization if done correctly can have huge benefits to businesses and other website owners. However, it takes a lot of time, effort and knowledge to do SEO well. It is estimated that 90 per cent of pages on the internet are invisible to search engines (Soulo, 2020). If done correctly, however, SEO can lead to increased visibility and reach as well as demonstrate competitive advantage and enhance reputation.

Table 18.2   Advantages and disadvantages of search engine optimization

Advantages	Disadvantages
• Increased credibility • Relatively low cost • Increased competitive advantage • Increased reach • Improves user engagement	• Requires time, knowledge and maintenance • Results are not guaranteed • Profit is not instant

Knight, 2022; Pencil Speech, nd; Muthoni, 2021

However, there are several disadvantages associated with SEO too. As we have discussed, SEO is not easy and requires specialized knowledge. It takes time to see results and there is no instantaneous fix to have a website appear highly ranked on the organic search results. Constant assessing as well as no guaranteed results are other disadvantages (Pencil Speech, 2022).

Paid search marketing

Organic search results are preferred by users and gain more overall clicks when generally searching the web for information. However, a study found that when people are searching the web with the intent to buy something (e.g. with commercial intent), 64.6 per cent of people click on paid search results (Kim, 2021).

KEY TERM
Paid search marketing

Paid search marketing affords businesses the opportunity to advertise within the sponsored listings of a search engine or a partner site by paying either each time their ad is clicked (pay-per-click) or less commonly, when their ad is displayed (CPM or cost-per-thousand).

SOURCE Sentance, 2018

Paid search marketing goes by a lot of different names but the most common ones are pay-per-click (PPC), search engine advertising and sponsored listings (Sentance, 2018). Paid search marketing has a number of benefits (Morris, 2021; Perricone, 2021; Sentance, 2018):

• campaign speed: paid search provides a quick entry to appear high on search engine results pages (SERPs)

- measurable and trackable results: statistics for paid search results in terms of impressions, clicks and conversions are readily available
- control over spending: businesses only have to pay if a user clicks on a link and can set a budget
- specific targeting opportunity: paid search allows for specific targeting including retargeting of visitors who previously did not complete a purchase
- suitable to fulfil a combination of goals: whether it is creating reach, awareness or reminding consumers, paid search can fulfil a number of different goals

There are different ad formats of paid search. These range from pay-per-click advertising on search engines to display advertising on websites as well as paid advertising on social media channels.

Activity 18.3

You have now been introduced to paid search advertising.

i. Visit iCrossing's YouTube channel and view the video 'UK case study: Ann Summers Sexy Paid Search'.

ii. Try to evaluate why this campaign has been so successful.

iii. Think of advantages as well as disadvantages of paid search marketing.

The pay-per-click business model

Unlike traditional adverts, businesses cannot simply pay a set amount of money for their advert to be prominently placed on search engine results pages. Instead, businesses have to be part of an *ad auction* which is 'an entirely automated process that Google and other major search engines use to determine the relevance and validity of advertisements that appear on their search engine results pages' (Wordstream, 2022a).

KEY TERM
Ad auction

The process that happens with each Google search to decide which ads will appear for that specific search and in which order those ads will show on the page (or whether or not any ads will show at all).

SOURCE Google Ads Help, 2022b

Each time an ad is eligible to appear for a search, it goes through the ad auction. The auction determines whether or not the ad actually shows and in which ad position it will show on the page.

Here's how the auction works:

1 When someone searches, the Google Ads system finds all ads whose keywords match that search.

2 From those ads, the system ignores any that aren't eligible, such as ads that target a different country or are disapproved based on a policy violation.

3 Of the remaining ads, only those with a sufficiently high Ad Rank may show. Ad Rank is a combination of your bid, ad quality, the context of the person's search, and the expected impact of extensions and other ad formats.

As you can see from the definition, the auction process is a relatively complex one which is why many businesses decide to outsource their PPC campaigns to agencies that are specialized in running successful paid search campaigns. Any business should have a basic understanding of how PPC campaigns work.

In order to understand more about how an ad auction works, we need to take a closer look at the ad rank. The ad rank depends on a number of factors: the bid amount, ad quality (click-through rate, ad relevance and landing page experience determine quality), user signals (such as location, device type and time of day), context of search, competitiveness of auction and ad extensions (inform the overall experience with the ad) (Osmundson, 2022).

Another relevant factor in PPC campaigns is the *quality score*.

KEY TERM
Quality score

Quality score is a diagnostic tool meant to give you a sense of how well your ad quality compares to other advertisers. This score is measured on a scale from 1 to 10 and a higher quality score means that an ad and landing page are more relevant and useful to someone searching for a particular keyword, compared to other advertisers.

SOURCE Google Ads Help, 2022c

The quality score is calculated based on the combined performance of three components (Google Ads Help, 2022c):

● expected click-through rate (CTR): the likelihood that an ad will be clicked when shown

- ad relevance: how closely an ad matches the intent behind a user's search
- landing page experience: how relevant and useful the landing page is to people who click on the ad

Each component is evaluated with a status of 'above average', 'average' or 'below average'. This evaluation is based on a comparison with other advertisers whose ads showed for the exact same keyword, over the last 90 days (Google Ads Help, 2022c).

The cost-per-click model

As we have now learnt, the quality score is essential for how and where an advert will appear on the paid search listings. One of the main advantages of paid search is that businesses only incur costs if there is an actual click on the advertisement. One common metric for businesses to determine the success of a PPC campaign is the *cost-per-click* amount (Perricone, 2021).

KEY TERM
Cost-per-click (CPC)

Cost-per-click is the amount that an advertiser pays for each click on an ad. CPC acts as a bid in an auction that determines where an ad will be placed. A higher bid equates to better ad placement. The CPC needs to be set at the maximum price one is willing to pay-per-click on an ad. What actually needs to be paid is determined by the following formula:

(Competitor's Ad Rank / Advertiser's Quality Score) + 0.01 = Actual CPC

The cost-per-click can vary tremendously across industries. For example, whereas the average cost-per-click for the legal industry is $5.88, the average cost-per-click for the dating industry is only $0.18 (Wordstream, 2022b).

Activity 18.4

You have now been introduced to how paid search works. As you might have noticed, it is a relatively complicated bidding system that establishes when and how an advert is displayed on the search engine results pages (SERPs).

i. Visit take some time to familiarize yourself with how cost-per-click works.

ii. Take a look at the infographic that shows the average cost-per-click in Google Ads across industries.

iii. Now revisit how the cost-per-click is calculated and try to think of reasons why the averages differ between industries.

There are a number of different ways in which a PPC campaign can be optimized (Payne, 2020; Schwartz, 2022):

- Optimize and update keywords regularly: The success of any PPC campaign depends on how well businesses know their target audiences' search behaviour including which keywords they are using. It is therefore important to regularly update a keyword list by researching relevant keywords as well as pausing underperforming keywords.

- Invest in good landing pages: Landing pages are the first thing that users see once they have clicked on a paid search ad. It is therefore essential to create a compelling landing page that persuades prospects to be converted into an actual sale. There are three elements of a PPC landing page that are known for converting prospects (Schwartz, 2022):

  o landing pages should be easily accessible and usable

  o the design should be appealing, simple and user-friendly and should load within three seconds or less

  o visitors should be encouraged to click and take action through clear and relevant calls to action (CTAs)

- Think about developing a remarketing (or retargeting) PPC strategy. A good way to boost conversions and strengthen a brand is to re-engage with a target audience by displaying highly relevant ads to prospects that have already visited a website.

Table 18.3 Advantages and disadvantages of paid search and PPC

Advantages	Disadvantages
• Campaign speed	• Requires time, knowledge and maintenance
• Measurable and trackable results	
• Control over spending	• Results are not guaranteed
• Specific targeting opportunity	• Profit is not instant
• Suitable to fulfil a combination of goals	

Knight, 2022; Morris, 2021; Perricone, 2021; Sentance, 2018

Advantages and disadvantages of paid search

We have now covered paid search and ways in which to optimize a PPC campaign. There are a number of benefits associated with paid search such as the speed in which a PPC campaign can be implemented, the measurable and trackable results, as well as the opportunity to target a very specific target audience.

Yet there are also drawbacks of paid search that need to be taken into consideration. Paid search is not a straightforward digital marketing channel and requires expert knowledge. It is also competitive and can get expensive, especially in industries with high average costs per click. While a campaign can be set up more quickly than improving organic search engine results, paid search can still be time-consuming as it requires constant monitoring including keyword research.

Display advertising

Besides paid search advertising, there are a number of different options for *display advertising* on the internet. These range from static banner ads on websites to interactive ads such as augmented reality ads on Facebook.

KEY TERM
Display advertising

Display advertising refers to the process of advertising a product or service through visuals like images and videos on networks of publisher websites such as the Google Display Network, Facebook, etc. Display ads are placed on relevant third-party websites in the form of banner, image and text ads.

SOURCE Muhammad, 2020

There are three basic categories of display advertising (DiSilvestro, 2018):

- **Site placement advertising**: This is when a marketer/advertiser chooses the site they would like to advertise on.
- **Contextual advertising**: This is when a marketer advertises a product or service on a website with similar content, for example promoting wedding dresses on a honeymoon destination website.

- **Remarketing advertising:** These ads appear when a user has already been to your website. A service uses cookies to track the visit, and then an ad would appear on another website they visit, ideally causing the user to return to your website.

Display advertising has been around since the beginning of the consumer internet, as they closely resemble the traditional form of print advertising, just within a digital context. The first static banner ad was published in 1994 in the web-based magazine HotWired (Muhammad, 2020). The opportunities for designing display adverts have come a long way since the 1990s which makes them a very interesting opportunity for any digital marketing strategy.

As opposed to paid search where the design of adverts is relatively standardized, display advertising comes in various different formats and sizes. Digital marketers have the choice between standard display ads similar to the first banner ad in 1994 and a range of *rich media ad* alternatives.

KEY TERM
Rich media ads

Rich media ads are display ads that use HTML5 technology to deliver advanced features like video, audio, expansion or polling. Rich media offers a more engaging experience that helps capture the attention of your target audience and drive conversions.

SOURCE Bui, nd

The advantage of rich media adverts lies in the opportunity to create brand awareness and engage with users. The key advantages of rich media creatives include the following (Google Studio Help, 2022):

- an engaging user experience leading to higher interaction rate
- increased conversions, click-throughs and view rates
- better metrics than traditional ads

There are many different display advertising formats to choose from (Bui, nd; Google Studio Help, 2022):

- **Static/standard banner ads:** A banner is a simple image ad that is served onto a web page. Static banner ads typically consist of a single image file with no audio, video or additional features.
- **Animated ads:** Animated ads can include videos and polite download technology, which waits for the web page to completely load before loading the creative.

- **Interactive ads:** Interactive advertisements provide embedded features that allow the audience to immediately interact with the product or service.

- **Video ads:** While video ads are primarily served through video content platforms like Netflix and YouTube, they can also be distributed through display ad networks.

- **Expandable ads:** A creative that expands beyond its initial dimensions over the top of another page or app content. Expansion can take place after a user interacts (for example, by click, tap or mouse-over) or automatically when the page loads (auto-expand).

- **Interstitial ads:** A creative that either floats on top of a page's content or appears as a full screen ad during natural transition points in mobile apps, such as during launch, loading and video pre-roll.

Activity 18.5

You have now been introduced to several forms of display advertising. As you can see, there are plenty of options for marketers to run a display advertising campaign in a number of different formats.

i. Visit Google's Richmediagallery.com and browse through the different examples of rich media campaigns.

ii. Pick two examples, one that you think is doing a good job at reaching new consumers, and one example that you think does not succeed in doing so.

iii. Provide justifications for your choices.

The effectiveness of display advertising

Display advertising is commonly visible on the internet and research suggests that the average US user sees around 63 display ads per day, which makes it roughly 1,900 display ads per month (Muhammad, 2020). The frequent exposure to display advertising can result in 'banner blindness' or advertising avoidance.

However, Hervet et al (2011) define banner blindness as 'the absence of fixation on banners' and find in their eye-tracking study that people seem to notice a banner ad when it is first presented as it seems to alter the structure of the presented website and catches the user by surprise. They also establish that once a consumer has been exposed to a banner ad, they tend to avoid looking at it (Hervet et al, 2011). The surprise element seems to be one of the reasons why new types of display ads that include an animated aspect are being so successful.

Ghose and Todri-Adamopoulos (2016) analyse a Big Data set and find that merely being exposed to display advertising makes consumers actively search for the advertised brand and product and makes them purchase a product. They also find that the duration of display advertising exposure makes the impact even bigger.

Hsieh and Chen (2011) researched contextual factors influencing the effectiveness of display advertising. They find that display ads on picture- or video-based web pages attracted greater attention than similar adverts on text-based and text-picture web pages. They explain those findings by the fact that users need be more involved in reading text-heavy websites and therefore pay lesser attention to display advertising (Hsieh and Chen, 2011).

Another study on the effectiveness of display advertising finds that commercial websites are better for the effectiveness of display advertising compared to social websites such as Facebook and LinkedIn (Auschaitrakul and Mukherjee, 2017). However, if businesses decide to place these ads on social websites, these should be placed on brand rather than personal pages.

The review on the effectiveness of display advertising summarizes that it is effective if:

- presented as a surprise (and changing the structure of the website)
- increased exposure duration
- user is cognitively less involved in the website
- picture- and video-based websites are more effective than text-heavy websites
- the context of placed ads is commercial rather than social

Arnold (2015) suggests the following three ways to ensure the effectiveness of display advertising:

- **Be compelling:** Ads have to be eye-catching enough to attract attention. Things like animation, the use of faces, brand colours and clear text help ads stand out.
- **Be concise:** At any given moment, someone might see a display ad and only pay attention to it for a moment. In that moment, a concise message ensures the message sticks.
- **Be clear:** Display ads tend to be relatively small, so there is not always a lot of space to work with. Avoid trying to say too much; the ad may just end up looking cluttered. Instead, clearly communicate a single marketing message about a single product.

The need for clarity goes for *calls to action* too, as users need to know exactly where to go next if they want to know more about a product or actually make a purchase.

KEY TERM
Call to action

A call to action (CTA) is a marketing term that refers to the next step a marketer wants its audience or reader to take. The CTA can have a direct link to sales. For example, it can instruct the reader to click the 'buy' button to complete a sale, or it can simply move the audience further along towards becoming a consumer of that company's goods or services. The CTA can suggest that the reader subscribes to a newsletter that contains product updates, for example. To be effective, a CTA should be obvious and should immediately follow the marketing message.

SOURCE Kenton, 2020

Brand reputation and display advertising

Despite several advantages, display advertising also comes with its challenges, one of the main ones being the management of brand reputation. The issue with display advertising is that it is often based on target audience interest rather than the location where the ad will appear (Rothfuss, 2022). Display adverts can end up in places that brands do not want to be associated with. This could be, for example, sites that contain sensitive content or fake news. Another issue might be that ads are shown on websites whose main purpose is to make money through display ads and as such do not provide much engaging content for the audience. Some display ad networks have policies against such behaviour.

For example, Google states (Setupad, 2021): 'Advertising and other paid promotional material added to your pages should not exceed your content. We may limit or disable ad serving on pages with little to no value and/or excessive advertising until changes are made.'

A good ratio between content and ads is recommended as 30 per cent of ads and 70 per cent of content with the focus on quality content to avoid high bounce rates. This ratio also depends on the layout of the website, the length of content and how visitors are using the pages (Setupad, 2021).

There are some steps that businesses can take to ensure that their display ads are appearing in the right places to the right people. Businesses that place display advertising should do the following (Rothfuss, 2022):

- Review ad publishers' network for options to opt out of ads appearing on websites containing sensitive content or dealing with specific topics (e.g. Facebook and Instagram let advertisers opt out of advertising on pages that contain news, politics, religious or gaming content).

- Constantly monitor the placement of ads to review if these show up on any unsuitable and potentially toxic social media pages, websites and YouTube channels.
- Update an ad placement blacklist preventing ads from appearing on those pages again.

Unilever is one of the biggest advertisers in the world and in order to gain more control and visibility over where its adverts are placed, it has created a network of Unilever Trusted Publishers. In collaboration with Unilever, this network of global, regional and local online publishers and platforms aims to transform online advertising into a more positive experience for the consumers online (Unilever, 2019).

Advantages and disadvantages of display advertising

In the previous section, we reviewed different formats of display advertising as well as looked into how effective they are. There are clear advantages associated with display advertising such as creative opportunities, especially with rich media and compared with search advertising opportunities. Display advertising is great for retargeting and remarketing and it is relatively easy to track clicking behaviour.

However, there are a number of drawbacks associated with display advertising such as people ignoring display advertising or blocking it. Statista reported that there were 763.5 million adblock users worldwide (Statista, 2021). Also, there is only a limited amount of time that users have to process a display ad which poses challenges to marketers.

Mobile marketing

Mobile marketing is another marketing channel enabled through technological development. It provides extensive opportunities to reach and engage with consumers.

Table 18.4   Advantages and disadvantages of display advertising

Advantages	Disadvantages
• Creative opportunities	• Often ignored by audience
• Attention	• Can be blocked
• Engaging user experience	• Limited time
• Retargeting opportunity	
• Easy to track and measure success	

Knight, 2022; Google Studio Help, 2022; Muriuki, 2016

KEY TERM
Mobile marketing

Mobile marketing is any advertising activity that promotes products and services via mobile devices, such as tablets and smartphones. It makes use of features of modern mobile technology, including location services, to tailor marketing campaigns based on an individual's location.

Mobile marketing is a way in which technology can be used to create personalized promotion of goods or services to a user who is constantly connected to a network.

SOURCE Kenton, 2022

The increased availability of mobile phones is contributing to an ever-increasing market size of mobile marketing. The Statista Research Department (2021a) has reported that the size of the global mobile marketing market is projected to grow from $11 billion to reach almost $58 billion by 2030. Mobile marketing can make use of significant and unique features that comes with mobile devices. Kumar and Mittal (2020) list the following:

- ubiquity: largescale adoption and the versatility of smart mobile devices across the world
- multiway communication: marketer to consumer, consumer to marketer, consumer to consumer communication along with interaction with the platforms serving these marketing campaigns to the customer
- 24 × 7 availability: mobile phone is normally switched on even while the target customer is sleeping or travelling, hence ensuring the delivery of marketing content anytime anywhere
- marketing channels: availability of multiple channels and tools for mobile marketing with the growth of smartphones with the latest features and enhanced computing powers
- personalization: offers high potential for highly personalized and localized campaigns with better targeting due to effective use of analytics

The previous features of mobile marketing demonstrate just how many opportunities there are to engage with an audience via mobile devices. In order for customers to be engaged, they need to see how mobile marketing creates value for them.

Creating value is challenging as mobile consumers differ in terms of what they want. Therefore, mobile marketing requires segmentation based on both demographic (e.g. age, gender and education) as well as the behavioural level (e.g. perceived value, shopping style and brand trust) (Persaud and Azhar, 2012).

Businesses have to understand that mobile devices have several uses for consumers and are much more than communication devices. Consumers for example use their smartphones for business, entertainment and social networking (Persaud and Azhar, 2012).

Types of mobile marketing strategies

There are different types of mobile marketing strategies. Their suitability to create value depends on the target audiences, industry and the budget available. One relatively new trend is the use of augmented reality in mobile marketing, making use of the interactive nature of mobile devices. Businesses offer, for example, ads that enhance the physical environment or let consumers sample products virtually (Garbi, 2016). Marrs (2022) highlights the following different types of strategies:

- **App-based marketing:** Different services help advertisers create mobile ads that appear within third-party mobile apps.

- **In-game mobile marketing:** In-game mobile marketing refers to mobile ads that appear within mobile games. In-game ads can appear as banner pop-ups, full-page image ads or even that appear between loading screens.

- **QR codes:** QR codes are scanned by users, who are then taken to a specific web page that the QR code is attached to. QR codes are often aligned with mobile gamification.

- **Location-based marketing:** Location-based mobile ads are ads that appear on mobile devices based upon a user's location relative to a specific area or business. For example, some advertisers may only want their mobile ads to appear when users are within a one-mile radius of their business.

- **Mobile search ads:** These are basic Google search ads built for mobile, often featuring extra add-on extensions like click-to-call or maps.

- **Mobile image ads:** Image-based ads designed to appear on mobile devices.

- **SMS:** SMS marketing involves capturing a user's phone number and sending them text offers.

CASE STUDY   L'Oréal

There are several unique features and different strategies of mobile marketing. Offering consumers the chance to virtually sample products has been made available by using augmented and virtual reality. L'Oréal is at the forefront of using virtual and augmented reality in a number of different ways, offering various apps that let consumers try products virtually or gain access to beauty advisors.

A press release from L'Oréal said (WBR Insights, nd):

> Did you ever imagine you could try on hundreds of looks in a matter of minutes? The latest revolution from L'Oréal Paris: virtual reality makeup that lets you apply every look and product to your image. Smile, change your expression, move your head – the makeup will follow! The result is stunning, just as if you're wearing it.

L'Oréal has also used augmented reality in mobile ad campaigns. For example, in 2018 L'Oréal launched a digital campaign using the hashtag #LifeAtCannesSummerEscape to introduce a new lipstick collection targeting consumers in India (InMobi, 2018). The idea behind the campaign was to offer a personalized consumer experience to consumers in India making them feel as if they were experiencing the Cannes Film Festival, which was actually taking place in France, in their own homes. L'Oréal utilized an interactive and immersive ad experience to allow Indian consumers to upload their pictures within the ad and virtually 'try on' different shades.

InMobi (2018) explain how the mobile advert worked:

- Facial recognition software allowed recognition of the user's face.
- As soon as the facial features of the consumer were captured, a carousel of the different lipsticks appeared and allowed users to experiment with the different shades. That way the consumer could instantaneously live the new look.
- Once the consumer liked a colour, they could click on it and were directed to the L'Oréal mobile website.
- Consumers were also encouraged to share their look on social media channels and to browse L'Oréal's website for more products.

The campaign resulted in high engagement with a number of target audiences across India. Within 20 days the campaign had been viewed by more than 700,000 women and had more than 2.4 million impressions (InMobi, 2018). The campaign received 19,000 clicks and on average consumers spent around 60–90 seconds engaging in the ad unit. More than 80 per cent of people who viewed the interactive ad visited L'Oréal's mobile website. Besides these successful brand engagement statistics, L'Oréal could use the collected data to identify consumer preferences.

Questions

a. Visit L'Oréal's YouTube site, find the video, 'Beauty for All: Retail consumer experience in your palm', and watch how L'Oréal India used augmented reality in a mobile marketing campaign.

b. Why do you think this campaign has been so successful?

c. Which of the five unique features of mobile marketing have been employed during this mobile marketing campaign:?:

- ubiquity
- multiway communication
- 24 × 7 availability
- marketing channels
- personalization

d. Do you see any potential ethical issues with this campaign?

In order for mobile marketing to be successful, there are some guidelines that can help when creating mobile marketing campaigns (Kumar and Mittal, 2020; Marrs, 2022):

- Offer clear and concise messages easily readable on small screens.
- Ensure consumers grant permission for mobile marketing activities to avoid campaigns becoming spam.
- Consider the audience to ensure relevant and personalized content.
- Optimize for location-sensitive content.
- Track results to determine campaign effectiveness.

Mobile marketing advantages and disadvantages

Mobile marketing offers several opportunities to digital marketers. These include message personalization, real-time customer interaction and location-based data. However, these advantages also raise some ethical questions. Mobile devices capture contextual information and other customer behaviour data about their users (Tong et al, 2020). Collecting such data, whether businesses have the right to collect it or not, does pose issues concerning consumers' privacy. If this collected data is available to the wrong people it can be used for identity theft or spamming (Kenton, 2022). But even if the data is kept and used by the intended people, some highlight that collecting data such as location can be perceived as too intrusive (Kumar and Mittal,

Table 18.5 Advantages and disadvantages of display mobile marketing

Advantages	Disadvantages
• Personalization opportunity • Easy access • Real-time customer interaction • Cost-effective	• Concerns about privacy and security • Annoyance • Little display

Knight, 2022; Kenton, 2022; Marrs, 2022; Nguyen, 2018

2020). The issue of mobile marketing being intrusive does not only concern the collection of data but also consumers being annoyed by campaigns that are not relevant to them. Advertising on larger devices can be ignored but the mobile phone is a very personal device for many, making consumers not wanting to be interrupted unless it is relevant to them (Nguyen, 2018).

Email marketing

Email marketing is one of the most commonly used digital marketing channels. The reasons are not surprising as email marketing is one of the most lucrative channels. A survey conducted by Statista in 2020 found that among marketers worldwide, the return on investment for every US dollar invested in *email marketing* was $36 (Statista Research Department, 2021b).

> **KEY TERM**
> Email marketing
>
> Email marketing is the process of targeting an audience and customers through email. It helps boost conversions and revenue by providing subscribers and customers with valuable information to help achieve their goals.
>
> **SOURCE** Perricone, 2022a

There are many benefits attached to email marketing, the high return on investment being just one of them. The overall effectiveness of email marketing as a marketing channel is mentioned by almost 80 per cent of marketers (Perricone, 2022a). This is not surprising as research has shown the influence of email newsletters on consumer purchases (Kumar, 2021).

Another benefit includes the number of email users worldwide. Despite a rise in chat apps and other mobile messengers, email remains an integral part of daily online life with roughly four billion global email users (Dixon, 2022). This is a huge number of potential readers who are opting in to receive business messages.

One of the main advantages associated with email marketing is that it is one of the few forms of digital channels where the media is actually owned by the business. This does not mean that the email channel itself is owned as businesses use a variety of email providers but the email contact list is owned and should consist of people who want to hear from a business (Riserbato, 2020).

Email marketing process

An email campaign requires some planning in order to be executed successfully and to reap the benefits of email marketing. The following six steps have been suggested by Perricone (2022a) as a way to build an effective email marketing campaign (Figure 18.2).

1. Define audience

As with many digital marketing channels strategies, it is essential to know and visualize an audience. Knowing what the consumer wants to gain from opting in to receive business newsletters is important for tailoring the content of an email campaign.

Figure 18.2 Email marketing process

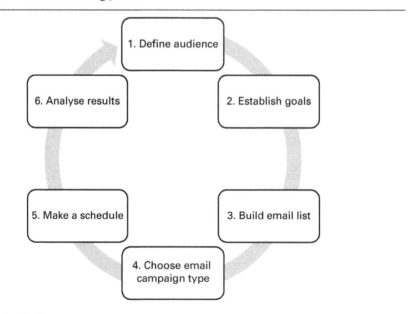

SOURCE Based on Perricone, 2022a

Consumers read email newsletters for a variety of reasons. Kumar (2021) highlights newsletters as a source of entertainment, engagement, interaction, shopping and information search, among others. This is important for businesses to consider when creating the content of a campaign.

The more businesses know about their audience the more the email campaign can be personalized. For example, personalizing an email's subject line to include the name of the message recipient leads to impressive results. Sahni et al (2018) find that adding the name of the message recipient to the email's subject line increased the probability of the recipient opening it by 20 per cent, which translated to an increase in sales leads by 31 per cent and a reduction in the number of individuals unsubscribing from the email campaign by 17 per cent.

Clyde (2020) stresses that businesses should establish both segmentation and suppression lists. A segmentation list includes those people who receive the email based on a group of consumers with similar needs, values and interests. The more specifically an email campaign is tailored to the readers' interests and current buying stage, the more successful the email will be (Clyde, 2020). A suppression list includes those individuals who should not receive an email for a particular campaign. There are a number of reasons why someone should be put on the 'do not send list'. This could be users who have not engaged with emails for a long period meaning that not including them could boost opening and click-through rates. Also, people should be on the suppression list if they have already interacted with the content that will be promoted in the email campaign (Clyde, 2020). It can be frustrating for consumers to receive an email for a particular product that is on offer if they have purchased it a couple of weeks prior to receiving the promotion.

Perricone (2022b) suggests the following ways in which an email list could be broken down into different segments:

- geographical location
- life cycle stage
- awareness, consideration, decision stage
- industry
- previous engagement with your brand
- language
- job title

Activity 18.6

We have now learnt about the benefits of email marketing and the importance of compiling a segmentation as well as a suppression list of contact to include and exclude in an email campaign.

i. Visit Campaign Monitor online and search for the article 'Rip Curl makes waves with email marketing'. Then click on the button 'Watch the video' to watch Ripcurl's video about their email marketing.

ii. Pretend to be the email marketing manager for Ripcurl. It is your job to compose an email marketing campaign to promote the latest boardshorts for men.

iii. Think of criteria, both demographic as well as behavioural, that should inform your segmentation as well as your suppression list. In other words, who could be a suitable target audience for the campaign and who would you choose to exclude?

iv. Provide justifications for your choices.

2. Establish goals

It is a good idea to set goals for each email campaign to evaluate the success. There are a number of metrics that are commonly used in email marketing and can be helpful in setting goals. These can differ quite dramatically between industries, and knowing industry benchmarks is important to set realistic goals (Perricone, 2022a). The most common metrics are:

- **Email open rate:** the email open rate is the percentage that measures unique opens compared to the total number of messages delivered to a list (Fryrear, 2020).

- **Click-through rate (CTR):** the CTR is the percentage of recipients who click on one or more links within an email (Green, 2022).

- **Click-to-open rate (CTOR):** the CTOR is the percentage of subscribers who clicked something in the email as related to the total number who opened it (Fryrear, 2020).

- **Unsubscribe rate:** the percentage of recipients who unsubscribe as related to the total number receiving the email. Unsubscribe rates are relatively low, averaging around 0.1 per cent (Campaign Monitor, 2022).

- Further information about these metrics can be found in the Additional Supporting Materials online.

Goals should not only contain metrics though. Businesses should determine more broadly what they are aiming to achieve with their campaign. For example, the CTR is a statistic that describes how many people are clicking onto a link which ultimately tells the campaign manager how relevant a campaign has been (Fryrear, 2020). The CTOR is an indication of how interesting the recipient finds the message, so while these metrics are relevant to set goals and to measure success, it is essential to see the bigger picture of what these statistics actually mean.

3. Build email list

Having an up-to-date email list with users who have given permission to receive relevant content is essential to successfully achieving the set goals. It used to be common practice to buy email lists and send emails to people who have not given their explicit permission. However, since legislation such as the General Data Protection Regulation (GDPR) has come into force, the practice of sending emails without the explicit consent of the recipient is against the law.

It is therefore important to build an email list of people who are happy to receive information. There are two ways in which brands can get people to sign on to their email list: by using *lead magnets*; and by creating an enticing opt-in form (Perricone, 2022b).

KEY TERM
Lead magnet

A lead magnet is something that attracts prospects to an email list, usually in the form of a free offer. The offer can take a number of formats, should be valuable to your prospects, and is given away for free in exchange for an email address. A lead magnet should be relevant, useful, and make the prospects' lives easier.

Types of lead magnets include e-book, whitepaper, infographic, report or study, checklist, template, webinar or course, and tool.

SOURCE Perricone, 2022b

The opt-in form is the form that prospects complete with their information to be added to the email list. There are some suggestions of how an opt-in form can be created (Perricone, 2022b):

- create an attractive design and attention-grabbing header
- make the copy relevant to the offer
- keep the form simple

A good email list should ensure that only recipients who are interested in engaging with a brand are on the list as this ensures high click-through and opening rates which in turn lead to more purchases (Kumar, 2021).

4. Choose an email campaign type

There are various kinds of email marketing campaigns and they differ in terms of which goals they aim to achieve. For example, sending out a newsletter to keep recipients up to date on a number of different topics is great for building relationships with consumers over time. If the content is relevant to the consumer, they will continue to read the newsletter. However, a promotional email offering a special, often time-sensitive deal is great for converting a recipient into a purchasing consumer. Hussain (2016) lists some of the types of emails that can be explored:

- new content announcement email
- product update email
- digital magazine or newsletter
- event invitation
- dedicated send to those who have previously signed up to something
- social media send
- transactional emails (confirmation email, thank you email, welcome email)
- co-marketing email

Most of these types of emails aim to either maintain a relationship with the consumers (e.g. transactional emails and newsletter), to engage consumers (e.g. dedicated social media send) or to convert recipients into buyers (e.g. product update or new content announcement). However, there is one type of marketing that can be used to reach and acquire new customers: the *co-marketing email*.

KEY TERM
Co-marketing email

Co-marketing is when two or more complementary companies partner together for some mutually beneficial task, event or other promotion. The main draw of co-marketing is to leverage the audience of another company to increase reach.

SOURCE Hussain, 2016

---

5. Make a schedule

Email marketers have to consider how often they are planning on compiling different types of email and how frequently they are going to send them. Recipients want to know when they can expect an update which is why it is crucial to be consistent once a schedule has been established.

There are some days that yield better results than others when it comes to email marketing metrics. So depending on what goal an email marketing campaign aims to achieve, different days and times are better suited than others.

Campaign Monitor (2022) found the following statistics which are useful to consider when making a schedule:

- Weekdays tend to perform the best, with the lowest engagement numbers falling on the weekend:
  - best day with highest email open rates: Monday (22.0 per cent)
  - best day with highest click-through rates: Tuesday (2.4 per cent)
  - best days with highest click-to-open rates: Wednesday and Tuesday (10.8 per cent)
  - email unsubscribe rates were virtually identical throughout the week (0.1 per cent)
- Based on the global averages by day shown above, the following are the worst-performing days for sending emails:
  - worst day with lowest email open rates: Sunday (20.3 per cent)
  - worst days with lowest click-through rates: Saturday & Sunday (2.1 per cent)
  - worst day with lowest click-to-open rates: Friday, Saturday, Sunday (10.1 per cent)

6. Analyse results

Another great benefit of email marketing is the ability to easily measure performance and therefore be able to improve results. There are activities such as *A/B testing* that can help improve results if metrics such as the click-through or open rate show that the email is not performing as well as anticipated (see also Chapters 3 and 22).

KEY TERM
A/B testing

A/B (or split) testing in email marketing describes having two different versions of the same content and testing whether consumers prefer option A or B. This allows marketers to choose the better-performing email to be sent in the main email campaign. Tests can vary in complexity: simple tests involving sending multiple subject lines to test which ones generate more opens; or more advanced tests which include completely different email templates to see which one generates more click-throughs. Variations can include headlines, email subject lines, images, colours, fonts, buttons or calls to action.

SOURCE Campaign Monitor, nd

Successful email marketing design

There is no doubt that the design of an email is crucial to its success. Research into the email components that influence consumer behaviour identifies subject line length, email size, purchase links, non-purchase links and branded banners as being of significance (Kumar, 2021). For example, shorter subject lines improve email open and click-through rates and the presence of links within the email positively influence consumers' purchases (Kumar, 2021). Sahni et al (2018) provide statistically significant results that show that personalizing an email increases open rates and sales. Clyde (2020) lists the following components that go to make an email campaign successful.

1. A clear call to action

Setting clear goals when planning a digital marketing campaign is crucial to be able to evaluate success. It also helps to streamline the design of an email as the email should contain a clear key action for the recipient to take. Such a call to action should be part of any email marketing campaign and is usually a link, a button, in-text instructions or a video (Clyde, 2020).

2. A relevant and intriguing subject line

Often the subject line is the first (and sometimes the last) thing that recipients see. It is therefore crucial to get it right. Clyde (2020) proposes the following dos and don'ts:

Do:
- be specific
- hint at the value of the email
- use an exciting or fun line
- include personalization tokens if possible, like name or company

Don't:
- use all caps – there's no need to shout at your readers
- include filler words like 'hey' or 'thanks'
- ask a yes or no question
- trigger spam filters with the use of too much punctuation or the word 'free'
- over-use punctuation of any kind

3. Good copywriting

The content of the email is as essential as a pleasing design. Most of the components of a good email such as writing style, length or language used requires some testing and experience will provide an answer to the question of what works best for a brand. However, some common rules such as checking for grammatical errors, avoiding typos and using correct punctuation are a good starting point.

4. Personalization

Personalizing an email as much as possible is a great way to engage the recipient and to make it feel relevant to them. As we have discussed earlier in this part of the chapter, things like the subject line and greeting can be personalized. Knowing and referring to the purchasing history of a recipient can be another helpful way to personalize an email. Perricone (2022b) suggests the following tips for personalizing an email:

- add a first name field in your subject line and/or greeting
- include region-specific information when appropriate
- send content that is relevant to your sales lead's life cycle stage
- only send emails that pertain to the last engagement a lead has had with the brand
- write about relevant and/or personal events, like region-specific holidays or birthdays
- end emails with a personal signature from a human (not the company)
- use a relevant call to action to an offer that the reader will find useful

5. Simplify the unsubscribe option

Email marketing campaigns are most successful if they reach an audience that has opted in to be receiving information from the business or brand. Therefore, it is good practice to enable an easy-to-unsubscribe option in every email sent for those who are not interested in receiving emails. This will ensure that the emails that are sent are only reaching those that are truly interested and eager to engage.

Table 18.6 Advantages and disadvantages of email marketing

Advantages	Disadvantages
• High return on investment	• Perceived as spam
• Effective	• Resource requirements
• Large amount of users	• Undelivered emails
• Owned channel	• Design problems
• Personalization	
• Measurable	
• Flexible design	

Knight, 2022; Clyde, 2020; Perricone, 2022a; Riserbato, 2020; NI Business Info, nd

Disadvantages of email marketing

There are many advantages associated with email marketing. Nevertheless, there are also some disadvantages that require consideration. For example, many email providers do not deliver emails with particular subject lines containing specific words and signs. Therefore, email marketers need to know exactly what is acceptable to avoid too many undelivered emails. Another issue concerns relatively low open rates as consumers often do not see the relevance of an email or perceive it as spam (NI Business Info, nd). Finally, design issues such as over-large pictures or differences in the email's appearance on different email providers sets a challenge for the email design team to ensure an aesthetically pleasing experience for all of the recipients.

Summary

In this chapter, we have covered several digital marketing channels. We started by reviewing affiliate marketing which explained the use of third-party websites to promote a brand. Then search engine marketing was covered differentiating between search engine optimisation and paid search options. We reviewed a number of display advertising options across the internet. We then looked into how mobile devices provide plenty of opportunities for marketers. This chapter finishes by outlining the advantages and disadvantages of email marketing, one of the oldest digital marketing channels.

Chapter review

Reflective questions

Q1 What are the differences between digital marketing channels?

Q2 What are the advantages and disadvantages of the different digital marketing channels?

Q3 Which digital marketing channels are particularly applicable to either reach new consumers, or engage/convert existing ones?

Key learning points

- The differences between digital marketing channels and platforms.
- The advantages and disadvantages of the different digital marketing channels.
- The suitability of digital channels for different goals.

References

Armitage, P (2021) 10 content curation tools every marketer needs, HubSpot, 2 August, blog.hubspot.com/marketing/content-curation-tools (archived at https://perma.cc/2NSB-GMZG)

Arnold, B (2015) Inside Google marketing: Banner ads can be creative and effective, Google Marketing Strategies, www.thinkwithgoogle.com/marketing-strategies/app-and-mobile/inside-google-marketing-creative-effective-banner-ads/ (archived at https://perma.cc/KQE6-TRKV)

Auschaitrakul, S and Mukherjee, A (2017) Online display advertising: The influence of website type on advertising effectiveness, *Psychology and Marketing*, 34(4), 463–80

Baker, K (2022) Social media marketing: The ultimate guide, HubSpot, 11 March, blog.hubspot.com/marketing/social-media-marketing (archived at https://perma.cc/Y3FC-HUXC)

Barnhart, B (2020) How to set (and achieve) meaningful social media goals, SproutSocial, 2 January, sproutsocial.com/insights/social-media-goals/ (archived at https://perma.cc/WLE3-CKXX)

Barnhart, B (2021) Building your social media marketing strategy for 2022, SproutSocial, 7 October, sproutsocial.com/insights/social-media-marketing-strategy/ (archived at https://perma.cc/3732-P8TA)

Beveridge, C (2022) What is user-generated content and why is it important, Hootsuite, 13 January, blog.hootsuite.com/user-generated-content-ugc/#What_is_user-generated_content (archived at https://perma.cc/7S73-7ESE)

Bhat, U (2018) Top 8 types of influencer marketing campaigns, Cloohawk, 9 July, www.cloohawk.com/blog/top-8-types-influencer-marketing-campaigns (archived at https://perma.cc/L8K8-X6MZ)

Big Commerce (nd) Affiliate Marketing 101: What it is and how to get started, Big Commerce Essentials, www.bigcommerce.co.uk/articles/ecommerce/affiliate-marketing/ (archived at https://perma.cc/9FHN-S49G)

Blau, P M (1986) *Exchange and Power in Social Life,* 2nd edn, Routledge, New York

Bui, B (nd) 8 types of display ads you need to know, Directive, directiveconsulting.com/blog/types-of-display-ads-you-need-to-know/ (archived at https://perma.cc/2PY2-FQMM)

Bushery, M (nd) Ultimate guide to real estate keywords, Placester, placester.com/real-estate-marketing-academy/real-estate-seo-keyword-planner-spreadsheet (archived at https://perma.cc/42EC-9VB6)

Campaign Monitor (2022) Ultimate email marketing benchmarks for 2022: By industry and day, www.campaignmonitor.com/resources/guides/email-marketing-benchmarks/ (archived at https://perma.cc/WKF7-P8AQ)

Campaign Monitor (nd) A/B Test your email campaigns, www.campaignmonitor.com/resources/guides/ab-test-email-marketing-campaigns/#:~:text=A%2FB%20testing%2C%20in%20the,campaign%20garners%20the%20best%20results (archived at https://perma.cc/84GZ-87AX)

Carmicheal, K (2019) The 12 types of content marketing in a marketer's arsenal, Hubspot, 19 September, blog.hubspot.com/marketing/content-marketing-types (archived at https://perma.cc/CV8D-GYXF)

Carmicheal, K (2022) Which social media metrics are marketers tracking? HubSpot, 25 January, blog.hubspot.com/marketing/social-media-metrics-ceos-cares-about (archived at https://perma.cc/63BX-C7W7)

Chappel, N (2022) The history of billboard advertising, Big Box, 12 January, www.bigboxadvertising.com/blog/historyofbillboardadvertising#:~:text=The%201889%20Paris%20Exposition%20revealed,standard%20format%20for%20billboards%20everywhere (archived at https://perma.cc/SFR6-S9UK)

Chen, J (2020) What is influencer marketing: How to develop your strategy, SproutSocial, 17 September, sproutsocial.com/insights/influencer-marketing/ (archived at https://perma.cc/9EF4-JYKW)

Chen, J (2021) The most important social media metrics to track, SproutSocial, 26 March, sproutsocial.com/insights/social-media-metrics/ (archived at https://perma.cc/2MTQ-P4ZV)

Chen, Y, Wang, Q, and Xie, J (2011) Online social interactions: A natural experiment on word of mouth versus observational learning, *Journal of Marketing Research*, 48(2), 238–54

Clyde, W (2020) 7 components of a successful marketing email, New Breed, 2 December, www.newbreedrevenue.com/blog/components-of-a-successful-marketing-email (archived at https://perma.cc/XQ6J-87FA)

Content Marketing Institute (2016) How Red Bull turned their content marketing into a media company, YouTube, www.youtube.com/watch?v=TvXAwYUVbZ0 (archived at https://perma.cc/4PGZ-NFFD)

Content Marketing Institute (2022) What is content marketing? contentmarketinginstitute.com/what-is-content-marketing/ (archived at https://perma.cc/4442-5NEL)

Cooper, P (2021) The best time to post on Facebook, Instagram, Twitter, and LinkedIn, Hootsuite, 19 May, blog.hootsuite.com/best-time-to-post-on-facebook-twitter-instagram/ (archived at https://perma.cc/H8SC-P6H8)

Dada, G (2017) What is influencer marketing and how can marketers use it effectively? *Forbes*, 14 November, www.forbes.com/sites/forbescommunicationscouncil/2017/11/14/what-is-influencer-marketing-and-how-can-marketers-use-it-effectively/?sh=69a05aa623d1 (archived at https://perma.cc/54FL-9Z9N)

Daugherty, T, Eastin, M and Bright, L (2008) Exploring consumer motivations for creating user-generated content, *Journal of Interactive Advertising*, 8(2), 16–25

Davis, D (2022) Social media marketing advantages and disadvantages, Social Planner, socialplanner.io/blog/social-media-marketing-advantages-and-disadvantages/ (archived at https://perma.cc/RAA5-JGDS)

De Oliveira, M J and Huertas, M (2015) Does life satisfaction influence the intention (we-intention) to use Facebook? *Computer Human Behaviour*, 50, 205–10

Digital Marketing Institute (2019) What is SEO and how does it work? 21 October, digitalmarketinginstitute.com/blog/what-is-seo#:~:text=Well%2C%20SEO%20stands%20for%20'Search,more%20people%20will%20see%20it (archived at https://perma.cc/YXQ9-FEAU)

Digital Marketing Institute (2021) 20 surprising influencer marketing statistics, 19 October, digitalmarketinginstitute.com/blog/20-influencer-marketing-statistics-that-will-surprise-you (archived at https://perma.cc/MWX5-EBU9)

Digital Marketing Institute (nd) Digital Marketing: What is it? Digital Marketing Institute (DMI), digitalmarketinginstitute.com/resources/lessons/social-media-marketing_social-media-marketing-concepts_7xoq (archived at https://perma.cc/5UW5-DVNN)

DiSilvestro, A (2018) A beginner's guide to display advertising, Search Engine Watch, 14 February, www.searchenginewatch.com/2018/02/14/a-beginners-guide-to-display-advertising/ (archived at https://perma.cc/5Q8S-QYFH)

Dixon, S (2022) Number of e-mail users worldwide 2017–2025, Statista, 2 August, www.statista.com/statistics/255080/number-of-e-mail-users-worldwide/ (archived at https://perma.cc/R6F5-WP9P)

Dollarhide, M (2021) Social media: Definition, effects and list of top apps, Investopedia, 31 August, www.investopedia.com/terms/s/social-media.asp (archived at https://perma.cc/F363-668B)

Duffy, D (2005) Affiliate marketing and its impact on e-commerce, *Journal of Consumer Marketing*, 22(3), 161–63

Evans, N J, Phua, J, Lim, J and Jun, H (2017) Disclosing Instagram influencer advertising: The effects of disclosure language on advertising recognition, attitudes, and behavioral intent, *Journal of Interactive Advertising*, 17(2), 138–49

Ferm, L and Thaichon, P (2021) Customer pre-participatory social media drivers and their influence on attitudinal loyalty within the retail banking industry: A multigroup analysis utilizing social exchange theory, *Journal of Retailing and Consumer Services*, 61, 1–11

Frankenfield, J (2022) Affiliate marketer: Definition, examples and how to get started, Investopedia, 5 July, www.investopedia.com/terms/a/affiliate-marketing.asp (archived at https://perma.cc/VF7U-YDDK)

Fryrear, A (2020) Measuring email campaign effectiveness with click-to-open rate and other marketing metrics, Sailthru, 26 February, www.sailthru.com/marketing-blog/written-measuring-email-effectiveness-ctor/#:~:text=Click%2Dto%2Dopen%2Drates,relevancy%20of%20a%20given%20email (archived at https://perma.cc/6G9V-9P9N)

Garbi, S (2016) Augmented reality and the future of mobile marketing, LinkedIn, 6 September, www.linkedin.com/pulse/augmented-reality-future-mobile-marketing-shlomo-garbi/ (archived at https://perma.cc/ZW5Q-LGMT)

Gardener, K (2020) Everything you need to know about affiliate tracking, AWIN, 9 June, www.awin.com/gb/affiliate-marketing/everything-you-need-to-know-about-affiliate-tracking (archived at https://perma.cc/FL9D-69R7)

Geyser, W (2022a) What is influencer marketing? The ultimate guide for 2022, Influencer Marketing Hub, 15 July, influencermarketinghub.com/influencer-marketing/#toc-6 (archived at https://perma.cc/6ELJ-VAE6)

Geyser, W (2022b) Influencer Rates: How much do influencers really cost in 2022? Influencer Marketing Hub, 26 July, influencermarketinghub.com/influencer-rates/ (archived at https://perma.cc/8557-QXD4)

Ghose, A and Todri-Adamopoulos, V (2016) Toward a digital attribution model: measuring the impact of display advertising on online consumer behaviour, *MIS Quarterly*, 40(40), 889–910

Google Ads Help (2022a) Choose the right campaign type, Google, support.google.com/google-ads/answer/2567043 (archived at https://perma.cc/TCR6-B77C)

Google Ads Help (2022b) Auction, support.google.com/google-ads/answer/142918?hl=en-GB#:~:text=The%20process%20that%20happens%20with,goes%20through%20the%20ad%20auction (archived at https://perma.cc/TP57-2ZXL)

Google Ads Help (2022c) About quality score, support.google.com/google-ads/answer/6167118?hl=en-GB#:~:text=Quality%20Score%20is%20a%20diagnostic,available%20at%20the%20keyword%20level (archived at https://perma.cc/CQV9-XGUT)

Google Rich Media Showcase (nd) www.richmediagallery.com/ (archived at https://perma.cc/2JEL-DW3X)

Google Studio Help (2022) What is rich media, support.google.com/richmedia/answer/2417545?hl=en#:~:text=Rich%20media%20is%20a%20digital,and%20engage%20with%20the%20content (archived at https://perma.cc/9379-5DPS)

Green, S (2022) What is an email CTR? How to calculate and improve it, HubSpot, 21 January, blog.hubspot.com/blog/tabid/6307/bid/34132/how-to-improve-email-clickthrough-rate-by-583.aspx (archived at https://perma.cc/S4FL-LMG8)

Grow Traffic (nd) What are the disadvantages of content marketing, www.growtraffic.co.uk/disadvantanges-of-content-marketing/ (archived at https://perma.cc/2YSZ-Q237)

Guttmann, A (2019) Affiliate marketing spend in the US 2010–2022, Statista, 6 March, www.statista.com/statistics/693438/affiliate-marketing-spending/#statisticContainer (archived at https://perma.cc/88LU-4AHA)

GWI (2022) The biggest social media trends for 2022, Global Web Index, www.gwi.com/reports/social (archived at https://perma.cc/H4KA-9LQB)

Gymshark 66 (2020) How to change your life in 66 days, YouTube, www.youtube.com/watch?v=vSa9eNvtCT0 (archived at https://perma.cc/PQE8-PHHC)

Gymshark (2021) What is #GYMSHARK66? 17 December, central.gymshark.com/article/what-is-the-gymshark-66-challenge (archived at https://perma.cc/6WJ5-SUCY)

Gynn, A (2022) 7 more ways to curate content like a pro, Content Marketing Institute, 27 April, contentmarketinginstitute.com/articles/how-to-curate-content/ (archived at https://perma.cc/897H-P8YT)

Haenlein, M, Anadol, E, Farnsworth, T, Huga, H, Hunichen, J and Welte, D (2020) Navigating the new era of influencer marketing: How to be successful on Instagram, TikTok, and Co, *California Management Review*, 63(1), 5–25

Hervet, G, Guerard, K, Tremblay, S and Chtourou, M (2011) Is banner blindness genuine? Eye tracking internet text advertising, *Applied Cognitive Psychology*, 25, 708–16

Hossain, M A, Kim, M and Jahan, N (2019) Can 'Liking' behaviour lead to usage intention on Facebook? Uses and gratification theory perspective, *Sustainability*, 11, 1–13

Hsieh, Y C, and Chen, K H (2011) How different information types affect viewers' attention on internet advertising, *Computers in Human Behavior*, 27, 935–45

Hughes, J (2021) Why first-party cookies are the future of affiliate marketing, Easy Affiliate, 13 December, easyaffiliate.com/blog/first-party-cookies-affiliate-marketing/?utm_source=rss&utm_medium=rss&utm_campaign=first-party-cookies-affiliate-marketing (archived at https://perma.cc/6FFR-AGLB)

Hussain, A (2016) 12 different types of marketing email you could be sending, HubSpot, 5 May, blog.hubspot.com/blog/tabid/6307/bid/33987/11-types-of-marketing-emails-you-could-be-sending-free-templates.aspx (archived at https://perma.cc/BEY9-WX8B)

iCrossing (2010) UK case study: Ann Summers Sexy Paid Search, YouTube, www.youtube.com/watch?v=eVU60NRuOJo (archived at https://perma.cc/44X8-XSXA)

Indig, K (2022) What is technical SEO: Your guide to getting started, Semrush, 7 February, www.semrush.com/blog/learning-technical-seo/ (archived at https://perma.cc/4BGG-V3WD)

InMobi (2018) L'Oréal: Beauty for all: Retail consumer experience in your palm [video], 19 August, YouTube, www.youtube.com/watch?v=2i94VdFZi0g&t=92s (archived at https://perma.cc/5ZLG-JBN8)

Itani, O, Krush, M, Agnihotri, R and Trainor, K (2020) Social media and customer relationship management technologies: Influencing buyer–seller information exchanges, *Industrial Marketing Management*, 90, 264–75

Iyer, Y (2022) How to develop an influencer marketing strategy, Wrike, 23 March, www.wrike.com/blog/influencer-marketing-strategy-guide/#What-is-influencer-marketing (archived at https://perma.cc/S7X5-6XSD)

Kagan, J (2022) Viral marketing, Investopedia, 28 March, www.investopedia.com/terms/v/viral-marketing.asp (archived at https://perma.cc/H4HX-ECGL)

Kagan, M (2016) 100 awesome marketing stats, charts and graphs, HubSpot, 20 October, blog.hubspot.com/blog/tabid/6307/bid/14416/100-Awesome-Marketing-Stats-Charts-Graphs-Data.aspx (archived at https://perma.cc/CEG4-TJ2G)

Kay, S, Mulcahy, R, and Parkinson, J (2020) When less is more: The impact of macro and micro social media influencers' disclosure, *Journal of Marketing Management*, 36 (3–4), 248–78

Kenton, W (2020) Call to action (CTA), Investopedia, 29 March, www.investopedia.com/terms/c/call-action-cta.asp (archived at https://perma.cc/NY7G-FAFZ)

Kenton, W (2022) Mobile marketing, Investopedia, 29 March, www.investopedia.com/terms/m/mobile-marketing.asp (archived at https://perma.cc/B6U4-5CP8)

Kerner, M (nd) Cookie, TechTarget, www.techtarget.com/searchsoftwarequality/definition/cookie (archived at https://perma.cc/FTR3-ZX8S)

Kim, L (2021) The war on 'free' clicks: Think nobody clicks on Google Ads? Think Again!, Wordstream, 19 November, www.wordstream.com/blog/ws/2012/07/17/google-advertising (archived at https://perma.cc/C4PB-P4EX)

Kumar, A (2021) An empirical examination of the effects of design elements of email newsletters on consumers' email responses and their purchase, *Journal of Retailing and Consumer Services*, 58, 1–13

Kumar, V and Mittal, S (2020) Mobile marketing campaigns: Practices, challenges and opportunities, *International Journal of Business Innovation and Research*, 21(4), 523–39

Latuca, A (2018) Diverse affiliate payment methods, AWIN, 23 August, www.awin.com/gb/ how-to-use-awin/diverse-affiliate-payment-methods (archived at https://perma.cc/ RNF6-STBR)

Leist, R (2021) The definition of SEO in 100 words or less, HubSpot, 1 April, blog.hubspot. com/marketing/what-is-seo (archived at https://perma.cc/C874-228E)

Leonard, J (2022) 7 pros and cons of content marketing, Business 2 Community, 13 July, www.business2community.com/content-marketing-tips/7-pros-and-cons-of-content-marketing-0266634 (archived at https://perma.cc/2R29-GCV7)

Li, F, Larimo, J and Leonidou, L (2021) Social media marketing strategy: Definition, conceptualization, taxonomy, validation, and future agenda, *Journal of the Academy of Marketing Science*, 49, 51–70

L'Or é al (2018) Beauty for all: Retail consumer experience in your palm, YouTube, www. youtube.com/watch?v=2i94VdFZi0g&t=92s (archived at https://perma.cc/X82P-U9J7)

Lyons, K (2021) What is search engine marketing and how does it work? Semrush, 13 August, www.semrush.com/blog/search-engine-marketing/ (archived at https://perma.cc/ H7VZ-Z9DA)

Marketo (2014) The definitive guide to engaging content marketing, go.marketo.com/rs/ marketob2/images/DG2ECM.pdf (archived at https://perma.cc/UJG5-XQQT)

Marrs, M (2022) What is mobile marketing and why does it matter so much? WordStream, 3 March, www.wordstream.com/blog/ws/2013/08/19/what-is-mobile-marketing (archived at https://perma.cc/DGA4-K9U2)

Martin, M (2022) The complete guide to content curation in 2022: Tools, tips, ideas, Hootsuite, 23 February, blog.hootsuite.com/beginners-guide-to-content-curation/ (archived at https://perma.cc/W4YU-QXD7)

Mazouri, H (2021) User-generated content: 5 steps to turn customers into advocates, SproutSocial, 14 July, sproutsocial.com/insights/user-generated-content-guide/ (archived at https://perma.cc/6AFL-8BQQ)

McLachlan, S (2021) How often to post to social media in 2022, Hootsuite, 16 June, blog. hootsuite.com/how-often-to-post-on-social-media/ (archived at https://perma.cc/MC8N-CKFH)

Mileva, G (2022) Top 8 affiliate marketing strategies for 2022, Influencer Marketing Hub, 21 June, influencermarketinghub.com/affiliate-marketing-strategies/ (archived at https:// perma.cc/RR3K-TNTE)

Morris, C (2021) 7 powerful benefits of using PPC advertising, Search Engine Journal, 8 February, www.searchenginejournal.com/ppc-guide/ppc-advertising-benefits/#close (archived at https://perma.cc/98SR-2BSZ)

Muhammad, F (2020) What is display advertising? Instapage, 10 November, instapage.com/ blog/display-advertising (archived at https://perma.cc/8CPN-T4S8)

Muriuki, S (2016) Display ads: Advantages and disadvantages, LinkedIn, 8 February, www. linkedin.com/pulse/display-ads-advantages-disadvantages-samuel-muriuki/ (archived at https://perma.cc/VS59-BNML)

Muthoni, J (2021) 10 key benefits of SEO for your business, *Forbes*, 14 June, www.forbes. com/sites/forbesagencycouncil/2021/06/14/10-key-benefits-of-seo-for-your-business/?sh=4a0171603fd0 (archived at https://perma.cc/4U49-NRH2)

Nguyen, H (2018) The pros and cons of mobile marketing, LinkedIn, 10 August, www.linkedin.com/pulse/pros-cons-mobile-marketing-ho%C3%A0ng-c%C3%B4ng/ (archived at https://perma.cc/2DWV-F66V)

NI Business Info (nd) Email marketing, www.nibusinessinfo.co.uk/content/advantages-and-disadvantages-email-marketing (archived at https://perma.cc/FUK4-J7YB)

Obar, J A and Wildman, S (2015) Social media definition and the governance challenge: An introduction to the special issue, *Telecommunications Policy*, 39(9), 745–50

Optimizely (nd) Search engine optimization, www.optimizely.com/optimization-glossary/search-engine-optimization/ (archived at https://perma.cc/92QM-7GMR)

Osmundson, B (2022) Get to know ad rank and learn 3 ways to improve it, Search Engine Journal, 22 June, www.searchenginejournal.com/what-is-ad-rank/257305/#close (archived at https://perma.cc/N2Q6-YHK3)

Pack, S (2017) Social media strategies: What is the 4-1-1 Rule and the 70-20-10 Rule? LinkedIn, 9 June, www.linkedin.com/pulse/social-media-strategies-what-4-1-1-rule-70-20-10-look-pack-pcm/ (archived at https://perma.cc/NT4Y-7W6A)

Papacharissi, Z and Mendelson, A (2011) Toward a new(er) sociability: Uses, gratifications, and social capital on Facebook, in *Media Perspectives for the 21st Century*, 212–30, Routledge, New York, NY

Patel, N (nd) Content marketing made simple: A step-by-step guide, neilpatel.com/what-is-content-marketing/ (archived at https://perma.cc/47SM-SHBK)

Payne, K (2020) 10 Strategies to optimise your PPC ads and boost sales, *Campaign Monitor*, 28 February, www.campaignmonitor.com/blog/email-marketing/10-strategies-to-optimize-your-ppc-ads-and-boost-sales/ (archived at https://perma.cc/825B-SSBW)

Pencil Speech (2022) Advantages and disadvantages of SEO in 2022, 25 February, pencilspeech.com/en/advantages-and-disadvantages-of-seo-in-2022/ (archived at https://perma.cc/T4XC-YBPX)

Perricone, C (2021) The ultimate guide to PPC marketing, HubSpot, 1 July, blog.hubspot.com/marketing/ppc (archived at https://perma.cc/ND9F-33Y6)

Perricone, C (2022a) The ultimate guide to email marketing, HubSpot, 23 March, blog.hubspot.com/marketing/email-marketing-guide (archived at https://perma.cc/NKR7-4HGX)

Perricone, C (2022b) The ultimate guide to email marketing: #Build your email list, HubSpot, 1 August, blog.hubspot.com/marketing/email-marketing-guide#build-your-email-list (archived at https://perma.cc/CVJ6-36QK)

Persaud, A and Azhar, I (2012) Innovative mobile marketing via smartphones: Are customers ready? *Marketing Intelligence and Planning*, 30(4), 418–43

Qualman, E (2018) Digital Transformation by Erik Qualman, YouTube, www.youtube.com/watch?v=pD2ojCPFU28 (archived at https://perma.cc/JNR2-ZH9Y)

Riserbato, R (2020) 12 Benefits of email marketing your marketing team must know, HubSpot, 25 February, blog.hubspot.com/marketing/benefits-of-email-marketing (archived at https://perma.cc/MK9Q-AFRK)

Rose, R (2016) The 2017 content marketing framework, Content Marketing Institute, 27 October, contentmarketinginstitute.com/2016/10/content-marketing-framework-profitable/ (archived at https://perma.cc/Y2S5-3CMA)

Rothfuss, A (2022) How to increase brand safety when advertising online, Comtogether, 18 January, comtogether.com/2022/01/18/how-to-increase-brand-safety-when-advertising-online/ (archived at https://perma.cc/Y3TU-N32J)

Rowley, J (2008) Understanding digital content marketing, *Journal of Marketing Management*, 24(5-6), 517–40

Sahni, N, Wheeler, C, and Chintagunta, P (2018) Personalization in email marketing: The role of noninformative advertising content, *Marketing Science*, 37(2), 236–58

Santora, J (2022a) Key influencer marketing statistics you need to know for 2022, Influencer Marketing Hub, 29 March, influencermarketinghub.com/influencer-marketing-statistics/ (archived at https://perma.cc/85HB-3GDQ)

Santora, J (2022b) 12 types of influencers you can use to improve your marketing, Influencer Marketing Hub, 15 July, influencermarketinghub.com/types-of-influencers/ (archived at https://perma.cc/9M2K-AAK3)

Schwartz, J (2022) How to optimize PPC campaigns to calculate the right bid, Gartner, 10 March, www.gartner.com/en/digital-markets/insights/ppc-optimization-strategies (archived at https://perma.cc/VCB9-YT3T)

Sentance, R (2018) What is paid search (PPC) and why do you need it? Econsultancy, 22 November, econsultancy.com/what-paid-search-ppc/ (archived at https://perma.cc/R689-KJ9K)

Setupad (2021) How many ads should I put on my website? 31 March, setupad.com/blog/how-many-ads-put-on-my-website/#:~:text=Sign%20Up-,What%20is%20a%20good%20ratio%20between%20content%20and%20ads%3F,and%2070%25%20of%20the%20content (archived at https://perma.cc/ELE9-GCKS)

Sides, G (2022) How to set and exceed social media goals, Hootsuite, 24 June, blog.hootsuite.com/smart-social-media-goals/ (archived at https://perma.cc/HT8Z-AJFL)

Soulo, T (2020) 90.63% of content gets no traffic from Google, Ahrefs, 31 January, ahrefs.com/blog/search-traffic-study/#:~:text=In%20other%20words%2C%20a%20whopping,breadth%20of%20the%20entire%20web (archived at https://perma.cc/TG6Q-DG9K)

Stamoulis, N (nd) Definition of a tracking URL, Brick Marketing, www.brickmarketing.com/blog/define-tracking-url (archived at https://perma.cc/EQ35-S3Y8)

Statista (2021) Adblocking: number of users 2013–2019, www.statista.com/statistics/435252/adblock-users-worldwide/ (archived at https://perma.cc/672Y-JFUW)

Statista Research Department (2021a) Mobile marketing market size worldwide 2020–2023, 1 December, www.statista.com/statistics/1002859/mobile-marketing-market-size-worldwide/ (archived at https://perma.cc/HP6F-WREW)

Statista Research Department (2021b) Email marketing ROI worldwide 2020, by industry, Statista, 18 October, www.statista.com/statistics/804656/email-roi-perception/ (archived at https://perma.cc/Y666-8NAP)

Steimle, J (2014) What is content marketing, *Forbes*, 19 September, www.forbes.com/sites/joshsteimle/2014/09/19/what-is-content-marketing/?sh=7997e56c10b9 (archived at https://perma.cc/3NFW-895X)

Techopedia (2020) Internet meme, 30 June, www.techopedia.com/definition/16944/internet-meme (archived at https://perma.cc/LH9X-TEJC)

Tellis, G, McInnis, D, Tirunillai, S and Zhang, Y (2019) What drives virality (sharing) of online digital content? The critical role of information, emotion and brand prominence, *Journal of Marketing*, 83(4), 1–20

Thaichon, P, Surachartkumtonkun, J, Quach, S, Weaven, S and Palmatier, R W (2018) Hybrid sales structures in the age of e-commerce, *Journal of Personal Selling*, 38 (3), 277–302

Tong, S, Luo, X and Xu, B (2020) Personalised mobile marketing strategies, *Journal of the Academy of Marketing Science,* 48, 64–78

Trustmary (2022) 80% of content marketing is targeted at the wrong target audience – avoid this common mistake, Trustmary, 22 April, trustmary.com/marketing/80-of-content-marketing-is-targeted-at-a-wrong-target-audience-avoid-this-common-mistake/ (archived at https://perma.cc/V38K-4XZP)

TurnTo Networks (2017) New study shows user-generated content tops marketing tactics by influencing 90 per cent of shoppers' purchasing decisions, 19 June, www.prnewswire.com/news-releases/new-study-shows-user-generated-content-tops-marketing-tactics-by-influencing-90-percent-of-shoppers-purchasing-decisions-300475348.html (archived at https://perma.cc/B7RR-C3NL)

Twin, A (2022) Key performance indicator, Investopedia, 12 June, www.investopedia.com/terms/k/kpi.asp (archived at https://perma.cc/RM33-CM2V)

Unilever (2019) Unilever unveils next phase in clean-up of digital advertising with creation of Unilever Trusted Publishers, Unilever, 28 March, www.unilever.com/news/press-and-media/press-releases/2019/unilever-unveils-next-phase-in-clean-up-of-digital-advertising-with-creation-of-unilever-trusted-publishers/ (archived at https://perma.cc/7UBL-8MXD)

Wang, Z, Hangeldiyeva, M, Ali, A, and Guo, M (2022) Effect of enterprise social media on employee creativity: Social exchange theory perspective, *Frontiers in Psychology*, 12, 1–9

WBR Insights (nd) Here's how L'Oréal is using augmented and virtual reality to create in-store experiences, Future Stores, futurestores.wbresearch.com/blog/loreal-augmented-reality-virtual-reality-in-store-experience-strategy (archived at https://perma.cc/5HKG-NPN6)

Wellman, M, Stoldt, R, Tully, M and Ekdale, B (2020) Ethics of authenticity: Social media influencers and the production of sponsored content, *Journal of Media Ethics*, 35(2), 68–82

Wordstream (2022a) Pay-per-click advertising: What is PPC and how does it work? Wordstream, www.wordstream.com/pay-per-click-advertising (archived at https://perma.cc/G7H7-M78B)

Wordstream (2022b) Cost-per-click, Wordstream, www.wordstream.com/cost-per-click (archived at https://perma.cc/6S3J-9GQP)

Ye, G, Hudders, L, De Jans, S and De Veirman, M (2021) The value of influencer marketing for business: A bibliometric analysis and managerial implications, *Journal of Advertising*, 50(2), 160–78

Yesiloglu, S, Memery, J and Chapleo, C (2021) To post or not to post? Exploring the motivations behind brand-related engagement types on social networking sites, *Internet Research*, 31(5), 1849–73

Zheng, R (2021) 10 best influencer marketing campaigns in 2021, No Good, 22 October, nogood.io/2021/10/22/best-influencer-marketing-campaigns/ (archived at https://perma.cc/LW2F-2SEC)

Zhu, Y and Chen, H (2015) Social media and human need satisfaction: Implications for social media marketing, *Business Horizons*, 58, 335–45

PART FIVE
Measurement and evaluation

Evaluation of digital marketing success

19

Dashboards and challenges of data-driven marketing

By the end of this chapter, you should be able to:

- briefly define what a digital dashboard is
- describe the components and characteristics that can make up a dashboard
- understand what FAIR data is
- explain in simple terms what challenges data-driven marketing holds for digital marketers

Introduction

Part Five (Measurement and Evaluation) of this book is underpinned by a managerial perspective, which informs the marketer if their strategy, related projects, campaigns, etc are running and performing as they should. While it is important to develop marketing strategies and integrate all of the background information obtained via research and all the components we have discussed thus far, a (digital) marketing project should ultimately result in a positive return on investment, whether monetary or in another form.

This chapter provides an overview of the tools marketing managers use to monitor projects, namely marketing funnels and digital dashboards. *Marketing funnels* provide basic stages for the marketing strategy that governs how objectives, tactics and other project elements come together to deliver. *Digital dashboards* are used to evaluate successes and failures of projects and ultimately gather insights for future strategies. These evaluations are used to create reports for businesses, clients and other stakeholder purposes. Thus, we will take a closer look at the platforms available for marketers to be able to accomplish that. We will also explore challenges of fair data that should be of paramount importance to the responsible and accountable marketer.

Marketing funnels

The AIDA model is regarded as the first marketing theory developed by St Elmo Lewis in 1898 and is, in essence, still the basis of all marketing and sales strategies (Ritson, 2016). AIDA stands for awareness, interest, desire, action. The AIDA model is often presented in a funnel form that illustrates how the marketing strategy is designed to guide the consumer on their customer journey from awareness to action (see Figure 19.1).

While some still apply the basic version of this traditional AIDA funnel, others prefer to use a revised version, which is more reflective of the complexity of modern consumption and customer-orientated marketing strategies (see The Customer Journey in Chapter 11). The revised marketing funnel (Marketing Funnel 2.0) consists of five stages: awareness, consideration, action, engagement and advocacy (see Figure 19.2). This funnel is also the most frequently used in digital and social media marketing strategies (Digital School of Marketing, 2021). This funnel is particularly attractive to digital marketers as it includes means of increasing engagement with customers via digital channels (such as social media), and subsequently brand advocacy (positive electronic word of mouth) and loyalty (retention of existing customers).

The stages of the funnel are:

- awareness: creating initial awareness in the mind of new customers
- consideration: implies inherent interest, because it necessitates the consumer moving from awareness to interest to considering your brand, despite being aware of other products from competitors

Figure 19.1   AIDA model

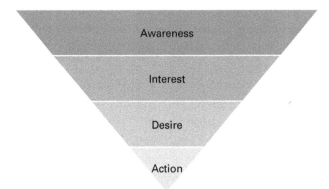

Figure 19.2   Digital marketing funnel

SOURCE Adaptation of Digital School of Marketing, 2021

- action: self-explanatory, marks the point of purchase
- engagement: increasing engagement with customers post-purchase to build relationships
- advocacy: increasing trust and loyalty to the point of positive brand advocacy via customers

Marketing funnels are useful for developing overarching strategies and dividing activities, tactics, channels and budgets into different stages. However, once the digital marketing strategy, project or campaign is implemented in the marketplace, marketers need to be able to monitor and evaluate its progress.

See Worksheet 6 in Additional Resources for a template you can use to create your own digital marketing funnel complete with objectives, channels and key metrics.

Digital dashboards

As a result of digital marketing and consumer activities online, marketers are faced with a challenge in the form of mountains of Big Data. In order to evaluate their digital marketing strategies, projects and campaigns, they need to know what the data says. This is where *digital dashboards* come in handy as primary reporting tools.

KEY TERM
Digital dashboards

Platforms with strategically selected collections of interrelated marketing metrics which enable marketers to interpret unstructured data and present them visually.

SOURCE Chan and Uncles, 2022

Marketers use these dashboards as project management tools to aid their processing of large amounts of unstructured data. Using the insights derived from their monitoring of the dashboards, marketers can identify and report on patterns of engagement and consumption across their digital marketing channels and campaigns (Chan and Uncles, 2022). Marketers use these evaluations to determine the levels of success or failure of marketing projects and to inform decision-making for developing future marketing strategies, objectives and projects. Marketing dashboards also allow marketers to determine the return on investment and other metrics (see Chapter 20) which can be used as a basis for future budget allocations.

Why do you need it?

Digital dashboards are essential for integrating digital marketing into traditional marketing projects (Kingsnorth, 2022). Digital dashboards give you an overview of the performance of the marketing strategy or campaign. The digital dashboard also informs you which elements or channels are not working and need attention or revised content and strategies to perform optimally.

> This dashboard must go beyond simply reporting and providing information that can meet detailed effectiveness monitoring objectives. A number of steps are crucial for its success, including adapting KPIs to objectives, selecting the 'right' platform, and developing an optimal user interface for the full appropriation of the dashboard.
>
> Flores, 2013

The advantage (and challenge) of digital marketing and dashboards is that you can adjust a suboptimal element quickly, even while the campaign is running.

Characteristics of good digital dashboards

There are a lot of customizable and highly specialized dashboard tools available on the internet, some for free and others for subscription fees. A lot of the functions and data processing to produce visual representations are automated. However, it is still necessary to apply analytical and strategic thinking to develop insights from the data and develop informed reports and recommendations.

Flores (2013) identifies seven key characteristics of a good dashboard:

1 relevant to purpose
2 standardized presentation of data/findings
3 overview vs specific findings (depending on purpose and SMART objectives)
4 fast turnaround of data

5 indicate profitability and ROI (return on investment)

6 up to date

Selecting a digital dashboard

The dashboard(s) you select depends on a number of factors:

- what you want to monitor
- the time period monitored
- which SMART objectives need to be met or reported on
- who the insights are being presented to
- whether it is an interim report for a project that is currently running or a report of final results after the project is complete
- whether you have a dedicated specialist and/or digital team
- the level of detail required – an in-depth review or general overview

---

Activity 19.1

i. Visit the Whatagraph.com website. Scroll down to 'Top 10 Types of Marketing Dashboard Examples (+ Templates)' to read Vaičiūnaitė's (2022) review of different dashboards including template examples.

ii. Then read 'The 19 Most Powerful Social Media Dashboards You Should Know' on Neal Schaffer's website (search for social media dashboards, click on the article with the title as above).

iii. In your groups, pick two dashboards to inspect and answer the following questions:

- What is the purpose of this dashboard?
- What does it monitor?
- Which channels can you include/integrate into the dashboard?
- Is it free or subscription-based?
- Is it easy to use?
- Do you need to use it with another dashboard to get a good understanding of the performance of a campaign? Why/why not?
- Does it have an automatic report function?
- What else does the dashboard offer?

In the last couple of years there has been a significant increase in the number of digital dashboards. The dashboards can be sub-divided into two categories: integrated overview and channel-specific. The following section provides an overview of the different types of digital dashboards, with a more detailed explanation of each.

Types of digital dashboards

There are two main types of dashboard (Kingsnorth, 2022; Schaffer, 2022; Vaičiūnaitė, 2021):

- Integrated overview dashboards:
    - key performance indicator (KPI) dashboards e.g. Geckoboard
    - chief marketing officer (CMO) marketing dashboards e.g. Dashthis
    - e-commerce marketing dashboards e.g. Klipfolio
    - online/digital marketing dashboards e.g. Whatagraph
    - social media or content marketing dashboards e.g. Hootsuite or Brandwatch.com
- Channel-specific dashboards:
    - website analytics dashboards e.g. Google Analytics
    - email marketing dashboards e.g. Mailchimp
    - search engine optimization (SEO) analytics dashboards
    - Google AdWords campaign studio dashboards
    - Amazon attribution dashboards
    - YouTube ads dashboards
    - Twitter Analytics
    - Facebook Analytics
    - Tiktok Analytics

Integrated overview dashboards

As the name suggests, integrated overview dashboards provide a broader overview of the project (or even all marketing activity if evaluating multiple projects). Integrated dashboards are more consolidative in their approach; they allow you to combine data from a broad range of sources e.g. social media, website and email, to give you both a strategic overview and a means to probe each channel in-depth.

Key performance indicator (KPI) dashboards e.g. Geckoboard, and chief marketing officer (CMO) marketing dashboards e.g. Dashthis, enable the digital marketer to see how the project is doing in terms of achieving SMART objectives or KPIs; sales, spending and budget; and ultimately the ROI. E-commerce dashboards such as Klipfolio are more business- than marketing-orientated, focusing more on objectives such as sales, bookings, etc. Online or digital marketing dashboards are similar, but do include more marketing information on the specific platforms used, e.g. Whatagraph.

Social media or content marketing dashboards, such as Hootsuite and Brandwatch, take it a step further by allowing you to integrate data from your social media channels, create and disseminate content, manage brand communities, allow for collaborations and track analytics all in one integrated platform. These dashboards integrate digital marketing measurement with customer relationship management (CRM) and customer engagement management (CEM), topics which were introduced in Chapter 11.

Channel-specific dashboards

Channel-specific dashboards are more niche in terms of the data provided for that specific channel. For example, email marketing dashboards such as Mailchimp provide data unique to the email database used for the project (read, links clicked, unsubscribed, etc). Email dashboards, such as Mailchimp, also allow for CRM and CEM.

Google AdWords and SEO are concerned with their respective content and how they perform to draw consumers to your platforms. SEO is concerned with the searchable and discoverable terms built into your content to optimize your website. Google AdWords gives information on the performance of Google AdWords campaigns.

Amazon Attribution also allows you to pull data from platforms outside Amazon, but provides a means of attributing which platform provides what kind of brand awareness and conversion to optimize your activity on Amazon.

Web analytics

Website analytics dashboards, e.g. Google Analytics, give an overview of all the activity related to your specific website, such as page views, number of visits, conversion rates, etc. Platforms like Dashthis and Klipfolio also allow website-specific dashboards, where you only include data widgets related to the website as marketing channel.

KEY TERM
Web analytics

Web analytics describes the reporting of activities on websites. It gets its information from traditional business intelligence and data mining processes. It provides information on how many visitors your site gets, how much time they spend on your website, and what they do while they are on your website.

SOURCE Lippa, 2012

Figure 19.3   Three focus areas within web analytics

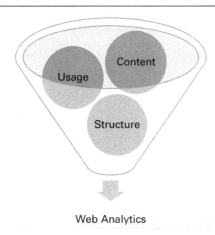

Web Analytics

According to Alghalith (2015), there are three focus areas within web analytics (see Figure 19.3). The widgets you select should capture data for each of these three areas to give a sufficient overview of website performance. It could also be argued that your SMART objectives for the website should also include measures for each of these three areas. Therefore, to evaluate the success of a website, you need to understand how the content is performing, how consumers use the content and whether the structure of your website is intuitive (more specific measures will be discussed in Chapter 20).

Social media analytics

Each social media platform has its own analytics feature for business accounts, for example number of viewers for videos on YouTube ads dashboards, and Facebook and Tiktok analytics for number of interactions, posts, etc. Most dashboards (whether individual or integrated) use a combination of metrics to measure the digital or social media marketing funnel stages – awareness, consideration, action, engagement and advocacy (see Figure 19.2) – which we will discuss in Chapter 20.

It is advisable to have an integrated digital marketing dashboard that combines data from different channels if you have an integrated marketing campaign (a campaign with multiple communication pieces across different channels at the same time such as a web page, digital banners, social media advertisements, social media posts, emails, etc).

Setting up digital dashboards

As indicated above, there are a variety of dashboards you can use. However, the process for setting up the dashboard is essentially the same, as outlined in the steps below.

Step 1: Select the type of dashboard that is most appropriate for your requirements and project. Use the factors above as a starting point for selecting your dashboard and deciding what needs to go into it.

Step 2: Design the dashboard and specific widgets. Most of the dashboards allow you to pick and arrange an assortment of widgets that can produce visual depictions of your data. When designing your dashboard keep in mind the user experience design discussed in Chapter 16.

Step 3: Determine the time period for capturing data.

Step 4: The widgets pull the data from your sources once you have integrated them into the dashboard. *Remember:* maintain and update the dashboard frequently.

Step 5: Depending on the dashboard and templates' functionality, you can generate results and preliminary reports based on the data presented in the widgets.

Step 6: Analyse the data. In order to work with the data and metrics in the dashboards, it is necessary to know what the different measurement metrics are and what they tell you about your marketing project. In Chapter 20 we will cover a broad range of measurement metrics that are applicable to digital marketers.

Step 7: Develop insights from the findings and create informed reports and strategic recommendations for future projects, budgets, media decisions, etc.

Activity 19.2

i. Using the information you gathered in Activity 19.1 and the steps above, create a quick outline of a dashboard for a fictitious digital marketing project.

ii. Things to include:
  - what your project is
  - what the SMART objective is that it needs to achieve
  - which channels are used in the project (e.g. social media, email and website)
  - which dashboard you are using and why (see your answers from previous activity)
  - who you are gathering information for
  - what time period you are measuring
  - what you are going to do with the visual data generated by the dashboard

Challenges of data-driven marketing

Digital marketing is, in essence, data driven. In other words, digital marketing strategies and projects cannot be developed, implemented or evaluated without the use of data. The insights from the data tell the marketer if the digital marketing effort is successful or not, both for profits (or conversions) and consumer engagement. Data-driven marketing is not without its challenges, especially when data is gathered and processed via machines and algorithms. An issue of growing importance is the ethical sourcing, usage and storage of consumer data by businesses. Therefore, the FAIR data concept was developed.

FAIR data

FAIR data consists of Findable, Accessible, Interoperable and Reusable data (Ali and Dahlhaus, 2022). Wilkinson et al (2016) present the FAIR data principles as guidelines for good data management and improved utility that:

> put specific emphasis on enhancing the ability of machines to automatically find and use the data, in addition to supporting its reuse by individuals.

FAIR data principles should be considered from the start and be integrated before implementation of data-driven projects (Wilkinson et al, 2016).

Findable

Findability is when machines are easily able to find data. Findability is achieved through consistent use of standard and indexable identifiers, such as (Ali and Dahlhaus, 2022):

- uniform resource locator (URL)
- digital object identifier (DOI) findability focuses
- uniform resource identifier (URI)

Accessibility

Accessibility requires easy access to data, by both machines and people. This access is subject to legislative conditions of access, data licensing and protocols. Accessibility is achieved through (Ali and Dahlhaus, 2022):

- access protocol
- access permission
- metadata permanency

Interoperability

Interoperability ensures that data is understood and processable across machines in standardized formats. This interoperability is achieved through (Ali and Dahlhaus, 2022):

- provision of raw data in syntactic and semantic structures
- communication via resource description frameworks or open-source frameworks that can transmit the data without loss

Reusability

Reusability stipulates that data is managed to such a high level that new users can reuse the data for new purposes, even after a significant amount of time has passed. This data curation requires (Ali and Dahlhaus, 2022):

- comprehensive, explicitly detailed and descriptive machine-readable metadata
- provenance metadata that enables tracking of all changes to original names, editions and parameters

---

EXAMPLE

CEDAR (The Center for Expanded Data Annotation and Retrieval)

CEDAR is a centre of excellence with the purpose of creating tools and technologies that will help data managers with the challenges of creating and enhancing metadata to meet the FAIR principles. These tools and technologies will be available via metadata templates from FAIRsharing's website (Fairsharing, 2022a):

> These templates will guide users to create rich metadata with unique and stable HTTP identifiers [FAIR] that can be retrieved using HTTP [accessible] ...in a variety of formats (JSON-LD, TURTLE, RDF/XML, CSV, etc) [interoperability]... These metadata will use community standards, as defined by the template, and include provenance and data usage [reusability].

SOURCE Wilkinson et al, 2016

Activity 19.3

Explore the summative statistics on the FAIRsharing platform and discuss the questions below in class. The statistics are available from the stats tab on the FAIRsharing website (Fairsharing, 2022b).

i.   Notice the breakdown of disciplines adopting the FAIR principles. Which ones are leading the way?

ii.   Can you find marketing or social media in those statistics?

iii. Should marketers be more actively contributing to FAIR data creation? Why?

Breaching consumer privacy

'Studies have highlighted both the fundamental shortage of marketing data professionals and the lack of knowledge regarding how much companies are currently using data-driven decisions in marketing' (Länsipuro and Karjaluoto, 2021).

Palos-Sanchez et al (2019) find that due to a general lack of training in accountable, ethical and responsible use of consumer data, some digital marketing practices can easily fall into the realm of unethical use of data and breach of consumer privacy. Programmatic advertising, for example, can easily be deemed invasive because of misuse of data obtained from consumer activity such as data garnered from geolocation and cookies (Palos-Sanchez et al, 2018).

This misuse of consumers' personal data can lead to significant consequences for the transgressing brands. Consumers may provide false information, conduct negative word of mouth, block brand communications, switch to competitor brands or even take legal action (Niemann and Schwaiger, 2016). For more detail on marketers' role in responsible and ethical use of data and protecting consumer privacy refer to Digital Accountability in Chapter 4 and Ethical Considerations in Chapter 24.

Nevertheless, consumers are aware that tailored digital content and offers from brands require them to offer some personal data. Niemann and Schwaiger (2016) conducted a study and found that consumers consider fair use of data in three justice categories: *distributive*, *procedural* and *interactional*.

KEY TERM
Distributive/procedural/interactional justice

Distributive justice: 'expectations a customer holds regarding the possible costs and benefits of providing personal data' and how it will be distributed.

Procedural justice: giving consumers a voice that determines 'whether the individual has control over personal information as manifested by the existence of voice (i.e. approval, modification) or exit'.

Interactional justice: 'transparency and disclosure of relevant information' that does not resemble an endless liability disclaimer.

SOURCE Niemann and Schweiger, 2016

Table 19.1 Fair uses of personal data

Distributive justice	• Limited overall amount of data saved • Limit the collection and usage of sensitive data such as financial, health and location information • No sharing or sales of information with third parties for secondary usage
Procedural justice	• Customers should provide permission for data to be collected • Customers should be able to modify the data they provide • Customers should be able to control how their data is used • Customers expect their data to be protected from unauthorized access
Interactional justice	• Concise, explicit statements about the use of their data

Niemann and Schwaiger, 2016

Table 19.1 sets out what users perceive as fair uses of their personal data.

CASE STUDY EU digital marketplace regulations

Thierry Breton, European Commissioner for the Internal Market, wrote that in July 2022 the European Union voted to adopt the Digital Services Act (DSA) and Digital Markets Act (DMA), which makes it the first single digital marketplace with explicit, enforceable regulations based on comprehensive standards (Breton, 2022).

The combined European Union marketplace has *circa* 450 million consumers, who will now enjoy more protection against illegal use of their data. Businesses will have to perform rigorous risk assessments, and have legal representatives in Europe. Governments – via dedicated teams – will now be able to enforce laws, apply sanctions, give fines and perform other procedures of regulation based on the framework set out by these standards (Breton, 2022).

Some of the implications are:

- increased consumer protection (and subsequently trust) in digital marketplaces
- increased protection for people on social networks, particularly children
- responsible management of content on businesses' digital channels
- stricter requirements against illegal content, such as:
  - counterfeit or dangerous products
  - incitement to violence
  - hate speech
- a guiding framework to ensure:
  - protection of fundamental rights
  - reduction of harmful content and disinformation
- an online advertising framework that:
  - limits data use to the essentials
  - safeguards vulnerable users
- opportunities for new businesses with products and services that cater to these acts and their requirements
- increased transparency around platforms' algorithms

SOURCE Breton, 2022

Activity 19.4

i. Read about the Digital Services Act (DSA) and Digital Markets Act (DMA) on the European Commission's 'Shaping Europe's Digital Future' web page.

ii. Discuss the following points in class:
   - Who was consulted in developing the Acts?
   - When do the Acts come into force?
   - Who will be affected?
   - What does this mean for marketers, businesses (brands) and their digital marketing?

Cookie-less digital marketing

Targeted marketing (like programmatic advertising discussed earlier) requires a large amount of consumer data to function. As discussed in Table 19.1 consumers have certain expectations with regard to fair collection, storage and usage of their data before they deem it a breach of privacy. *Cookies* or cookie tracking is one activity tracking practice that has recently come under fire and as a result is facing increasing restrictions across the web.

KEY TERM
Cookie

A cookie is information that a website puts on a user's computer. Cookies store limited information from a web browser session on a given website that can then be retrieved in the future. They are also sometimes referred to as browser cookies, web cookies or internet cookies. Cookies can be accessed by the browser user, the site a user is on or by a third party that might use the information for different purposes. Common use cases for cookies include session management, personalization and tracking.

SOURCE Kerner, nd

Due to consumer protection laws such as the General Data Protection Regulation (GDPR), websites need to inform visitors about the types of data they are collecting via cookies and require consumer permission to collect cookies beyond the minimal functional level (Strycharz et al, 2021). This is why there is an explosion of pop-up windows as soon as you land on a website. However, as also seen from Table 19.1 above, consumers do not want overly dense and unmanageable disclaimers in order to enter a website (and often just scroll down to the end of the page to give permission to collect cookies, without reading the mountain of legal jargon preceding it).

In a bid to be more conscientious and accountable to consumers, Google has decided that they will 'stop the use of third-party cookies in Chrome by the end of 2023' (Cookiebot, 2021). While this limitation on third-party cookies is welcome, this does not signify the end of tracking, targeted marketing or even cookies. The following example illustrates the ways in which tracking and cookies continue.

EXAMPLE
A world without cookies? Not yet...

Cookies allow organizations to obtain and use data about your online activity. Tracking should be subject to innovative privacy measures, for example, banning third-party cookies and any other technology that could breach consumer privacy (Kingsnorth, 2022). While Google is stopping the use of third-party cookies in Chrome (Cookiebot, 2021), this does not signify the end of cookies altogether. It is a step in the right direction but it is not exactly the end of cookies or the tracking of consumer activity online. Google will still track your activity on its own platforms and there are ways around the limitation of third-party cookies. Facebook, for example, used a combination of first-party cookies and pixels that allowed them to continue to monitor EU citizens' online activity.

SOURCE Cookiebot, 2021

Summary

This chapter kicked off the Measurement and Evaluation part of this book. It provided an overview of the tools marketing managers use to monitor projects, evaluate successes and failures, and ultimately gather insights for future strategies, namely digital dashboards. We explored the different types of digital dashboards and their purposes, the characters of a good dashboard and how to set up your dashboard. These dashboards are carefully studied by marketing managers, so that they can evaluate their marketing strategies, projects and campaigns. The findings from their dashboard analyses are used to create reports for business, client and other stakeholder purposes. We also introduced the FAIR data principles and explored other challenges related to the responsible use of data, namely the results of breaches to consumer privacy, the end of third-party cookie tracking on Google Chrome and the new digital protection Acts in the EU that will have significant implications for marketers and businesses (and the digital platforms such as digital dashboards and social media that they use).

Chapter review

Reflective questions

Q1 How can you ensure your dashboard is constantly updated, maintained and properly monitored?

Q2 What are the benefits and disadvantages of having a digital dashboard?

Q3 How can you ensure your data is FAIR?

Q4 What will the lack of cookies mean for data-driven marketing strategies?

Key learning points

- A digital dashboard can be defined as a platform with strategically selected collections of interrelated marketing metrics which enables marketers to interpret unstructured data and present them visually (Chan and Uncles, 2022).

- There are many different digital dashboards, such as CMO, e-commerce, social media and email dashboards. It is up to the digital marketer to strategically select which channels to include and monitor to enable evaluation and reporting on digital marketing projects.

- FAIR data should be findable, accessible, interoperable and reusable and this approach should be adopted from the start of a project.

- Challenges of data-driven marketing provide opportunities for digital marketers to demonstrate their responsible and accountable approach to obtaining and managing consumer data for ethical digital marketing projects.

References

Alghalith, N (2015) Web analytics: Enhancing customer relationship management, *Journal of Strategic Innovation & Sustainability*, 10(2), 1–7

Ali, B and Dahlhaus, P (2022) The role of FAIR data towards sustainable agricultural performance: A systematic literature review, *Agriculture*, 12(2), 1–17

Breton, T (2022) Sneak peek: how the Commission will enforce the DSA & DMA, LinkedIn, 5 July, www.linkedin.com/pulse/sneak-peek-how-commission-enforce-dsa-dma-thierry-breton/ (archived at https://perma.cc/2AA3-JQCV)

Chan, K and Uncles, M (2022) Digital media consumption: Using metrics, patterns and dashboards to enhance data-driven decision-making, *Journal of Consumer Behaviour*, 21(1), 80–91

Cookiebot (2021) Google ending third-party cookies in Chrome, Cookiebot, 17 January, www. cookiebot.com/en/google-third-party-cookies/ (archived at https://perma.cc/B9MC-WGSC)

Digital School of Marketing (2021) What are the stages of the social media marketing funnel?, Digital School of Marketing, 31 March, digitalschoolofmarketing.co.za/blog/ what-are-the-stages-of-the-social-media-marketing-funnel/ (archived at https://perma.cc/ AA95-JR79)

European Commission (2022) Shaping Europe's digital future page, European Commission, digital-strategy.ec.europa.eu/en/policies/digital-services-act-package (archived at https:// perma.cc/2GQB-ETJT)

Fairsharing (2022a) Home page, Fair Sharing, fairsharing.org/ (archived at https://perma.cc/ B5GV-UPCU)

Fairsharing (2022b) Fairsharing summary statistics, Fair Sharing, fairsharing.org/summary-statistics (archived at https://perma.cc/483S-7WNN)

Flores, L (2013) *How to Measure Digital Marketing: metrics for assessing impact and designing success,* Springer, London

Kerner, M (nd) Cookie, TechTarget, www.techtarget.com/searchsoftwarequality/definition/ cookie (archived at https://perma.cc/A42C-6LVU)

Kingsnorth, S (2022) *Digital Marketing Strategy: An integrated approach to online marketing,* Kogan Page, London

Länsipuro, H and Karjaluoto, H (2021) Data-driven marketing processes: Boundaries and how to overcome them, in *Contemporary Issues in Digital Marketing,* ed O Niininen, 22–31, Routledge, London

Lippa, G (2012) FAQ's web analytics, Data and Marketing Association, 14 June, dma.org. uk/article/faqs-web-analytics (archived at https://perma.cc/D533-A2NC)

Niemann, A and Schwaiger, M (2016) Consumers' expectations of fair data collection and usage-a mixed method analysis, in *2016 49th Hawaii International Conference on System Sciences* (HICSS), 3646–655

Niininen, O (ed) (2021) *Contemporary Issues in Digital Marketing,* Routledge, London

Palos-Sanchez, P, Saura, J R and Martin-Velicia, F (2019) A study of the effects of programmatic advertising on users' concerns about privacy overtime, *Journal of Business Research,* 96(3), 61–72

Ritson, M (2016) Mark Ritson: If you think the sales funnel is dead, you've mistaken tactics for strategy, *Marketing Week,* 6 April, www.marketingweek.com/mark-ritson-if-you-think-the-sales-funnel-is-dead-youve-mistaken-tactics-for-strategy/ (archived at https:// perma.cc/7J4C-8ADG)

Saura, J R, Palos-Sánchez, P and Cerdá Suárez, L M (2017) Understanding the digital marketing environment with KPIs and web analytics, *Future Internet,* 9(4), 1–13

Schaffer, N (2022) The 19 most powerful social media dashboards you should know, Neal Shaffer, nealschaffer.com/social-media-dashboards/ (archived at https://perma.cc/2FHQ-VV4J)

Strycharz, J, Smit, E, Helberger, N and van Noort, G (2021) No to cookies: Empowering impact of technical and legal knowledge on rejecting tracking cookies, *Computers in Human Behavior,* 120, 106750

Vaičiūnaitė, D (2022) Top 10 types of marketing dashboard examples (+ templates), Whatagraph, 14 December, whatagraph.com/blog/articles/marketing-dashboard-examples (archived at https://perma.cc/LL4H-JF4Z)

Wilkinson, M D, Dumontier, M, Aalbersberg, I J, Appleton, G, Axton, M, Baak, A, Blomberg, N, Boiten, J W, da Silva Santos, L B, Bourne, P E and Bouwman, J (2016) The FAIR guiding principles for scientific data management and stewardship, *Scientific Data*, 3(1), 1–9

Data analytics and metrics

20

By the end of this chapter, you should be able to:

- briefly define attribution, data analytics and metrics
- explain in simple terms how you can attribute success to particular marketing elements
- describe the value of metrics for data-driven marketing
- understand the implications of irresponsible application of data analytics and metrics

Introduction

In order to work with the data provided in the dashboards, it is necessary to know what the different measurement metrics are and what they tell you about your marketing project. Thus, in this chapter we will cover a broad range of measurement metrics that are applicable to digital marketers. We will define key concepts such as data analytics, attribution and metrics. Lastly, we will finish the chapter on a critically reflective note, considering the challenges that the digital marketer faces when overwhelmed by the sheer volume of metrics or when metrics are at odds with the cultural differences of differing marketplaces.

Attribution

As Kingsnorth (2022) notes, a consumer usually interacts with multiple marketing elements or touchpoints on the customer journey before the desired action is achieved. One of the challenges for marketers, particularly where integrated and complex digital marketing campaigns are concerned, is figuring out which marketing element was responsible for motivating the consumer to action.

KEY TERM
Attribution

Identifying which marketing element was responsible for motivating the consumer to action that achieves the desired outcome, e.g. purchasing the product, subscribing to the newsletter, engaging with a social media post etc.

SOURCE Charlesworth, 2021

Attribution may seem like an unnecessary complication when a strategy or campaign is deemed successful. However, *attribution* is helpful in determining which marketing elements are most successful or profitable and which needs revision or even exclusion from future strategies. Attribution then also plays a role in informed budget allocation strategies. Applying data analytics and metrics to digital marketing projects offers marketers a means to determine this attribution, especially where multiple channels are reviewed together (see Chapter 22 for more detail).

EXAMPLE
Understanding attribution: key for sharing-economy marketing strategies

Sharing-economy business models (as discussed in Chapter 12) have caused significant disruption to market economies and are increasingly altering consumer attitudes towards product ownership. Opting for borrowing and lending products instead of outright ownership causes significant disruption to traditional business models, which has been exacerbated by digital marketing and the increasing possibilities of channel-specific marketing such as mobile applications (Key, 2017).

The content- and data-driven foundations of digital marketing highlight the empowered position of the consumer, who can dictate how and when they consume from brands and even whether brands are allowed to communicate with them (Key, 2017).

When consumers deem marketing communications intrusive they are likely to look for ways to prohibit brands from communicating with them, opting for solutions such as ad blocking software, opting out of communication channels such as email newsletters, or even deleting mobile applications (Key, 2017). This then means that consumers hold individualized channel power (Key, 2017).

Sharing-economy marketing models rely heavily on tailored content across different marketing channels (think of Airbnb, Spotify, Uber, Vinted and the different ways in which they communicate and operate on digital channels). In an increasingly competitive and communication-cluttered digital space, it is crucial for marketers to understand the potential of each marketing channel and also whether their communication efforts via these channels are effective or not. Therefore, understanding attribution is key to successful marketing strategies and determining the means for managing consumers' channel power in a positive manner.

Data analytics

Data analytics gives marketers the tools to work with Big Data to develop better digital marketing strategies and campaigns.

KEY TERM
Data analytics

Identifying patterns in the data to acquire insights about project performance and consumer behaviour and inform future strategy and budget development.

SOURCE Charlesworth, 2021

Flores (2013) lists those KPIs that marketers should concern themselves with to get a better understanding of the performance of a strategy or campaign:

- growth in awareness
- increased market share (or even obtaining or maintaining the leading market share)
- price in relation to competitors
- reduced or minimal number of complaints
- growth or maintained customer satisfaction
- increased or streamlined distribution
- increased availability of product or service
- increased total number of customers
- increased perception of quality or appreciation of brand
- increased loyalty or retention of existing customers
- increase perception of quality in relation to competitors

We have previously discussed the components required for a digital marketing strategy (Chapter 2) and the SMART objectives and KPIs that form the foundation of measuring success (Chapter 14). When you evaluate the success of the campaign, SMART objectives and KPI, you get to an overall assessment – was the campaign a success or not? This is done by determining the return on investment.

Return on investment (ROI)

While there are many nuanced measures to determine the specific results of one or more objectives or performance of channels, campaign elements, promotions, sales, etc (which we will discuss in more detail next) the overall insight most clients are interested in is the *return on investment* or ROI.

KEY TERM
Return on investment (ROI)

A performance measure used to evaluate the efficiency of an investment... calculated by comparing the spending on digital marketing to the sales increases.

SOURCE Saura et al, 2017

The formula for determining the ROI is as follows:

ROI = (Gain from Investment – Cost of Investment) / Cost of Investment

Not all ROI is financial, but that doesn't mean it has no value. According to Hug (2021) branding is an investment providing:

- **Client loyalty:** Professional, relevant branding encourages brand loyalty and repeat business.
- **Client trust:** Professional design conveys a message of quality and consideration, meaning customers will trust your brand as one that operates to a high standard at all times.
- **Differentiation:** Well-considered branding differentiates your business from the millions of others and makes it easily recognizable.
- **Positioning:** Proper branding makes it possible to position your brand for the correct target market and strike a chord with your audience.
- **Clarity:** Professional branding provides clarity of message and helps explain your offering.

However, this only gives a broad overview of the marketing strategy and/or campaign's success when it comes to digital marketing. Determining ROI in digital marketing is challenging. As mentioned above, there are a lot of other more nuanced measures you can use to determine results of specific parts of the strategy or campaign, collectively termed *metrics*. As discussed in the previous chapter, integrated dashboards (or simultaneous review and analysis of channel-specific dashboards) have a selection of channels brought together in one platform for performing some analytics. This mean that you will have the opportunity to strategically select which channels and metrics are most relevant for the insights you are seeking to find.

Metrics

Digital marketing is linked to an increasing array of measurement *metrics* to determine success. The selection of measures used is a strategic choice in itself, something that both challenges and inspires marketing and business managers. According to Saura et al (2017) 'Appropriate, accurate and timely digital marketing metrics are critical for a company to assess whether they are achieving their objectives, or whether the selected strategy is appropriate to achieve organizational goals.'

KEY TERM
Metrics/e-metrics (for online application)

Standards of measurement that determine the success or failure of a business, either overall (such as sales revenue or gross margin) or for a specific component of the business (such as click-through rate or number of conversions for marketing projects).

SOURCE Charlesworth, 2021

Research and development of metrics occurs every day. As the digital marketing world evolves and channels or platforms change frequently, that means that metrics are frequently in need of change. So why do we then bother with them? Mintz et al (2021) did an extensive study on the use of metrics on a global scale and summarized the main purposes of metrics (as identified in theory and by almost 150 marketing practitioners), as follows:

- clarifies which channel and KPI will be assessed (and how)
- informs strategy developments to acquire the desired results
- holds managers accountable

- empowers employees working with metrics
- positively impacts on company performance

Activity 20.1

i.   We have already discussed KPIs, but the Simplilearn video provides a quick refresher and ties KPIs to digital analytics.

ii. Take five minutes to watch the 'Digital Analytics KPI – Digital Marketing Tutorial For Beginners' video on Simplilearn's website (Simplilearn, 2017).

What is measured?

As we mentioned above, digital metrics have evolved over time and new ones are developed on a regular basis. The selection discussed next provides an overview of the most likely metrics you would encounter, covering what they measure and how to go about it. These digital marketing metrics can be tied to the different stages in the digital marketing funnel (Hanlon, 2021) (see Figure 19.2 in Chapter 19). However, this greatly depends on your customer journey, marketing channel strategy (which channel is used where in the campaign, some even more than once, for example in an introductory email, reminder email, confirmation email, etc). Your metrics should ultimately be linked to the KPIs as set out in your original marketing strategy. As we saw from the list of main purposes of metrics above, if a metric is not linked to a KPI, you will not know if it is successful or not.

Frequently used metrics

There are useful metrics that can work across different digital marketing channels. What is necessary here is to define comparable SMART objectives for each channel. For example:

Get 10 per cent of leads from Instagram advertisement in July

vs

Get 35 per cent of leads from website form in July

Determining the success for each of these will not only tell you whether they reached their objective, but also which one was more successful (or not).

Click-through rate

The most frequently used metric to determine success in digital marketing is *click-through rate* (closest to an overview result, and can also be used in conjunction with ROI).

> **KEY TERM**
> Click-through rate (CTR)
>
> A metric that measures the number of clicks advertisers receive on their ads per number of impressions.
>
> **SOURCE** Saura et al, 2017

The formula for determining the CTR is:

$$CTR = \text{Number of Clicks} / \text{Impressions}$$

CTR can be used for a number of channels. For example, it can tell you how many people clicked on a link or button on digital advertisements, emails, website links, promoted content or general content on social media. When viewing the CTR for all channels, you get an overview of the level of engagement with your digital marketing campaign (and to some extent can attribute the relative success of each marketing channel).

However, as you can see from the formula, you need to know how many impressions your content got before you can get the answer. What are impressions? See Table 20.1 for the explanation and formula.

Once you know the impressions and CTR, there are a number of other regularly used metrics that give you a broad overview of the performance of your digital marketing channels and campaigns. These other metrics can also be found in Table 20.1

Table 20.1 Frequently used metrics

Metric	Formula
Impressions When digital marketing content, e.g. search engine marketing (SEM) content or display advertisements, are viewed by consumers, they make an 'impression' on them. This is calculated by multiplying 1000 with the cost of the campaign and then dividing the result by CPM (cost per thousand impressions – see next formula).	Impressions = (1000 × cost) / CPM

(continued)

Table 20.1   (Continued)

Metric	Formula
Cost per thousand impressions (CPM) As the name implies, this metric gives you the cost of obtaining a thousand impressions. It is calculated by multiplying 1000 with the cost of the campaign and then dividing this by the number of impressions.	CPM = (1000 × cost) / number of impressions
Cost-per-click (CPC) This metric gives you the average cost-per-click on your content. It is calculated by dividing the cost of the campaign by the number of clicks.	CPC = cost / number of clicks
Cost-per-lead (CPL) When a potential customer engages with your content, for example in downloading, subscribing or making an enquiry, this is considered as generating a lead. Cost-per-lead tells you how much you are spending for every lead created. This is calculated by dividing the cost of the campaign by the number of leads generated.	CPL = cost / number of leads
Conversion rate Conversions are successfully completed actions that are not necessarily buying a product or service: for example, if you wanted consumers to click on a button, enter a competition, download content, share content or indeed purchase the product. They are calculated by dividing the number of conversions by the number of impressions. This is then multiplied by 100 to get the percentage.	Conversions = (number of conversions / number of impressions) × 100
Churn rate Rate of customers lost over a certain period of time. It is calculated by dividing the number of customers lost with the number of customers at the start of the period. This is then multiplied by 100 to get the percentage.	Churn rate = (number of lost customers / number of customers at start of period) × 100

EXAMPLE

Do I have to do all these calculations myself?

Bogna Szyk and Mateusz Mucha created an *Online Marketing Conversion Calculator* that resides on Omnicalculator.com (2022a). With this handy tool they have automated a lot of the calculations above, which is very helpful for those who struggle with mathematical equations or even those who need to get the results in a hurry. However, it is always a good idea to at least know what the metric measures and how it is done (what the formula consists of).

They also give a practical overview of how the calculations work together, to give you results for reporting on campaign success vs money spent. In the website they explain:

- how to calculate select metrics for each stage of the digital marketing funnel, e.g. impressions, leads and leads to customers (conversion rate)
- costs of digital marketing, e.g. CPM, CPC, cost per lead and cost per customer
- return on investment, including revenue, ROI and revenue per click/per lead/per customer
- a function for more advanced calculations such as number of orders per customer and total revenue

Activity 20.2

i. Visit the Omnicalculator (2022a) website.

ii. Search for 'Online Marketing Conversion Calculator' to read their case study and explore the calculators.

iii. Then go to the Omnicalculator (2022b) website to find other automated calculators. Try searching for the items below to find their automated calculators:

- CTR
- CPM
- CPC + CPM
- churn rate

Website metrics

There are a number of metrics for websites that can give you an abundance of data about the performance of your website.

Offsite vs onsite analytics

Before we delve into the metrics for assessing website performance, it is worth distinguishing between *offsite analytics* and *onsite analytics*, as described in the Key Term box.

KEY TERM
Offsite/onsite analytics

Offsite analytics: Analytics that are not based on access to your own data. The results are determined with limited data and provide a superficial view and aggregate measures for your website performance in comparison to competitors, for example monthly traffic and keywords.

Onsite analytics: Analytics that are based on your own data. The data generated by your website provides rich data for determining your website performance, such as actual number of visitors, landing page and other activity on site.

SOURCE Hanlon, 2021

Some metrics are visible on your dashboard, for example on Google Analytics, and can be used to do some onsite data analysis on the performance of your website. These are discussed in Table 20.2.

As mentioned in Chapter 19 the dashboard does this calculation and provides you with the numbers. However, it is up to the data analyst or marketer reviewing the data to generate findings for reports and recommendations for future marketing efforts. Having the exit pages, for example, can tell you that the most exited page might need some revising as it might be causing customers to abandon your site. Even so, if it is the last page when a desired action has been completed, e.g. the confirmation page after a purchase has been completed, then you need to examine other exit pages with a high exit rate.

Activity 20.3

i. Go and explore website-specific Omnicalculator (2022b) automated calculators.

ii. Try your hand at determining the results for the items below by searching for them on the website:

 - exit rate

 - bounce rate

Table 20.2 Website metrics

Metric	Formula
Unique visitors Number of unique visitors to your website within a specific period. This is measured by adding up the number of times your website (or IP address) has been entered into a browser	This is found by checking the web analytics for your website
Returning visitors The number of visitors that come back to your website are return or repeat visitors	This is found by checking the web analytics for your website
One page visitors Visitors who only visit one page	This is found by checking the web analytics for your website
Return visitors rate (RVR) This is the average rate at which visitors return to your website. This is calculated by dividing the number of returning visitors by the number of unique visitors within a specific time period (monthly, bi-annually, etc). This is then multiplied by 100 to get the percentage	RVR = (number of returning visitors / number of unique visitors) × 100
Pageviews The number of pages viewed by the visitor	This is found by checking the web analytics for your website

(continued)

Table 20.2   (Continued)

Metric	Formula
Average time on page The average time a visitor spends on a specific page	This is found by checking the web analytics for your website
Session duration The average time a visitor spends on a website before exiting	This is found by checking the web analytics for your website
Clickstream An overview of the pages a visitor browsed during their session on your website	This is found by checking the web analytics for your website
Exit pages The last page a visitor browses before leaving your website	This is found by checking the web analytics for your website
Exit rate The rate at which visitors exit your web page (a specific page)	Exit rate = number of exits / number of pageviews
Bounce rate Bounce rate should not be confused with exit rate. A bounced page is one that was left immediately, where an exit page has a longer visit duration. This is calculated by dividing the number of one page visitors by the number of unique visitors	Bounce rate = number of one page visitors / number of unique visitors

Email metrics

While you might think that email is an old, less exciting marketing channel, it is still very relevant. Email marketing forms an essential part of any digital marketing campaign, particularly where development and maintenance of customer databases and customer relationship management is concerned. Email marketing has its own set of metrics, and a couple of them can be viewed and analysed on your dashboard (when sending emails through an automated customer relationship manager (CRM) system such as Mailchimp).

Table 20.3   Email metrics

Metric	Formula
Total unique recipients Total number of recipient email addresses on your mailing list that the mail was sent to	This is found by checking your email dashboard
Total unique opens Total number of emails opened by unique recipients	This is found by checking your email dashboard
Total opens The total number of opens (Note: this includes when one user opened the mail multiple times)	This is found by checking your email dashboard
Open rate The percentage of emails opened by unique recipients. This is calculated by dividing the total unique opens by the total unique recipients. This is then multiplied by 100 to get the percentage.	Open rate = (total unique opens / total unique recipients) × 100
New subscriber The number of new subscribers on a mailing list (usually by month)	This is found by checking your email dashboard
List growth rate The average rate of new subscribers over a specific period. This formula requires a couple of numbers, calculated in three steps. 1. Subtract the number of unsubscribes and 'marked as spam' from new subscribers. 2. Divide the answer from 1 by the total number of subscribers in the list. 3. This is then multiplied by 100 to get the percentage.	List growth rate = [(new subscribers – unsubscribers – spam complaints) / total number of subscribers] × 100
Total emails delivered The number of emails successfully delivered per mail	This is found by checking your email dashboard
Bounced email The number of sent emails that are undeliverable due to faulty or deactivated email addresses per mail	This is found by checking your email dashboard

(*continued*)

Table 20.3 (Continued)

Metric	Formula
Bounce rate for email Not to be confused with bounce rate for websites. Bounce rate for email is the percentage of emails bounced per mail sent. This is calculated by dividing the total bounced emails by the total unique recipients. This is then multiplied by 100 to get the percentage.	Bounce rate = (all bounced emails / total unique recipients) × 100
Unsubscribe rate The percentage of recipients who unsubscribed from your mailing list. This is calculated by dividing the total number of unsubscribes by the total emails delivered successfully	Unsubscribe rate = total number of unsubscribes / total emails delivered
Marked as spam The number of recipients who marked your mail as spam	This is found by checking your email dashboard
Spam rate The number of recipients who reported your email as spam in a specific period. This is calculated by dividing the total marked as spam by the total emails delivered. This is then multiplied by 100 to get the percentage	Spam rate = (total marked as spam / total emails delivered) × 100
Click rate for email Number of clicks from one mail. This is calculated by dividing total clicks by total emails delivered. This is then multiplied by 100 to get the percentage	Click rate = (total clicks / total emails delivered) × 100
Conversion rate for email Similar to conversion rate from Table 20.1. Just replace impressions with total emails delivered. Thus this is calculated by dividing the number of conversions by the number of emails delivered. This is then multiplied by 100 to get the percentage	Conversion rate = (number of conversions / total emails delivered) × 100
Viral rate or email sharing rate The number of emails passed on to other addresses. This is calculated by dividing the total share by the total emails delivered. This is then multiplied by 100 to get the percentage.	Viral rate = (total shares / total emails delivered) × 100

There are many different platforms that offer integrated services with email, social media, etc. The video in Activity 20.4 will give you a taster of how one of these CRM systems works and how you can glean the insights about your digital marketing campaign's performance using the built-in metrics' results generated from the campaign data.

Activity 20.4

i. Take 30 minutes to watch the 'Mailchimp Tutorial 2022: How to use Mailchimp step by step for beginners' video by Dorothy Tutorials, showing how to use Mailchimp (Dorothy Tutorials, 2022).

ii. Ask yourself the following questions:

   – What are the benefits of using a CRM system?

   – Do you think the automated processes help or hinder digital marketers? Why?

Social media

Social media metrics can either be found on each platform's analytics page or be integrated into your dashboard (see Chapter 19). However, the main metrics to be aware of (that may determine which widgets you select and inspect) remain the same (Table 20.4).

Activity 20.5

i. Search for the Engagement Rate calculator on Omnicalculator (2022b) website.

ii. Use the drop down menu to change the calculator from daily ER, ER by views, ER by reach, ER by impressions, ER by posts.

Activity 20.6

i. In your groups, create your own digital content that will result in some data for practising analytics skills you learnt about above. Decide what you want to create, but make sure that you have access to the data. A good example would be to create your own blog on a free site, such as Blogger. Populate your website with some content, for example a couple of blog posts over the course of a month.

ii. Pick at least three metrics from above. Things to look for:

- What did you select?
- Why is this metric appropriate?
- What do you see in your data?

Table 20.4 Social media metrics

Metric	Formula
Impressions The number of impressions on users your post creates (this can be multiple for the same user)	This is found by checking your social media dashboard
Reach The number of unique users your post reaches	This is found by checking your social media dashboard
Reach rate The percentage of followers who see your post. This is done by dividing the reach by the followers. This is then multiplied by 100 to get the percentage	Reach rate = (reach / followers) × 100
Growth rate The percentage of growth in your social media audience over a specific period. This is done by dividing the number of new followers in the time period by the total number of followers. This is then multiplied by 100 to get the percentage.	Growth rate = (new followers / total number of followers) × 100
Engagement rate (ER) The average rate of engagement for a piece of social media content. There are different types of engagement rate, depending on what you want to calculate. The different types of ER and their formulas are provided below.	
Daily ER	(Total daily engagements on a post / Total followers) × 100
ER by views	(Total video engagements / Total video views) × 100
ER by impressions	(Total post engagements / Total impressions) × 100

(*continued*)

Table 20.4 (Continued)

Metric	Formula
ER by posts	(Total post engagements / Total followers) × 100
ER by reach	(Total post engagements / Reach per post) × 100
Share of voice The market share on social media vs your competitors. This is done in stages. 1. Collect your and your competitors' total mentions across all social media channels. 2. Add all the mentions from 1 together to get the total industry mentions. 3. Divide your mentions by the industry mentions. 4. This is then multiplied by 100 to get the percentage.	Share of voice = [(all your mentions across social media) / (total industry mentions by adding up all mentions for you and your competitors)] × 100

Challenges of metrics for digital marketing

Credibility of data

There are a number of challenges linked to digital marketing metrics, not least the fact that there is no independent auditing for these measures (Charlesworth, 2021). Apart from the possibility that numbers may be manipulated to make the data look good, there are also fake accounts on digital channels. Fake accounts appear as unique visitors and can thus impact the results.

FAIR data use and adblockers

Another challenge is the regulations around FAIR use of data (as discussed in Chapter 19). This is made even more challenging when paired with related consumer attempts to protect themselves, for example, using adblockers to prevent spamming while browsing the internet (Charlesworth, 2021). While adblockers are useful for consumers, they are problematic for data generation and metrics, as they prevent cookies from recording their activity (such as website visitors).

Lack of marketing research and metrics skills in marketing practice

Flight (2021) conducted a study with practitioners and found that marketing practitioners often do not learn how to conduct market research and analyse data using metrics. While marketing is popular for its creative aspect, such as advertising, the quantifiable skills needed to prove the benefit and profit resulting from a campaign, like applying metrics, are scarce – even though over 98 per cent of marketing practitioners rely on data to inform their decision-making and strategy development (Flight, 2021).

Customer relationship management vs data-driven decisions

Data analytics and the myriad of metrics available to influence digital marketing decision-making has profoundly changed the way marketers develop strategies and practices and even how they manage customer relationships (Volrath and Villegas, 2021). When reviewing the profit- and results-driven purpose of these practical solutions vs strategic models (such as customer journeys) and customer-orientated value via marketing, the synergy is not always clear (Volrath and Villegas, 2021).

Summary

We explored the different measurement metrics you can use in evaluating the success of your marketing project, across different marketing channels: website (or web analytics), email and social media. We defined key concepts, such as data analytics, attribution, metrics, onsite and offsite analytics. We explored the most frequently used metrics across these channels, including formulae where appropriate. Finally, we also reflected on the use of digital marketing metrics through a contemporary lens, considering the challenges that the digital marketer faces such as credibility, FAIR data, adblockers and their compatibility with consumers' realities in modern marketplaces.

Chapter review

Reflective questions

Q1 How do you attribute success or failure to a marketing element?

Q2 Why do we need to measure marketing project success?

Q3 How do we view all of the metrics in one place?

Q4 What does data analytics and metrics offer the digital marketer?

Key learning points

- Attribution can be defined as identifying which marketing element was responsible for motivating the consumer to action that achieves the desired outcome, e.g. purchasing the product, subscribing to the newsletter, engaging with a social media post, etc (Charlesworth, 2021).

- Data analytics can be defined as identifying patterns in the data to acquire insights about project performance and consumer behaviour and inform future strategy and budget development (Charlesworth, 2021).

- Metrics can be defined as standards of measurement that determine the success or failure of a business, either overall (such as sales revenue or gross margin) or for a specific component of the business (such as click-through rate or number of conversions for marketing projects) (Charlesworth, 2021).

- Application of data analytics and metrics allows for the comparative review of different marketing elements, enabling the marketer to determine what was most and least successful, i.e. enabling the marketer to attribute success to particular marketing element(s).

- Metrics enable processing of Big Data into valuable insights that can report on the success and inform development of future data-driven marketing initiatives.

- Irresponsible application of data analytics and metrics can result in erroneous findings, false representations of the campaign and consumer data, and ultimately uninformed future marketing efforts that are less effective or even damaging to the business.

References

Charlesworth, A (2021) *Absolute Essentials of Digital Marketing*, Routledge, London

Dorothy Tutorials (2022) Mailchimp Tutorial 2022: How to use Mailchimp step by step for beginners, www.youtube.com/watch?v=tZKYiiQP57I (archived at https://perma.cc/A66Q-N7XR)

Flight, R L (2021) Linking practitioner dilemmas and research metrics across an integrated marketing curriculum, *Journal of Marketing Education*,43 (3), 317–32.

Hanlon, A (2021) *Digital Marketing: Strategic planning and integration*, Sage

Hug (2021) Recognising the true ROI of business branding, Hug London, huglondon.com/insights/recognising-the-true-roi-of-business-branding (archived at https://perma.cc/H2BT-MJWG)

Key, T M (2017) Domains of digital marketing channels in the sharing economy, *Journal of Marketing Channels*, 24(1-2), 27–38

Kingsnorth, S (2022) *Digital Marketing Strategy: An integrated approach to online marketing,* Kogan Page, London

Mintz, O, Currim, I S, Steenkamp, J E M and de Jong, M (2021) Managerial metric use in marketing decisions across 16 countries: A cultural perspective, *Journal of International Business Studies*, 52(8), 1474–500

Omnicalculator (2022a) Online Marketing Conversion Calculator, www.omnicalculator.com/finance/online-marketing-roi#costs-of-internet-marketing (archived at https://perma.cc/2BW4-DTE2)

Omnicalculator (2022b) Your life in 2,906 free calculators, www.omnicalculator.com/ (archived at https://perma.cc/8EWM-QCER)

Saura, J R, Palos-Sánchez, P and Cerdá Suárez, L M (2017) Understanding the digital marketing environment with KPIs and web analytics, *Future Internet*, 9(4), 76

Simplilearn (2017) Digital analytics KPI: Digital marketing tutorial for beginners, YouTube, www.youtube.com/watch?v=DnXr8Yf8M_k (archived at https://perma.cc/5CX7-ALRL)

Simplilearn (2022) Digital marketing tools and techniques 2022, YouTube, www.youtube.com/watch?v=zBD-wxaUm1Q (archived at https://perma.cc/8JJB-PFTN)

Vollrath, M D and Villegas, S G (2021) Avoiding digital marketing analytics myopia: Revisiting the customer decision journey as a strategic marketing framework, *Journal of Marketing Analytics,* 10(2), 106–13

Digital marketing audit

By the end of this chapter, you should be able to:

- briefly define marketing audit
- understand the benefits of conducting a marketing audit
- explain in simple terms the marketing audit process
- describe the different types of marketing audits

Introduction

Due to the competitive nature of the modern marketplace and the developments in digital environments, conducting marketing audits is becoming an important part of the marketing strategy development process (Wymbs, 2011). In this chapter, we will explore the concept of marketing audit and all the different audits a marketer can undertake in the process. We will cover the history of marketing audit including the different eras in its development. Thereafter we will have a brief overview of the reasons for conducting a marketing audit before delving into the process. We will explore digital marketing audits more closely, including website, SEO, content, social media and email audits. We end the section with a practitioner-based interview, where we get an insider peak of applying theory to practice when conducting a marketing audit.

The digital marketing audit

What is a marketing audit?

Marketing audits are essentially rigorous reviews to evaluate how a company's marketing is doing in the marketing environment and to determine the most effective allocation of resources (Wilson, 2005). According to Kotler et al (1989) *marketing audits* are control processes with four basic characteristics:

- broad focus (including horizontal (comprehensive) and vertical (in-depth) audits)
- independence (objectively conducted by internal or external auditors)
- systematic (orderly and rigorous process)
- periodic (occurring regularly, both in good and bad times)

KEY TERM
Marketing audit

A comprehensive, systematic, independent and periodic examination of a company's – or business unit's – marketing environment, objectives, strategies and activities, with a view to determining problem areas and opportunities and recommending a plan of action to improve the company's marketing performance.

SOURCE Kotler et al, 1989

Marketing audit processes and approaches can differ between industries and teams, but each marketing audit essentially consists of a detailed list of questions answered in a systematic way to determine the 'health' of the marketing activities for the company.

Marketing audits should include considerations of both internal and external factors that may impact on the state of marketing activity within the company. For example, if there is a recession and subsequent marketing budget cuts, the budget for marketing spending would not be as good as the pre-recession budget, which may have a knock-on effect on the success of campaigns. Marketing audits should also be done in good and bad times, to get a consistent overview of the performance (and growth vs decline) and efficacy of marketing activity for the company.

Kotler et al (1977) identified six components of the marketing audit:

- marketing environment audit: macro- and micro-environment review
- marketing strategy audit: strategy review in relation to opportunities and threats
- marketing organization audit: review of the marketing department in relation to other business functions
- marketing systems audit: review of the systems and procedures for developing and implementing marketing activity
- marketing productivity audit: review of the cost and return on investment for marketing productivity

- marketing function audit: review of overall marketing function in relation to previous audit findings

When marketing audits are done, marketers can determine which resources provide the best results and which do not, which subsequently informs future resource allocation or removal. Resources can broadly be categorized according to time, money and people. Where resources are allocated, these can either remain the same, be increased or decreased depending on the level of success of the particular marketing function. Where a specific function is essential or performs well, more resources could be allocated, e.g. more budget and team members required for the marketing research team when entering new markets. Where a specific function or channel does not provide meaningful results, resources can be reduced, e.g. reduced budget for print and distribution of physical advertisements and posters, and reallocation of more budget to the social media marketing budget.

History of the marketing audit

Marketing audit as a concept has been around (and applied) for decades, but did not receive a lot of management attention until the 1970s (Kotler et al, 1989). By the 1990s the marketing audit was regarded as an effective business tool (Rothe et al, 1997). Rothe et al (1997) identified six eras of the marketing audit. As illustrated in Figure 21.1 these six eras of marketing audit are split into decades that reflect the definition and use of marketing audits in business (Rothe et al, 1997).

Figure 21.1   Six eras of marketing audit

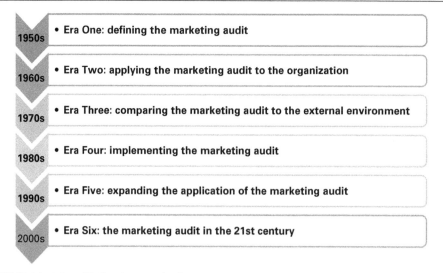

1950s	• Era One: defining the marketing audit
1960s	• Era Two: applying the marketing audit to the organization
1970s	• Era Three: comparing the marketing audit to the external environment
1980s	• Era Four: implementing the marketing audit
1990s	• Era Five: expanding the application of the marketing audit
2000s	• Era Six: the marketing audit in the 21st century

SOURCE Adaptation of Rothe, Harvey and Jackson, 1997

The six eras are: definition (1950s), application (1960s), comparison to external environment (1970s), implementation (1980s), expansion (1980s), and marketing audit in the 21st century (2000s). Given the time of the publication of their study, the sixth era was their conceptualization of what marketing audits would look like from 2000 onwards.

Rothe et al (1997) characterize marketing audits in the 21st century as seeking more global perspectives, being more sustainability-focused, having more formal acknowledgement of the marketing auditor role, being more integrated as a normal part of the marketing department, and being more essential to the evaluation (and justification) of resource allocation. Three decades on, we see that they were right in their predictions. With the increased use of digital channels in marketing and blurring of geographic boundaries, the need for global perspectives is crucial. Green marketing audits are growing in importance to reflect sustainability efforts of the company (Chen and Yang, 2019 – see Example Green Marketing Audit Criteria later in this chapter). Marketing audits for resource allocation are a regular feature and norm in most marketing departments, with a responsibility for justifying strategic and budgetary decisions (Wilson, 2005).

What is a digital marketing audit?

In digital environments, marketing audit scopes are broadened to include inspections of the respective digital channels and their performance. While traditional marketing audits should not be replaced by digital audits, we will focus on the types of audits used when reviewing digital marketing activities. Hence, we refer to the *digital marketing audit*.

> **KEY TERM**
> Digital marketing audit
>
> A rigorous review of a company or business unit's digital marketing activity across channels such as website, SEO, social media and digital advertisements.

Why would you conduct a digital marketing audit?

Digital marketing audits are challenging and can be daunting, as it is necessary to critically review and reflect on the marketing activity and whether it was successful or not. However, they are useful and offer many benefits (Point Visible, 2022):

- identify weaknesses or potential frustration points for consumers' journeys caused by marketing activity

- discover potential opportunities for growth
- ensure marketing activity is in line with company objectives
- improve team morale
- reveal strengths to build on
- increase return on investment

How do you conduct a digital marketing audit?

Digital marketing audits should follow a systematic and rigorous process of reviewing marketing activity. Conducting digital marketing audits also often rely on the same data sources for generating findings about marketing performance, namely dashboards (see Chapter 19). Although you have pulled your data from the dashboard and subjected them to their various digital marketing metric measures (see Chapter 20 to determine the campaign and strategy performance), the digital marketing audit provides a broader overview. The digital marketing audit allows for comparative review of all the digital marketing activity.

As mentioned above, the process differs from team to team, but there are a number of key components of the marketing audit process that are consistent across teams and traditional and digital audits. The marketing audit process typically involves four main steps:

1 set objectives and scope of audit
2 gather data
3 analyse
4 report

Types of digital marketing audits

Digital marketing audits generally consist of five key areas or channels, namely website (including content), SEO, SEM and paid media, social media, and email. The remainder of this chapter introduces each type and provides a brief overview of how and what to do for each audit.

As mentioned above, marketing audits typically rely on marketing dashboards' data and evaluation of a couple of marketing metrics too. If you need a refresher on metric terms, review Chapter 20 again. Where relevant, new terms will be explained.

Website audit

A website audit revolves around a thorough review of your website. This audit does not only cover the functionality of your website (for example, links and buttons go to where they are meant to when you click on them), it also covers a review of the content (informative, updated and correct information) and the overall user experience (for example, easy-to-navigate website). Therefore, the key components of a website audit are:

- traffic audit
- user experience (UX) audit
- content audit

Traffic audit

For the traffic audit, you can use your website dashboard (such as Google Analytics) to develop findings. In essence, you have to determine insights such as: the number of visitors to your website, which pages they visit, how many times they visit, which pages receive the most visitors and which ones have the highest bounce rate.

Review the findings for each of these metrics (separately and as a whole unit), evaluate them against the marketing and business objectives and draw conclusions. Typical conclusions answer questions such as:

- Is the traffic satisfactory or do you need to revise your strategy to attract more visitors to the website?
- Which web pages are successful?
- Which web pages are unsuccessful or cause consumers to leave (what is causing the problem)?

Content audit

Content audits are reviews of the written content or copy that appears on the website. Content audits include review of all the content, from headlines to paragraphs right down to the footer at the bottom of the page. Depending on the industry and level of complexity on the website, some content audits might be more challenging than others. A simple website, with a low number of web pages (e.g. a website for a small, local charity) will be easier to audit than a website with multiple pages, sub-pages and big chunks of content (e.g. a medical website that has information on a number of illnesses and treatments that need to be verified by a medically trained audit team member).

Content audits require a thorough read through of all content, including checking for clarity, consistency and being correct. Once all content has been reviewed, typical questions can include:

- Is there any content that is hard to understand that needs revision?
- Does the content match the company tone and language?

- Does the content match the company mission and values?
- Are there any incomplete or incorrect pages that need content revision?
- Are there any outdated pages that need content revision?
- Are there any obsolete pages that need content removal?
- What is the purpose of the content?
- Who is the content for?

User experience audit

KEY TERM

User experience (UX)

User experience design is the process design teams use to create products that provide meaningful and relevant experiences to users. This involves the design of the entire process of acquiring and integrating the product, including aspects of branding, design, usability and function.

SOURCE Interaction Design Foundation, 2020

User experience (UX) audits can give you insights into: which parts of the website are functioning well, which parts are easy or difficult to navigate, etc (see also Chapter 16). User experience draws from web design and the audits typically involve a review of the design principles associated with the discipline. Memon (2019) provides a list of key UX principles to review when conducting a UX audit:

- meeting users' needs
- determining where the team is in the website design process
- creating a clear information hierarchy
- consistent design
- increasing accessibility
- designing with the users' environment in mind
- prioritizing usability
- simplistic approach
- avoid hard-to-understand language
- carefully consider typography in design

- integrate feedback received
- confirm good UX and functionality before going live
- design the navigation to put the user in control
- include personality in the design
- employ visual grammar principles
- design with a narrative in mind

The principles outlined above can be used to ask typical questions when conducting a UX review, for example:

- Is the UX consistent?
- Is the usability good?
- Is the navigation intuitive?
- Is the language easy to understand?
- Is the flow of information logical and prioritized (information hierarchy)?
- How accessible is my website?
- Does the UX allow the user to be in control?

Activity 21.1

i. In a group, pick a website and review three of the pages for that website using some of the key UX principles by Memon (2019).

ii. Is it a good website? What would you change and why?

iii. Discuss your answers with the class (remember, screen shots of the web pages analysed).

SEO audit

Search engine optimization (SEO) audits review the performance of the company's SEO efforts on search engines. Good SEO practices improve website rankings. The higher the ranking, the higher up the list of results when consumers search for something related to your business (or client's business). Website audit and SEO audit often go together, as a bad website will negatively impact SEO performance (and vice versa).

The typical things to review for an SEO audit include:

- on-page SEO audit
- local search audit

- keyword audit
- website load speed
- broken links

On-page SEO audit

As with website audits, SEO audits rely on reviewing digital dashboards such as Google Analytics. Using dashboards, marketers can conduct on-page SEO audits to review the quality and usefulness of their websites. For example, do the keywords for SEO attract visitors as intended? Typical questions to answer here include:

- Does the web page provide a quality experience?
- Is the web page useful to consumers?
- Do the SEO-linked keywords on the page provide the desired results?

Local search audit

SEO audits also involve a bit of 'field work' in, for example, testing search processes, keywords and links. This type of work is associated with local search audits and provides the marketer with an overview of the results from conducting local searches using the keywords linked to the SEO marketing strategy. Typical questions include:

- Does our website or the specific web page appear when searching for the keywords in the search engine?
- Who else appears in the results list?
- Where do we appear on the results list?
- (If SEO marketing was employed in the form of sponsored content), does the sponsored result appear at the top? Does it drive traffic to the website as intended?

Keyword audit

A good content audit also inherently informs on the status of keyword performance, as consistent and clear use of keywords should successfully direct visitors to the website. Typical keyword audits involve reviewing the keywords used or underutilized key words that lead visitors to the website. Typical questions to answer here include:

- Are the keywords being used?
- What are the keywords not used for SEO?
- Are the keywords being used correctly and efficiently?
- Which keywords are most effective?
- Which keywords face the most competition from other businesses?

Website load speed

Website load speed evaluates the time it takes for the website to load. According to Monaghan (2022) the ideal load speed for e-commerce websites is 1–2 seconds – any longer and your bounce rate and competitors' chances to steal your customer increases. There are two typical questions to answer here:

- What is the load speed?
- If it is too long, what can we do to improve it?

Broken links

Broken links are often only found when testing links. While it is harder to do on websites where there are a lot of links to internal or external pages, for SEO it is easier to test. When a link appears based on SEO keywords searched, the auditor checks if the link works as intended. Typical questions include:

- Is the link working?
- Is the link directing the visitor to the right page or content?

Activity 21.2

Hill (2022) developed a 15-step audit checklist for SEOptimer that combines some website and SEO audit questions for review. The website audit checklist article on the SEOptimer website provides his overview of each of the 15 steps and includes a downloadable template for a website audit.

i. Take some time to read the article.

ii. Download the template for use (and customization) for your own website audit.

Search engine marketing (SEM) audit

Search engine marketing (SEM) is the marketing activity employed on search platforms, such as Google. SEM is paid marketing, such as Google Ads, and involves a number of routes to driving customers to your website and/or other online company channels.

According to Imarc (2022a) there are a number of different SEM strategies available to marketers on the Google platform:

- **Search campaigns:** Advertisements appear directly within keyword search results, measured via PPC.

- **Display campaigns:** Advertising via Google Display Network (GDN), for example banner advertisements on websites, apps and videos.

- **Smart campaigns:** Automated optimizations for targeting, displaying Google Ads to audiences their algorithm determines as appropriate for your business.

- **Discovery campaigns:** Discovery campaigns uses relevance, extended reach, visually appealing ad formats and machine learning to bolster Google's algorithm ability to optimize your campaign in achieving a goal. Available in different formats and on Google Discover, YouTube Mobile and Gmail.

- **Dynamic campaigns:** Dynamic campaigns or Dynamic Search Ads (DSAs) rely on machine learning to enable algorithms to automatically create headings, determine landing pages and set bids for targeted advertising.

The key insights required from SEM audits are to determine:

- what the results are (i.e. the conversion rate)
- which SEM can be attributed with successful conversion
- whether it delivers good ROI

As mentioned in Chapter 20 attribution is defined as identifying which marketing element was responsible for motivating the consumer to action that achieves the desired outcome (Charlesworth, 2021). Attribution is a useful tool for SEM audits. Marketers use *attribution models* to monitor their conversion goals for SEM marketing.

KEY TERM
Attribution model

A rule, a set of rules, or a data-driven algorithm that determines how credit for conversions is assigned to touchpoints on conversion paths.

SOURCE Google, 2022

EXAMPLE
Google

Google provides some attribution models as useful tools for marketers to use. Google (2022) distinguishes between two types of attribution models:

- rules-based models (following fixed rules regardless of conversion type)

- data-driven models (calculate conversion from each click and thus distribute credit for each conversion type)

Rules-based models have a number of rules marketers can follow:

iii. first interaction model – attributes credit to the first click

iv. last interaction model – attributes credit to the last click

v. linear model – equally distributes the credit for conversion across all clicks

vi. time decay model – attributes more credit to later clicks that occur closer to conversion.

vi. position-based model – attributes 40 per cent of the credit to the first and last click each, while the rest is distributed across the rest of the clicks on the path to conversion

Data-driven models follow only one rule:

i. Data-driven model attributes individual credit to each marketing point according to conversion type

SOURCE Google, 2022

Question

a. Visit the Google Analytics website.

b. Search for the article about the two types of attribution models (Google, 2022).

Social media audit

The trickiest part about social media audits is deciding what the purpose is of your social media marketing. It is important to set clear objectives for each channel and for all the different content you put onto your social media channels. Marketing activity differs per industry and per channel. In determining the success of your social media marketing, you need to know which channel(s) you are using, whether you are employing promoted (paid) or organic content, who your target audience is and what you are trying to achieve with it.

As with websites, using the social media platforms' analytics dashboards allows the marketer to review a lot of the performance results for social media marketing activity. The most common things to evaluate here are click-through rate (CTR), cost-per-click (CPC) and conversion rate (see Chapter 20) It is also useful to conduct a content audit of your social media for each channel and each piece of content.

Typical questions to ask here are:

- Is this piece of social media marketing delivering a good CTR?
- Is this piece of social media marketing delivering a good CPC?
- Is this piece of social media marketing delivering a good conversion rate?
- How does it compare to other social media marketing attempts on the same channel?
- How does it compare to social media marketing activity on other channels?
- Who is the content aimed at?
- Do the social media marketing activities achieve the objectives set?

Activity 21.3

There are endless possibilities in terms of the questions to ask of a social media audit. Digital agency Imarc (2022b) developed a social media marketing audit checklist that covers a range of questions across different types of social media marketing. This checklist is available as a downloadable template on their website.

i. Go to the Imarc.com website, and download the template for use (and customization) for your own social media marketing audit.

ii. Take some time to read through the checklist. Can you spot different types of content? The importance of creativity?

Email marketing audit

Email marketing audits also have an abundance of data and measurable results, particularly if you are using a database and a customer relationship marketing (CRM)-based platform, such as Mailchimp. The general performance of mails (e.g. open rate, click-through rate) all offer good ways to audit the email marketing activity. However, audits of your email marketing activity also review the status of your database and CRM system, for example determining list quality and delivery rate. It is also useful to conduct a content audit of your emails, just like with websites and social media. Typical questions can include:

- How is (each) email performing?
- How many subscribers?

- How many open the email(s)?
- How many mark the email(s) as spam?
- What is the delivery rate of email(s)?
- What is the quality of the content list (how many emails are undeliverable due to outdated lists)?
- What is the purpose of the content?
- Who is the content for?
- Is there any content that is hard to understand that needs revision?
- Does the content match the company tone and language?
- Does the content match the company mission and values?
- Do the links in the email work?

EXAMPLE
Green marketing audit criteria

Chen and Yang (2019) used a decision-making approach, in conjunction with practitioners, to develop criteria (a checklist) for conducting a green marketing audit. A green marketing audit tests a company's sustainability via four main components: its mission, answering to stakeholders, marketing activities, and environmentally friendly competencies (Chen and Yang, 2019).
   The criteria, divided into those four components, are:

- Mission and goals:
  - developed a clear mission statement dictating environmental awareness throughout business functions
  - integrated a green approach as a central value
  - integrated tackling environmental issues as a goals of the company
  - prioritized environmental preservation and green management
  - educated employees about the importance of green business practices
- Global green competence:
  - developed green products and services that can compete on a global scale
  - implemented green marketing initiatives that reflect national green perspectives and environmental preservation agendas
- Stakeholders' requirements
  - adhered to environmental policy and legislation

- complied with required standard(s) of environmental preservation
- met stakeholders' requirement for environmental preservation
- met society's requirements for green practices and responsibilities
- improved the sustainable development of the company
- satisfied customer expectations for green products and practices
- Green marketing activities
  - considered the environment in product design
  - used ecological and green materials for manufacturing
  - used recycled, cleaned and repurposed materials in packaging, where possible

SOURCE Chen and Yang, 2019

Note: a sustainability audit could build on this by also including a focus on social initiatives and checklist items.

Activity 21.4

i. Take the Green Marketing Audit Checklist in the example box above, pick a company of your choice and see if you can answer some of the questions.

ii. Take a look at their mission and values on their website, stakeholder reports, newspaper articles and press releases about their activities (particularly CSR activities).

iii. How many could you answer?

iv. Discuss your answers in the class.

PRACTITIONER INPUT
Hannah Quirke

Vectorise Marketing is a UK-based training, coaching and marketing agency led by founder and owner Hannah Quirke. The interview below offers her answers to some key questions about working with clients on audits, reviews of business and strategy development.

Can you give us some background information about Hannah and Vectorise?

I have run a marketing consultancy since 2005. The business is a small consultancy which is a wobbly wheel in format, in other words I am the sole consultant at the centre of the wheel and the sole point of contact with the client. Then radiating from the wheel in order to deliver the projects I am supported by freelance designers, copy writers and administrators. Services provided through the business include marketing, training and business support.

Which clients do you work with?

There are two main strands to the business. First, we work on business support programmes with either growing or start-up businesses. Their motivations vary considerably. Those at growth stage have sometimes looked to secure external investment and need to demonstrate a strategic marketing growth plan or market potential. Others at start-up stage are looking to break into new markets as an unknown brand.

Secondly, the business specializes in consulting and working with independent financial advisory firms with no more than 25 staff. They have seen a huge increase in their professional indemnity insurance and so their running costs have increased and they often have a declining client base with elderly clients. Over recent years the landscape for financial advice has changed and resulted in our client base shrinking.

Do you think marketing audits are still useful?

Yes. Without an evidence-based approach, objectives are not well thought through and the implications involve mismanaging the expectations of the client for whom we are planning marketing activities. Additionally, audits act as a sense check with the client to ensure that everyone understands their resource availability and how it is aligned with their ambitions. One of the biggest challenges working with small businesses is that they say they want to grow, and indeed they want to generate more income, but haven't got the capacity internally to service it. So they are in fact a barrier to their own growth. Audits help them understand that and what needs to be done to overcome barriers.

Have you ever conducted a marketing audit?

Yes absolutely, where we are creating a strategic marketing plan it is always the first stage of the process. However, I don't usually explicitly refer to this first step as an audit. When we are only commissioned to design and deliver on a campaign, we don't do an audit, but work from a specific brief from the client, using their and our insights.

What is your typical process to follow when conducting a marketing audit?

Ultimately, the marketing framework I use is the SOSTAC [(situation, objectives, strategy, tactics, action and control)] framework. So the marketing audit informs the situation analysis and from here objectives are agreed.

What do you typically evaluate?

External evaluations, covering a wide range of factors, from competitors to growth or market opportunities. Internal evaluations, where we consider the values, mission, ambitions, resources and capacity they have as a business. Based on our evaluations we can make informed decisions and provide strategic recommendations.

We need to ensure that recommendations are congruent with the organization and that where there are discrepancies between the ambition and the current resource these can be identified and discussed. We sometimes find that specializing to serve a niche market may be better than expanding the volume of activity (where we have small businesses). In one marketing audit, we identified a niche area for a local accountancy practice, where there was a high influx of immigrants coming over from a specific country. These immigrants were setting up their own businesses. Our client could specialize and serve this community well. Without the marketing audit, we would not have found this solution.

How do you report the results to clients?

In the form of a report and a follow-up discussion. Company directors for small organizations tend to be less interested in reading reports from cover to cover, so it is beneficial to facilitate a discussion to go over the details. Ideally there should be a discussion both before and after the audit. In this way the audit acts as a fact-finding mission from which a series of recommendations and actions can be agreed.

What are the usual outcomes from marketing audits?

Most frequently, the audit informs the business priorities and marketing objectives for the next 12 months. Sometimes they have highlighted where additional resource is required. They are also an excellent way to gauge whether there will be a partnership approach with the client or a one-off project.

Summary

In this chapter we explored the concept of marketing audit, including its historical developments and eras. After a brief overview of the reasons and benefits of conducting a marketing audit, we were introduced to the different types of marketing audits, such as website, SEO, SEM and paid media, social media and email audits. Lastly, we read about conducting a marketing audit from an experienced marketing specialist, giving us an insider peek at applying theory to practice.

Chapter review

Reflective questions

Q1 Why is it becoming important to conduct marketing audits?

Q2 When should marketing audits be done?

Q3 How are marketing audit results communicated?

Q4 What are the potential implications of marketing audit results?

Key learning points

- The marketing audit can be defined as a thorough examination of all the marketing activities of a business to improve performance (Kotler et al, 1989).

- There are many benefits in conducting a digital marketing audit, such as identifying strengths and weaknesses, opportunities for growth, streamlining marketing activity and objectives, improving team morale and increasing return on investment.

- The digital marketing audit process follows four key steps:

  a set objectives and scope of audit

  b gather data

  c analyse

  d report

- There are different types of marketing audits that focus on key aspects of the digital marketing strategy. Website, SEO, SEM, social media and email audits all provide nuanced insights of the status of their respective part of the marketing strategy as a whole.

References

Charlesworth, A (2021) *Absolute Essentials of Digital Marketing*, Routledge, London

Chen, H C and Yang, C H (2019) Applying a multiple criteria decision-making approach to establishing green marketing audit criteria, *Journal of Cleaner Production*, 210, 256–65

Google (2022) Attribution reports and attribution models, support.google.com/google-ads/topic/7279627?hl=en&ref_topic=3119145 (archived at https://perma.cc/68HP-J9Q2)

Hill, T (2022) 15 step website audit checklist (& PDF template), www.seoptimer.com/blog/website-audit-checklist/ (archived at https://perma.cc/8FU5-X3PA)

Imarc (2022a) How to perform search engine marketing, iMarc, www.imarc.com/blog/how-to-perform-a-search-engine-marketing-sem-audit (archived at https://perma.cc/8VKX-DTFV)

Imarc (2022b) Social media audit checklist, Imarc, www.imarc.com/writable/files/pdf/Social-Media-Audit-Checklist.pdf (archived at https://perma.cc/TT23-7MZQ)

Interaction Design Foundation (2020) User experience (UX) design, www.interaction-design.org/literature/topics/ux-design#:~:text=User%20experience%20(UX)%20design%20is,%2C%20design%2C%20usability%20and%20function (archived at https://perma.cc/LP95-SK9P)

Kotler, P H, Gregor W T and Rodgers W H (1977) The marketing audit comes of age, *Sloan Management Review,* 18(Winter), 25–43

Kotler, P H, Gregor W T and Rodgers W H (1989) The marketing audit comes of age, *Sloan Management Review,* 30(Winter), 49–62

Memon, M (2019) 16 important UX design principles for newcomers, Springboard, www.springboard.com/blog/design/ux-design-principles/ (archived at https://perma.cc/BVK7-XLZS)]

Monaghan, M (2022) Website load time statistics: Why speed matters in 2022, Website Builder Expert, www.websitebuilderexpert.com/building-websites/website-load-time-statistics/#:~:text=So%2C%20how%20fast%20should%20a,seconds%20before%20abandoning%20a%20site (archived at https://perma.cc/5REX-3E3J)

Point Visible (2022) How to perform a digital marketing audit, Pointe Visible, www.pointvisible.com/blog/what-is-a-digital-marketing-audit/ (archived at https://perma.cc/4DS2-YP7Q)

Rothe, J T, Harvey, M G and Jackson, C E (1997) The marketing audit: Five decades later, *Journal of Marketing Theory and Practice*, 5(3), 1–16

SEOptimer (nd) SEO audit and reporting tool, SEOptimer, www.seoptimer.com (archived at https://perma.cc/YGA7-S6XW)

Unger, R and Chandler, C (2012) *A Project Guide to UX Design: For user experience designers in the field or in the making, New Riders*, Indianapolis, IN

Vectorise (2022) Home page, Vectorise, www.vectorise.uk/ (archived at https://perma.cc/27X9-3RY7)

Wilson, A (2005) *Marketing Audit Handbook,* Kogan Page, London

Wymbs, C (2011) Digital marketing: The time for a new 'academic major' has arrived, *Journal of Marketing Education*, 33(1), 93–106

Managing, testing and improving campaigns 22

By the end of this chapter, you should be able to:

- explain in simple terms what the strategic approaches to managing digital marketing campaigns are
- understand the methods employed by digital marketers to improve campaigns
- describe Kelley's 3S approach: search, site and social
- briefly define A/B testing

Introduction

A digital marketing campaign's success relies heavily on the strategic planning that goes into the initial stages of development. Digital marketing requires an intricate strategy, including stages, channels, KPIs and metrics. Now, apart from having a well-thought out digital marketing strategy and detailed planning sheets and visualizations of the whole process, things can (and will) inevitably go wrong. The luck and challenge of digital marketing is that it is possible to spot and fix those campaign elements that are not performing as they should. Some of these improvements can be done before the digital marketing campaign goes live (e.g. testing the success of different colours, headlines or designs), but most of them require constant monitoring and a quick responsiveness when the campaign is live. In this chapter we will take a look at the main methods employed by marketers for improving campaigns.

Management practices for improving digital marketing strategies

Each digital marketing channel domain requires a unique, but shared, skill set, that when combined creates a synergy in the digital environment not possible in traditional marketing channels

Key, 2017

Key components/insights needed to improve campaigns

- digital marketing strategy
- SMART objectives and KPIs
- digital dashboard for monitoring metrics related to campaign/channels
- relevant audits of specific channels (before, during and after the campaign or project)
- testing campaign variables
- implementing improvements in a timely manner

As we have learnt throughout this book, digital marketing relies heavily on data. In the list above we see the key components needed for improving campaigns. Each component provides insights that are essential for making informed strategic decisions. We also learnt that Big Data can be daunting for digital marketers and that digital dashboards and metrics help marketers to deal with Big Data. According to Singaraju and Niininen (2021), being able to do Big Data analysis is becoming a critical skill for marketers to augment business performance and growth. They provide a categorization of Big Data that is helpful for initializing the analytical process.

Big data involves three analytical categories (Singaraju and Niininen, 2021):

- descriptive (what has already happened in the past)
- predictive (estimating what is likely to happen in the future)
- prescriptive (what can be done to improve where needed)

Metrics analysis revolves around the descriptive data of campaign and channel performance in the past. Predictive analyses are developed based on findings from the descriptive category and comparison to KPIs and previous campaign data. This chapter focuses on prescriptive analysis and illuminates the ways in which digital marketers can improve strategies and campaigns. These prescriptive recommendations can either be done through strategic approaches or specific digital marketing techniques, we will take a look at both below.

Strategic approaches for digital marketing management

Pinball strategy

Hollensen et al (2017) note that digital marketing strategy is like playing pinball. The digital marketplace is dynamic and chaotic, ever changing. The digital marketer 'loses' control of the content once it is out there. The digital marketing campaign content (the 'marketing ball') is passed around the marketplace and often accelerated by users on social media, that essentially functions as the 'bumpers' on the pinball board. Sometimes the marketing ball comes back to the brand. When this happens the digital marketer manages the interactions and sends the content back out into the marketplace – so they use the flippers to engage and throw it back into the digital marketplace.

A key consideration to keep in mind for the digital marketer is that you cannot know the outcomes in advance. Digital marketers need to be prepared to respond in real time to the spin put on the ball by consumers, while maintaining a positive impact for the brand.

RACE plan

A digital marketing strategy represents a combination of many marketing models, such as AIDA, social media funnel, customer journeys, etc. Usually each strategy and its visualization would include stages, channels, KPI and sometimes even the metrics. One very helpful and free template is the RACE plan (Chaffey and Bosomworth, 2015; Chaffey and Ellis-Chadwick, 2019) (see Activity 21.1).

The RACE plan summarizes the key digital marketing activities that need to be managed as part of the digital marketing strategy. This plan (or visualization thereof) combines the funnel, customer journey in stages, channels, KPI suggestions and even some key metrics you can use. The RACE model name stems from the authors' interpretation of the consumer journey and marketing funnel, and stands for: Reach > Act > Convert > Engage. When you go into the template file (Activity 21.1), you will see there is a 'pre-phase' called planning. The plan phase links back to the opening sentence of this chapter – a digital marketing campaign's success relies heavily on the strategic planning that goes into the initial stages of development.

There is also a RACE planning framework that provides a more detailed flowchart which shows how this plan can be applied, from SWOT analysis and market research to objective and strategy development, to project management and specific marketing tactics suggested for each stage.

Activity 22.1

i. Visit the Smart Insights (2022) website and search for the digital marketing plan template.

ii. On this web page you will find more background information on the RACE plan as well as downloadable templates for the plan visualization with the funnel/ customer journey stages, channels, KPI and key metrics suggestions.

Digital marketing methods for improving campaigns

McCarthy (2022) notes there are six methods for improving digital marketing campaigns:

- tailoring
- targeting
- triggering
- monitoring
- testing
- revising

Tailoring

A lot of market and consumer research goes into informing the initial strategic development for digital marketing campaigns. Having all the background information allows you to develop robust marketing strategies that are tailored to engage your desired target audience and meet your marketing objectives. As we saw in Part Three – Consumer Behaviour, Chapter 10 – the most frequently used method for tailoring strategies is to develop a detailed customer persona. While these do not always guarantee success, having all the background information makes it easier to change tactics or strategies when things do not work or need improvement. Does your customer persona give you opportunities to tailor the campaign or content in a different way? Perhaps rewording a headline or social media post, coming up with a different concept, etc?

Targeting

Once you have your (re)tailored customer persona, you can start to build a customer journey for your target audience (see Chapter 11). Again, you need to base your customer journey on insights gathered about the consumer, the marketplace and the channels you have at your disposal. The customer journey works in conjunction with detailed media plans and time lines that match the target audience's consumption and media behaviour. For example, a young mother with toddlers will scroll specific social media channels, watch television and shop at different times to a first-year student at university. Your marketing strategy needs to build in these insights to ensure you are making the right targeting decisions.

Now, once your campaign is live in the marketplace, you can monitor your consumer progress through the journey. You can also start to gather insights on which channel or touchpoint can be attributed with the most successful engagement and conversion rates. You will remember we defined attribution in Chapter 20. If you see that one or more of the touchpoints are becoming frustration points that are causing consumers to abandon your customer journey, you can revise their use, place in the journey, content and timing.

Gopaldas and Siebert (2022, p3) say customer journeys 'should not always be effortless or predictable' . They developed a customer journey matrix with four archetypes: routines, joyrides, treks and odysseys. If your customer journey is not as effective as it should be, perhaps tailoring it more towards your target audience is advisable. Targeting the customer journey according to one of these archetypes could be a useful exercise.

Figure 22.1   The customer journey matrix

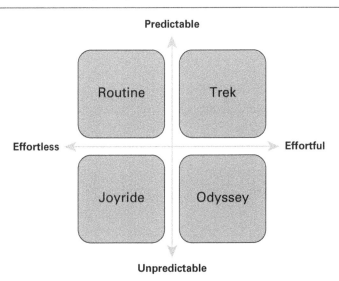

SOURCE Gopaldas and Siebert, 2022

According to their matrix, as seen in Figure 22.1 the archetypes can be categorized according to predictability and effort, as follows (Gopaldas and Siebert, 2022):

- **Routines:** The routine journey works well for fast-moving consumer goods (FMCG) that are used regularly, products that do not require that much thinking or effort along a complicated journey, for example, chewing gum or dishwashing liquid. Streamlining (removing non-value-added touchpoints) and consistency (making it easier to learn and automatically complete the journey) are recommended as key improvement areas for customer journeys adopting a routine approach.

- **Joyrides:** Joyride journeys are suitable for products that offer escape from routines and entertainment, unpredictable yet still effortless, for example streaming movies or music. Streamlining is recommended to mitigate frustration points, but you need to ensure endless variation (e.g. new content or even consumer generated content) to keep the consumer engaged.

- **Treks:** Treks, as the name implies, are viable for long-term goals and journeys that take a long time to complete, for example completing a course at college or saving enough money for a house deposit. Adding goal-posting (achievable goals along the journey via interactive user experiences such as apps) is recommended or eventually converting treks to odysseys.

- **Odysseys:** Odysseys are those journeys that are unpredictable and exciting, and require a lot of effort on the consumer's part, for example training for a marathon or mastering photography. Adding substantive variation (a variety of functional excitement points or challenges) and journey tracking (means to track your progress) is recommended.

SOURCE Gopaldas and Siebert, 2022

Triggering

McCarthy (2022) notes that employing trigger marketing can significantly increase the success of your campaign, and outlines key steps for employing a *trigger marketing* method to improve campaigns.

KEY TERM
Trigger marketing

Sending emails or campaigns at specific points in a customer's engagement life cycle – can significantly increase your chance of success.

SOURCE McCarthy, 2022

The key steps of trigger marketing are (McCarthy, 2022):

1 Determine key stages of customer journey e.g. discovery or renewal.

2 Add additional layers and touchpoints to keep them engaged.

3 Employ marketing automation tools such as CRM systems.

Monitoring

Measuring your campaign performance via metrics analysis gives you the most concrete information about the success or failure of your campaign (see Chapter 20). We already touched on the necessity of monitoring digital marketing via dashboards (see Chapter 19) employing a pinball approach to managing campaigns and evaluating the customer journey (in the Targeting section above). However, there are useful methods for monitoring activity more thoroughly. One such method is social listening. We already introduced the concept of social listening in Chapter 9, but here is a more detailed overview of the concept and how to apply it.

Social listening

According to Li and Bernoff (2011) consumer activities online create a groundswell of information sharing into which marketers can tap to improve understanding of consumer needs that are often more explicit than when they engage with companies, brands or other marketing efforts. Li and Bernoff (2011) also recommend monitoring or 'listening' to the internet to find out who's saying what, where, to whom and (more importantly) why. This is what is known as social listening.

While social media and other new digital technologies provide challenges to marketers in terms of data management and accountability, it also provides ideal opportunities to 'listen' to consumers and online communities. Social listening should be approached in an ethical manner, and can be used to improve communication with consumers and even co-creation of value in terms of marketing and brand experiences for consumers. This in turn bolsters customer journey experiences.

EXAMPLE
Five-step plan for social listening

Step 1: Find out who your customer are and where they engage online.

Step 2: Determine which customers are the opinion leaders influencing group activity.

Step 3: Monitor key engagement areas for what is being said/shared. For example, where service encounters or brand interaction points occur such as on social media platforms or brand chatrooms.

Step 4: Draw on experience and skilled employees or external sources that know the customer, social media and online dialogues.

Step 5: Allocate the job of social listening to a dedicated interpreter who can convert data into insights.

SOURCE Bernoff and Li, 2011

Kelley's 3S approach: search, site and social

Another means of monitoring digital marketing activity is employing Kelley's (REF) 3S approach (Richardson, 2019). Kelley's 3S approach consists of monitoring in three key areas: search, site and social. This strategy is used to monitor the performance of all the digital marketing channels involved in the campaign (these are then linked to dashboard monitoring and metrics analysis).

According to Richardson (2019), the three Ss monitor consumer behaviour within three distinct digital marketing areas:

- search: search engine analytics and behaviour
- site: website analytics and visitor behaviour
- social: social media behaviour

Search   This is related to search engine marketing and how consumers in the early stages of their customer journey can be drawn to the specific business. *Note:* the aim of search engine marketing is not to focus on search engine optimization (SEO) or pay-per-click (PPC), but rather on monitoring the consumers' journey (Richardson, 2019).

Site   As the name implies, site refers to consumer activity related to the website including geographic and time-related information. While traditional internet access was geographically tied to static computers in fixed locations, the adoption of smartphones and widely available internet connection means geographic locations can change constantly, even for the same users, coming to your brand platforms or websites multiple times. Knowing where website traffic comes from is very useful for marketing strategy monitoring and improvements. The top data insights marketers look for when monitoring site activity are:

- in-bound links
- exit pages
- efficacy of search engine terms
- means of accessing site (desktop, laptop, tablet, phablet, smartphone, TV)
- browser used (Chrome, Firefox, Safari, etc)

Social   Social monitoring is related to behaviour on social media and often occurs via platform specific dashboard monitoring e.g. Facebook Analytics. Here marketers pose similar questions as in the other Ss, so they can start to build a more detailed picture of the customer. Here marketers seek to identify:

- common interests
- sentiment in relation to brands
- purchases
- experiences
- stage of family life cycle
- lifestyle choices
- frequency of posts
- how active they are on different networks
- how much influence they have (influencers)
- social mentions

The insights derived from analysing this behaviour informs customer personas and customer journeys as it provides more understanding into consumers' digital behaviour.

Testing

Testing, as part of monitoring and improving campaigns, plays a big part in digital marketing campaign success. There are a whole range of things you can test by simply monitoring their success in engagement and conversion rates (e.g. website, email, social media story, sponsored digital advertisement). There are also other means of testing, such as providing two options of the same content with slight variations. The most frequently used form of testing on digital marketing in this instance is *A/B testing*.

A/B testing

> **KEY TERM**
> A/B testing
>
> A/B (or split) testing in email marketing describes having two different versions of the same content and testing whether consumers prefer option A or B. This allows marketers to choose the better-performing email to be sent in the main email campaign. Tests can vary in complexity: simple tests involving sending multiple subject lines to test which ones generate more opens; or more advanced tests which include completely different email templates to see which one generates more click-throughs. Variations can include headlines, email subject lines, images, colours, fonts, buttons or calls to action.
>
> **SOURCE** Campaign Monitor, nd

As it is possible to quickly change something that is not working, e.g. a headline or image, this means this part of campaign monitoring is probably used the most. In an ideal world testing should be done before the campaign goes live, but often this happens during a live campaign. It is also useful to conduct A/B testing before and during campaigns, as there can be more factors at play in a live environment (i.e. competitor marketing, marketplace events, etc).

> **Activity 22.2**
>
> Pun (2022) have 10 great examples of A/B testing from different brands that resulted in positive outcomes.
>
> **i.**   Visit the Design for Founders website (Pun, 2022).
> **ii.** Search for 'Here Are 10 Fascinating A/B Testing Examples That Will Blow Your Mind' to see a range of examples where this form of testing was applied successfully.

Refine

The last step in the process for improving a campaign is one that occurs as you are reviewing your digital marketing strategy, implementation, activity and performance.

By applying the previous steps, you will inadvertently already be refining the digital marketing campaign when it is live in the marketplace.

When the campaign has finished, another round of reflection is required to assess the overall success. Reviewing the data generated from the digital marketing activity, via dashboards, audits and comparison to marketing objectives, gives you a broader overview of its success. This retrospective review allows you to create reports for the marketing team, for review with other departments and management and with clients. The review of the digital marketing activity will then also enable the marketer to refine the digital marketing strategy – either for other campaigns or new iterations of the same campaign. Refining the digital marketing strategy will also enable the marketing team to justify future allocation of marketing budgets to certain campaigns and hopefully lead to even more success in achieving marketing and business objectives.

Activity 22.3

i.   In a group, take some time to find a digital marketing campaign. It can be any campaign from any brand. Make sure that it has content on at least three digital marketing channels, e.g. Facebook, Instagram and website.

ii. Using the steps outlined in this chapter, evaluate the campaign.

iii. How would you improve the marketing strategy and/or campaign?

iv. Discuss the questions below to complete the activity:

   – Can you figure out who they were targeting? How is the content tailored?

   – Is it necessary to retarget/apply more tailoring to the content?

   – Would the campaign benefit from some engaging triggers?

   – What would you need to monitor to make informed decisions? How?

   – What would you need to test to make informed decisions? How?

   – Make at least two justified recommendations for revising the strategy and/or campaign.

Summary

In this chapter we explored the main methods employed by marketers for improving campaigns. We introduced approaches to managing digital marketing campaigns, i.e. the pinball and RACE strategic approaches. We adopted practitioner-based steps in the monitoring and improving of digital marketing campaigns and strategies, weaved in with practical application of theoretical models such as the more nuanced customer journey matrix, social listening, Kelley's 3S approach and A/B testing.

Chapter review

Reflective questions

Q1 What is the benefit of a detailed digital marketing strategy for managing a campaign?

Q2 Why is effective engagement with Big Data becoming an essential skill for digital marketers?

Q3 How can digital marketing managers ensure positive engagement with consumers using the pinball strategy?

Q4 Why is it necessary to do campaign testing and improvements while digital marketing campaigns are live?

Key learning points

- The strategic approaches to managing digital marketing campaigns require a lot of planning, hands-on managing, customer engagement and quick responses, and the ability to apply improvements to campaigns quickly.

- The main methods employed by digital marketers to improve campaigns are: tailoring, targeting, triggering, monitoring, testing and refining.

- Social listening allows the marketer to gain more insights into the customers' wants and needs and how to integrate this into future strategies.

- Kelley's 3S approach – search, site and social – is used to monitor the performance of all the digital marketing channels involved in the campaign. These are then linked to dashboard monitoring and metrics analysis.

- A/B testing can be defined as: '[testing] two different versions of a page or a page element such as a heading, image or button. A/B testing is aimed at increasing page or site effectiveness against key performance indicators including click-through rates, conversion rates and revenue per visit' (Saura et al, 2017).

References

Campaign Monitor (nd) A/B test your email campaigns, www.campaignmonitor.com/resources/guides/ab-test-email-marketing-campaigns/ (archived at https://perma.cc/45WK-424X)

Chaffey, D and Bosomworth, D (2015) Digital marketing strategy planning template, images.template.net/wp-content/uploads/2016/06/27115818/Digital-Marketing-Strategy-Template.pdf (archived at https://perma.cc/KA7J-G8VQ)

Chaffey, D and Ellis-Chadwick, F (2019) *Digital Marketing: Strategy, implementation and practice*, Pearson, London

Gopaldas, A and Siebert, A (2022) What you're getting wrong about customer journeys, *Harvard Business Review*, July–August, hbr.org/2022/07/what-youre-getting-wrong-about-customer-journeys (archived at https://perma.cc/8GT2-2DDT)

Hollensen, S, Kotler, P and Opresnik, M O (2017) *Social Media Marketing: A practitioner guide*, Opresnik Management Guides

Key, T M (2017) Domains of digital marketing channels in the sharing economy, *Journal of Marketing Channels*, 24(1–2), 27–38

Li, C and Bernoff, J (2011) Groundswell: Winning in a world transformed by social technologies, Forrester Research, Boston, MA

McCarthy, K (2022) 6 proven marketing strategies to improve your campaigns, Act On, act-on.com/blog/6-marketing-strategies-to-improve-your-campaigns/ (archived at https://perma.cc/9Z7J-ULK4)

Niininen, O (ed) (2021) *Contemporary Issues in Digital Marketing*, Routledge, London

Pun, H (2022) Here are 10 fascinating A/B testing examples that will blow your mind, Design for Founders, designforfounders.com/ab-testing-examples/ (archived at https://perma.cc/WSK5-5H5N)

Richardson, N (2019) *Sustainable Marketing Planning*, Routledge, London

Saura, J R, Palos-Sánchez, P and Cerdá Suárez, L M (2017) Understanding the digital marketing environment with KPIs and web analytics, *Future Internet*, 9(4), 76

Singaraju, S and Niininen, O (2021) Understanding Big Data and its application in the digital marketing landscape, in *Contemporary Issues in Digital Marketing*, ed O Niininen, 9–21, Routledge, London

PART SIX
Legal and ethical considerations

Ethical considerations

23

By the end of this chapter, you should be able to:

- distinguish between ethics, business ethics and digital marketing ethics
- explain advertising fraud and list the different types of advertising fraud
- differentiate between mis- and disinformation and explain their relevance to digital marketing
- elaborate on the importance of protecting vulnerable groups in the digital world

Introduction

This chapter deals with the ethical consideration of digital marketing. We will start this chapter by looking at ethics in general before moving on to discuss how digital marketing ethics relate to business ethics. There are several ethical challenges in the digital space and as we have learnt before, legislation concerning the internet is relatively slow to catch up. *Remember:* some of the problems legislators are facing is that the internet is borderless and allows many activities to go on unnoticed. We will therefore review some ethical issues of digital marketing such as ad fraud, fake news, vulnerable groups on the internet and accessibility. One way for businesses to demonstrate their care for ethical issues is to follow the guidelines of corporate digital responsibility (CDR) that we will review in great detail towards the end of this chapter.

Ethics, business ethics and (digital) marketing ethics

Laws and regulations are in place to ensure that illegal business practices are not taking place. There are clear lines that a business cannot cross without being held responsible by a country's government. The digital marketing landscape is a relatively recent one with the internet only being widely available since 1995 (Science and Media Museum, 2020). The exponential growth of the internet and fast technological changes make it very difficult for laws and regulations to keep up.

Due to the absence of clear legal standards, online business decisions currently often have to be guided by ethical principles. Ethics in its most general form refers to knowing what is right and what is wrong. It is guided by a moral compass that decides what humans ought to do concerning obligations, benefits to society and fairness (Velasquez et al, 2010). Organizations are formed of human beings and as such the employees' own personal ethics will determine on which side of those moral principles they will do business.

There are times when individuals need to set their own ethical guidelines aside and act in the best interests of the firm, which is when *business ethics* problems arise in a corporate environment.

KEY TERM
Business ethics

Business ethics is the study of appropriate business policies and practices regarding potentially controversial subjects including corporate governance, insider trading, bribery, discrimination, corporate social responsibility and fiduciary responsibilities. The law often guides business ethics, but at other times business ethics provide a basic guideline that businesses can choose to follow to gain public approval.

SOURCE Twin, 2021

There are strong arguments for why businesses should follow the basic guidelines of conducting ethically sound business practices.

Today, businesses are more transparent than they have ever been and that is to some extent because we are living in the Information Age, with information readily available and just one online search away. The Information Age, also referred to as the Computer Age, Digital Age or the New Media Age, is the idea that 'access to and the control of information is the defining characteristic of this current era in human civilisation' (Tucci, 2014). This means that one scandal or breach of ethics will be visible to a large audience and can be associated with a business/brand for years. On a more positive note, the high visibility through the internet allows consumers to see businesses' efforts to act ethically, which provides an impetus for ethical business behaviour.

Sumlin et al (2021) find that the ethics environment within a business positively impacts organizational performance demonstrating that adhering to corporate ethics has tangible outcomes of strong business performance.

In summarizing, drivers for businesses to act ethically can be seen in the following:

- to comply with legal requirements (if available)
- to meet demands of consumers and other stakeholders
- to enhance business performance

There are different ethical challenges in the various departments of a business. For example, the accounting department will have different ethical guidelines from the marketing department. Table 23.1 highlights some of the corporate ethics issues dealt with in the various business departments.

Table 23.1 Corporate ethics according to different business departments

Business department	Unethical behaviour example
Finance department	• Taking part in manipulative financial practices such as fraud, bribery or insider trading • Knowingly withholding financial information or non-disclosure of invisible risks and expenses • Producing misleading information about financial products • Exploiting tax loopholes
Human resources department	• Hiring personnel for the wrong reasons • Having no consideration for diversity and inclusion • Preferential treatment of some employees • Allowing for different pay for similar jobs • Taking part in exploitation practices
Marketing department	• Communicating wrong or misleading claims about a product/service • Providing incomplete product information • Running culturally insensitive advertising • Collecting consumer data and invading privacy for corporate gain
Research and development department	• Claiming innovative breakthrough without due consideration for the inventor • Limiting the information disclosure • Not adhering to ethical considerations in clinical trials and animal research

(*continued*)

Table 23.1   (Continued)

Business department	Unethical behaviour example
Operations/production department	• Unsustainable production methods particularly with regard to the environment • Using unrenewable energy sources • Producing pollutants • Over-exploitation of natural resources • Unsustainable waste management

Knight, 2022; some content based on Alton, 2017

Activity 23.1

We have outlined several unethical business practices.

i. Visit Ethicalconsumer.org and search for three businesses that you might have suspected in the past of unethical behaviour.

ii. Review the unethical behaviours that they have been accused of.

iii. Try to arrange those unethical behaviours according to the different business departments.

iv. Could you find any unethical marketing practices? If so, what were those?

Ethical issues in digital marketing

As you have seen previously, there are some unethical marketing practices concerning misleading product claims (e.g. reduced fat products that are high in sugars instead), withholding product information (e.g. burgers made from horse meat) and insensitive adverts (e.g. limited body diversity in underwear adverts). Unethical marketing behaviour used to be mainly concerned with fair advertising activities such as how business competitors are treating each other, but today, unethical behaviour in the digital marketing context often relates to data privacy concerns. Some 84 per cent of global consumers fear that their personal data is not secure (Nakka, 2020). Whereas 63 per cent of global consumers would accept display ads on websites in return for access, once they understand how their personal data is shared with advertisers to serve those targeted ads, that percentage falls to 36 per cent (Nakka, 2020).

In 2020, the World Federation of Advertisers (WFA) published a report on Data Ethics: The Rise of Morality in Technology to outline good ethical practices for advertisers. The four key principles are (WFA, 2020; Nakka, 2020):

1 respect: respect for users and their interests

2 fairness: be inclusive, acknowledge diversity and eliminate bias

3 accountability: robust local and global governance and effective remedy for data ethics failure

4 transparency: be open, honest and transparent about data practices

Industry partners of the WFA agree that it is essential to start treating consumer data ethically. For example, Conny Braams, Chief Digital and Marketing Officer for Unilever, has been quoted saying the following:

> The advertising, marketing and media industry must look beyond regulation and champion the ethical use of consumer data. We have a responsibility to inspire trust in our brands and our use of data, and raise ethical standards to drive positive change in society.
>
> WFA, 2020

In the following sections, we will be reviewing further unethical behaviours that play a crucial role in digital marketing.

Advertising fraud

Online advertising is one of the fastest-growing and most lucrative industries in the digital world. High revenue attracts criminal activity and there are figures that suggest that by 2023, *ad fraud* will result in $100 billion in losses for the worldwide digital advertising industry (Device Atlas, nd).

KEY TERM
Ad fraud

Ad fraud is an attempt to deceive advertising platforms into thinking that fake activity on the network is real user behaviour for the purpose of financial gain. Malicious actors typically use bots in order to implement ad fraud, although there are a variety of other methods used to get advertisers and ad networks to pay them for fake activity including some that involve real humans. In short, ad fraud refers to any attempt to disrupt the proper delivery of ads to real users and the intended audience.

SOURCE Singular, nd

There are several types of ad fraud. Some are targeting the end-consumer and others are targeting the advertisers, and digital marketers need to be aware of how to prevent, spot and resolve advertising fraud:

- **Click fraud:** This is one of the most common forms of ad fraud and usually refers to *bots* or *botnets* that target pay-per-click (PPC) ads. Bots or botnets can perform human-like activities like clicking on links or liking social media posts. They can generate clicks that are not from real users and therefore waste advertisers' budgets. Such fake clicks are also used to inflate visitor numbers to websites and social media profiles aiming to make them seem more popular than they are (Device Atlas, nd).

KEY TERM
Bots/botnets

Bots are software apps or programs hosted on unsuspecting computers which perform a wide range of activities online. Botnets are groups of bots that are hosted on different computers that can do human-like activities. Bots and botnets are sophisticated software programs that can be used for click-automation to generate income for fraudsters.

SOURCE Singular, nd

- **Domain spoofing:** This is another common application of ad fraud and relates to the imitation of a legitimate company's website or email. These fake domains are used to defraud both users and advertisers. A closely imitated website can be used to make advertisers believe that they are advertising on an actual business website when in reality they are not. Domain spoofing is also used to ask users for sensitive information (e.g. payment details) as the user believes they are using the correct domain.

- **Ad stacking:** Ad stacking is another fraudulent activity used by scammers to generate ad revenue. It involves fraudsters stacking multiple ads on top of one another. The viewer only sees the top ad, and the impression counts for the served ad and hidden ads in the stack. Ad stacking is another network trick used to deceive advertisers (Device Atlas, nd).

Some of the examples of ad fraud are illegal as well as unethical. The most pressing issue with these fraudulent activities in the digital marketing landscape is the difficulty in differentiating between real and fake information. The limited technical knowledge of users and businesses means that those who can may use that fact to their advantage. Fou (2020) has created an Excel spreadsheet that covers most of the ad fraud opportunities with examples (Fou, 2020). (Towards the end of Fou's article click on the Excel spreadsheet to view the types and techniques of ad fraud and their purpose.)

Activity 23.2

We have now learnt about the different kinds of advertising fraud. One way of creating fake clicks is through click farms.

i. Visit Today's YouTube Channel (#TodayShow) and search for the video 'Inside click farms and their impact on social media'.

ii. Who is acting unethically in this example? Why do you think click farms are such common practice?

Mis- and disinformation and 'fake news'

The spread of misinformation, disinformation and 'fake news' is another unethical behaviour that utilizes the fact that verification of online information is difficult. Around the year 2016, the terms fake news and *misinformation* caught momentum in relation to the presidential election in the United Sates and the Brexit vote in the UK. 'Fake news' is a term that was first popularized by Donald Trump and was used to refer to media spreading misinformation (Fearon, 2017).

KEY TERM
Misinformation

Misinformation pertains to information that is false, inaccurate or misleading. *Note* to be misleading, the information itself need not be false, but may be presented out of context.

SOURCE Treen et al, 2020

The main difference between misinformation and disinformation is seen in the lack of prevailing intent. This means that disinformation differs from misinformation in that disinformation is deliberately created with the intent to mislead (University of Michigan Library, 2022).

Misinformation ranges from having no intention to cause harm where, for example, people might make fun of a fact that they have come across online. Say, for example, a user might come across a post on social media where people still believe that the earth is flat. That user (despite the fact that they do not believe the statement to be factual) might share the post, potentially with a sarcastic comment to make fun of the fact that some people still believe that the earth is flat. Some recipients of that shared post might not read the sarcastic comment and merely read the content of the post. Some of those readers might believe what they have read. This is just one example of how misinformation can spread despite the fact that no harm was intended.

The other end of the spectrum is fabricated and manipulated content. Fabricated content is classified as 100 per cent false with the intent to deceive and cause harm. Similarly, manipulated content describes when genuine information or imagery is manipulated to deceive (Wardle, 2017).

There are many more forms of misinformation and it is important to look at the spread of misinformation from a business point of view.

The impact of mis- and disinformation on digital marketing

The spread of mis-/disinformation and fake news has several impacts on digital marketing from a business and consumer point of view. Consumers get most of their information through online channels such as social media channels and other websites.

This holds true for most of the consumer journey going through the pre-purchase, purchase and post-purchase stages. Information search is essential during the pre-purchase stage where consumers are searching for information about potential products, reading reviews and comparing prices. When purchasing the product, consumers are also exposed to information online, for example during e-commerce purchases. Finally, during the post-purchase stage, consumers might share their experiences with the purchased products in the form of reviews.

All of these stages are important for digital marketers to consider and the involvement of digital marketing activities differs, depending on which stage the consumer is in.

In the following, impacts of misinformation on digital marketing activities are highlighted, based on Fearon (2017):

- Consumers have lost trust in the information they receive online both in the form of paid (e.g. advertisements) and earned (e.g. social media posts) content. This makes it harder for digital marketers to communicate their benefits to the consumers and impact the consumers' purchase decisions.

- Content that consumers are exposed to online is difficult to control for digital marketers. Associations between branded content (e.g. advertisements on search channels or on social media channels) and external content which might be seen as misinformation or fake news can have a bad impact on brands. This can lead to reputational damage through the association of controversial content with a brand.

- Digital marketers are under a lot of pressure to create engaging content for consumers and the nature of misinformation is that it is engaging. Digital marketers are constantly needing to verify the authenticity of the information they are sharing.

- If a brand is associated with fake news or misinformation, the negative effects of reputational damage can last long after it has been corrected and resurface at a later date. Therefore, preventing a situation where negative coverage could be amplified should be taken into account when marketing content online.

There are several recommendations for how digital marketers can prevent the negative impact of misinformation. Digital marketers are encouraged to accept the situation that the online space is one that is hard to control so instead of trying to control it businesses need to find ways to deal with such a lack of control (Kemp, 2017). This can be done, for example, by establishing contingency plans in case of negative publicity.

Other recommendations based on the limited control include the application of channels that are still more controllable by digital marketers. For example, the chance of gaining negative associations from external content is less likely during an email marketing campaign than it is for an advertisement campaign on a social media channel. Several large companies such as Starbucks, *The Guardian* and Walmart are withdrawing from online advertisement as these businesses are worried about being featured next to extremist or questionable content (Solon, 2017).

A final recommendation is a focus on quality rather than quantity when it comes to content creation. Rather than posting and sharing a lot of content which could include the possibility to spread misinformation, digital marketers should focus on building long-lasting relationships by sharing authentic content (Fearon, 2017).

Activity 23.3

We have outlined several impacts of mis-/disinformation and fake news on digital marketing practices.

i. Think of buying a product online and start looking into different brands that might sell your chosen product.

ii. You are now in the pre-purchase phase and are searching for information online.

iii. Such information includes comparing prices, looking at different brands and product features and reading reviews.

iv. Please use social media channels as well as websites when searching for information.

v. Write down all of the times and places where you are exposed to external content that could be mis-/disinformation or fake news.

vi. Has the exposure to such external content influenced your product choice?

Vulnerable groups on the internet

The accessibility of information online is another cause of ethical concern. Young audiences, including children, have access to the same information as adults. This is unique to the digital world as there are several constraints in the 'real' world that prevent children from being exposed to information that could harm them. This also applies to purchasing products that are age restricted.

Young adults are spending a lot of time online, with the UK Government reporting that 12- to 15-year-olds are spending over 20 hours a week online (Dempsey, 2022). Out of the same group, 79 per cent state that they have experienced at least one potentially harmful experience online in the previous year (Dempsey, 2022). Harmful experiences can mean a lot of different things and mainly refer to online bullying, sexual harassment, exploitation or hacking. While these potentially harmful experiences are not to be dismissed, being exposed to too many advertisements when using social media and apps is children's top concern (Livingstone et al, 2017).

Digital marketing and in particular online advertisements are designed to impact behaviour, to elicit an emotional response to influence preferences (Gabrijelčič Blenkuš, 2017). As we have learnt in previous chapters, one reason for the effectiveness of digital marketing campaigns is understanding of the consumer through the collection of data. While this does not necessarily have to be a bad thing for consumers, it does pose the ethical question of how ethical the targeting of young consumers is. Some voice concerns that social media is designed to be addictive and this is extremely problematic for vulnerable groups in society. Given the ability of specific targeting in digital marketing, children are increasingly targeted when they play games, go on social media or use apps, and being exposed to digital advertising when online may harm children by leading to child obesity, hurt to their self-image, increased use of tobacco products and alcohol (Blumberg and van der List, 2021).

The responsibility to protect children from harm online lies with many stakeholders. Parents, schools, the government and businesses as well as internet and social media providers are all called upon to make the digital world a safe space for children and young adults. Table 23.2 highlights the responsibilities of those who have to keep children safe online and outlines tools and policies that help to protect children online (these are UK based).

Digital marketers need to be aware that it is their responsibility that advertisements for age-restricted products have to follow the same strict content rules online and on social media as in traditional media such as TV (Advertising Standards Authority, nd). Examples of ad targeting restrictions apply to products and services like alcohol, gambling and foods high in fat, salt or sugar.

Table 23.2 Responsibilities and policies to protect children from harm online

Responsible group	Responsibilities	Tools and policies to protect children
Parents	• Ensure regulated access • Provide children with digital literacy • Childproof digital devices • Restrict access to certain pages • Be aware of what children are watching • Be a safe space for children to voice their concern	• The Child Exploitation and Online Protection Centre – free education to keep children safe online, www.ceop.police.uk/Safety-Centre/ • NSPCC – www.nspcc.org.uk/keeping-children-safe/online-safety/
Schools	• Educate children and parents on internet safety • Provide children with digital literacy • Be a safe space for children to voice their concern	• The Child Exploitation and Online Protection Centre – free education to keep children safe online, www.ceop.police.uk/Safety-Centre/ • www.nspcc.org.uk/keeping-children-safe/online-safety/
Businesses	• Ensure that children are not directly targeted • Limit the exposure of advertising content to young and vulnerable groups • Follow professional standards	• The Advertising Standards Authority (ASA), www.asa.org.uk/static/uploaded/6829937c-f185-4be6-9455e501af1df1e3.pdf
Internet and social media providers	• Prevent underage access • Clearly communicate age policy • Implement age policy by checking users • Monitoring conversations on platforms • Offer quick recovery plan for reported violation of rules	• Video age verification plan on Instagram, www.bbc.co.uk/news/technology-61828900

(continued)

Table 23.2   (Continued)

Responsible group	Responsibilities	Tools and policies to protect children
The government	• Monitor the online landscape • Offer help and guidance to schools • Implement legal restrictions to protect children online • Impose fines for non-compliance • Prevent access to markets for non-compliance • Fund charities that keep children safe online	• The Online Safety Bill will introduce a duty to protect children from harmful or inappropriate material • www.gov.uk/government/publications/online-safety-bill-supporting-documents/online-safety-bill-factsheet

Summary

In this chapter, we have learnt about the importance of complying with ethical standards. We have differentiated between general ethics, business ethics and have specifically looked into ethical questions for digital marketers. We have reviewed advertising fraud and covered the different types of advertising fraud. These included click fraud, domain spoofing and ad stacking. We have thoroughly reviewed misinformation and how it differs from disinformation. We have learnt that there are several different types of misinformation and that these differ in the impact on businesses and the consumer. This chapter also considered vulnerable groups online, mainly children and young adults. We have outlined how these vulnerable groups need to be protected and questioned who is responsible for protecting these groups.

Chapter review

Reflective questions

Q1 What is the difference between ethics, business ethics and digital marketing ethics and why are they important to consider?

Q2 What are the different types of advertising fraud?

Q3 What is mis- and disinformation, and why are they important for digital marketers to consider?

Q4 Who is responsible for protecting vulnerable groups online?

Key learning points

- There are different ethical challenges in the various departments of a business. Unethical behaviour in the digital marketing context often relates to data privacy concerns.

- There are several types of ad fraud. Some are targeting the end-consumer and others are targeting the advertisers, and digital marketers need to be aware of how to prevent, spot and resolve advertising fraud.

- The spread of misinformation, disinformation and fake news is another unethical behaviour that utilizes the fact that verification of online information is difficult.

- The responsibility to protect children from harm online lies with many stakeholders.

References

Advertising Standards Authority (nd) Regulation of online advertising: A briefing, www.asa.org.uk/static/uploaded/6829937c-f185-4be6-9455e501af1df1e3.pdf (archived at https://perma.cc/K4DA-TGT6)

Alton, L (2017) How much do a company's ethics matter in the modern professional climate? *Forbes*, 12 September, www.forbes.com/sites/larryalton/2017/09/12/how-much-do-a-companys-ethics-matter-in-the-modern-professional-climate/?sh=dfbcf4d1c790 (archived at https://perma.cc/3JQF-X3E8)

Blumberg, D and van der List, L (2021) The threat of digital advertising to children, UC Davis Health, 29 March, health.ucdavis.edu/blog/kids-considered/the-threat-of-digital-advertising-to-children/2021/03 (archived at https://perma.cc/PUU8-ZVCV)

Dempsey, M (2022) What parents need to know to keep their kids safe online, BBC, 27 June, www.bbc.co.uk/news/business-61577187 (archived at https://perma.cc/C5BL-VPAL)

Device Atlas (nd) Advertising fraud: Meaning, prevention and detection, deviceatlas.com/blog/advertising-fraud-meaning-prevention-and-detection (archived at https://perma.cc/BD4U-DY63)

Fearon, A (2017) The impact of fake news on digital marketing, LinkedIn, 9 October, www.linkedin.com/pulse/impact-fake-news-digital-marketing-amon-fearon/ (archived at https://perma.cc/S5KR-87T2)

Fou, A (2020) Digital ad fraud explainer for digital marketers, *Forbes*, 4 June, www.forbes.com/sites/augustinefou/2020/06/04/digital-ad-fraud-explainer-for-marketers/?sh=3124d5516e41 (archived at https://perma.cc/2R5T-TLQX)

Gabrijelčič Blenkuš, M (2017) Digital marketing to children: A new public health challenge, *EuroHealthNet Magazine*, 13 November, eurohealthnet-magazine.eu/digital-marketing-to-children-a-new-public-health-challenge/ (archived at https://perma.cc/BBV5-JJX6)

Kemp, N (2017) Marketing in the age of the troll, Campaign Live, 25 January, www. campaignlive.co.uk/article/marketing-age-troll/1420757 (archived at https://perma. cc/7UZH-P3FP)

Livingstone, S, Davidson, J and Bryce, J (2017) Children's online activities, risks and safety, UKCCIS, October, assets.publishing.service.gov.uk/government/uploads/system/uploads/ attachment_data/file/759005/Literature_Review_Final_October_2017.pdf (archived at https://perma.cc/FQ8B-U3FK)

Nakka, S (2020) Concerns about unethical practices in digital marketing, LinkedIn, 22 November, www.linkedin.com/pulse/concerns-unethical-practices-digital-marketing-sanket-nakka/ (archived at https://perma.cc/B77Q-YEKM)

Science + Media Museum (2020) A short history of the internet, 3 December, www. scienceandmediamuseum.org.uk/objects-and-stories/short-history-internet#:~: text=Consequently%2C%20the%20number%20of%20websites,around%2010%20 million%20global%20users (archived at https://perma.cc/RGR6-BGAA)

Singular (nd) Ad fraud, www.singular.net/glossary/ad-fraud/ (archived at https://perma.cc/ Q5CC-XRBR)

Solon, O (2017) Google's bad week: YouTube loses millions as advertising row reaches US, *The Guardian*, 25 March, www.theguardian.com/technology/2017/mar/25/google-youtube-advertising-extremist-content-att-verizon (archived at https://perma.cc/3TMC-GSZR)

Sumlin, C, Hough, C and Green, K (2021) The impact of ethics environment, organizational commitment, and job satisfaction on organizational performance, *Journal of Business and Management*, 27(1), 53–78

Today Show (2019) Inside click farms and their impact on social media [video], YouTube, www.youtube.com/watch?v=YZhlU2_YsPE (archived at https://perma.cc/UYP6-KXMZ)

Treen, K, Williams, H and O'Neill, S (2020) Online misinformation about climate change, WIREs Climate Change, 11, e665, 1–20

Tucci, L (2014) Information Age, TechTarget, March, www.techtarget.com/searchcio/ definition/Information-Age (archived at https://perma.cc/RH42-8MRQ)

Twin, A (2022) Business ethics: Definition, principles, why they're important, www. investopedia.com/terms/b/business-ethics.asp (archived at https://perma.cc/9C3W-JD4C)

University of Michigan Library (2022) Research guide fake news and propaganda, guides. lib.umich.edu/fakenews (archived at https://perma.cc/HQ48-5NGK)

Velasquez, M, Andre, C, Shanks, T and Meyer, M (2010) What is ethics, Markkula Center for Applied Ethics at Santa Clara University, 1 January, www.scu.edu/ethics/ethics-resources/ethical-decision-making/what-is-ethics/ (archived at https://perma.cc/3Q7B-C7DB)

Wardle, C (2017) Fake news. It's complicated, First Draft, 16 February, firstdraftnews.org/ articles/fake-news-complicated/ (archived at https://perma.cc/JNB6-R3MY)

WFA (2020) WFA launches world's first guide on data ethics for brands, World Federation of Advertisers, wfanet.org/knowledge/item/2020/06/01/WFA-launches-worlds-first-guide-on-data-ethics-for-brands (archived at https://perma.cc/N84X-HV2P)

Sustainability in the digital world   24

By the end of this chapter, you should be able to:

- briefly explain the difference between CSR and CDR
- outline in detail what CDR (corporate digital responsibility) entails
- explain how social media can be utilized for corporate sustainability messaging
- explain in your own words how the digital landscape and technology can help to achieve a more sustainable planet

Introduction

In this chapter, we will be reviewing how businesses need to consider sustainability in the digital age. We will be covering how the concept of corporate social responsibility has been extended and adjusted to fit the digital context with the advent of corporate digital responsibility. We will be looking into the necessity for businesses to consider their sustainability strategy and cover individual dimensions of sustainability messaging. The environmental context of sustainable strategy refers to the treatment of the environment, the social context highlights the need for change in society, inequality and deprivation and the economic context focuses on strong economic performance. We will review how social media provides a platform for businesses to communicate their sustainability efforts. Here, we will review how consumers want these messages to be communicated. We will then review global sustainability initiatives that champion digitization and digital technologies as the way forward in achieving a sustainable planet.

Sustainable corporate behaviour

Since the 1970s, businesses have applied the concept of *corporate social responsibility* (CSR) (see also Chapter 4). CSR describes the idea that businesses have an obligation to contribute to the needs of society as they exist due to public consent (*CSR Journal*, 2019). Because of this, businesses have an obligation to ensure their actions enhance society and the environment rather than contributing negatively to them (Fernando, 2022).

KEY TERM
Corporate social responsibility (CSR)

Corporate social responsibility is a self-regulating business model that helps a company be socially accountable to itself, its stakeholders, and the public.

SOURCE Fernando, 2022

This responsibility towards people and the planet can be seen as two dimensions of a sustainable business strategy, namely the environmental and the social context. In Chapter 12, you were introduced to the triple bottom line as a pro-sustainable business strategy. The triple bottom line (Elkington, 1997) is a concept that is based on the 3Ps: *profit*, *planet* and *people*. The idea around the triple bottom line is that businesses need to address all three in order to be successful. The pursuit of profits alone is seen as short-sighted and instead businesses are being held accountable by all their stakeholders in terms of responsible business and actions that do not damage the environment or society.

Corporate digital responsibility

One of the main global business trends that is having a major impact on society is digitization. Wade (2020) states that sustainability deals with humanity's relationship with the natural world, while digitization concerns relationships in the virtual world. He further elaborates on the risk that unethical digital practices have on society and the planet and stresses that both concepts (sustainability and digitization) have to be considered together (Wade, 2020). While both the government and society are starting to consider both, businesses are encouraged to join the debate (Wade, 2020).

One way of ensuring that businesses are merging both their sustainability efforts and digitization is described in the concept of *corporate digital responsibility (CDR)* (see also Chapter 4). This concept, similar to corporate social responsibility, is seen as a self-regulating business model that helps businesses to be held accountable to stakeholders and the public for actions in the digital world.

KEY TERM
Corporate social responsibility (CSR)

Corporate digital responsibility (CDR) is the set of shared values and norms guiding an organization's operations concerning four main digital technology and data processes. These processes are: creating technology and data capture; operation and decision-making; inspection and impact assessment; and refinement of technology and data.

SOURCE Lobschat et al, 2021

Some argue that corporate digital responsibility is, in fact, a subset of corporate social responsibility (Wade, 2020). Closer aligned to the definition of CSR, The International CDR Manifesto defines CDR to be a 'set of practices and behaviours that help an organization use data and digital technologies in a way that is socially, economically, technologically and environmentally responsible' (Corporate Digital Responsibility, 2021).

Despite this minor difference of opinion, CDR guides business in the responsible use of data. It aids in setting out standards for businesses to self-regulate their accountability to be good to society and the planet while ensuring profits are high enough to have sustained business. The International CDR Manifesto is based on collaborations between an international group of academics, corporate practitioners and published authors to set out principles that guide businesses on their CDR journey. The following seven guidelines have been established (Corporate Digital Responsibility, 2021):

1 **Purpose and trust**: Clear and unambiguous public statement of intent to positively impact planet and society, in conjunction with clarity of purpose.

2 **Fair and equitable access for all**: A commitment to equity, diversity and inclusion in the organization and extended supply chain, ensuring that resultant products and services are accessible and consumable by all.

3 **Promote societal well-being**: A stronger focus on protecting personal data, supporting improved privacy balanced with identity, addressing digital poverty in access to skills and understanding and protecting all of society from harmful consequences of digital products and services.

4 **Consider economic and societal impact:** Considering the economic and societal impact of decisions within the organization.

5 **Accelerate progress with impact economy:** Take steps to improve consumer demand of ecologically and societally better products, support and incubate more cleantech, greentech, organic and low-waste supply chain SMEs and invest in sustainable and societal impact initiatives.

6 **Creating a sustainable planet to live:** Understand and report corporate impact against the UN Sustainable Development Goals or similar. To innovate and go beyond Carbon Negative, to innovate and solve biggest challenges.

7 **Reduce tech impact on climate and the environment:** Implement an environmental IT strategy, understand consequence of technology, shift energy use to renewables, mitigate and minimize impact and minimize use of offset.

Activity 24.1

You have now learnt about the term corporate digital responsibility. PricewaterhouseCoopers (PwC) is one of the Big Four accounting firms and the second-largest professional services network in the world.

i. Visit the PwC (2022) website and read about the services that PwC offers to their clients with regard to corporate digital responsibility and digital ethics.

ii. What does PwC consider to be the key components of responsible digitization?

iii. How do these components compare to the seven guidelines of the International CDR Manifesto?

iv. What are the differences and what are the similarities?

Lobschat et al (2021) describe the role and relevance of CDR in marketing management as dealing with consumer data privacy and protection and the impact of AI. They further stress the unintended side effects of digitization as crucial to consider as prerequisites for sustainable digital societies and environments (Montag and Diefenbach, 2018; Scholz et al, 2018).

Those organizations that implement CDR practices are realizing that sustainable practices are not only good for the environment but also for profits. For example, Unilever's Sustainable Living Brands account for more than 75 per cent of the company's growth (Wade, 2020). In addition to investing in sustainable products, Unilever is at the forefront of realizing the need for a digital responsibility framework (Unilever, 2019a).

CASE STUDY   Unilever

Unilever is one of the biggest global advertisers, owning brands such as Ben & Jerry's, Dove, Hellmann's, Marmite, Persil and Pot Noodle. In total, Unilever owns about 400 brands around the world and pledges to make sustainable living commonplace (Unilever, nd).

Unilever is a strong supporter of corporate digital responsibility and has implemented a number of different activities over the years to ensure that companies are purpose-led and help to solve global challenges rather than just selling products (Unilever, 2019a). In order to do so, Unilever has implemented a number of digital initiatives that aim to assist in solving challenges.

In February 2018, Unilever announced the launch of the Responsibility Framework to broaden Unilever's approach to partner engagement by covering three key areas (Unilever, 2019b):

- **Commitment One – Responsible Platforms:** Unilever will not invest in platforms or environments that do not protect our children or which promote anger, hate or create division in society. We will prioritize investing only in responsible platforms that are committed to creating a positive impact in society. This includes engagement on brand safety, fake news, influencer transparency and fraudulent activity on the platform.

- **Commitment Two – Responsible Content:** Unilever is committed to creating responsible content, initially tackling gender stereotypes in advertising through #Unstereotype, and championing this across the industry through the #Unstereotype Alliance. This also includes a focus on how platforms are vetting and monetizing content that goes live on platforms.

- **Commitment Three – Responsible Infrastructure:** Unilever will only partner with organizations that are committed to creating a better digital infrastructure and improving the consumer experience. This includes engagement around One Measurement system, consumer data protection, and infrastructure for managing key platform issues with third-party verification implementation.

Another area in which Unilever sees the need for change is influencer marketing. Influencer marketing has been growing rapidly and lacks control mechanisms to avoid bad practices such as fake followers, bots, fraud or other dishonest business models (Unilever, 2018). Keith Weed, Chief Marketing Officer (CMO), said in June 2018:

> At Unilever, we believe influencers are an important way to reach consumers and grow our brands. Their power comes from a deep, authentic and direct connection with people, but certain practices like buying followers can easily undermine these relationships.

As a result, Unilever announced in June 2018 the following three commitments to make influencer marketing more responsible:

- Transparency from Influencers (we will not work with influencers who buy followers).
- Transparency from Brands (our brands will never buy followers).
- Transparency from Platforms (we will prioritize partners who increase transparency and help eradicate bad practices).

In January 2019, Unilever publicized its aim to develop a Cross-Media Measurement Model to help businesses measure and understand campaign impact across the media landscape (Unilever, 2019b). In order to establish a global system operating across multiple markets that puts privacy and consumer experience first, Unilever has partnered with Facebook, Google, Twitter, Kantar Media and Nielsen (Unilever, 2019b).

A final corporate digital responsibility initiative that Unilever aims to tackle is the global problem of click fraud. Unilever is establishing a Trusted Publisher Network as Keith Weed, Chief Marketing Officer at Unilever, states that it is important to rebuild trust across the industry (Unilever, 2019a). This network of global, regional and local online publishers and platforms will be carefully chosen by Unilever and include checks around ad fraud, ad experience, traffic quality and data access (Unilever, 2019a). Unilever hopes to gain more control over the placement of the ads and who is watching them – people not bots.

As you can see from the initiatives explained throughout the case study, Unilever is committed to making the online advertising space a fairer place to improve their control and to deliver a better experience to the consumer.

Questions

a. Visit the 'Planet and Society' page of the Unilever.com website and the other Unilever sources in the References to review some of the CDR initiatives that the company is undertaking.

b. Why do you think that Unilever is so committed to implementing CDR activities?

c. Write down three benefits of CDR activities for the business and three benefits for the consumer.

d. Can you think of any challenges that businesses such as Unilever might face when trying to implement CDR initiatives?

Sustainability messaging on social media

We have now considered a number of corporate digital responsibility initiatives implemented by private businesses. A study by IBM shows that 7 out of 10 customers care about the sustainability efforts of their favourite brand (Haller et al, 2020) and it is, therefore, crucial to understand the role of digital technology in facilitating the exchange between corporate sustainability messages and the consumer.

Haller et al (2020) have researched what consumers are looking for in brands with regard to sustainability efforts and found the following:

- 53 per cent find it very important that brands provide products and services that help simplify life

- 50 per cent want brands that offer 'clean' products
- 45 per cent find it very important that brands are sustainable and /or environmentally responsible

Given the importance that consumers are placing on sustainability efforts, businesses need to find new ways to spread the word about their sustainability story and these new ways include social media. Leidermann (2019) stresses that for businesses to share their sustainability story on social media provides an opportunity to produce compelling content and to create an emotional connection with the audience.

The influence of consumers has grown tremendously with social media as it allows consumers and consumer groups to directly put pressure on government and businesses (Langley and van den Broek, 2010). There is no question that consumers care about the sustainability efforts of the brands that they are buying; instead, we need to understand how such sustainability messages need to be communicated to resonate with the consumer.

Activity 24.2

We have looked into the rise of importance of sustainability for the consumer.

i. Visit *The Guardian* newspaper and search for the article 'Consumer put firms under pressure to lead the way in sustainable living' by Melissa Davis.

ii. What seem to be the different sustainability efforts that companies are making?

iii. Make a list of all of the initiatives that you can identify in the article and try to analyse which part of the triple bottom line (people, planet, profit) they align to.

From the business's point of view, it would already be a positive outcome if the audience believes there to be shared values between the brand and the consumer based on sustainability communications on social media. However, an even better outcome would be for the consumer to share those sustainability communications so that the message is not just received by single consumers at a time but by a larger audience instead.

There are a number of studies that try to understand how content needs to be presented in order for it to be shared more frequently. For example, Tellis et al (2019) find that positive emotions of amusement, excitement, inspiration and warmth increase sharing. In a sustainability context, Sparks et al (2013) study online reviews' persuasiveness and find that vague content is less persuasive than specific content about the sustainability efforts of the brand.

A study by Knight et al (2021) specifically looks into what makes consumers share corporate sustainability messages on social media channels. They look into the importance of sustainability information quality vs source expertise. In simpler words, the study tries to understand whether consumers care more about WHAT is communicated or WHO communicates the message. The study concludes that both factors are indeed important for sustainability messages to be shared by consumers. However, consumers require fewer information quality pointers in order to share sustainability messages if these seem to stem from a source that is trustworthy and an expert in their field. This finding is supported by research that shows how sustainability certification strengthens consumers' beliefs (Sparks et al, 2013). A lack of such source credibility can lead to scepticism among consumers and can result in consumers using social media channels to question the sustainability of business operations and to call out companies for *greenwashing* (Pearson et al, 2016) (see also Chapters 5 and 12).

KEY TERM
Greenwashing

Greenwashing is the process of conveying a false impression or providing misleading information about how a company's products are more environmentally sound. Greenwashing is considered an unsubstantiated claim to deceive consumers into believing that a company's products are environmentally friendly. Created by Jay Westerveld in 1986, the term is used to describe companies' efforts to claim to be pro-sustainable to mislead consumers and cover up questionable environmental records.

SOURCE Kenton, 2022; Kopnina, 2019

In order to get sustainability communication on social media channels right, Leidermann (2019) provides the following 'to-do' list on how to promote sustainability successfully on social media:

- Listen to what is happening on social media first to determine how your business fits into the larger conversation.

- Every social media message should ultimately help address a broader issue you are aiming to solve.

- Focus on the *why* instead of the *what* you are doing, so avoid publishing self-serving content.

- Incorporate sustainability messaging with overall content.

- Highlight human stories and trigger engagement by exemplifying emotions.
- Use social media as a platform for positive change.

Sustainability initiatives in the digital world

We have now considered corporate digital responsibility initiatives implemented by private businesses and learnt how the consumer wants to be informed about sustainability messages. Private businesses are just one of the important groups of stakeholders that are required in the transition to a more sustainable world. A study by the World Economic Forum and PwC found in 2020 that two-thirds of the 169 targets supporting the global Sustainable Development Goals could be positively influenced by using digital technology applications (PwC, 2020). The study has tested digital technology applications such as artificial intelligence (AI), blockchain, the Internet of Things, 5G and drones. There seems to be an agreement that the future of humanity and the health of planet Earth depends to a large extent on how digital technologies are used and adopted (CODES, 2020).

This tremendous potential for utilizing technology for sustainable development stresses its relevancy. Besides private businesses, both politics and consumer initiatives need to be involved to actually reach the full potential.

From a global policy point of view, there are several initiatives that aim to aid in sustainable development from a digital, technological point of view.

Coalition for Digital Environmental Sustainability (CODES)

The Coalition for Digital Environmental Sustainability (CODES) was established in March 2021 in response to the UN Secretary General's Roadmap for Digital Cooperation (CODES, 2020).

The following groups are the co-founder of CODES:

- United Nations Environment Programme (UNEP)
- United Nations Development Programme (UNDP)
- International Science Council
- German Environment Agency
- Kenya Ministry of Environment and Forestry
- Future Earth
- Sustainability in the Digital Age (SDA)

The main purpose of CODES is to advance digital sustainability, understood as the design, development, deployment and regulation of digital technologies to accelerate environmentally and socially sustainable development, while mitigating risks and unintended consequences (CODES, 2020). Three shifts have been identified in the CODES (2020) Action Plan that are necessary to achieve this purpose:

- Shift 1: enable alignment
- Shift 2: mitigate negative impacts
- Shift 3: accelerate innovation

From a digital marketing point of view, CODES (2020) has identified a number of problems that need to be addressed for Shift 2 to be implemented. The Action Plan stresses the importance of addressing consumption drivers as overconsumption hinders sustainable development. The Action Plan sets out that persuasive technologies and practices that accelerate consumption need to be considered in future policies (CODES, 2020). Examples of persuasive technologies are very prominent in digital marketing and describe, among others:(1) product customization; (2) influencer endorsements; (3) personalized advertising; (4) digital nudging; and (5) 24/7 opportunities for purchasing.

Another problem that has been identified that prevents sustainable development is the spread of misinformation about sustainability on digital channels. We have covered the problem of misinformation in Chapter 23 and it is particularly a problem for topics such as climate change, biodiversity loss and pollution. The spread of misinformation around these topics can affect consumer trust and hinder collective action as well as result in a wider gap between divided groups (CODES, 2020). If we consider that false news stories are 70 per cent more likely to be retweeted than true news stories and it takes around six times as long for a true news story to reach the same amount of people as a false news story (Vosoughi et al, 2018), there is no wonder that combating the spread of misinformation is essential in the strive towards a more sustainable world.

Activity 24.3

You have now learnt about the Coalition for Digital Environmental Sustainability and learnt about persuasive technologies that are commonplace in digital marketing. These include (1) product customization; (2) influencer endorsements; (3) personalized advertising; (4) digital nudging; and (5) 24/7 opportunities.

i. Think about your latest purchase that you have done online.

ii. Consider the five persuasive technologies that we have outlined.

iii. How many of these have influenced your purchase and how have they done so?

iv. Do you believe a restriction of such persuasive technologies would aid in the development of a more sustainable planet?

Sustainability in the Digital Age (SDA)

Sustainability in the Digital Age is an initiative that was established by Future Earth. Future Earth is an international, interdisciplinary research network of scientists, researchers and innovators collaborating for a more sustainable plant (Future Earth, nd). The SDA initiative aims to discover opportunities and challenges when using digital technologies to strive towards global sustainability (SDA, nd). Its core aim is to establish multi-stakeholder partnerships and support actions that make this vision a reality. Some of the following organizations are collaborators with the SDA:

- UN Environment Programme
- Office for Artificial Intelligence
- UK Science & Innovation Network
- Grantham Institute Climate Change and the Environment (Imperial College London)
- Barcelona Supercomputing Centre

SDA (nd) state that they 'work to leverage the digital age to drive societal transformations towards a more sustainable equitable world'. They aim to achieve this through three areas:

- research and innovation
- training and networks
- policy, standards and best practices

Summary

In this chapter, we have learnt about the importance of responsible business behaviour. We have briefly introduced corporate social responsibility and have reviewed in detail how corporate digital responsibility can aid responsible business practices. We then moved onto the importance of social media channels when communicating sustainability messages and analysed how consumers would like to be informed about sustainability efforts. We then outlined a number of global sustainability initiatives which believe that technology and the digital world can make a real difference to achieving a more sustainable planet.

Chapter review

Reflective questions

Q1 What is the difference between corporate social responsibility (CSR) and corporate digital responsibility (CDR) and why are they important to consider?

Q2 What are the main aspects of CDR and how do they differ between sources?

Q3 Why is social media a good channel for businesses to talk about their sustainability efforts?

Q4 How do consumers want to be informed about corporate sustainability messages on social media?

Q5 How can digital technologies aid the attempt to become a more sustainable world?

Key learning points

- Corporate social responsibility (CSR) describes the idea that businesses have an obligation to contribute to the needs of society, as they exist due to public consent.

- One way of ensuring that businesses are merging both their sustainability efforts and digitization is described in the concept of corporate digital responsibility (CDR).

- Given the importance that consumers are putting on sustainability efforts, businesses need to find new ways to spread the word about their sustainability story and these new ways include social media.

References

CODES (2020) Action plan for a sustainable planet in the digital age, Coalition for Digital Environmental Sustainability, wedocs.unep.org/bitstream/handle/20.500.11822/38482/CODES_ActionPlan.pdf (archived at https://perma.cc/GY98-QLSA), or doi.org/10.5281/zenodo.6573509 (archived at https://perma.cc/X9G6-WD9F)

Corporate Digital Responsibility (2021) The International CDR Manifesto: The seven core principles of the international definition of corporate digital responsibility, corporatedigitalresponsibility.net/cdr-manifesto (archived at https://perma.cc/YDC4-ZGBG)

CSR Journal (2019) A brief history of corporate social responsibility in the US, *CSR Journal*, 26 September, thecsrjournal.in/a-brief-history-of-corporate-social-responsibility-in-the-us/#:~:text=Although%20responsible%20companies%20had%20already,Social%20Responsibilities%20of%20the%20Businessman (archived at https://perma.cc/B9NB-LVML)

Elkington, J (1997) *Cannibals with forks. The triple bottom line of 21st century*, Capstone, Oxford

Fernando, J (2022) Corporate social responsibility, Investopedia, 7 March, www.investopedia.com/terms/c/corp-social-responsibility.asp (archived at https://perma.cc/KN3P-ZDFF)

Future Earth (nd) futureearth.org/ (archived at https://perma.cc/VN7K-4MTW)

Haller, K, Lee, J and Cheung, J (2020) Meet the 2020s consumers driving change, IBM Institute for Business Value, June 2020, www.ibm.com/downloads/cas/EXK4XKX8 (archived at https://perma.cc/6XAK-AKMN)

Hanauer, D (nd) Corporate digital responsibility and digital ethics, Digitization demands value awareness and responsible action, PricewaterhouseCoopers, www.pwc.de/en/sustainability/corporate-digital-responsibility-and-digital-ethics.html (archived at https://perma.cc/6UV4-A9H8)

Kenton, K (2022) Greenwashing, Investopedia, 22 March, www.investopedia.com/terms/g/greenwashing.asp (archived at https://perma.cc/9DQQ-KL57)

Knight, H, Haddoud, M Y and Megicks, P (2021) Determinants of corporate sustainability message sharing on social media: A configuration approach, *Business Strategy and the Environment*, 31, 633–47

Kopnina, H (2019) Greenwashing or best case practices? Using circular economy and cradle to cradle case studies in business education, *Journal of Cleaner Production*, 219, 613–21

Langley, D and van den Broek, T (2010) Exploring social media as a driver of sustainable behaviour: Case analysis and policy implications, *Internet Politics and Policy Conference*, 16–17 September, Oxford

Leiderman, S, (2019) How to promote your sustainability story on social media, Sustainable Brands, 5 March, sustainablebrands.com/read/marketing-and-comms/how-to-promote-your-sustainability-story-on-social-media-as-a-b2b-company (archived at https://perma.cc/R42V-DXKY)

Lobschat, L, Mueller, B, Eggers, F, Brandimarte, L, Diefenbach, S, Kroschke, M, and Wirtz, J (2021) Corporate digital responsibility, *Journal of Business Research*, 122, 875–88

Montag, C and Diefenbach, S (2018) Towards homo digitalis: Important research issues for psychology and the neurosciences at the dawn of the internet of things and the digital society, *Sustainability*, 10(2), 415

Pearson, E, Tindle, H, Ferguson, M, Ryan, J and Litchfield, C (2016) Can we tweet, post, and share our way to a more sustainable society? A review of the current contributions and future potential of #Socialmediaforsustainability, *Annual Review of Environment and Resources*, 41, 363–97

PwC (2020) Over two-thirds of sustainable development goals could be bolstered by emerging tech, including AI and blockchain, PricewaterhouseCoopers, 17 January, www.pwc.com/gx/en/news-room/press-releases/2020/blockchain-sdgs-wef.html (archived at https://perma.cc/5SME-6Y2E)

Scholz, R W, Bartelsman, E J, Diefenbach, S, Franke, L, Grunwald, A and Helbing, D (2018) Unintended side effects of the digital transition: European scientists' messages from a proposition-based expert round table, *Sustainability*, 10(6)

SDA (nd) Who we are, Sustainability in the Digital Age, sustainabilitydigitalage.org/who-we-are/ (archived at https://perma.cc/9ZS6-ACMH)

Sparks, B, Perkins, H and Buckley, R (2013) Online travel reviews as persuasive communication: The effects of content type, source, and certification logos on consumer behavior, *Tourism Management*, 39, 1–9

Tellis, G, MacInnis, D, Tirunillai, S and Zhang, Y (2019) What drives virality (sharing) of online digital content? The critical role of information, emotion, and brand prominence, *Journal of Marketing*, 83(4), 1–20

Unilever (2018) Unilever calls on industry to increase trust, transparency and measurement in influencer marketing, 18 June, www.unilever.com/news/press-and-media/press-releases/2018/unilever-calls-on-industry-to-increase-trust-transparency-and-measurement-in-influencer-marketing/ (archived at https://perma.cc/YXF7-XF6B)

Unilever (2019a) Unilever unveils next phase in clean-up of digital advertising with creation of Unilever Trusted Publishers, 28 March, www.unilever.com/news/press-and-media/press-releases/2019/unilever-unveils-next-phase-in-clean-up-of-digital-advertising-with-creation-of-unilever-trusted-publishers/ (archived at https://perma.cc/7AQY-X47W)

Unilever (2019b) Unilever leads efforts to develop a cross media measurement model for brands, Unilever, 29 January, www.unilever.com/news/press-and-media/press-releases/2019/unilever-leads-efforts-to-develop-a-cross-media-measurement-model-for-brands/ (archived at https://perma.cc/W3V4-MUNY)

Vosoughi, S, Roy, D and Aral, S (2018) The spread of true and false news online, *Science*, 359, 1146–51

Wade, M (2020) Corporate responsibility in the digital era, *MIT Sloan Management Review*, 28 April, sloanreview.mit.edu/article/corporate-responsibility-in-the-digital-era/ (archived at https://perma.cc/GQ9Z-J7KP)

Legal considerations

By the end of this chapter, you should be able to:

- briefly explain the relevance of data protection and privacy laws
- outline in detail the principles of the GDPR
- explain how and why online advertising is regulated
- explain in your own words why it is essential for businesses to avoid discrimination in the digital world and ensure equal access for everyone
- briefly outline the relevance of intellectual property laws

Introduction

In this chapter, we will be reviewing which laws are having an impact on digital marketing. Laws offer a framework to ensure legal business behaviour and digital marketing requires many legal considerations. This is mainly to ensure compliance with the law as well as to prevent unlawful marketing practices. For example, we have all come across cookies online as companies use cookies to track consumer behaviour in order to personalize content. Data protection and privacy laws set out what companies are allowed to do with the data they are collecting through cookies. Another set of laws deals with advertising standards that apply to the digital context. Other digital marketing activities that are affected by legal issues are, for example, the protection of digital assets or the use of trademarks online.

In this chapter, we will cover data protection and privacy laws, intellectual property laws, consumer marketing and advertising laws, and finally disability and discrimination laws.

Data protection and privacy law

Data protection and privacy laws are essential for businesses to know when operating online. One of the main advantages of digital marketing is that of creating personalized messages for consumers. The amount of personal information that is collected from consumers allows for highly effective targeting. Personal information can be collected in two ways, either by directly asking customers or by indirectly tracking them.

According to Freedman (2022), consumer data that businesses collect can be broken down into four categories:

- **Personal data:** This category includes personally identifiable information such as social security numbers and gender as well as non-personally identifiable information, including IP address, web browser cookies, and device IDs (which both laptops and mobile devices have).

- **Engagement data:** This type of data details how consumers interact with a business's website, mobile apps, text messages, social media pages, emails, paid ads and customer service routes.

- **Behavioural data:** This category includes transactional details such as purchase histories, product usage information (e.g. repeated actions), and qualitative data (e.g. mouse movement information).

- **Attitudinal data:** This data type encompasses metrics on consumer satisfaction, purchase criteria, product desirability and more.

Questions relating to the capturing, usage, storage and deletion of consumer data are regulated through data protection and privacy laws. The European Union's General Data Protection Regulation (GDPR), the UK's General Data Protection Regulation (UK GDPR) and the California Consumer Privacy Act (CCPA) are some of the most prominent laws that regulate how businesses capture, store, share and analyse consumer data. The CCPA is similar to GDPR regulation but rather than consumers having to opt in to allow for personal data to be collected, the CCPA requires consumers to opt out of data collection (Freedman, 2022).

General Data Protection Regulation (GDPR)

The European Union's GDPR sets rules for data capture, storage, usage and sharing for companies and it is applicable to any business that targets or collects the personal data of EU citizens (Freedman, 2022). When the UK left the European Union on 1 January 2021, the EU GDPR was replaced by the UK GDPR. The UK GDPR is almost identical to the original EU GDPR but it adapts the European rules to the UK domestic legal system (Nistico, 2021). The most notable difference is the age at which people are able to provide consent for the use of their personal data, which is 16 years old in the EU and 13 years old under the UK's law (Torry-Cook, 2021). It is important for companies to know their obligations, as non-compliance with the GDPR principles results in fines of up to €20 million or up to 4 per cent of annual revenue, whichever is higher (Freedman, 2022).

Both the UK GDPR and the EU GDPR have seven key principles:

1 lawfulness, fairness and transparency

2 purpose limitation

3 data minimization

4 accuracy

5 storage limitation

6 integrity and confidentiality

7 accountability

The UK GDPR distinguishes between a *controller* and a *processor* of data to recognize that not all organizations involved in the processing of personal data have the same degree of responsibility.

KEY TERM

Controller/processor

Controller: the natural or legal person, public authority, agency or other body which, alone or jointly with others, determines the purposes and means of the processing of personal data.

Processor: a natural or legal person, public authority, agency or other body which processes personal data on behalf of the controller.

SOURCE ICO, nd a

The seven key principles apply to controllers and processors of data. The first six principles set out that data shall be (ICO, nd b):

i. Processed lawfully, fairly and in a transparent manner in relation to individuals.

ii. Collected for specified, explicit and legitimate purposes and not further processed in a manner that is incompatible with those purposes; further processing for archiving purposes in the public interest, scientific or historical research purposes or statistical purposes shall not be considered to be incompatible with the initial purposes.

iii. Adequate, relevant and limited to what is necessary in relation to the purposes for which they are processed.

iv. Accurate and, where necessary, kept up to date; every reasonable step must be taken to ensure that personal data that are inaccurate, having regard to the purposes for which they are processed, are erased or rectified without delay.

v.   Kept in a form which permits identification of data subjects for no longer than is necessary for the purposes for which the personal data are processed; personal data may be stored for longer periods insofar as the personal data will be processed solely for archiving purposes in the public interest, scientific or historical research purposes or statistical purposes subject to implementation of the appropriate technical and organizational measures required by the GDPR in order to safeguard the rights and freedoms of individuals.

vi   Processed in a manner that ensures appropriate security of the personal data, including protection against unauthorized or unlawful processing and against accidental loss, destruction or damage, using appropriate technical or organizational measures.

The seventh principle refers to the controller and sets out the following:

vii. The controller shall be responsible for, and be able to demonstrate compliance with, paragraph (I) (the six principles mentioned before).

Activity 25.1

You have now learnt about the principles of the General Data Protection Regulation (GDPR).

i.   Visit the EU's GDPR website (European Commission, nd) and click on the questions that relate to the individual principles of the GDPR.

ii. After having clicked on one of the questions take a look at the examples given for each of the principles.

iii. Review some of the examples to get a better understanding of each of the principles.

Online advertising law/consumer marketing laws

Advertising standards are regulated by the Advertising Standards Authority (ASA) whose purpose is to make advertising in the UK responsible and to protect against misleading, harmful and offensive advertising in traditional media such as TV as well as online (ASA, nd). In 2017, there were double the number of cases of online complaints compared to TV complaints (ASA, nd).

The ASA regulates not just typical advertising formats such as display adverts online but also newer forms of advertising such as influencer and affiliate marketing. The following are some relevant examples of what the ASA is regulating (ASA, nd):

- Restricting ads for food and drink products that are high in (saturated) fat, salt or sugar (HFSS): Advertisers are banned from targeting children with HFSS ads across all non-broadcast media, including on children's websites, apps, 'advergames' and social media platforms including Facebook, YouTube, Instagram, Snapchat and Twitter.

- Enforcing a strict burden on advertisers in targeting age-restricted ads online: Tougher standards require that advertisers show they have used social media targeting tools to direct ads away from users who are likely to be younger than they claim. For example, advertisers might choose to actively exclude web users whose browsing history shows they are interested in clothing brands of particular appeal to children.

- Gambling ads that target or appeal to children online are banned: Ads cannot exploit children or other vulnerable people, including through advertising content which appeals particularly to young people or which reflects youth culture. Among other restrictions, ads cannot suggest gambling provides an 'escape', can solve financial worries, or can enhance personal qualities.

The UK Government sets out 'The consumer protection from unfair trading regulations' (UK Government, nd) and specifies that consumers cannot be misled or harassed by any of the following:

- false or deceptive messages
- leaving out important information
- using aggressive sales techniques

Laws set out frameworks that businesses need to adhere to in order to ensure lawful business practices. For digital marketers, it is important to provide true facts while not ignoring relevant information. As such it is crucial to avoid any form of *misleading advertising*.

KEY TERM
Misleading advertising

Under the consumer law advertising is seen as misleading if it involves false, misleading or deceptive information that is likely to cause the average consumer to act in a way they might otherwise not. Advertising may also be considered misleading if important information that the average consumer needs to make an informed decision is left out. Misleading advertising covers claims made directly to consumers by manufacturers, distributors and retailers, as well as in advertisements, catalogues, websites.

SOURCE CCPC, nd

Some of the following are examples of misleading advertising (CCPC, nd; Bella, 2021):

- false claims about products and services: e.g. a product is a different colour, size or weight to what is advertised

- misrepresenting product prices: e.g. products are advertised at sales prices but turn out not to be

- not providing or leaving out important information: e.g. the product advertising does not state how long a product will last

- misrepresenting the way the goods or service are supplied: e.g. free delivery is advertised, but the delivery actually involves some sort of fee or charge

- creating a false impression about a product or service: even if the information given is correct, e.g. the product is advertised as looking much bigger than it in reality is

- misrepresenting any aspect about the advertiser: e.g. the business is presented as being a member of a trade association, when they are actually not

---

Activity 25.2

We have now reviewed different forms of misleading advertising.

i. Visit *The Guardian* newspaper and search for the article 'Nivea's latest "white is right" advert is the tip of a reprehensible iceberg' by Afua Hirsch.

ii. Take a look at what Nivea is accused of.

iii. Compare it to the misleading advertising examples and try to determine which aspect of misleading advertising the Nivea advertisement is accused of.

Disability and discrimination law

Businesses should ensure that they make their website and general online presence accessible to everyone – including those with disabilities, long-term illnesses or other impairments. This is to ensure an inclusive and non-discriminatory approach. Research has shown that an accessible website has many advantages for brands (Recite Me, 2020a):

- 86 per cent of users with access needs would spend more if there were fewer barriers

- building more brand ambassadors and loyalty through accessible websites

- the annual online spending power of people with access needs is now £24.8 billion in the UK and $490 billion in the United States
- demonstrating corporate social responsibility and community support
- better SEO results

SEO best practices and conformance to the Web Content Accessibility Guidelines (WCAG) already overlap more than people think, and early indicators suggest that Google and other search engines will soon be incorporating accessibility factors into their algorithms.

Tim Berners-Lee, the inventor of the World Wide Web, founded and is leading the World Wide Web Consortium (W3C) whose objective is to develop standards for the World Wide Web. In 1999, the W3C established the first set of *Web Content Accessibility Guidelines (WCAG 1.0)* to establish accessibility standards that would be recognized and applied across the world (Shaw Trust Enterprises, 2018).

KEY TERM
Web Content Accessibility Guidelines (WCAG)

The Web Content Accessibility Guidelines, commonly referred to as WCAG, are a set of standards that are developed internationally by the World Wide Web Consortium (W3C) in order to create a set of guidelines that are regarded across the world as the recognized set of accessibility standards. Beginning in 1999 with WCAG 1.0, the standards have been updated every so often to keep up to date with technological advancements and research into cognitive impairments and disabilities. In 2008, WCAG 2.0 was published, which completely overhauled the initial set of standards. In June 2018, W3C released an updated version of 2.0, aptly named WCAG 2.1.

SOURCE Shaw Trust Enterprises, 2018

There are a number of different barriers that can make a website inaccessible. These barriers range from visual impairments, colour blindness, ADHD, dyslexia and hyperlexia to mobility and physical impairments. Among some of the problems that make websites inaccessible are the following (Recite Me, 2020b):

- not easy to use on a mobile
- cannot be navigated using a keyboard
- have inaccessible PDF forms that cannot be read using screen readers
- have poor colour contrast that makes the text difficult to read
- do not have adequate link descriptions and/or alt text descriptions on images
- use images containing text that is unreadable by speech synthesizer software

The Web Content Accessibility Guidelines (WCAG) establish a minimum of guidelines to which businesses should adhere. It is the law in most places that businesses do not treat those with disabilities less favourably, and besides implementing the WCAG set by the W3C, businesses will have to check regionally which regulations have to be applied. Some relevant laws include the following (Recite Me, 2020a):

- the Equality Act of 2010 (UK)
- the European Accessibility Act (Europe)
- the Americans with Disabilities Act (USA)

The Equality Act of 2010 (UK)

The Equality Act was established in 2010, updating and including information that had previously been found in other antidiscrimination laws such as the Equal Pay Act of 1970 and the Disability Discrimination Act of 1995 (Recite Me, 2020b). The Equality Act of 2010 provides a legal framework that businesses need to adhere to in order to make their websites accessible and inclusive.

The Equality Act of 2010 applies to websites and in the UK both public- and private-sector organizations must ensure that digital resources are accessible (BOIA, 2022). While the Act does not contain a technical standard, businesses are encouraged to use WCAG as a resource to design accessible websites and mobile apps. It is noted that any content conforming with the most recent version of WCAG (currently WCAG 2.1) can demonstrate compliance with the Equality Act of 2010 (BOIA, 2022).

There are four cornerstones that require inclusive websites to be (Recite Me, 2020b):

- perceivable: accommodating for various sensory differences in vision, sound and touch so that users can comprehend and consume the information in a way that is perceivable to them
- operable: user interface and navigation components on a website must be usable by all
- understandable: both website information and the operation of the user interface itself must be consistent and understandable
- robust: the website must be standards compliant and able to function using all applicable technologies, including assistive software

The Bureau of Internet Accessibility has produced a Website Accessibility Checklist, to ensure that businesses know what to check for WCAG2.1 A/AA compliance. Worksheet 7 in Additional Resources provides an extract from the original checklist which can be helpful when reviewing websites for accessibility.

> ## Activity 25.3
>
> You have now been introduced to the Equality Act of 2010. As you have heard, there are several different impairments that can make it harder for people to use the web.
>
> i.   Think of a website that you are frequently using.
>
> ii. Visit the Toptal.com website (Toptal, 2022), that simulates how colour-blind people might perceive a website.
>
> iii. Type the URL of your chosen website into the search field.
>
> iv. Play around with the various filters and make notes on how the use of colours on your chosen website could be improved to make it more accessible.

Intellectual property laws

A final legal consideration that businesses need to follow is that of intellectual property laws. Such laws protect digital assets such as text, photographs, video, artwork and music. If businesses want to use any such digital assets, they need to ensure that permission and licences are sought from authorized owners before doing so.

To avoid any problems when using digital assets in digital marketing campaigns, Bella (2021) recommends the following:

- only use original multimedia content
- read licence details for any content
- opt for common creative materials that are free to use
- seek permission from content creators
- purchase and use licenced photos
- don't use photos with recognizable trademarks, landmarks, logos or people
- while not required by the law, always credit and attribute original authors

Summary

In this chapter, we have learnt about the importance of knowing laws and regulations that apply in the digital marketing context. Among the most prominent areas that concern both businesses and consumers are the data protection and privacy laws. We have reviewed the UK and EU GDPR as some of the most essential laws that, if not followed, can result in vast fines for businesses. We have reviewed online advertising laws and learnt that the digital space is also subject to advertising standards and businesses need to be mindful of how and where they can promote their products online. We have further reviewed disability and discrimination laws and should know how important it is for businesses to build websites that allow equal access for all users. Finally, this chapter covers the need for following intellectual property laws to ensure that any digital assets used in digital marketing strategies require permission from an authorized party.

Chapter review

Reflective questions

Q1 Why is it important to know data protection and privacy laws and what are the most prominent of such laws that businesses need to be aware of?

Q2 What are the main principles of the GDPR?

Q3 How and by whom is digital advertising regulated and why is it essential for businesses to know of such regulations?

Q4 Why is it essential for businesses to avoid discrimination in the digital world and ensure equal access for everyone?

Q5 How can businesses ensure legal use of digital assets such as music, pictures or artwork?

Key learning points

- The relevance of data protection and privacy laws is essential for businesses to consider.

- Both the UK GDPR and the EU GDPR have seven key principles: lawfulness, fairness and transparency; purpose limitation; data minimization; accuracy; storage limitation; integrity and confidentiality; and accountability.

- Advertising standards are regulated by the Advertising Standards Authority (ASA) whose purpose is to make advertising in the UK responsible and to protect against misleading, harmful and offensive advertising in traditional media such as TV as well as online.

- Businesses should ensure that they make their website and general online presence accessible to everyone – including those with disabilities, long-term illnesses or other impairments.

- Intellectual property laws protect digital assets such as text, photographs, video, artwork and music.

References

ASA (nd) Regulation of Online Advertising: A briefing, Advertising Standards Authority, www.asa.org.uk/static/uploaded/6829937c-f185-4be6-9455e501af1df1e3.pdf (archived at https://perma.cc/YQ2Q-MNGG)

Bella, C (2021) If you are doing digital you need to know these legal issues, UK Business Blog, 17 April, business.clickdo.co.uk/legal-issues-in-digital-marketing/ (archived at https://perma.cc/PJE8-J67H)

BOIA (2022) The Equality Act of 2010 and British Standards for Web Accessibility, Bureau of Internet Accessibility, 24 February, www.boia.org/blog/the-equality-act-of-2010-and-british-standards-for-web-accessibility (archived at https://perma.cc/G34K-YCDA)

CCPC (nd) Misleading advertising, Competition and Consumer Protection Commission, www.ccpc.ie/consumers/shopping/misleading-advertising/ (archived at https://perma.cc/5Y7Y-MHCR)

Elkington, J (1997) *Cannibals with forks. The triple bottom line of 21st century,* Capstone, Oxford

European Commission (nd) ec.europa.eu/info/law/law-topic/data-protection/reform/rules-business-and-organizations/principles-gdpr_en

Freedman, M (2022) How businesses are collecting data, Business News Daily, 29 June, www.businessnewsdaily.com/10625-businesses-collecting-data.html (archived at https://perma.cc/Z2A7-MH6A)

ICO (nd a) Controllers and processors, Information Commissioner's Office, ico.org.uk/for-organisations/guide-to-data-protection/guide-to-the-general-data-protection-regulation-gdpr/key-definitions/controllers-and-processors/ (archived at https://perma.cc/SVL8-57EJ)

ICO (nd b) The Principles, Information Commissioner's Office, ico.org.uk/for-organisations/guide-to-data-protection/guide-to-the-general-data-protection-regulation-gdpr/principles/ (archived at https://perma.cc/EL4N-FPC8)

Nistico, A (2021) How to apply with EU GDPR, UK GDPR and Data Protection Act, EU GDPR Academy, 25 May, advisera.com/eugdpracademy/blog/2021/05/25/how-to-comply-with-eu-gdpr-uk-gdpr-and-data-protection-act/ (archived at https://perma.cc/3RD7-V5DS)

Recite me (2020a) How to improve brand reputation through being inclusive, 7 September, reciteme.com/news/how-to-improve-brand-reputation-through-being-inclusive (archived at https://perma.cc/UH7Z-EJZ2)

Recite me (2020b) Understanding the equality act and website accessibility, reciteme.com/news/understanding-the-equality-act-and-website-accessibility (archived at https://perma.cc/RT48-GWGE)

Shaw Trust Enterprises (2018) WCAG 2.1 changes explained, disability services, www.accessibility-services.co.uk/2018/12/20/wcag-2-1-changes-explained/ (archived at https://perma.cc/XK6E-9CPR)

Toptal (nd) Colorblind webpage filter, www.toptal.com/designers/colorfilter (archived at https://perma.cc/RWW3-DQRS)

Torry-Cook, S (2021) UK GDPR vs EU GDPR: The essential information you need, Signable, 29 April, www.signable.co.uk/uk-gdpr-eu-gdpr-businesses/ (archived at https://perma.cc/6BTT-YL7D)

UK Government (nd) Marketing and advertising: The law, www.gov.uk/marketing-advertising-law/regulations-that-affect-advertising (archived at https://perma.cc/7QPJ-RHY6)

ADDITIONAL RESOURCES

Worksheet 1

Template for macro-environmental analysis

	Broad overview of all forces prevailing in the macro-environment	Specific description of forces particularly relevant to the business under investigation	Critical assessment of the impact of identified forces on the business	Determine whether the identified forces are an opportunity or threat	If threat, determine how it could be overcome. If opportunity, determine how could it be turned into a competitive advantage
Technology forces					
Economic forces					
Social/cultural forces					
Environmental forces					
Political/legal forces					

Worksheet 2

Template for positioning statement

For ... (target customer)	
who ... (statement of need or opportunity)	
the ... (product name)	
is a ... (product category)	
that ... (statement of key benefit/compelling reason to buy).	
Unlike .... (primary competitive alternative)	
our product... (statement of primary differentiation)	

SOURCE Moore, 2014

Worksheet 3

Creating customer personas

Customer persona	Demographics	Psychographics	Webographics	
Short biography *Fictional name, picture – humanize the target audience*	Age, gender and family status	Personality, values, attitudes and beliefs	Digital literacy	Communication channels *e.g. which social media, when active*
	Cultural background and affiliations	Lifestyle and hobbies	Digital consumption activity	Favourite brands
Geographics *Geographic segmentation based on regions living and working in, climate or urban vs rural, etc*	Occupation, income and education	Likes and dislikes	Other *Other useful information specific to brand or marketing objectives*	

Worksheet 4

Creating customer journeys

Customer journey starts. Map all possible digital and traditional touchpoints where interaction with brand can occur, e.g. newsletter, email, billboard, social media advertisement, etc.

Two things to keep in mind:

1 efficacy , benefits and disadvantages of each communication channel for achieving your objectives.

2 how feedback from the customer can be used to create insights for improving the customer journey to attract and retain customers (from every phase)

Pre-purchase phase	Purchase phase	Post-purchase phase
DIGITAL		
TRADITIONAL		

Worksheet 5

Detailed website review

Use the following workbook to check corporate and commercial websites according to best practices.

	User Experience (UX) Checklist					
	Useful content:	**Usable site:**	**Desirable website** (evokes emotion and appreciation):	**Findable content:**	**Accessible content for everyone:**	**Credible content:**
Morville (2004) notes that for any user experience to be meaningful and valuable, the information provided must fulfil the following points. Review the chosen website and write your conclusion in the last column						
	Entertainment and visual appeal (Henderson, 2022)	**Reliability** (Nielson, 2020)	**Personalization**	**Information quality**	**User empowerment**	**Privacy/security**
Six success factors for website design from the consumer's perspective have been identified	website use of colour aesthetically pleasing images website content	'Error prevention' (Principle 5) states that good error messages are important, but the best designs carefully prevent problems from occurring in the first place	Are there aspects of personalization on the website? If so, do they work?	(Korgaonkar et al, 2009) The website provides objective information The website helps users research products and services	Korgaonkar et al, 2009) referred to user empowerment as the website user being able	Is there any information on the website that relates to the assurance of privacy and security?

(continued)

User Experience (UX) Checklist

layout website navigation	'Recognize, diagnose and recover from errors' (Principle 9) states that error messages should be expressed in plain language (no error codes), precisely indicate the problem, and constructively suggest a solution.	The information presented on the website seems fair and accurate	to *control* the following: opportunities for interaction how fast to go through the website order and/or sequence of information access
Online value proposition	Can you observe a clear online value proposition? For example, are any of the following services mentioned? ☐ Free shipping ☐ Free returns ☐ Multiple return options (in-store, postal, pick-up, etc) ☐ Amount of brands/products to choose from ☐ Price matching the competition ☐ Try before you buy ☐ Discounts for particular segments ☐ Exclusivity		

| 18 best practices for e-commerce websites (based on Khan, 2022 and Huynh, 2021) | ☐ Use big and clear images/360 degrees view
☐ Use demonstration videos
☐ Review options for augmented reality
☐ Add a prominent call to action
☐ Ensure easy navigation between pages
☐ Create urgency by applying the scarcity principle
☐ Ensure clear pricing
☐ Display logos/badges to instil trust
☐ Use real customer reviews
☐ Have a stock meter and keep it updated | ☐ Write clear product descriptions using the language of your target audience
☐ Help users to find similar products on your site to allow for upselling/cross-selling
☐ Outline clear shipping and returns policy
☐ Enable live chat and/or chatbots for 24/7 customer support
☐ Review your website's speed
☐ Offer diverse payment methods
☐ Offer subscription and loyalty programmes
☐ Offer personalized product recommendations | |
| **Overall conclusion:**

Based on the above analysis write your conclusion of the detailed website analysis | | | |

Worksheet 6

Template for digital marketing funnel stages with objectives, channels and key metrics

CLIENT: _____

PROJECT: _____

TIME PERIOD: _____

STAGE	OBJECTIVES	CHANNELS	METRICS
1. Awareness			
2. Consideration			
3. Action			
4. Engagement			
5. Advocacy			

Worksheet 7

Website accessibility checklist

The Bureau of Internet Accessibility has produced a Website Accessibility Checklist. This is to ensure that businesses know what to check for WCAG2.1 A/AA Compliance.

The following workbook is an extract from the original list and can be helpful when reviewing websites on their accessibility.

☐	Alternative text is provided for all content that is not text
☐	Captions are provided for multimedia both live or pre-recorded
☐	Information is presented the same for everyone indifferent to how the website might be viewed or used
☐	Information is easily distinguishable from background
☐	All functionality is operable through a keyboard interface
☐	The user is in control of time limits when reading something
☐	Content avoids too excessive flashing
☐	Users are assisted to find content and navigate through the site
☐	Content is readable and understandable
☐	Actions taken by users can be reversed in case of an error having been made

INDEX

Bold page numbers indicate figures, *italic* numbers indicate tables.